We All Have A Share

A Catholic Vision of
Prosperity through Productivity

by

Richard C. Haas

"Of his fullness we have all had a
share—love following upon love."
John 1: 16

ACTA Publications
Chicago, Illinois

We All Have a Share
A Catholic Vision of Prosperity through Productivity
by Richard C. Haas

Richard Haas is a journalist and businessman with career-long experience in both the daily newspaper industry and the Catholic press. He is currently the business manager for *Commonweal* magazine in New York City.

Edited by Gregory F. Augustine Pierce
Cover design and artwork by Emil Antonucci
Typesetting by Garrison Publications
Printed by Evangel Press

Unless otherwise indicated, scripture selections are taken from the New American Bible (NAB).

Copyright © 1995 by ACTA Publications
                       4848 N. Clark Street
                       Chicago, IL 60640
                       312-271-1030

Year 00 99 98 97 96 95
Printing 7 6 5 4 3 2 1

ISBN: 0-87946-103-9

Library of Congress Number: 94-073613

Printed in the United States of America

Table of Contents

In loving memory of

John R. Haas

(December 11, 1908 – July 3, 1970)

Introduction

The physicists' pursuit of a "unified theory" that explains all physical events has its parallel in the lives of all thoughtful Christians. We want a guide we can apply to every occasion, an incentive which will motivate every action.

Jesus' commandment, "Love one another as I have loved you," should serve as this all-purpose rule of life. Since most of us, however, devote a major portion of our time and energies to an endeavor we regard (at best) as morally neutral or (even worse) directly contrary to our religious convictions—that is, to "making money"—Christians often lack the sense of leading whole, integrated, unified lives.

The purpose of this book is to present a vision of economic life built around the concept of productive relationships. This vision is at the same time faithful to the Christian tradition and successful in the marketplace. Its thesis is this: Once we recognize that our religious notions of loving relationships can apply in the economic sphere as well as they do in our personal lives, we can start to experience economic activity as one of the primary ways in which we respond to Jesus' mandate on how we are to live.

I write as a businessman and a journalist, not as a philosopher or theologian, but I am attempting to follow in the Catholic intellectual tradition, particularly the tradition of sacramental theology. By offering its members the *certainty* that we are witnessing signs of God's presence in the seven official sacraments (Baptism, Reconciliation, Eucharist, Confirmation, Matrimony, Holy

Orders, and Annointing of the Sick), the Catholic Church provides the faithful with an invaluable spiritual resource. This same sacramental "sensibility" can help us detect God's presence and acknowledge God's absence in the various aspects of our lives outside of the Church's liturgical setting.

Despite this rich theological tradition, however, few Catholic writers have attempted to view economic activity in sacramental terms. As a result, we have been deprived of a rich metaphor for our relationship with the all-loving God. The thrust of this book, then, is sacramental. My intention is to show how the symbols of God's love abound in economic life.

Three aspects of God's love affair with creation seem evident as we consider the economy:

(1) God's love is demanding. God shares with us the divine essence and, in so doing, calls us to transcend our own limits and interests. The economic expression of each person's transcendence is productivity, the ability to produce more than he or she consumes—to generate, in other words, value in excess of cost.

(2) God's love is bountiful. Just as children are the fruit of a loving sexual union, prosperity is the fruit of loving economic relationships. Economic activity is not a "zero sum game." There is no limit to what the economy can produce if it operates in the way God intends.

(3) God's love is free. It is freely given and must be freely accepted. The economy provides one of the most exciting arenas for witnessing the interplay between freedom and commitment. Productive, prosperity-creating relationships are only possible within a climate of economic freedom.

For the Christian, reality's *organizational* structure is Trinitarian: a community of perfect fullness to which we are all invited. The basic *operating* procedure of this structure is the Paschal Mystery: the ongoing life-through-death struggle that opens our way to conscious participation in the Trinity. And the fundamental *motivating* principle of life is hope: the longing for a lasting reward based on faith in, love for, and the freedom of our divine benefactor.

In this book's sacramental view, energetic participation in the economy becomes a way for Christians to deepen their appreciation for the Trinity, the Paschal Mystery, and the virtue of hope. I try to emphasize the essentially sacrificial character of all worthwhile economic activity, and I see the goal of economic activity as a state of universal prosperity that mirrors the Trinity. Because the virtue of hope tempers reward-seeking behavior with respect for the freedom of other persons, I believe it transforms economic activity from a selfish pursuit into an opportunity for love.

The first part (Chapters 1-4) presents productivity as the focal point around which a comprehensive Catholic understanding of economic relationships can be constructed. The intent here is to replace the language of self-interest, the normal way of explaining economic behavior, with the language of productivity, a concept that draws attention to the human capacity for creativity and self-transcendence. The second part (Chapters 5-7) examines freedom as the prequisite for productivity. This section proposes a proper understanding of sinfulness, competition and commitment as critical to a full comprehension of economic freedom. Finally, the third part of the book (Chapters 8-11) identifies specific steps individuals, managers, government and Church can take to make productivity and, therefore, prosperity more abundant.

PART I: BEYOND SELF-INTEREST

A New Model of Economic Relationships

• **Productivity: The Search for Surplus Value**

• **A Trinitarian View of Prosperity**

• **Mutuality in Marriage and in the Marketplace**

• **Pursuing Prosperity in a Spirit of Poverty**

Of his fullness we have all had a share
—love following upon love.

John 1:16

PRODUCTIVITY: THE SEARCH
FOR SURPLUS VALUE

"Greed is good."

With these three words, financier Ivan Boesky, one of the archetypal villains of the 1980s, articulated the main reason followers of Jesus Christ continue to have reservations about economic activity. It is unfortunate that many religious people agree with Boesky's blunt assessment. They, too, believe that without humanity's instinct for acquisitiveness, economic progress would not occur. Thus, those who suspect that greed and economic interactions are inseparably linked find themselves faced with two equally unattractive options: justify greed by pointing to economic advancement as its positive by-product (the Boesky approach) or refrain from—or at least minimize—economic activity (what we might call the monastic approach).

If Boesky is right, if greed must be the driving force in economic affairs, constructing a Christian philosophy of economic life is impossible, since there can be no positive Christian view of greed. For this reason, the primary challenge faced by anyone attempting to offer a Christian vision that *encourages* rather than *discourages* economic activity is to construct a theory of economic motivation that goes beyond greed or even its more neutral pseudonym, "self-interest."

The second major roadblock in the way of developing a distinctively Christian approach to economic life is the prevalent belief that prosperity is a limited commodity that must be fought over and is one of the major sources of human conflict.

ECONOMIC GOODNESS

The Catholic faith contains powerful antidotes to the idea that economic activity demands both greed and limits. Our belief in the God who is the source of all goodness provides us with two universally valid criteria for testing the presence of goodness wherever we look for it—in the economy or anywhere else. First, goodness is always one, and second, goodness is always unlimited.

The first characteristic tells us that goodness is *never* associated with conflict and contradictions. In other words, what is bad for you can never be good for me, and what is bad for me cannot be good for you. We cannot reach the good by pursuing an evil.

The second characteristic insures that goodness is never associated with shortages. There is *always* enough goodness for all. Our core Catholic beliefs—the Trinity and the Incarnation—instruct us that love cannot be contained. We believe that love is overflowing, abundant, inexhaustible. It is infinite. It is God.

Through Jesus Christ, each and every one of us is promised a share in the fullness of life. In St. John's Gospel we read: "Of his fullness we have all had a share—love following upon love. For while the law was given through Moses, this enduring love came through Jesus Christ."

Thus, those of us who approach the economy from a Catholic perspective are in a position to craft a vision of economic life as truly good—another endeavor that provides a sign (a sacrament, if you will) of the link between fullness, abundance and loving relationships.

Although this approach may appear to some as the ultimate exercise in "voodoo economics," linking economic expansion to loving relationships is not as preposterous as it might seem. When we focus on the most critical question about the economy—how can we make it *grow?*—we start to recognize that we are dealing with a living organism. Since the economy is a collection of living people, why are the notions of generation and multiplication, which are central to the study of biology, not applicable to the study of economics as well?

By emphasizing the reality and importance of human fruitfulness, Catholics have an opportunity to foster organic, natural, "pro-life" thinking about the expansion of wealth. An appropriate starting point for a distinctively Catholic look at economic life is productivity, the most fundamental of all economic concepts.

Reflection on productivity in light of such fundamental Catholic beliefs as Creation, the Trinity, and the Eucharist offers a way of comprehending wealth formation as a *generative* rather than an *extractive* process. The new understanding of productivity that flows from such reflection provides a conceptual framework that transforms the economy from an arena of *conflict* into an opportunity for *community*. In this way, the focus on productivity can lead to a new appreciation for humanity's economic instincts. By recognizing voluntary productivity as a form of self-denial absolutely essential to economic development, we can see human longing for prosperity as another sign of grace drawing people together. If we find that our economic urges are fully satisfied only in productive relationships, then economic activity becomes an expression of humanity's best—not worst—instincts.

Establishing a connection between wealth formation and productive relationships provides the basis for a people-oriented guide to a more prosperous society. As we will see in the final section of the book, the notion of productivity as fruitfulness suggests changes in worker attitudes, management practices and governmental economic policies that can foster more widespread prosperity. A more refined notion of productivity also leads to new economic arguments in favor of key elements in the Catholic social justice tradition, particularly the notions of a living wage and the preferential option for the poor.

MORE THAN EFFICIENCY

That religious thinkers have left reflection on productivity to economists is unfortunate, since productivity is a subject much broader than a simple mathematical measurement of output per worker. It is a topic filled with wonder. Productivity touches upon the most mysterious of all human capacities, the ability of women and men to transcend their physical limits. Whether approached from an economic or a religious starting point, the study of productivity must grapple with the most fundamental of all moral questions: What prompts people to extend themselves for others?

A religious perspective offers a way of eliminating the confusion and contradictions which mark current thinking about productivity. Certainly one argument in favor of elevating discussions on productivity to a higher plane is the current state of economic uncertainty in the world.

So is productivity *good* or *bad?*

As long as productivity is viewed as a technical concept measured by output-per-worker, contradictory answers to this question can be given. On the one hand, improved productivity offers workers their only chance to enjoy non-inflationary income growth. Only if they produce more can they expect to get paid more. Viewed from the standpoint of worker salaries, the higher the productivity level the better. Case closed. Productivity is good.

Yet the economist's proverbial "on the other hand" must be interjected. As output per worker increases, fewer employees are needed to produce the same level of goods and services. For this reason, organized labor has viewed productivity improvement efforts with great scepticism. Indeed, the union practice known as "featherbedding" is a deliberate attempt to lower productivity so that high levels of employment can be maintained. Even though useless tasks are degrading to the workers involved, "featherbedding" is defensible under the limited logic of productivity used by management as well as labor. So long as one side in the labor-management debate advocates productivity improvements as a way to trim employment rosters, the other side will resist them for this very reason.

Companies are correct to recognize that their profitability depends upon the productivity of their workers. Yet managers who rely on the conventional output-per-worker measurement are tempted to see the elimination of workers as their ultimate goal. Indeed, if the formula commonly used to monitor productivity is valid, the attitude that management's goal is to minimize employment is quite understandable.

The conventional formula, (P)roductivity = (O)utput ÷ (W)orkers, suggests two ways to raise productivity: (1) increase the volume of output; (2) reduce the number of workers.

At first glance, the anti-worker bias inherent in this method of measuring productivity may not be visible, since this formula establishes a direct relationship between productivity and either variable. Comparable adjustments to either output or workers should have the same effect on the level of productivity. Therefore, option 1 and option 2 above appear to be equally beneficial.

The underlying mathematics of this formula, however, actually tells organizations that the way to maximize productivity is to minimize the number of workers. According to this formula, the value for "P" approaches infinity as the value for "W" approaches zero.

Do businesses really operate according to this logic? The frequency with which the term "downsizing" appears in the news provides ample evidence that many managers do, indeed, subscribe to this narrow and dangerous view of productivity. Their obsession with efficiency has created a spectre overshadowing the entire economy. In the last few years alone, such restricted management thinking has inflicted severe hardship on hundreds of thousands of displaced workers. And if this misguided pursuit of efficiency is allowed to run its course, the profitability of downsized companies and the prosperity of the economy as a whole will be threatened. Programs designed to minimize the size of the work force are removing from the economy the only true source of wealth creation—working people.

PRODUCTIVITY AS CREATIVITY

The proper measurement of productivity is not the *volume* of output, but the *value* of output. Mathematically speaking, productivity is not a *quotient* but a *remainder*. Productivity is much more closely aligned to such economic concepts as wealth and profitability than to efficiency. Productivity is the spread—the difference, the gap—between the value of an item (a good or a service) and the cost of producing that item. Even under the most precise economic definition, to be *productive* is to be *creative*, for productivity exists only when the value of output exceeds the cost of input. By definition, the productive person transforms the lesser into the greater. Productive men and women add value that did not exist prior to their efforts.

Our society's refusal to accept the miraculous—to acknowledge the human capacity for something-from-nothing creativity—blocks the application of this proper definition of productivity. As a result, meaningful discussion about real economic development is very difficult. We cannot articulate a coherent prescription for true economic growth unless we recognize the *creation* of new wealth in the strictest sense of the word. Furthermore, the traditional view of productivity is reinforced by analytical limitations. Determining the precise net value employees contribute to an organization is much more difficult than calculating the number of cars assembled or insurance claims processed.

CATHOLIC CONTRIBUTION

Disputing those who underestimate men and women's economic power and reversing the misunderstandings which glorify the workerless economy are among the most significant contributions Catholic thinkers can make to a new vision of prosperity through productivity. Michael Novak, one of the few Catholic philosophers working in this field, has noted that Catholics bring to economic discussions a strong belief in creation. Catholics see themselves both as creatures of an all-loving God and as co-creators of God's reign on earth. In *The Catholic Ethic and the Spirit of Capitalism*, Novak proposes Pope John Paul II's 1991 encyclical *Centesimus Annus* (*The One Hundreth Year*) as the culmination of Catholic thought on the importance of creativity in economic life. In it, the pope regards the acting person—the creative person—as the "decisive factor" in the economy.

How do we translate Catholic thinking about human creativity into a prescription for economic growth and a spirituality of economic interactions? To put it simply, we must emphasize over and over the importance of people in the economy! Only when the reality of wealth's creation is accepted does the productive worker (the one who generates value in excess of cost) receive the recognition he or she deserves.

SURPLUS VALUE

The alternate definition of productivity we are presenting, (P)roductivity = (V)alue of Output - (C)ost of Input, avoids the fallacy of the zero workforce, but it does raise the so-called "surplus value" question which has captivated economists since the time of Karl Marx. How is it possible for an economic item (either a product or a service) to have a value in excess of its cost? If indeed such surplus value does exist in the economy, where does it come from?

To Marx and his followers, the presence of surplus value at the end of an economic process was incontrovertible evidence that someone along the way did not receive his or her due. Although the victim is always a person, shortchanging the inventor of a machine fits in as well with Marx's theory as underpayment to a worker operating that same machine. In any case, for the Marxist, any surplus value is a surefire sign of exploitation.

For other economists, surplus value is an illusion. They acknowledge that companies enjoying temporary monopolies are able to charge prices that exceed costs, but they regard these prices as a sign of market dominance rather than inherent value. Sooner or later, they argue, competition will force the price to equal the cost, since ultimately cost determines value. If these economists are correct and the generation of economic value in excess of costs is truly impossible, then true economic advancement also is an illusion.

Opposing these two conflicting views of value creation is an understanding of a worker's productivity—the gap between value produced and compensation received—as his or her generous contribution to the economy. Establishing such a theory is extremely important if we are to fashion an approach to economic growth that favors maximum rather than minimum employment. The challenge faced by those trying to articulate a more people-oriented conception of the economy is to show that surplus value is neither illusory nor an automatic sign of exploitation.

THE NEED FOR SACRIFICE

One thing is clear. We cannot talk about this type of productivity only in terms of self-interest.

In their hearts, the best of this nation's economists, politicians, journalists and business people know the answer to our most troubling economic questions. Listen to their speeches, read their interviews and columns. Peeking out from under the hard-nosed, pragmatic covers they hide beneath is their vague awareness that the solution to this nation's economic problems (as well as most of its other social ills) requires use of words like "sacrifice" and "selflessness." Yet, because the prevailing understanding of economic motivation is limited to the single concept of "self-interest," those who set the public agenda lack the courage to translate their insights into the real cause of our economic problems into realistic policy recommendations. They fear that any program that appeals to motives other than financial self-interest will be labeled idealistic, soft-headed and unworkable.

When managers believe that workers are motivated solely by financial self-interest, however, what can they possibly say to their employees that will prompt them to expand their output of uncompensated value? Do they really think that the spread between worker costs and worker value can be widened without resort to some form of coercion? When it is explained only in the language of self-interest, productivity is indeed an exploitative concept.

An expanded vocabulary is one of the beneficial contributions religious thinkers bring to economic discussions. Using religious language, an inquiry into the true nature of productivity can lead to drastically different conclusions from those of conventional economists. When "grace" is factored into the equation and the ability of women and men to transcend their immediate financial interests is accepted, productivity can become an expression of human creativity—the explosive force which makes true (not just illusory) expansion of the economy possible. Productivity, in this view, is a manifestation of humanity's greatest strength and its most mysterious gift: the capacity to transcend physical limitations by creating new realities. When words like "creativity" and "transcendence" are substituted for the language of self-interest, "voluntary productivity" is no longer a linguistic absurdity. Quite simply, unselfishly motivated productive participants in the economy give more than they get. They are willing and able to produce value far in excess of cost. Such productive workers are the real-life equivalent of the goose who lays a golden egg.

One of the amazing conclusions of this radically different understanding of productivity is this: Since each productive worker adds new value to the economy, *a society is not maximizing its prosperity so long as one potentially productive person remains unemployed.*

Such an ethereal idea as "the creative capacity for self-transcendence" may seem like a rather shaky foundation on which to base a program of economic expansion. But is this approach any more unrealistic than telling workers the way to improve everyone's standard of living is for some of them to lose their jobs?

As long as productivity improvements are based primarily on employment reductions, the U.S. will have an economy which is stagnant at best. The output-per-worker measurement may rise, but the total pool of economic value—the true gauge of the nation's economic health—will stay capped at its current level. Only when we start measuring economic activity by the total value that can be contributed by *all* potential workers will we be able to establish the real connection between maximum employment and sustained economic progress. My hope is that the rest of *We All Have a Share*, which amplifies this single theme, will encourage a shift in the way we think about the economic concept called productivity. Defining the type and level of prosperity that can result from a new approach—one that is steeped in Catholic social teaching and sensibilities—could truly be a blessing for all people.

A TRINITARIAN VIEW
OF PROSPERITY

In the previous chapter, I noted how some traditional economic terms like "productivity" and "self-interest" often lead to confusion. I also suggested that words taken from religious language, such as "creativity," "contribution," "sacrifice" and "self-denial," offer a way to bring new clarity to economic thought. In this chapter, however, I will be shifting to some of the language problems experienced by the Catholic Church itself. For, despite the issuance of numerous pastoral letters and social encyclicals, neither popes nor bishops have found the words to speak convincingly to the American people about economic affairs.

The effectiveness of the Catholic Church's communication on this issue might improve dramatically if it offered a clear answer to the most fundamental of all economic questions. Before the Church tries to tell individuals, corporations or nations how to lead their economic lives, it should answer this question: *What's the real point of economic life?*

THE WHY OF ECONOMICS

The first lesson now learned by every MBA is MBO—Management By Objectives. One of the most succinct summaries of this method was presented several years ago by Kenneth Blanchard and Spencer Johnson in their business classic, *The One Minute Manager*. If we take a "minute" at the start of an endeavor to state our goal, then management can be as easy as one-two-three, they explained. Once the goal is in place, management merely furthers the objective by praising positive behavior and by reprimanding those who stray from the course.

This simple, three-part management model (goal setting, praising, reprimanding) has considerable relevance to our examination of economic life from a Catholic perspective. Because Catholic social doctrine lacks an unequivocal statement about the *objective* of economic activity, the Church never seems quite certain about the economic actions it should be *praising* and those it should be *reprimanding.*

Pope John Paul II's 1987 encyclical *Sollicitudo Rei Socialis* (*On Social Concerns*) offers a good illustration of this problem. Had Blanchard and Johnson been asked to review the letter before it was released, they may have offered some suggestions about its organization. "Emphasize the goal," would have been their likely advice. Instead of starting with the objectives of economic activity, the pope opens with a stern reprimand. John Paul starts by blasting both "underdevelopment" and "superdevelopment."

Later in his letter, the tone shifts dramatically and the pope offers praise for economic initiative and courage—two themes he takes up much more extensively in his 1991 letter *Centesimus Annus* (*The One Hundreth Year*). Toward the end of *Sollicitudo Rei Socialis*, he writes: "There is no justification, then, for despair or pessimism or inertia. Though it be with sorrow, it must be said that just as one may sin through selfishness and the desire for excessive profit and power, one may also be found wanting with regard to the urgent needs of multitudes of human beings submerged in conditions of underdevelopment through fear, indecision and, basically, through cowardice."

This paragraph summarizes the moral dilemma Catholic social teaching finds in economic life. Christians are warned about the economic extremes they should avoid—"selfishness and the desire for excessive profit and power" on the one hand and "fear, indecision and...cowardice" on the other. Preoccupation with dilemmas, however, can leave the faithful with a "damned if I do, damned if I don't" attitude that makes them unreceptive to the full potential of Catholic social thought. The MBO practitioners tell us that goals are reached when people are praised for going down the right road and reprimanded for going down the wrong one. They are not reached when people get stuck at the intersection.

That the Catholic Church should be unclear about the goal of economic activity is not surprising in light of the uncertainty within the economics profession itself. Is the primary focus of economics coping with shortages or expanding wealth? Is aggregate demand or the initiative of suppliers the driving force in the economy? Do we push or do we pull to keep the economy on track? Each side in these debates has its own "school" of economics. With or without a religious perspective, economic theory is not a subject that offers universally accepted answers.

For their part, the U.S. Catholic bishops offered a summary statement to the "why" question in their 1986 pastoral letter *Economic Justice for All*. "Every perspective on economic life that is human, moral and Christian," they said, "must be shaped by three questions: What does the economy do for people? What does it do to people? And, how do people participate in it?"

Yet questions—no matter how thought provoking—are not goals. Management theorists would say the bishops are setting "constraints" rather than suggesting "objectives." The bishops are saying, in effect, that Americans can pursue whatever economic goals they choose and can structure their economy any way they want, as long as they show proper concern for people. This approach is certainly in harmony with the Catholic tradition. Both the bishops in their pastoral letters and the popes in their social encyclicals have been reluctant to endorse any particular form of economic organization. Thus, Church leaders have confined their economic commentary to norms and guidelines. Independent of clearly stated goals, however, such guidelines can become very confusing.

An Obvious Answer

What, then, should be the goal of all economic activity?

I am tempted to say that the answer to this question is obvious. Memories of a discussion held many years ago about the "goal" of drinking alcoholic beverages, however, make me aware that "obvious" is a very subjective term. In the winter of 1965, Wernersville, Pennsylvania, was hit by a heavy snowstorm which blocked rural roads near the Jesuit novitiate I was attending. For an entire day, we seminarians shoveled snow so that fuel trucks could service freezing homes and residents requiring medical attention could drive to the hospital. That evening the Master of Novices arranged for us to be served hot toddies (the only alcoholic beverages we would receive for two years). As he was passing by the kitchen table where we were sipping our drinks, I remarked to another novice, "I can't feel the alcohol." The next day, my comment became the subject of a long discussion about the evils of alcoholism. People (like me) who wanted to drink until they "feel it" obviously had a problem. I attempted to defend my simple assertion that one drank alcoholic beverages to receive a pleasant, relaxing, physical sensation, but my argument was not accepted. To accept my "feel it" theory would open the door to inebriation being the "goal" of drinking, I was told. Drinking alcoholic beverages could have as its end socializing and conviviality, but it should have nothing to do with seeking physical sensations.

My intention back then was not to argue with the novice master. He was the first person I had ever met who was openly committed to a life of holiness, and I will always admire him. Nor am I looking today for a quarrel with the U.S. Catholic episcopate and our wonderful pope. The appropriateness of their writing on social issues cannot be challenged. They issue a powerful appeal for Catholics to take our economic responsibilities seriously. Yet I believe both the complexity and ambiguity of Catholic teaching on economic life could be reduced if it started with the "obvious."

ECONOMIC HAPPINESS

Economic activity is no different than any other aspect of life, which has one simple goal: happiness. This is so obvious that it needs to be reiterated. The specific objective of economic activity is happiness. Saying that economic activity has something to do with "development" or with "improving the lot of humankind" is not convincing enough for anyone. The Church should state clearly and consistently that the goal of economic activity is universal prosperity leading to universal happiness.

In my novitiate discussion, I was unsuccessful in convincing others that my "feel it" theory did not lead—directly or necessarily—to drunkenness as the goal or end of drinking. I expect my arguments about prosperity to be criticized on similar grounds—namely, that they promote selfishness and greed and are little more than an echo of the discredited "Gospel of Prosperity" that equates holiness with financial success. Spared the intimidating gaze of a novice master, however, I will try to explain why a focus on prosperity through productivity actually leads to a most demanding course of economic involvement and provides the most appropriate way to appreciate the sanctifying potential of economic life.

Developing a proper understanding of prosperity is the key to this argument. A simple definition will not suffice, but it does provide a good starting point. Prosperity's root meaning is the fulfillment of our hopes (*pro-spero*). Prosperity is more than an economic condition; it is also an attitude—the exact opposite of despair (or *de-spero*), the abandonment of hope. Prosperity is a state of plenty which is never visited by the greedy, since they are incapable of saying "enough." Prosperity's connection with the virtue of hope is the insight that achieving fulfillment depends a great deal on the intended source of one's satisfaction.

One reason I find the concept of prosperity so appealing and so important is that its notion of "fullness" closely parallels my understanding of God. The Creator had in the act of Creation a "why," an objective. That goal, which has been revealed to us in the Scriptures, is to unite the human with the divine, to give us all a share in the fullness of God. For the Christian, the search for this fullness begins with the person who made God visible to us—Jesus Christ, the Anointed One, the Messiah, "the Way, the Truth, and the Life."

THE TRINITY AND THE *ECONOMIA*

The central revelation of Christ's life, death and resurrection is Trinity: God as Creator, God as Redeemer, God as Sanctifier. Although this is the foundation of our Christian faith, the relevance of the Trinity to the problems of daily life is largely ignored. Fortunately, theologians such as Catherine Laguna are responding to the need for a Trinitarian spirituality that emphasizes the practicality of this doctrine. In her book, *God For Us: The Trinity & Christian Life*, Laguna consistently uses the term *"economia"* to describe God's plan of salvation. She suggests that we can find within the mystery of the Trinity powerful clues to the true nature of all happiness, including economic happiness.

The first lesson of the Trinity, one with direct economic application, is that love is *expansive*. Love is *always* fruitful. There are three persons in the Trinity—not one, or even two. The love between the Father and Son is something real, a Holy Spirit "in addition to" either of the other divine persons.

By *incarnating* the love between God and us—thereby making it visible—Jesus revealed to us the fullness of love found only in God. *Poverty* was an important part of Christ's message, but *shortages* were not. He spoke of *fullness* and *completeness*—the fullness of life, the completeness of joy. Through Jesus Christ we all have a share of God's fullness. This is one powerful message of the doctrine of the Trinity.

A second lesson of the Trinity, the importance of relationships, is even more directly related to the concept of productivity. If each of us is an independent economic agent and if each of our transactions must stand on its own economic merits, productivity makes little sense. There is then no long-term payback for generating value in excess of cost, since we are only measuring "gains" against our own subjective situation. In the context of relationships, however, productive behavior becomes much more understandable.

Our failure to understand this practical application of the doctrine of the Trinity is particularly unfortunate since the central problems of our day are relationship issues. Relationships come in many varieties: husband and wife; parent and child; the individual and the state; the rich and the poor; workers and managers; stockholders and board members; borrowers and lenders; developing nations and developed nations; the pope and bishops; bishops and priests; priest and parishioners. Yet the basic conflicts in these relationships are often quite similar.

For those struggling with these relationship issues, the revelation of Jesus Christ about the Trinity provides a most important framework in which to resolve difficulties. Jesus taught that God is a God of relationships. The relationship among Father, Son and Holy Spirit is not one of static equality; instead, the Trinity pulsates with the rhythm of surrender and exaltation. Christ not only delivered this message, but also invited us to join in that three-in-one relationship that grounds all reality. Our faith in one God with three divine persons eliminates the most perplexing problem arising from relationships: the tension between love and freedom.

In his letter to the Philippians, St. Paul tells us how Jesus handled this "problem." Christ emptied himself. He abandoned all claim to parity, forsaking the rights of Creator to become a creature. Jesus "did not believe equality with God something to be grasped at." This emptying, however, did not result in the destruction of Christ's divinity; it confirmed it. "Because of this, God highly exalted him and bestowed on him the name above every name, so that at Jesus' name every knee must bend in the heavens, on the earth, and under the earth, and every tongue proclaim to the glory of God the Father: JESUS CHRIST IS LORD!"

Thus, the Trinity provides us with a compelling lesson on love's explosive force. In a loving relationship we forsake our parity with our partners and "empty" ourselves. The promise of the Trinity is that each person's fullness is enhanced—not diminished—within such an arrangement. The Father being Father does not threaten the Son. The Son does not threaten the Father. Neither of them threaten nor are threatened by the Spirit. Theirs is a relationship of total harmony, the combination of perfect individuality and perfect oneness.

We neither can nor need to understand the complete meaning of this mystery. As believers, however, we should recognize the solution the Trinity offers to the dilemma that love poses: Will I lose my identity, my individuality and my freedom if I surrender myself to a loving relationship? While teaching us that emptiness is a pre-condition for fullness, the lesson of the Trinity also reminds us that the rewards of a loving union are always worth the risks.

Within the Trinity, then, we find both the basis for a Christian understanding of prosperity and a guide to reaching our objective. The goal we aspire to is a state of fullness, a state of sufficiency, a state of grace. Belief in the Trinity helps us understand that behavior within loving relationships conforms to the backward logic of the cross, which redefines the meaning of self-interest. To die is to live, to lose is to find, to surrender is to be free.

The power of relationships, therefore, is the key to a Catholic understanding of economic expansion. Alone, each person is confronted with personal limitations and material shortages. Within relationships—within community—the expansive power of love is released, just as it is in the Trinity.

Jesus showed how, when passed through the right hands, five barley loaves and a couple of dried fish are enough to satisfy the multitudes. When shared among people, finite matter can acquire infinite usefulness. Harmony with other persons is the key to harmony with the material order.

ECONOMIC VERIFICATION

What could be more impractical than to introduce the Trinity into a discussion of contemporary economics? Yet the attempt to overcome material limitations—while also seemingly impractical—is at the center of all economic theories. Indeed, economists have verified that the alchemists were right all along: There is a way to turn base matter into gold! Monetarists focus on the role of central banks in creating wealth by expanding the money supply. For them, the only limit on the amount of money that can be created soundly is the number of sound loan proposals. Keynesians, followers of British economist John Maynard Keynes, emphasize the role of government spending in stimulating demand. The only limit they place on the economy is the number of worthwhile projects which can be created.

Traditional capitalists and neo-traditional "supply-siders" highlight the importance of the production function. Producing an item, they say, generates sufficient wealth to buy the item. If the item is useful, it will create its own market. On the other side of the economic spectrum, Marxists stress the value added by labor.

Each of these economic theories has its distinctive features, but all of them posit some form of initiative that allows economic participants to organize the material order in a way that transcends its limitations. What could be more Trinitarian? Economics is not a physical science; it is a social science. As was noted earlier, economics also should be regarded as a life science, since an economy is capable of actual growth. The way an economy grows is through human relationships that are modeled on the Trinity.

This assertion can best be verified by the way the size of the economy is measured. Gross domestic product (GDP), which has replaced gross national product (GNP) as the government's preferred economic measurement, tabulates the total number of economic interactions—not just the amount of money, raw materials, or people in the economy. The GDP number will expand—even if population and raw material supplies remain stable—as long as creative ways of exchanging goods and services can be discovered. Like the Trinity, the economy is sufficient to itself.

PERSONAL VERIFICATION

Thirty years ago, I would have considered the literal creation of new wealth an interesting but unverifiable theory. Since then, however, my career has provided too many conclusive experiences for me to deny the expansive power of a creative idea coupled with human cooperation. The key event which started my transformation from newspaper writer to newspaper manager occurred in 1975 in Charleston, West Virginia, when I was asked to coordinate the *Sunday Gazette-Mail*'s annual "Progress Edition." John McGee, president of Charleston Newspapers, suggested delaying the issue so that we could re-focus it on the state's then booming coal industry. Because of his simple suggestion, the edition more than doubled in size that year.

In keeping with McGee's idea, we transformed the news content of the edition from cursory reviews and generalized statements to an analytical overview of the West Virginia economy—with particular emphasis on coal. As the edition's coordinator, I was asked to make presentations to the newspaper's advertising staff, explaining news plans and offering reasons why readers would find our reports informative. Throughout the newspaper building, an enthusiastic spirit developed among writers, editors, photographers, sales and production people—all intent on making the edition something special. And it was! The 100-page "Progress '75" showed what good things can happen when people take a concept, implement it, and market it successfully. The newspaper's employees, readers, advertisers and owners all benefited from a cooperative effort that stemmed from a good idea.

A second verifying experience was my tenure at the *Asbury Park* (N.J.) *Press*, which has been one of the nation's fastest growing daily newspapers during the past 40 years. Even though its market's growth has been considerable, this has not been the only factor behind the *Press'* success. When the Jersey Shore began its transformation from a resort area to a populous suburb of New York City after World War II, there were four small daily newspapers based in Red Bank, Long Branch, Asbury Park and Toms River. The first to fall by the wayside was The *Long Branch Record,* which folded in 1975. Around that same time, the *Red Bank Register*, apparently destined for expansion, moved to a modern plant in nearby Shrewsbury. Yet, despite the backing of a succession of large corporate owners, this paper was unable to capitalize on the rapid growth and exceptional affluence of its part of the Shore market. It, too, is now out of business. The *Toms River Observer*, situated in Dover Township, the market's largest municipality, has been kept alive by two large newspaper chains, but its circulation has stagnated despite the tremendous growth of the towns where it is distributed.

In contrast to the experience of the three other papers, the *Press*, which until 1985 was located in Asbury Park, one of the few genuinely poor towns in the market, has quadrupled in size and is now the second largest newspaper in New Jersey. Again, a concept and cooperation have been the deciding factors. The newspaper's owners, the late Ernest Lass and the current chairman, Jules Plangere, Jr., recognized that the success of the *Press* depended upon its distinctiveness and pursued a clearly defined growth program. Unlike the Red Bank/Shrewsbury and Toms River papers, the *Press* refused to consider itself a local paper. On the other hand, it made no pretense of being a major metropolitan newspaper like the *New York Times* or the *Star-Ledger* of Newark, which also circulate in the market. The *Press* consciously decided to become a regional newspaper—much more comprehensive than the locals and much more local than the "metros." Because of close cooperation among all departments in executing this strategy, *The Press* has thrived by following this "middle" way.

Where did the added pages of the *Gazette-Mail* "Progress Edition" or the added circulation of the *Asbury Park Press* come from? They came, in one sense, from nowhere. They were the result of the expansive power of the good ideas and the cooperative relationships of the people involved.

PROSPERITY NOT AN ILLUSION

Recognizing the organic, even "miraculous," nature of wealth's expansion can give new legitimacy to a religious perspective on the economy. For the believer, acknowledging prosperity as something that is created by the interaction of people of good will provides another opportunity to appreciate the expansive force of divine love. Yet prosperity is far more than an idealistic notion. The material component of economic happiness also must be acknowledged.

St. James had fitting words for those who would equate prosperity merely with a state of mind. "If a brother or sister has nothing to wear and no food for the day, and you say to them 'Goodbye and good luck! Keep warm and well fed,' but do not meet their bodily needs, what good is that?"

The U.S. bishops, echoing the teaching of Pope John XIII in his encyclical *Pacem In Terris* (*Peace on Earth*), address this same issue in their economic pastoral: "A number of human rights also concern human welfare and are of a specifically economic nature. First among these are the rights to life, food, clothing, shelter, rest, medical care and basic education. These are essential to the protection of human dignity." Any definition of prosperity that does not include such material essentials would be meaningless.

As important as a person's material status, however, is his or her reaction to that status. An essential ingredient in prosperity is personal satisfaction. If our definition of prosperity is "hopes fulfilled," then prosperity also cannot be identified merely with wealth or affluence. The wealthy person is not prosperous so long as he or she is controlled by an "all consuming desire" for more things. People are prosperous as long as they can say, "We have enough."

From the Gospel parable of the widow's mite through the papal encyclicals on social justice, Christian writers have employed the distinction between giving from one's "abundance" and giving from "necessities." The church "is obliged" to do both, Pope John Paul II has stated. Within this distinction, however, is an essential link between true prosperity and true generosity. All acts of sharing, even the poor widow's, involve the "I have enough" statement. Giving from one's "necessities" creates recognition of one's "abundance." Only the full glass overflows.

PROSPERITY AND GENEROSITY

An unequivocal endorsement of prosperity as the goal of economic activity would have important implications for the Catholic Church in the U.S. and around the world, for affirming prosperity is a key step toward cultivating generosity.

Several reports dealing with Catholics' economic status and their giving habits underscore the distinction between the affluence and the prosperity of American Catholics. One of the most comprehensive of these studies was the 1987 analysis of survey data, *The American Catholic People*, by George Gallup, Jr., and James Castelli. "For the first time in the history of the nation," they wrote, "the proportion of Catholics in 'upscale' groups (upper income and education levels) matches the proportion of Protestants." Using the percentage of families with incomes above $40,000 and the percentage of persons employed in business/professional occupations as their benchmarks, the authors ranked Catholics the third most affluent Christian denomination in the U.S., behind only Episcopalians and Presbyterians.

While the Gallup and Castelli research showed that the typical Catholic in the U.S. has an economic situation equal to or exceeding that of the typical Protestant, their findings also indicated that Catholics say that they need more to get by than Protestants claim they need. When asked for an assessment of the amount of money needed by a family of four, Catholics responded to surveys with a figure seven percent higher than the Protestant response.

The fact that the sense of needing more has not been removed by Catholics' rising incomes may be one reason why studies have shown that Catholics' growing affluence has not been reflected in their contributions. Noted sociologist Rev. Andrew Greeley and others have documented that Catholics share a substantially lower percentage of their incomes with their churches than do their Protestant brethren. Because Catholics are not sharing their increased good fortune, the Church is struggling to maintain educational and social service programs that thrived in the past.

In his book, *Catholic Contributions*, co-written by Bishop William McManus, Greeley states that Catholics have been using their contributions to express dissatisfaction with Church policies. My own explanation of the disparity between income growth and contributions is much more straight forward. Catholics were once quite proud of their *poverty,* but we are now ashamed of our *affluence*.

Affirming prosperity—that sense of fullness which propels thankfulness and generosity—would allow faithful Catholics to reconcile their economic advancement with their religious beliefs. Then we could in good conscience both enjoy and share our economic abundance. If American Catholics continue to hear "it is more blessed to be needy" (which, in my opinion, is a perversion of Jesus' teaching), they will continue to feel needy. Preoccupied with our needs, we lose sight of the gifts we should be offering the rest of the world.

As will be explained more fully in subsequent chapters, greed has no place in a Christian vision of prosperity. Instead, the Christian recognizes the reinforcing relationship between generosity and prosperity. By sharing, we reaffirm our prosperity. Through our acts of giving, we proclaim that we have enough. And once we acknowledge our prosperity, we are then obliged to share. Before the glass can overflow, it must be full. Once the glass is full, everything added must overflow.

At the heart of our Catholic faith is a recognition that the force for goodness we call grace draws us to the fullness found only in the Blessed Trinity, the three-in-one relationship that provides a framework for all our personal relationships. This attraction to fullness, represented by the drive toward prosperity, provides the "why" of economic life. This energy does not stimulate selfishness but instead prompts us to form economic relationships that are productive—that is, marked by generosity and self-giving.

MUTUALITY IN MARRIAGE
AND IN THE MARKETPLACE

Pondering the mystery of the Trinity is an appropriate warm-up exercise for tackling that most mysterious of all economic phenomena: the mutually profitable exchange in which both parties simultaneously give more than they get and get more than they give. Although it is challenging, the attempt to explain this mystery is an important step in this development of a Catholic version of economic growth that maximizes respect for all human persons.

In the previous chapter, I tried to show that reflection on the dynamics of the Trinity, as revealed to us through the life, death and resurrection of Jesus Christ, provides a way of understanding the creative force unleashed through loving, self-surrendering relationships. In this chapter, I will focus on another Catholic concept which also suggests the qualities that make all personal relationships—including our economic ones—fruitful and productive: that of mutuality.

Examining mutuality in human affairs takes us to the next level of insight into the sanctifying potential of pursuing prosperity through productive relationships. Studying the husband-wife sexual relationship, for example, shows how personal relationships can be both sacrificial and rewarding at the same time. Applying this insight to the buy-sell relationships of the marketplace can provide several hints about the possible integration of economic activity into a full Christian life.

THE MUTUALITY OF SEXUALITY

According to Catholic tradition, the family—father, mother and child—is the best human representation of the Trinity. It also can be most visible symbol of love's expansive force. The child literally embodies the love the mother and father have for each other. Their love becomes another person, totally distinct from the father and the mother but still connected in very integral ways.

In our society, we never talk about a shortage of children. In fact, our culture is geared to controlling their number. Our preoccupation with contraception prevents us from deriving an important economics lesson from marital sexual activity. The productive act of a new child's creation should serve as a conclusive testament to the multiplying effects of mutual love.

In a society where peace rather than war between the sexes reigned, the union of wife and husband would serve more readily as the model of all human interactions. Regardless of our particular views about sexual bliss and turmoil, however, our overall attitude toward the wife-husband relationship has profound implications for our approach to economic life. Accepting the possibility of true mutuality in marriage is essential if we are to embrace the possibility of mutuality in the economic realm.

In male-female sexual intercourse the sensation of pleasuring and the sensation of being pleasured are indistinguishable. We do not still ask whether being the female or the male participant in the sexual act is more enjoyable. We have reached a point in our cultural development where we recognize the absurdity of such a question. Determining whether the man or the woman profits most from the transaction—that is, receives more than he or she gives—is impossible. Both the woman and the man can achieve satisfaction through a sexual union. Each offers a sexual identity that complements the other's. Their pleasure is mutual.

How many of life's problems would disappear if we saw sex in its full symbolic—indeed sacramental—significance? How many of our views would change if we recognized that sex is not something exceptional but rather the most intense expression of the very basic human reality that all personal transactions, guided by love, are meant to be mutually satisfying, mutually fulfilling, and mutually expansive?

Many religious reservations about economic life, for instance, would fade if the possibility of mutually profitable exchanges were better appreciated. In fact, all transactions contributing to economic improvement involve some form of more-for-less exchange. In other words, some form of profit is the source of all prosperity. The Catholic Church has carefully avoided outright condemnation of profits. Nevertheless, the frequent use of the modifier "excessive" in official Church documents suggests that profit is something taken *from* others rather than something shared *with* others.

If all persons are the same, with the same needs and the same gifts, then someone must win and another must lose in every economic exchange. Instead of applying the notion of mutual satisfaction to such a transaction, our instinctive reaction is to employ another sexual expression. "One of the parties is getting screwed," we say. If sex is "screwing" (that is, an act in which one partner's pain is the source of the other's pleasure), then applying its concept of mutuality to other areas of human relationships will be impossible. Yet sex need not be "screwing." Because of the radical differences between women and men, the sexual act can be a mutually satisfying exchange of pleasure, especially in the context of a lifelong, committed relationship.

Pleasure in lovemaking is not a limited commodity to be divided between the lovers. We do not say the wife's pleasure detracts from her husband's or that the husband's excitement diminishes his wife's. Just the opposite is true. We recognize the important contribution each lover's enjoyment adds to the couple's mutual sexual satisfaction.

MUTUAL PROFIT

The concept of mutual profit closely parallels the notion of mutual pleasure found in the sexual act. Both are grounded on the fundamental individuality of every human person. Each person's sexuality—not only his or her anatomy, but personality as well—is a visible sign that every person possesses unique gifts and unique needs. Yet, at the same time, we know that all men and all women are both gifted and needy, that all men and all women have both the ability to satisfy and the desire to be satisfied.

Once gender differences come to be appreciated as a great source of mutuality, other signs of difference within the human community can acquire new meaning. Racial characteristics, for example, also should be celebrated—for they, too, are important marks of individuality. The variety of skin colors in the world shows us there are not just two prototypes of humanity, but an unlimited number. For Catholics schooled in St. Paul's doctrine of the Mystical Body of Christ, gender and race are important reminders of the unique way each person brings the human community nearer to its goal of fullness. In Paul's first letter to the Corinthians, we hear: "The eye cannot say to the hand, 'I do not need you,' any more than the head can say to the feet, 'I do not need you.' Even those members of the body which seem less important are in fact indispensable."

This understanding of human diversity can help economic transactions become much more intelligible. Suddenly, what seemed impossible becomes possible. Because of diversity, both buyer and seller can profit from a single transaction. Once the mutuality of humanity is accepted, the mutuality of commercial transactions can be accepted as well. Profit does not exist before a transaction. It is created by the commercial relationship. Profit occurs when one person receives something of greater value for something of less value. Since every person is unique, the individual's possessions and needs also are unique. Therefore, value is a highly personal concept and can be created on both sides at the same time!

For example, the person who sells a car, house or share of stock obviously values cash more than those particular possessions. Because value is a relative notion, the seller profits from the transaction—almost regardless of the original price paid for the items being sold. Buyers thus perform a real service by allowing sellers to liquidate their investment. On the other side of the transaction, the purchaser values the car, house or share of stock more than the money he or she pays for it. Thus, the seller also has performed a real service for the buyer by making the exchange.

VALUE, NOT COST

If cost were the only component of value, then mutuality would be difficult—if not impossible—to achieve. The seller would be unable to offer something whose worth exceeded the price paid for it. Yet value ultimately is determined by the buyer's needs, not the seller's costs. Successful companies thus search for innovations that will make their products more useful without increasing the costs of production proportionately.

For example, every newspaper and magazine I have worked for attaches a premium (either a higher price or special conditions) on an advertisement that appears on its back cover. Is it wrong for publications to charge more for a back cover advertisement than for one placed on an inside page? After all, the cost of producing any one page is identical. Both research and common sense, however, verify the fact that ads appearing on the back cover attract much higher readership. As an example, if the readership increase enjoyed by a back-cover ad is 50 percent, then such an ad should be worth 50 percent more than an interior ad. However, when the premium charged for that same back-page placement is less than 50 percent—25 percent, for instance—both the advertiser and the publication profit. The advertiser literally gets more readership than it is paying for, and the publication picks up additional revenue not offset by any additional cost.

This book is being written with the assistance of word-processing software that came stored on plastic diskettes which cost only a few cents to manufacture. Should the cost of production dictate the price? Is it wrong for a company to charge dollars rather than pennies for its product? The answer is (and should be) no. The usefulness of the product should be the only relevant consideration to determining its value.

Every industry contains situations in which companies can provide extra value for their customers at little or no extra cost. These "extras" are the foundation of all profit and, therefore, all prosperity. In an exchange that mirrors the husband-wife relationship, buyer and seller come together and create value which did not exist and would not exist outside of their mutuality.

In the economic area—as in the sexual area—the question, "Who is getting the best deal?" often is irrelevant. The only meaningful test is mutuality. Do both partners profit from the exchange? Do both partners experience satisfaction? If the answers are "yes," other questions are pointless. Anyone who has witnessed the joy on both sides of a table when a mutually acceptable sale/purchase of a house is concluded knows that mutual satisfaction is attainable within economic affairs.

Sex as Sacrifice

Reflecting on sexual relationships also can help us recognize the sacrifice required to sustain long-term, mutually satisfying economic relationships.

Appreciation of the full range of gender differences between a husband and a wife is only one source of sexual satisfaction in marriage. For the relationship to be sustained, the true equality of the marriage partner must be acknowledged as well. Over time, however, affirming a partner's equality requires abandonment of any false sense of superiority. Through their mutual abandonment, husband and wife achieve the Trinitarian experience: the sense of absolute equality and absolute unity that enhances rather than diminishes each partner's individuality.

The Catholic Church has been criticized for being preoccupied with sexual morality. When sex is recognized as the archetype of all human relationships, however, the attention the Church pays it does not seem excessive. The technical definitions of "fruitfulness" and "mutuality" may be open to theological debate, but the Church's insistence that these characteristics be present in every sexual act stems from an unassailable objective.

The Church wants to preserve sex as an expression of giving, not of taking. One of the most serious problems with casual sex is that it confuses reciprocal abuse with mutuality in a way that infects other personal relationships, particularly economic ones. Many consumers, for instance, are susceptible to fraud because they operate according to the "you-can-screw-me-if-I-can-screw-you" philosophy. In contrast, productive economic relationships follow the self-surrender model of loving sex. Accepting another person as the source of our economic satisfaction requires us to abandon all pride and self-sufficiency.

Through its teaching on sexuality, the Catholic Church is reminding us that the logic of the cross offers the only true secret of success. Harmony in the family, in the business enterprise, and in society as a whole is achieved only through the Trinitarian cycle of emptying and exaltation. The possibility of everyone winning is created by a universal willingness to lose. Through the Paschal Mystery, Christ turns the notion of self-interest on its head. Those seeking true life must accept self-denial and even death as being in their ultimate self-interest.

ECONOMIC UNEVENNESS

If we claim to be a truly free society, constructing a view of the economy around the concept of selfishness is impossible. Equally unrealistic is an attempt to build an economy characterized primarily by evenness and balance. Participants in a free economy do not usually undertake an action when their benefits merely equal their costs; they act when the prospect for excess exists. Buyers buy and sellers sell when they can get more than they already have. Like husband and wife, they go beyond the half-way point. The market does not function when Value = Price but only when Value > Price. In a truly free economy, only companies which give their customers more than they feel they pay for can stay in business, and only workers whose efforts exceed their wages will have employment. Yet the opposite conditions also will prevail in a genuinely free economy. Only buyers who pay more than actual cost will be able to make purchases and only employers who overcompensate will be able to attract good workers.

Within a context of freedom and respect for other persons, the drive toward economic advancement becomes a powerful stimulus for economic generosity expressed as productivity. Because fruitfulness is a condition of relationships and not of individuals in isolation, the longing for prosperity as a sense of fullness and harmony with the material order becomes a powerful magnet attracting people together. The economic instinct, no less than the sexual instinct, draws persons into community. The desire for more that stimulates economic activity is not something which should be condemned. Instead, a religious perspective on economic life should help us recognize this pervasive impulse as a precondition for productive, self-surrendering behavior.

A love/rape distinction may be helpful in understanding the significance of more-seeking (profit-seeking) behavior. Not all sexual activity is loving. Both assault and seduction can lead to sexual intercourse. Sex can be hurtful. Yet despite the vulnerability and the potential for pain associated with sex, the church has consistently spoken St. Paul's words to married couples: "Wives should submit to their husbands . . . . Husbands, love your wives, as Christ loved the Church. He gave himself up for her . . . ." The submissiveness of the lover leaves both the man and the woman open to exploitation, but it also provides an invitation for a loving response.

PROSPEROUS VULNERABILITY

Prosperity-seeking behavior also involves both vulnerability and the potential for exploitation. Yet this approach to economic life represents an invitation to love as well. The prosperous economy is based not on obligations, but on gifts. I ask you to give me something more than I have, but I offer you more than you have. Economic activity is transformed from self-seeking to other-serving behavior when the value a buyer can derive from a product—rather than the cost of producing the product—becomes the key determinant of price in the marketplace. I will be glad to buy from you as long as my evaluation of your wares is higher than your price. You should be eager to sell to me as long as my payment is higher than your cost of production. When these conditions exist, the relationship is mutually productive—value exceeds cost on both sides of the transaction.

As this example illustrates, mutuality in economics—as in sex—requires respect and understanding. For you and I to enter into a mutually profitable relationship, we must know each other's needs well enough so that we can create value for the other person in a way that does not exceed our respective costs. As Pope John Paul II noted in *Centesimus Annus*, the "ability to perceive the needs of others and to satisfy them" is among the most important skills needed for participation in the economy. Later chapters in this book will explain in more detail the link between productive behavior and satisfying the demands of the market.

In Catholic social teaching, justice supersedes charity as an economic virtue. "Charity is not enough," the U.S. bishops stated in their pastoral letter *Economic Justice for All*. If the term charity means sharing only one's excess, then the bishops are correct.

Charity is not enough. If, however, we identify charity with the fullness of Christian love—a love that propels us to give our work, our talents, and even our life—then charity is the *only* solution needed to the problem of poverty. Loving one's neighbor as oneself is the key to fashioning the mutually demanding, mutually fulfilling relationships that are the source of prosperity for all.

PURSUING PROSPERITY IN A SPIRIT OF POVERTY

Although the New Testament writers present Jesus as a man (and God) of fullness, they also present him as a man (and God) for the poor. Thus, any attempt to establish prosperity as the proper goal of economic life must acknowledge the Catholic Church's strong tradition of evangelical poverty. An examination of contemporary social justice literature, filled with references to the "preferential option for the poor" and Christianity as a "counterculture religion," suggests the strong Catholic tradition of identification with the poor is getting even stronger.

Reflecting on the Church as a "soothsayer"—that is, an institution charged with helping its faithful read the signs of the times—presents a way to resolve the apparent contradiction between the prosperity approach to economic life and concern for the poor. This reflection also leads to insights about the interaction of priests, religious and the laity in the Church and completes the foundation for a productivity-centered view of economic relationships.

The Catholic Church carries out the soothsayer mission through her system of sacraments. For Christians, Jesus' life, death and resurrection were incontrovertible signs of God's love for us. Catholics believe the sacraments provide the certain signs that Christ remains present through the Spirit. The sacraments signal God's presence in life's most basic experiences: at birth, at death, in forgiveness, in the union of husband and wife, in the passage from youth to adulthood, in the selection of leaders, and—most importantly—in the sharing of food and drink.

Sacraments as Sign Language

From the sacraments flows an approach to life that marks a distinctively Catholic way of viewing reality—in Andrew Greeley's terminology, the "Catholic imagination." Participation in the Church's sacraments provides Catholics with an opportunity to "practice" noticing symbols in a way that encourages proficiency in God's sign language.

Among the most effective teachers of this peculiarly Catholic form of communication are those who have dedicated themselves to religious life through their vows of poverty, chastity and obedience. The interaction of these vowed religious with the rest of the faithful harmonizes the cultural and the countercultural elements within the Christian community. By their willingness to forego such important human experiences as sexual enjoyment, material prosperity, and personal freedom, priests, brothers and sisters offer themselves as signs. The signs they offer, however, are not necessarily meant for emulation as much as to illuminate the true nature of our own human reality. Vowed religious remind Christians that all of us are not yet fully alive. They tell us we are leading a Pinocchio existence, waiting to forsake our wooden ways for the complete joy of the reign of God.

Chastity and Sexual Activity

For example, the witness of religious chastity and priestly celibacy is obviously not a call to universal sexual abstinence. This much is apparent. The Christian community would disappear within a single generation if such an invitation were accepted! The chaste religious does not say to the married couple, "Join me in forsaking sex." Rather, the wise religious encourages the Christian couple to engage in sexual activity with eagerness and joy. Yet, by his or her own chastity, the religious also is cautioning the couple that sex is primarily a sign of a greater reality.

Making love in the Christian community (in the presence, if you will, of chaste abstainers), wife and husband are challenged to clarify the signals they send through their sexual encounters. What does their bodily contact reveal about the nature and depth of their love for one another? What does their physical union say about the nature and depth of God's love for us? The witness of dedicated chastity raises such questions for sexually-active Christians. Without such coaching from the sidelines, married couples would lose a rich source of meaning in their love lives.

The Catholic community is starting to decipher this sign-language communication between celibates and the sexually involved. A number of writers including Greeley, Pope John Paul II, and several Marriage Encounter enthusiasts have contributed greatly to this new understanding. As the Catholic theology of marriage has moved beyond sexual minimalism, we have come to see the important connection between ecstasy and self-transcendence. We know that embracing another person provides a unique opportunity to embrace our creaturehood in a truly salvific way. Now the challenge is to develop a parallel theology of *economic* passion that accentuates the importance of a joyful, satisfying relationship with the material world.

VOLUNTARY POVERTY AND ECONOMIC ACTIVITY

The witness of those who have voluntarily chosen a life of identification with the poor (outstanding examples being St. Francis of Assisi, Mother Teresa and Dorothy Day) is extremely important to the development of what Rev. John C. Haughey, S.J., has termed "the holy use of money." Yet how can we understand the religious poor as models for those of us who are active in the marketplace in a way that does not distort the distinction between religious and secular vocations? If the counter-sign analogy for religious chastity has validity, the message of voluntary religious poverty to the Christian community echoes its exhortation: Engage in economic activity; pursue prosperity with joy and enthusiasm; but remember that economic life is primarily a sign of a greater reality. Like good, wholesome sex, the pursuit of prosperity can be a powerful response to the unifying and expansive nature of God's love. Economic interaction can draw people together in truly creative ventures that multiply nature's abundance.

The counter-signs of evangelical poverty and chastity (more about obedience in a later chapter) also help those outside religious life understand how they are to become united in Christ's passage through death to life. All of life vibrates with the rhythm of the Paschal Mystery, the unavoidable paradox of rising by dying. Priests and religious adopt renunciation as a form of death on their journey toward life. They seek to transcend their selfishness through their vows. The rest of the Christian community, however, also must respond to Christ's call for conversion, his invitation to transcendence. That lay people are not asked to take vows of poverty and chastity does not mean that they are permitted to wallow in selfishness. For most lay people, however, the journey to the new life that exists beyond self-centeredness passes through the very regions vowed religious have pledged to avoid.

Still, the presence and example of vowed religious in the Church encourages the laity to appreciate the human ability to transcend self-interest. In their first draft of the never-to-be published pastoral letter on women's concerns, the U.S. Catholic bishops wrote of women religious: ". . . their choice of life is a validation of the human capacity to love without guarantee of exclusive love in return." This ability to give without the guarantee of getting in return is particularly important in the economic sphere (as we shall see in a later reflection on investment). The risk-taking involved in all forms of economic initiative parallels the religious' willingness to love without a guarantee of being loved.

SIN AS DISTORTION

Finally, the disciplined lives of religious alert the laity to the ever-present tendency of sin to pervert humanity's natural drives. The economic instinct, no less than the sexual instinct, can draw persons into community. But when freedom and respect are no longer present in relationships, the sexual and economic energies that bind people together are distorted into forces of conflict and destruction. Without the critical element of surrender, the sexual urge degenerates into lust and the economic urge degenerates into greed. Both of these sins are manifestations of our attempts to gain what another person has without sharing of ourselves. The witness of vowed religious serves as a reminder that in economic relationships, as in sexual relationships, the humility associated with accepting a partner as equal is the key to sustained satisfaction.

This dialogue—one that should be taking place constantly among priests, religious and the laity—provides a way of summarizing the distinctively Catholic view of economic relationships that takes us beyond the limitations of self-interest. In the sacramental approach, the drive toward prosperity is seen as the economic sign of life's pervasive pull toward fullness in community. Sustained satisfaction of this instinctive urge, which parallels sexual attraction, can only be achieved through productivity, which is the economic expression of self-surrender characterized by a willingness to generate value in excess of cost. To gain wide acceptance, however, this outlook on economic life requires religious affirmation.

As we have seen, contemporary thinking in the Church recognizes that the witness of chastity and celibacy helps married persons maximize true sexual joy. Vowed religious affirm sexuality as a stimulus to love in a way that helps wives and husbands avoid the temptation to lust. Truly satisfying sexual activity always involves self-surrender, priests and religious proclaim. Now, a similar theological development is needed in the economic sphere. The embrace of evangelical poverty must be seen as affirmation and encouragement for the economic impulse—not a denial or denigration of it.

PART II: FREEDOM

The Pre-Requisite for Productivity

- **Fear, Sin and Self-Destruction**

- **Competition: Outdoing One Another in Honor**

- **Spending Freedom in Commitment**

Of his fullness we have all had a share
—love following upon love.

John 1:16

FEAR, SIN, & SELF-DESTRUCTION

Fostering—even discussing—productivity, the gap between what is given and what is received, only makes sense in the context of freedom. In a free society, productivity is a gift. Outside of a free society, however, productivity is rightfully seen as a sign of exploitation. Thus, the search for a fully Catholic understanding of prosperity through productivity leads to one of the most fundamental of all human rights: our freedom. Before we can talk intelligently about the specific steps individuals and society can take to promote greater productivity, we must construct a religious framework of freedom into which recommendations can be placed.

The element which poses the greatest restriction to our freedom is sin. The principle manifestation in our economy of sin is fear. Only by acknowledging the impact of sin-fear on the economy can we develop an appreciation for the connection between economic security and true economic freedom.

SELF-DESTRUCTIVE BEHAVIOR

The traditional defense of a free enterprise system is that the multiplicity of self-interested behaviors eventually interact in a way that produces the maximum good. The logic of this argument would be solid, except for one critical flaw: People are capable of, and regularly practice, self-destructive behavior. The entire debate between advocates of economic freedom and proponents of economic regulation is actually a discussion about the appropriate way for society to cope with sin. Without the tendency of economic participants to ignore their own interests and engage in practices that are hurtful both to themselves and to others, there would be no need for any form of economic controls. Any comprehensive view of the economy must, therefore, take sin and self-destruction into account.

As new supervisors quickly learn, the most difficult employees to manage are rarely the most ambitious. Quite often those with clear goals are willing to expend considerable effort and endure considerable pain to reach them. Praising these workers' farsightedness often is the only management involvement required. In contrast, the most difficult employees to supervise are those who have become so embittered and cynical that they despair of ever having their personal interests recognized. These workers are unwilling to commit themselves to goals. Instead, they regularly engage in various forms of economic "suicide." Their view of work—if not life—has become so skewed that they pursue actions that are patently opposed to their self-interest. Inevitably they must be severed from the organization that employs them.

I speak from experience. One of the great disappointments of my career was having to terminate a graphic artist who had more flair than any person with whom I have worked. In the three years we were associated, however, he consistently practiced obstructionist behavior. Getting promotional material through the art department he supervised became an unending battle. Even though intolerable, his behavior was understandable. I was the third person hired as marketing manager in the eight years he had worked for the company. Every time the job became vacant, he thought it would become his. His feelings of discouragement and disappointment became so strong that he no longer could function effectively.

I repeatedly tried to assure him that, with my recommendation, he could become my successor. His behavior would improve for a brief time and then the self-destructive actions would resume. "Why does he keep pulling these stunts?" I asked myself. After three years, I ran out of explanations and recommended that he be fired.

A short time later, I found myself following a pattern remarkably similar to this man's in my own career. When my business skills began to be challenged, my confidence evaporated. My response to questions about my ability to manage a major project was a fear-induced set of stunts that were no less self-destructive than those of the artist I had fired for doing the same thing.

COLLAPSE OF A CAREER

My undoing at *The Asbury Press* was "the system."

In 1982, the newspaper got involved with one of the most talked about newspaper efforts of the period: Total Market Coverage (TMC). This program had the same basic appeal as President Reagan's Star Wars defense system: Computers will protect us! Newspapers tried to outflank competition from direct mail companies who were attracting advertising from Sears, Kmart, and other companies that traditionally distributed circulars inside local newspapers. The newspaper defense strategy was to develop a mailing list of every residence in its territory. This would allow advertisers to achieve that blissful state of TMC—subscribers would get their circulars in the newspaper while non-subscribers would get them through the mail. This combination was supposed to be much less expensive than distribution completely through the mail.

The main requirement for a TMC program is a circulation information system (CIS) that keeps track (theoretically) of every home in the market and reports who is getting newspaper delivery and who is not. We did not have such a system at *The Press*, but the CIS project manager (me) gave assurances that the newspaper could develop such a system in less than a year. As the uncompleted project entered its *fourth* year, I was ushered out the door.

At the start of the project, I had looked forward to serving as the middle man who spoke both marketing lingo and computer-ese. I understood the advertising importance of CIS, and I also considered myself more than an amateur in the data processing field. I had picked up my MBA at a school which stressed quantitative analysis (among other things, I had researched the application of computerized "least time" models to newspaper delivery systems). With the encouragement of the Charleston Newspapers data processing department, I had written several programs to analyze market research information.

At *The Asbury Park Press*, however, the attitude of the data processing department toward outsiders playing with their computers was quite different. Even though I had helped computerize job scheduling in the marketing department and been one of the first in the company to use a dormant word processing package imbedded in the computer system, I was told to keep my hands off the new CIS computers. Had I obeyed that simple directive, my career would have followed a different course. Yet I was not content to be a respected marketing or circulation professional; I wanted to be a computer whiz as well.

My first foray behind "enemy" lines went very well. The project schedule was seriously affected at the outset when we made the decision to construct our data base internally—management had balked at purchasing a list of all the homes in the two-county market. Data Processing Manager Tom Cosgrove and his boss, Systems Director Anthony Ordino, wanted our first key deadline postponed indefinitely. This would give them time to develop a method of entering and verifying the 325,000 address records which would comprise the base. Not wanting to blow my first major project management assignment by missing an important deadline, I made an end-run around them and went directly to their most talented programmer, Leo Zachek. By appealing to his programming vanity—"You're the best, Leo! Work some of that Zachek magic!"—I coaxed him into writing a data entry program I had devised. Utilizing the fact that the 325,000 addresses—an unmanageable number given our time constraints—were clustered on only 18,000 streets, we created a way to build our base in only six weeks. We met our first project check point. From a team-unity standpoint, however, developing the data-entry routine was stupid. We had done what Cosgrove and Ordino said could not be done. They accused me of jeopardizing the project with my "April 10th" mentality (a reference to the first deadline date). Yet the Haas-Zachek system was so simple to learn that we were able to use personnel from throughout the company to enter addresses. No one could question the air of excitement about CIS this created. When we encountered another delay a few months later, I had no hesitancy in going directly to Zachek.

CIS required a radical accounting adjustment for the circulation department. Previously, only two issues mattered: (1) How many newspapers did each carrier (or retail outlet) receive each day? (2) Did the newspaper eventually get paid for these newspapers? Thus, the newspaper allowed carriers to change their orders or "draw" on a daily basis.

The new system tracked subscriber information as well as carrier information. Each home in the base was assigned one of seven service codes. No longer was it sufficient to know that Johnny Jones needed 25 Sunday newspapers. Now we needed to know Johnny's "product mix" as well—18 seven-day customers, two Saturday-Sunday customers, and five Sunday-only customers, for instance.

Before record keeping could be shifted from the old computer to the new CIS, each carrier's daily draw had to be converted into service-code information. Ordino and Cosgrove wanted the circulation department to institute an elaborate survey and verification procedure involving each of the newspaper's 3,300 carriers. Such an approach, I argued, would be incredibly time consuming and inherently inaccurate—given the bookkeeping practices of the typical 12-year-old carrier. My department's unspoken fear was that the carriers would not be able to account for all of the newspapers they received. If the Ordino-Cosgrove logic were adopted, circulation would fall and bonus levels would be more difficult to achieve. Again, I "out-systemmed" the systems people. Even though the old arrangement had unlimited flexibility in theory, the carrier draw figures followed clear patterns. I predicted that an approximation method could be devised that would account for virtually every newspaper delivered. No, said the systems people, such an approximation method cannot be devised. Yes, said the circulation manager. I'll show you. I wrote the routine, which Zachek translated into the appropriate computer language, and that is how the infamous "Haas algorithm" was created. As predicted, the routine was highly efficient and accounted for more than 99 percent of the newspapers handled by the youth carriers. The algorithm kept the project moving. As I write this 10 years later, I am sure that algorithm is being blamed for every flaw that still remains in CIS (the goal of a true TMC program has long been abandoned). That certainly was the case during my final two and one-half years at *The Press*.

UNDER THE "PLUS SIGN"

One of the most valuable lessons in human relationships that I took away from my seminary experience was the frequently repeated counsel: "Give your brother the plus sign." In other words, always interpret a person's behavior in a positive light. During my early years at *The Asbury Press,* I definitely operated under the "plus sign." I was surrounded by an atmosphere of goodwill that made success easy. In time I came to believe that I could walk on water. After taking on the challenge of CIS, however, I learned that beneath the surface of the water on which I was walking lurked an incredible quagmire. ("Quagmire" was the apt description of circulation departments John McGee used when I told him I was leaving Charleston Newspapers for a job in Asbury Park that offered greater circulation involvement).

Had CIS required only a change in bookkeeping procedures, its installation would have been simple. Before *The Press* could implement its new program, however, it had to gain access to the route lists of the independent news dealers, who controlled about 20 percent of the newspaper's circulation. This step required a complete restructuring of the newspaper's legal relationship with its delivery force. Along with mounting tension between the circulation and systems departments, year one of the CIS project included the following: lengthy negotiations with 30 news dealers; a threatened dealers' "strike;" an anti-trust investigation by the state attorney general's office into our new distribution contracts; and $800,000 in un-budgeted delivery fees. Coaching us through these complications was Hugh Morrison, a Washington, D.C., antitrust specialist and a partner in the law firm of Cahill, Gordon & Reindell.

His inspiration kept me afloat for three years. Morrison advised us that any agreement with the dealers over the route-list issue would affect the newspaper's ability to settle other aspects of dealer relations. Thus, he forced us to formulate in a very brief time a long-term strategy for gaining full control of *The Press'* home delivery operation. The new contracts eliminated dealer service charges, but the dealers' lost income was replaced by a schedule of fees from the newspaper.

Morrison gave us the simplest, most valuable legal advice of all: The way to avoid entanglements is to avoid damaging other people's rights. He did not try to show us how to hurt the dealers with impunity. He educated us about the full range of rights dealers had established in other situations and challenged us to harmonize our program with the dealers' legally-protected interests. In addition, he also reminded us that the law sets only a *minimum* floor for behavior and does not preclude generosity. To the majority of questions posed—"Can we do this? Do we have to do that?"— his response was: "That is a business decision." He never once said: "I'll show you a way you won't have to do that." Instead, he acknowledged and encouraged *The Press'* desire to deal fairly with the dealers who had provided the newspaper with a very low-cost distribution system for many years.

ENCOUNTER WITH TERROR

Persuading all the dealers to sign the newspaper's new distribution contract gave me a false sense of security. I was sinking deeper into the quagmire but did not know it. In year two of the project, I received my first serious lesson in business "hardball." With financial aid from the bank which handled all of *The Press'* business, an Asbury Park businessman (I will call him "Jefferson" since he was the third in a succession of disagreeable characters) acquired one of the newspaper's new distributorships and installed his son to run it. Despite the unprecedented fee structure, father and son soon discovered the newspaper delivery business involved more work and less money than they anticipated. They wanted the newspaper to buy out their contract. Eventually, *The Press* did just that—but not before I was exposed to intimidating tactics I did not learn about in business school (and not even in the seminary).

I knew nothing about the Jeffersons before their take-over of the distributorship. In my naiveté, I thought the bank recommendation was all I needed to know, since I could not conceive of anyone more frightful than their predecessor, "Adams" (character number two in the drama). Adams had been instrumental in the downfall of a *New York Times* circulation director, and I was extremely glad to be rid of him. Had he not been seriously ill at the time, our 1983 dealer negotiations would have been much more difficult. Even in his weakness, however, Adams was strong enough to initiate a New Jersey antitrust complaint against the newspaper.

At our first meeting, the elder Jefferson was charming. He good-naturedly diffused any conclusions one might draw from his

Italian heritage or his business interests in cigarette vending machines and boardwalk amusements. He did not mention the fact
that he had been indicted once for engaging two people to torch a
Maryland racetrack. (Maybe I should not mention it, either, since
the charges were dismissed.) Later, after my nothing-could-be-
worse illusions were shattered, I discovered the news department
had a file on Jefferson. When I read the yellowed press clipping
about the indictment, his threats of "trouble" if *The Press* did not
go along with his demands—either give him free newspapers or
buy out his contract—took on new meaning. At a farewell dinner—a peace offering he extended after the newspaper acceded
to his demands—Jefferson gave an angry discourse on the link
between ethnic discrimination and New Jersey's "alternate"
economy. "For years, bankers treated people in the amusement
business like dirt," he said. "Where was I to go for financing?
Then along comes Disney and Six Flags and they're treated like
big stuff. They are in the same business as I am—amusements.

"Do you think a little guy can get bank financing to open a
bar?" he asked. "But we know that bars are a great place to sell
cigarettes. That's why we try to help guys open bars."

The newspaper delivery service the Jeffersons owned for a
brief period had been a source of trouble to *The Press* for several
years. Its original owner, "Washington," had once embarrassed
the newspaper's publisher by raising prices and eliminating porch
delivery in the publisher's neighborhood. In 1982, the newspaper
could have solved the problem for $15,000 by foreclosing on
Washington's long overdue newspaper bill. Instead, to avoid the
write-off (and to prevent Washington from making good on a
suicide threat), the delivery service was allowed to pass first to

Adams and then to the Jeffersons. Two years later, buying out the Jeffersons' contract cost *The Press* $150,000.

ON PROBATION

My reputation at the newspaper fell by the difference in those two amounts. A few weeks after the settlement with the Jeffersons was reached, I was placed on probation.

Actually, the situation could have been worse. After a heated meeting with the general manager, my boss, Charles Ritscher, alerted me to the fact that my job was in jeopardy. Did I want him to try to save it or should he negotiate a severance arrangement? The choice was mine, he said, shortly before we left the office for the weekend.

I talked the situation over with my wife that evening and we both decided that I should do everything possible to salvage my Press career. I arranged a meeting with Ritscher at his home on Sunday afternoon.

Together, we analyzed the frequent stupidity of my actions. My preoccupation with who was right and who was wrong was creating a lot of trouble, he said. If the group wanted to make a wrong move, that was the group's prerogative. I had to accept circulation's link to other departments and the fact that I was not the top man at the newspaper, Ritscher said.

A week later, I was presented with a list of ten performance deficiencies to be corrected within six months.

After reviewing the memo, I met one-on-one with the publisher and the general manager. Next I wrote a two-page response memo, which probably sounded like the "I'll try to be good" statement of a spanked little boy. I commented on one charge that I displayed a "subliminal resistance to authority" and pledged my loyalty and obedience to the company. I apologized for "being a source of interdepartmental tension rather than a catalyst for inter-departmental cooperation." I also drew the connection between my fears and my negative behavior:

"Ironically, coming face-to-face with the fearful prospect of losing my job has made me less fearful and nervous. The open-ness with which you shared your assessment of me has given me a much better sense of your essential decency and compassion. I see that I've been reacting with unnecessary nervousness to the almost war-like rhetoric we use sometimes to express our com-petitive intensity."

Unfortunately, I am better at analyzing problems than cor-recting them. Fear continued to be a serious issue for me during my remaining time at *The Press*.

Limiting my response memo to general "change of heart" statements would have been a smart move. Instead, I listed six specific objectives I planned to accomplish during the probation-ary period. I accomplished points two through six without diffi-culty, but point number one—completion of CIS and support of TMC—remained an elusive goal. A year later, Ritscher asked me why I had not taken that opportunity to disassociate myself from the "system." I was puzzled by the question since I had never even considered that option—one that was so obvious he had not even suggested it.

Year three of CIS started with a congressional "investiga-tion." A woman complained to now deceased Congressman James Howard that CIS-mandated procedural changes for carriers were in violation of her grandson's rights. Our changes were quickly unchanged. From there, the situation deteriorated even more rapidly. Cosgrove, the data processing manager of whom I had become quite fond despite our differences, quit in a huff. I recommended that one of my closest assistants become more actively involved in the CIS project. Instead, I was told to fire him. By the end of the year, I trusted few people and few people trusted me. I tried to save myself, but I could not. Instead of reaching out for whatever lifelines might be available, I turned inward, relying only on my own resources. In my lonely panic, I lacked the buoyancy to survive. I sank into the quagmire and never emerged.

SELF-DESTRUCTIVENESS IN SOCIETY

Not everyone actively pursues the demise of his or her own job, but more general signs of economic absurdity abound. The overwhelming evidence of self-destructive behavior in our society provides tremendous empirical support to those who argue against the self-correcting nature of a free-market economy. The unwillingness of most middle income families to live within their incomes, for example, eventually drives the cost of housing beyond the means of many families. Executives' urge to provide their families with more and more luxuries leads to work patterns which destroy families. The market may foster the creation of wealth, but it also supports rampant drug abuse and sexual exploitation. In addition, the market does little to prevent millions of persons from living in degrading poverty. In the face of society's self-destructive practices, the logic of controls becomes very appealing.

Eliminating freedom from the marketplace, however, is not the solution to self-destructive behavior. Fear, not freedom, is the negative force which must be uprooted if people are to replace self-destructive behavior with the self-expanding behavior of love. Activating the benefits of freedom in the market necessitates diminishing the power of fear in our economy.

IDOL OF INNOCENCE

For most of my life, I regarded my timidity—my lack of self-confidence, my fear—as a sign of meekness and humility which placed me in harmony with the innocent Jesus. As a result, I clung to a variety of juvenile behavior patterns and ways of thought that compounded my fears, but which, I thought, brought me affinity with the broken and beaten Jesus. Juvenile behavior, I rationalized, was essentially innocent behavior. Had not Jesus said, "Let the children come to me"?

Only recently have I begun to see my fears in all of their ugliness. In his book, *Healing Wounded Emotions: Overcoming Life's Hurts*, Rev. Martin Padovani describes the therapeutic journey on which he has led numerous people, including me, who are troubled by the pain of a failed marriage. With his sure guidance, I developed the courage to look beneath the surface of my behavior and confront the terrors of the deep. The interplay between sexual and economic uncertainties in my own life became quite evident. With Padovani's help, I was able to see that my compulsion to be recognized as a manager was intertwined with my more basic desire to be accepted as a man. With increasing clarity, I have come to see my fears as signs of bondage to a variety of idols, most particularly the idol of my own perfection.

The terrified little boy is not an existential reality that I can use to justify all of my behavior. The terrified little boy is a posture I adopted quite consciously at an early age to maintain my pretense of omnipotence. I have come to see fear, guilt and anxiety as continuous "protection" payments to an idol who promises to ward off my fallibility.

ORIGINAL SIN

Coming face to face with this idol has stimulated in me a new understanding of that old starting point for spiritual reflection, original sin. If, as Pope John Paul II says, our economic problems stem from "the structures of sin," then understanding the nature of sin becomes an important *economic* concern. My emerging conception of original sin goes like this: Our entry into the world triggers two strong but conflicting experiences. On the one hand, we sense our frailty. At the same time, we become aware of our freedom and power. These two conflicting experiences tug at us, and we vacillate between an image of ourselves as creature and one of ourselves as creator. Both viewpoints can muster strong empirical support: I am weak but I can control. On our own, we cannot reconcile both creaturehood and freedom. Thus, we develop a seemingly perfect solution to the dilemma, which is idolatry. We become creatures of a creature-made creator. We worship a god we ourselves fabricate. Instead of preserving our freedom, however, this delusion traps us and enslaves us in what we call sin. The idol becomes more and more demanding as the evidence of its existence becomes weaker. To diffuse the wrath of our idol, we often "sic" it on other individuals, groups and nations.

The destroyer of this delusion is Jesus Christ, who has shown himself as both God and man—at once the Son of the Father and one with the Father. In Christ, creature and creator are reconciled. The message of Jesus Christ, normally presented as the Good News, is actually a bad news/good news statement. Through his life, death and resurrection, Jesus tells us that we must first accept the bad news that we are not God—that we are only a creature—before we can embrace the good news that we are called to be children of God, colleagues of the Son in the ongoing work of creation. For the believer, the idol no longer has a role to play. Yet lacking perfect faith and perfect love, we continue to employ the idol's service. Thus, St. John tells us: "Love is not yet perfected in one who is afraid."

FEAR AS A SIGN OF EVIL

I include this personal discourse on fear because I see little evidence that any group within our economy recognizes fear as a true sign of evil. Quite the opposite is the case. The "lean and mean" business strategy which has led to so many layoffs in recent years is predicated, in part, on an attempt to raise productivity through intimidation. Trimming unneeded positions from the work force is only half the goal of these programs. Inflicting fright on the remaining workers is equally important in many cases. Faced with the threat of joining their former colleagues on the unemployment lines, those who have kept their jobs are expected to work even harder.

What are we to make of the way homelessness and other highly visible signs of poverty are tolerated in our society? Are not the destitute made to play the same role as the misbehaving child who is made to stand in the corner in full view of his or her classmates? Poverty will never be eliminated in the U.S. if its painful consequences are viewed as constructive—that is, as long as fear is regarded as a useful mechanism for controlling economic behavior. In an economy in which employers believe employees will not work as hard to reach economic heaven unless they face the very real possibility of falling into economic hell, highly evident examples of poverty and unemployment serve an important, even if unfortunate, function.

Would these examples of economic torment be allowed to exist if the utter immorality of the use of fear were recognized as a universal religious principle? Despite the superficial evidence of fear's link to discipline and proper order, for the Christian, at least, it can never be a stimulant of true productivity. Again, St. John says it best: "Love has no room for fear. Rather, perfect love casts out all fear." Fear is associated with greed, jealousy, hatred and loneliness. Fear can never be associated with love.

ABOLITION OF FEAR

Abolishing fear goes hand in hand with abolishing poverty, and the Catholic Church is especially well-equipped to lead this abolition campaign. There are several specific steps the Church can take to diminish the fear that prevents all people in our society from enjoying the freedom necessary for true prosperity. Here are three of them.

First, the Church must continuously preach the bountifulness of God's love, of which a prosperous society is a splendid manifestation. Once prosperity is viewed organically, as something created through loving human interaction, the main source of fear in the economy—shortages—can be eliminated. The Church need not invent a new economics—the economics of the loaves and the fishes will do just fine. Catholic theology should foster understanding of the expansive, procreative role humanity plays in the economy—a role detected by all serious economists.

In one of my early newspaper columns, I raised this question: What would we get if the Church combined the U.S. bishops' economic pastoral with the in-vitro fertilization document ("Instruction on Respect for Life in Its Origins") that came out a few months later? My conclusion was that such a combination would lead to a better understanding of economics as a life science and a deeper appreciation for love's creative power.

Studying the ethical dimensions of in-vitro fertilization raises our awareness that the cause and effect relationship between lovemaking and baby making has never been perfect. Not all sexual acts leading to conception are loving, and not all sexual expressions of genuine love lead to conception. The new bio-medical technologies further confuse the cause-and-effect link by providing all sorts of new answers to the question: Where do babies come from? The Church's teaching, however, remains clear. The normal and best way to create a baby is through the loving union of husband and wife.

Approaching economics from this perspective of biology can help us appreciate the fact that wealth is created, not extracted. Certainly, we can find in the economy instances where exploitation leads to success (the economic equivalent of rape). We also see decent, hard-working people who experience poverty and failure (the economic equivalent of infertility). Yet, too often, we fail to ask whether these situations are exceptions or norms.

Rape, infertility and test-tube technology do not blind Christians to the God-given connection between love and procreation. Why should the economic version of these problems block awareness into the God-given connection between love and prosperity?

(A much funnier treatment of the link between baby making and economic theory can be found in "Raising Arizona," one of the Coen brothers' early films. Normally, kidnapping is no laughing matter, but the Nicholas Cage character, who carries the shortage mentality to its absurd extreme, makes the movie hilarious. He easily graduates from robbing convenience stores to stealing a baby. In his view, those who do not have are entitled to take from those who do. Eventually, he discovers there is a much more enjoyable way to obtain a baby than kidnapping.)

A second major step in the Church's war on fear must be the explicit renunciation of fear in all of its applications. Another film, "The Mission," contains a scene in which the business world responds to the church's socio-economic teaching. Father Santiago, played by Robert DeNiro, denounces a slave trader's use of the lash as a motivational instrument. The accused turns and reminds Santiago of the Church's frequent reliance on fear to change its members behavior. "What are a few cuts across the back," the trader asks "in terms of what you offer them—eternal damnation of imprisoned souls?"

A church condemning fear as an economic force must purge fear from its own program for motivating moral behavior. Ironically, the Church's social justice literature is one of the worst offenders in this area. Painting economic life as something negative and malevolent can only be regarded as frightening. The success of the base communities in Latin America and of Mother Teresa's followers throughout the world suggests an alternative approach. Their starting point in helping the poor is embracing poverty and entering the economy without horror or fear.

Finally, to combat fear with its associated feelings of powerlessness, the Church must preach a doctrine of economic purity. Helping the poor resist economic exploitation as a form of personal defilement must be encouraged.

One of the heroes of my Catholic grade school in the 1950s was St. Maria Goretti, who protected her chastity to the point of death. Her approach would probably be regarded as extreme by most rape prevention counselors. The canonization of Maria Goretti, however, underscores the Church's unflinching defense of sexual purity. Yet Maria's death-defying, 'I will not submit to rape,' also has relevance to the Church's economic teaching. All assaults on the dignity of the human person demand active resistance. Just as forced sex must never be accepted, defilement and assault in the marketplace must also be resisted.

A consistent ethic of dignity, purity and modesty demands advocacy of courage in all areas. Both the poor and the affluent can benefit by hearing from the Church that no one need succumb to fear. The Church should teach that grace is available to resist all fear-induced forms of exploitation.

A Theology of Liberation

To resist fear is to resist the idolatry that is behind all forms of slavery. Any person or institution attempting to control others through fear has established himself, herself or itself as an idol. All such abuses of power are blasphemous, since those wielding the power have misused what ultimately comes from God. By highlighting the religious implications of exploitation—both sexual and economic—the Catholic Church is in a unique position to mobilize the moral outrage against any system that sustains itself through fear. Any truly Catholic view of economic freedom, therefore, must be predicated on a "theology of liberation" that recognizes fear as a force of enslavement that derives its power from a conspiracy between institutional idolatry and individual self-destructiveness.

Liberation from fear is what keeps the posture of economic generosity from deteriorating into one of subservience. Only when coupled with courage can generosity be the source of economic fruitfulness.

COMPETITION: OUTDOING ONE ANOTHER IN HONOR

If we resist internal domination by our own idols and external attempts to manipulate and exploit us through fear, we enter the marketplace in an entirely new and different frame of mind. Suddenly, competition—the hallmark of a free economy—acquires a positive meaning and becomes a strong stimulant for good.

In his letter to the Romans, St. Paul described the Christian approach to competition: "Love one another with brotherly affection; outdo one another in showing honor (RSV)." The challenge of the Christian in the marketplace is not to match the service offered by others, but to "outdo" all others or to "anticipate one another in respect (NAB)."

The author of the letter to the Hebrews expressed a similar notion when he wrote: ". . . let us consider how to stir up one another to love and good works." Thus, Christians in the marketplace seeking to outdo the competition in honoring and respecting customers become the force which stirs up the rest of the economy to love and good works.

The market can be exploitative only to the extent participants are motivated by fear. For only fear propels a person to adopt or acquiesce to self-destructive behavior. By refusing to interact economically with those intent upon such slavery, people can redirect the entire market force.

The Christian who has purged fear (or is seriously trying to purge fear) from his or her life resists defilement and proclaims to the market: "I will not submit to economic rape." Adopting this stance can be as simple as saying: "I will not accept poor service. I will go without lunch rather than wait 45 minutes in a 'fast food' line." On the other hand, living without fear can be as difficult as saying: "I will not accept such abusive treatment. I will seek another job if this practice continues."

As long as this posture against fear is maintained, generosity alone can serve as the only effective inducement to economic activity.

Freedom and fearlessness do not produce a laid-back, easy-going, static economy. The combination leads to the highly competitive situation of which St. Paul speaks. Suddenly, the only viable economic behavior is "anticipation." The key to attracting more customers is to offer them more respect than the competition does. In the free and fearless economy, only beneficial products, services and prices provide business with a competitive edge.

In recent years, I have had the opportunity to work with two of the leading Catholic journals of opinion in the U.S., the Jesuit-run *AMERICA* and the lay-run *Commonweal*. As a result, I often am asked about the need for two somewhat similar publications. While some Church leaders might have a different answer to this question, my response is always that two journals of opinion are much better than one. There exists between the two magazines a spirit of both collegiality and competition. In programs that will benefit either the Church or the Catholic press in general, the two magazines are more than willing to cooperate. In presenting thought-provoking articles to readers, however, each magazine wants to be the anticipator—the first with the news. Through this sense of competitive anticipation, *AMERICA* prods *Commonweal* and *Commonweal* pushes *AMERICA* to higher levels of Catholic journalism. The fact that several thousand readers subscribe to both publications suggests that competition benefits both magazines, their customers, and the Church.

Marketing Revolution

With economic advancement and continued defense of their liberty—by consumer advocates as well as by the armed forces—American consumers have become more fearless and more demanding. The business response to these changing consumer attitudes has triggered two major developments, neither of which has received significant attention in Catholic social justice writings.

The first has been termed a "marketing revolution." "The economic revolution of the American economy since 1900 has in large part been a marketing revolution caused by the assumption of responsibility for creative, aggressive, pioneering marketing by American management," Peter Drucker wrote in *The Practice of Management*. Although Drucker traces American marketing back to Cyrus McCormick in 1850, Drucker's own work in 1954 greatly advanced the science of meeting consumer needs, which is marketing. He was one of the first to articulate the radical shift in business focus that became known as the "marketing concept." For Drucker, "there is only one valid definition of business purpose: to create a customer."

"Fifty years ago," he wrote, "the typical attitude of the American businessman toward marketing was still: 'The sales department will sell whatever the plant produces.' Today it is increasingly: 'It is our job to produce what the market needs.'"

Marketing, Drucker explained, is a much broader concept than selling. "It encompasses the entire business. It is the whole business seen from the point of view of its final result, that is, from the customer's point of view."

The paramount question within the market-driven company is: What does the consumer need? Once businesses became serious about asking this question, they developed a multiplicity of techniques to determine the answer—random surveys, market tests, focus groups, shopper panels, exit interviews, and many more. The market research techniques differed, but the process was always the same. Business was saying, "We want to know what type of products and services consumers need."

In Drucker's view, the marketing company never panders to the customer and is not trapped by current tastes and technology. In an almost exact parallel of St. Paul's concept of "anticipation," Drucker describes "innovation" as the logical outgrowth of a market orientation. "It is not enough for the business to provide just any economic goods and services; it must provide better and more economic ones. It is not necessary for a business to grow bigger; but it is necessary that it constantly grow better."

Critics of the market system attempt to argue that consumers have no real choice; that the difference between a Ford and a Chevrolet, for instance, is so minor as to be meaningless. Yet those within the system—particularly those involved directly in marketing and sales—know first-hand that true choices abound. I have known talented, hard-working salespeople who have spent days, weeks, months and, in one case, even a year without making a major sale. Such people know without a doubt that customers are rarely forced to buy. Were the consumer in bondage to the market, there would be no reason for the increased refinements in marketing techniques and the intense attention paid to sales training.

One of the most popular sales trainers, Zig Ziglar, structures his entire program around a basic message about customer service. "You can get anything in life you want," Ziglar says, "if you just help enough people get what they want." Such teaching respects both the freedom and the fearlessness of the market. Success, Ziglar is saying, occurs only through the true satisfaction of others' needs. This should be a maxim religious leaders can endorse without reservation. In its best manifestations, marketing is a loving process—for it involves an intense effort to discover unmet buyer needs which can only be satisfied by "gifts" from the seller.

Marketing involves effort. Those who want to build and sell a better mousetrap must work at it. Many popular business books chronicling new ventures show in exciting detail the sweat and sacrifice involved in developing a new product. Two of the best are Tracy Kidder's Pulitzer Prize-winning *Soul of a New Machine*, which tracks the day-to-day progress of Data General Corporation's computer engineers as they race to create a 32-bit microprocessor, and *The Making of McPaper* by Peter Prichard, which describes the Gannett Co.'s seven-year, $450 million struggle to launch *USA Today* and make that innovative newspaper profitable. Both books are recommended reading for anyone seeking to learn how the marketing spirit animates business progress.

THE EXCELLENCE MOVEMENT

The second, more recent, American business development is a refinement and reformation of the first. Not all parts of the American economy took Drucker and his marketing concept to heart. The automobile industry was typical of those segments of American business which continued to emphasize internal product development instead of market research. Large cars produced large profit margins. Thus, large cars were manufactured and small cars were ignored.

Meanwhile, sophisticated marketing became identified with slick advertising. Innovation was confined to catchy sales slogans. Convincing the market that "all pain relievers (or whatever) are not alike" became the dominant concerns of too many businesses. They tried to trick customers into thinking "old" is "new" and "same" is "better" through advertising, even—or especially when—their claims were not true.

The mid-1970s energy crisis highlighted the pitfalls of this failure to anticipate market needs. The U.S. automobile industry lost market share to more fuel-efficient Japanese models, and then it watched as the imports strengthened their U.S. position even after gasoline prices declined. The imported cars acquired a market reputation for being better—not just cheaper—than American cars. There may have been less than a dime's worth of difference between a Ford and a Chevrolet in the 1960s. Ten years later, however, car buyers were offered substantial differences between a Honda and any American-made car.

The near bankruptcy of the Chrysler Corporation in 1979 was a consciousness-raising event for many parts of the American business community. Since then, the watchwords at U.S. companies have become "quality" and "excellence" as businesses sought to restore America's competitiveness in the world economy. The movement advocating these two principles was catalyzed by the 1982 work *In Search of Excellence* by Robert H. Waterman, Jr. and Thomas J. Peters. The two most important "Lessons from America's Best-Run Companies" (the book's subtitle) discovered in the authors' search were: (1) get "close to the customers;" and (2) achieve "productivity through people." The way these two lessons are presented in their book, these rules could easily be read as, "love your customers and your employees as yourself."

Through several follow-up books, Tom Peters has continued to be a leading spokesman for the movement advocating business excellence through superior customer service and inspired leadership of employees. If grace is defined as "the force in our lives pressuring us to do good," then what Peters writes about is grace. In his view of the economy, increased automation and international competition are not negative factors. Rather, they are positive forces pressuring American business toward increased customer and employee concern. His heroes are companies which offer their customers "unexpected" levels of service. In this, Peters, too, echoes St. Paul. For both businesses and individuals, *anticipation* is the wisest market strategy.

Anticipation

The marketing revolution and the excellence movement point to the competitive market's tremendous potential for stimulating good. A Catholic economic vision must promulgate the value of the anticipator, who loves customers with the affection of a brother or sister and who strives to outdo the competition by showing customers respect. In a free and fearless market, business always will flow to such a person. Love can only flourish in a context of freedom, and, within an atmosphere of freedom, love always will be expressed competitively. Don't lovers always search for ways to be more loving? In the case of economic activity, this means working to develop innovative products and services that are even more satisfying of true human needs.

It is fear that gives power to the cutthroat tactics so deplored by free market critics. The Catholic Church should be encouraging people to enter the free market and enjoy the rousing, striving, anticipating, outdoing form of competition that can be created by fearless love.

SPENDING FREEDOM IN COMMITMENT

In their pastoral letter on the economy, the U.S. bishops devote one of the five main sections to cooperation, which they see as the opposite of competition. At the beginning of their call for "A New American Experiment: Partnership for the Public Good," they write: "Today a greater spirit of partnership and teamwork is needed. Competition alone will not do the job. It has too many negative consequences for family life, the economically vulnerable, and the environment."

What the bishops fail to acknowledge, however, is that competition and cooperation are not necessarily incompatible. In fact, competition *devoid of fear* is a powerful stimulus toward generosity. It is a force stirring up good works in the marketplace. Still, the bishops are correct that freedom protected by a system of competing interests is not an absolute. Freedom is a prerequisite for love—not a substitute.

GUIDES FOR COMMITMENT

The two models of commitment we analyzed earlier—vowed religious and married couples—can serve as useful guides in formulating a view of the economy that incorporates both competition and cooperation. The two groups highlight the interplay between freedom and commitment in human relationships.

Like poverty and chastity, the religious vow of obedience delivers a clear—but contrarian—message to the Christian community: Freedom is a gift which is meant to be spent. As with everything considered precious, it is the exchanging of the gift that establishes its value. Since freedom is an essential condition for love, its value is priceless. Without the willingness to expend freedom through loving commitments, however, its value is unknown. So long as fear and self-interest are our only guides, we can never be free—we are always subject to manipulation. Only love, the willingness to give without guarantee of a return, establishes our freedom.

The commitment of religious vows is singular and permanent, once and for all. Vowed religious do not need the trappings of personal and financial independence to experience their freedom. All duties and obligations can be traced to their free exchange. The right to make certain choices was abandoned; a life of special union with Christ through the Church was selected. "Take and receive, O Lord, my liberty," the followers of St. Ignatius sing as they pronounce their vows. They tie this offer with an appeal for Christ to keep his side of the bargain. "Only Thy grace, Thy love on me bestow."

Now, it should be obvious but it must be emphasized that the witness of religious obedience is in no way meant to be an endorsement of authoritarian societies or controlled economies. Yet the strong tradition of religious obedience in the Church does provide a framework for evaluating economic freedom. Those who have forsaken personal liberty remind the rest of us that it is the choices made—not merely the freedom to choose—that establishes a society's moral character.

Married life, the other primary way in which Christians "spend" their freedom, shows there is a clear correlation between the strength of commitment and the intensity of generosity. With good reason, most people do not expose themselves to strangers. To present oneself nude to an unknown person is not an invitation to be loved. People cannot truly surrender themselves to strangers, since surrender requires trust, which can only be developed over time.

Within the context of marriage's for-better-or-for-worse bond, however, surrendering oneself to another person is not an irrational proposition. Sexual activity which is loving always contains a measure of surrender. Sex without surrender will always be "screwing"—mutual taking instead of mutual giving. The Church's strong prohibition against sexual intercourse outside of marriage is based on the quite reasonable conviction that without the permanency of marriage real sexual surrender is absurd. No one who understands the powerful nature of the sexual exchange would offer himself or herself for anything less than an enduring commitment. In this sense, the Church's sexual morality provides a high form of "consumer protection."

Economic Commitment

Economic expressions of love—the many manifestations of productivity—also involve surrender. The investments necessary for a profitable and prosperous economy require partners to lay down their interests for each other. Customers, employers, employees and colleagues must love with the affection of brothers and sisters if prosperity is to be maximized.

Surrendering oneself to an *economic* stranger, however, is no less an invitation to exploitation than exposing oneself sexually. There is nothing loving in such behavior. Surrender only expresses loving generosity when it is coupled with trust. "I will subordinate my interests to yours," the lover says, "when I can trust you not to 'screw' me. When I love, I expect you to love me in return."

Thus, participants in the economy require the protection and security of commitments if they are to become productive. Commitments make surrender in the marketplace both loving and expected. Forcing an economic partner to justify the benefits of every interaction, on the other hand, deprives that person of the opportunity to be truly generous. The "prove that you love me" mentality is antithetical to love—in economic as well as in affectionate relationships.

Although discussing economic partners as "lovers" may seem strange, most business arrangements acknowledge the correlation between commitment and generosity. The reality is present, even if the terminology is not. For example, in most cases long-term contracts earn both providers and customers the best deal.

The Monitor, the diocesan newspaper I worked for in the late 1980s, provides a good case study of this principle. Like most newspapers, it offers substantial discounts to every-issue advertisers. At one point, its prices went from $10 per column inch (the price charged to one-time advertisers or "strangers") down to $5 per column inch (the price paid by "friends" who advertised in every issue). *The Monitor*'s "friends" rate was profitable. On the other hand, its "strangers" rate was still not exploitative.

The value of commitments explains this economic miracle. Because its subscribers pay in advance for 50 issues, *The Monitor* is obliged to publish a minimum number of pages, even if no advertising is sold for a particular issue. Thus, the base of advertising provided by committed customers represents in some sense a gift. Every dollar received offsets a cost that would be incurred with or without advertising. The paper acknowledges the gift from advertisers by offering a substantial rate reduction.

On the other hand, when a newspaper must expand its size to accommodate occasional advertisers, the cost of printing and distributing the extra pages of advertising is high. Neither *The Monitor* nor any other publication should have qualms about charging strangers a price based on these incremental costs. Most successful publications couple their relatively high prices for occasional advertisers with incentives that invite those customers to become regular advertisers and enjoy the financial advantages of economic friendship.

In their pastoral letter on economic justice, the American bishops encouraged all participants in the economy to explore the benefits of such friendships, which they describe as "partnerships." Within the individual company, the bishops note, job security and ownership participation must accompany requests for greater worker productivity. Likewise, protection of shareholder rights must go hand in hand with appeals for greater investment on their part.

The bishops also extend the partnership analogy to firms within industries, states within regions, sectors within the national economy, and nations within the world economy. All of their suggestions encourage economic participants to "spend" freedom in exchange for more productive and prosperous committed relationships.

Unfortunately, several years after the pastoral, there is little evidence that the bishops' message about the importance of cooperative commitment has been absorbed by U.S. businesses. More and more companies, confusing productivity with efficiency, have replaced full time workers with part-timers and temporaries. In doing so, however, they have adopted employment programs that are *antithetical* to long-term productivity—at least from a Catholic viewpoint.

The managers responsible for this switch from friends to strangers have eliminated all possibility and potential for employee generosity. When workers are reduced to the status of replaceable machines, productivity cannot happen. In and of itself, a machine's contribution to an enterprise is always neutral. The machine's owner only gets back what was paid for. Thus, businesses which treat their employees as machines can never expect worker value to exceed worker cost. Any company that refuses to treat its employees generously—by compensating them with security and appreciation, as well as with a paycheck—will never enjoy the benefits of a committed, generous workforce.

In many ways the great financial scandals of the eighties—the savings and loan crisis, the insider trading debacle, the attempted cornering of the government securities market—can all be read as testaments to the breakdown of business loyalties. Prominent Catholic layman Thomas Johnson, former president of Chemical Bank in New York City, has called the preoccupation with short-term results Wall Street's number one "temptation to misbehavior." I heard him address a conference on "Identifying Ethical Issues in the Financial Services Industry," sponsored by the Jesuit office of Faith and Justice, shortly after the initial revelation of the insider trading scandals. In his presentation, Johnson noted the tremendous pressure toward improper behavior created by customers themselves who change investment fund managers on the basis of a single quarter's results.

AN EXAMPLE OF COMMITMENT

Offering a sharp contrast to the short-term investment approach is Berkshire Hathaway's "billion dollar man" Warren Buffett, who was named by *Forbes* magazine in 1993 as the richest person in America. His phenomenal success challenges several common business notions. A few years ago, *Fortune* magazine described his ability to outperform the stock market for more than 30 years as a "statistical aberration so rare that it practically never happens." Of more interest to our discussion is Buffet's reputation for integrity and decency, which confound those who believe great wealth can be achieved only through greed and power.

Profiles of Buffett leave little doubt that he is a man who believes in committed relationships. In a *Fortune* magazine article, "The Inside Story of Warren Buffett" (April 11, 1988), Carol J. Loomis described Buffett as a manager "solicitous of the talent working for him" and as an investor who regards some companies as a "permanent" part of his portfolio. Of the Berkshire Hathaway textile company which now exists only in name, Loomis wrote: "Buffett nursed the business for 20 years while deploring the benightedness that had taken him into such industrial bogs as men's suit linings, in which he was just another commodity operator with no edge of any kind. Periodically, Buffett would explain in his annual report why he stayed in an operation with such poor economics. The business, he said, was a major employer in New Bedford, Massachusetts; the operation's managers had been straightforward with him and as able as the managers of his successful businesses; the unions had been reasonable."

Although Buffett initially became a millionaire buying and selling investment "bargains," he has become a billionaire because "he has tended to buy good managements and stick with them," Loomis said.

At the start of her glowing tribute to Buffett, Loomis admitted she wrote "with something less than total objectivity" since she has been a friend of his for more than 20 years. Perhaps, I should put in a similar disclaimer. Like me, Buffett got his early business training as a "paper boy." Unlike me, he is in the Newspaper Carrier Hall of Fame. Hearing his induction address to the International Circulation Managers Association in 1985 was one of the most memorable experiences in my short-lived circulation career. Buffett credited his circulation experience with providing both the seed capital for his investment partnership and the people skills he has used throughout his business career.

REBUILDING BUSINESS RELATIONSHIPS

Even though unemployment represents a painful severing of business relationships, overcoming unemployment often requires building upon those same business friendships. Having been in the job-search market twice in the last ten years, I speak with first-hand knowledge.

The personal experience which provided the strongest confirmation of business friendships was a five-month period of unemployment following my departure from *The Asbury Park Press*. Past connections provided the foundation for a tremendous range of future options, and in this way the experience deepened my appreciation for the link between commitments and freedom. For a time, I had the feeling that half of the people at *The Press* were working to find me a new job. John Van Pelt, the newsroom graphics editor whom I had originally hired for the marketing department, typeset my resume and designed stationery. Richard Orloff, whom I had promoted into the research manager's position, helped me document *The Press'* growth during my tenure. George Hamilton, the production and distribution manager, referred me to an executive search firm with which he had worked. Bob Nelson, who replaced me as marketing manager when I went to the circulation department, distributed my resume at a meeting of the International Newspaper Promotion Association. My ex-boss, Charles Ritscher, made calls and provided references, and Lori McGregor, my former secretary who now worked for Ritscher, prepared several cover letters to be mailed with my resumé. Several of *The Press'* distributors phoned and sent notes of encouragement. One provided the name of a contact at the *New York Daily News*.

Although I had worked for only two newspapers (a low figure for many circulation professionals), I was able to put together a mailing list of industry contacts that exceeded 100 names—people I had met at seminars and conventions, suppliers, recruiters, and people I knew only by reputation. Help came from the strangest places. One salesman, whose business with *The Press* I would have curtailed had I stayed, provided three job leads.

I drew up a list of 14 newspapers between White Plains, New York, and Philadelphia, Pennsylvania, that I thought might offer a job similar to the one I had held. Through letters, persistent telephone follow-ups, and the intervention of friends, I was able to get interviews with 12 of the 14 companies. Getting each interview was a mini-victory and visiting so many newspapers in succession was an educational experience. Each circulation department was structured differently, but all shared the same basic problems associated with getting a newspaper into the hands of the reader. Just having the chance to exchange views with circulation officials at *The New York Times*, *New York Daily News*, *Newsday*, *The Star Ledger* of Newark, and the *Philadelphia Inquirer* was a thrill.

Carlton Rosenberg, then circulation director at *The Inquirer* who went on to become corporate circulation director for the Gannett Company, offered something to me just as important as a job. He offered personal understanding and compassion. He had lost his job in one of the *New York Daily News'* many management shake-ups, he told me, and made a practice of offering whatever encouragement he could to those going through similar experiences. Although he did not have a specific opening in his department, he had his key assistants spend time with me and arranged for me to take the Knight-Ridder Company's (the parent company of the *Inquirer*) management assessment test. Rosenberg's actions were among the most comforting gestures of kindness I received during that period.

Also reassuring was a consulting assignment from Creative Data Systems, the software company that had designed *The Press'* circulation "system." Company president Dann Kroeger and his assistant Fred Petty, who was in charge of the Asbury Park project, had been aware of the problems surrounding installation of their program. They wanted any information that would help their other clients prevent similar occurrences. Creative Data paid me to fly to Kansas and conduct a two-day workshop for their circulation installation teams. By the end of the session, Petty and I had developed a unity of thought we had not enjoyed during our three years on the CIS project.

None of these business friendships led to a job. But the sense of belonging to such a supportive industry eased my fears about the future, and the generous severance arrangement I received from *The Press* reduced my concerns about the present. These extended business relationships, which lasted well beyond actual employment, gave me the freedom and security to reflect upon my deepest aspirations. I tested potential involvement with the Catholic press through consulting assignments at *AMERICA* magazine and *The Monitor*, and, after completing a project at the latter publication, I accepted a full-time position there.

GETTING "LOCKED IN"

Despite the evidence of the economic value of commitment, there remains strong the cynical opinion that making commitments means getting "locked in" to bad situations. Lazy employees, higher prices, and sloppy service are among the economic ills thought to be linked to binding business relationships.

Once again, the experience of both vowed religious and married couples offers guidance to those uneasy about economic commitments. These paragons demonstrate the unbreakable circle in which love and freedom swirl. Commitments consume freedom, but they enhance it as well. By freeing lovers from their fears, commitments allow them to become truly generous. In addition, the satisfaction of a loving relationship provides a standard against which the value of freedom can be measured. Love is what freedom can "buy."

Relationships cease to be loving when they cease to be free. As soon as one side of the relationship gives his or her freedom, the other must return it. The security of relationships becomes a sham when each person's freedom is not preserved. When religious and married people see themselves as trapped, in fact, the joy of commitment turns into the bitterness of imprisonment.

By displaying the respect for freedom that must accompany all commitments, vowed religious and married couples offer another lesson for the person seeking to become economically productive: Love never asks for guarantees. Therefore, all love involves a risk. Committed people do become economically vulnerable. Yet they assume a posture of vulnerability because they expect to be loved and respected in return.

For this reason, the married person abused by a spouse, the priest or religious abused by the Church, or the generous person abused by his or her economic partners send messages of negativism and despair throughout society. The exploitation of those made vulnerable by circumstances, rather than choice, sounds an even louder warning to those contemplating commitments. If the preponderance of evidence suggests that vulnerable people will be "screwed," society has little chance of inspiring the expressions of economic surrender so essential to true prosperity.

So are commitments "worth it?" I believe that it is in the Church's interest to encourage "yes, indeed" as the answer. For only the security offered by freely-entered-into commitments can provide the environment needed to foster prosperity through productivity.

PART III: THE VALUE ADDED IS LOVE

Practical and Prayerful Ways to Stimulate Productivity

• **Becoming Productive: The Responsibility of the Individual**

• **Inspiring Productivity: The Management Challenge**

• **Securing Productivity: The Role of Government**

• **Sanctifying Productivity: A Spirituality for Economic Life**

Of his fullness we have all had a share
—love following upon love.
                                        John 1:16

BECOMING PRODUCTIVE: RESPONSIBILITY OF THE INDIVIDUAL

In the first section of this book, I presented a three-part argument: (1) The goal of economic activity is prosperity; (2) the key to universal prosperity is universal productivity—i.e., a willingness on the part of all economic participants to give more than they get; (3) productivity makes sense economically only in the context of a mutual relationship in which partners simultaneously give more than they get and get more than they give.

In the second section, I tried to show that a climate of freedom was absolutely essential to the furtherance of productivity. Furthermore, I noted that the struggle for freedom is a struggle against sinfulness that requires a sense of fearlessness, a spirit of anticipation and innovation, and a willingness to make binding commitments.

In this third and final section, I will attempt to spell out some of the ways that individuals, employers, government and the Church can foster the productive relationships which spawn prosperity. Each chapter in this section is structured around a question. Individuals are encouraged to ask: How can I lead a more productive life? Employers: How can we inspire workers to lead more productive lives? Government officials: How can we structure a secure society that will motivate productive behavior and provide productive roles for all persons—including those presently "unproductive"? And finally, the Church: How can we develop a spirituality that highlights the identification between virtue and productive behavior?

RETURN TO THE MARRIAGE PARADIGM

Vatican II's *Constitution on the Church in the Modern World* offers an exhortation on married love that, when applied to economic love, provides a framework for answering all four of the above questions. The chapter on "Fostering the Nobility of Marriage and the Family" looks at the union of husband and wife from three perspectives that show how marriage has evolved from a natural impulse into a social institution and finally into a sacrament. The primary experience, the council fathers remind us, is the "conjugal covenant" between the couple themselves. Next, through the institution of marriage, society protects this covenant so that it can enhance the "dignity, stability, peace and prosperity of the family itself and of human society as a whole." Finally, "Christ . . . the Spouse of the Church comes into the lives of married Christians through the sacrament of Matrimony." Through the sacrament, "authentic married love is caught up into divine love."

Just as the magnetism of a man's and a woman's sexual differences attracts them into a single conjugal covenant, the multiplicity of the material needs of individuals and employers draws them into numerous economic covenants. In order for prosperity to flourish, the institutional protection of society and the sanctifying assistance of the Church, which have long been offered to sexual relationships, must be extended to these economic relationships as well.

LIFE AS A CURVE

The many spiritual components of productivity start to become apparent as soon as individuals adopt a posture towards the economy of giving instead of taking.

One of the most enduring lessons I took away from my business school training was the importance of curves. Very few aspects of the economy can be explained in terms of straight-line relationships. Virtually all forms of business analysis involve the study of non-linear or multi-variable situations. Reducing per-unit production costs while increasing volume, for instance, is one of the surest approaches to profitability. In this case, the favorable cost variable compounds the benefit of expanding volume. On the other hand, the combination of rising production costs and increasing volume often form the fast track to insolvency. Here, volume growth multiplies the negative impact of the cost trend.

When these compounding variables are plotted graphically, they form a curve, which is the normal result of depicting most economic phenomena.

An important first step for an individual who wants to lead a more productive life is learning this lesson of the curve. Too often in the business of our personal lives, we view reality only in straight-line terms. We expect tit-for-tat, one-for-one, direct cause-and-effect relationships. If our exertion does not earn a direct and immediate payoff, we consider it to have been in vain. We are reluctant to examine other variables which can offset or multiply our efforts. Why does one person's labor lead to so little output, while another's yields so much? Ultimately, the answer lies in the fact that each person is at a different point on the great curve of life, and the formula for this curve is a very complex equation.

Religious believers should be attuned to this "curve" paradigm, since we recognize that God's love for us is not a quid-pro-quo affair. Surely, God's love for us is unconditional and cannot be earned through circumcision, Mass attendance, or any other

religious rite. And, while we believe that our prayers will be answered and our good behavior rewarded, the response seldom
happens immediately or directly.

INDETERMINATE REWARDS

A concomitant feature of a free economy is an indeterminate
system of rewards, which, as often as not, follows a curve rather
than a straight line. When properly understood and accepted, such
a system can be seen as an expression of the divine calculus, another reflection of God's unbounded love. The very uncertainty
of the reward system becomes the factor which converts self-interest into self-extension and from there into love.

The normal inspiration for the economic generosity identified with productivity is the expectation that our actions will be
reciprocated. In any relationship that respects the freedom of each
partner, however, there can be no guarantee that generosity will
be returned. People who govern their economic behavior only on
the basis of self-interest parcel out their service according to a
calculated plan. They carefully compute the cost-benefit ratio and
extend themselves only when the prospect of a favorable response
is very high. Such people, however, can never maximize their return through this approach. They have no way of knowing what
the response would be from those to whom they did not extend
themselves. This supposedly self-interested behavior has cut them
off from the possibility of innumerable benefits.

The only sure-fire approach to *maximizing* return-on-invest-
ment is to abandon straight-line expectations and to surrender
ourselves to the reality of the curve. While we place our hope in
the overall correlation between effort and reward, we accept the
fact that our reward curve can be downward sloping as well up-

ward sloping at any point in time. This acceptance of a reality that is spiritual as well as economic allows us to extend ourselves graciously at every occasion—that is, to offer everyone we meet the opportunity of loving us in return. Genuinely productive people know there is a general link between the generous life and the good life. They are not preoccupied, however, with calculating the correlation coefficient for every act.

In looking for specific examples of productive behavior, we need not examine only the lives of saints. Four of the most basic job classifications in our economy provide models that explain what is necessary for personal productivity. An examination of the craftsman, marketer, manager and investor will show us that productivity involves effort, attention to the needs of others, responsibility, and—most importantly—risk taking. As we have seen in the lesson of the curve, there are no guarantees in relationships marked by mutual freedom, but there are no limits to rewards either.

THE CRAFTSMAN

The example of the craftsman shows us the importance of mastering skills. A master craftsman is more likely to be productive than a novice, just as a skilled scientist is more likely to be productive than a starting graduate student. Proficiency contributes to productivity. Traditionally, the Church has emphasized this point through its strong commitment to education. In the Catholic tradition of education, schools and colleges are not simply places in which students prepare to get good jobs. Rather, education is seen as a refinement of one's gifts and skills leading to greater giving and service. In fact, as we shall see throughout this chapter, the definition of a productive person matches closely the ideal Catholic school graduate—well-educated, well-disciplined and committed to unselfish service.

The shift in our economy away from manufacturing and towards services has received extensive attention in both economic and social justice literature. Quite often, religious critiques of this trend describe new service positions as "dead end jobs." While I was working at *The Monitor,* the Diocese of Trenton's weekly newspaper, the New Jersey Council of Churches issued a report, *Reshaping New Jersey,* which was produced at the height of a state-wide economic boon. At the time, the increase in total wages in the service industry was running 65 percent ahead of the total loss in wages in the manufacturing sector. Nevertheless, the Council concluded that the manufacturing-to-services shift was a sign of "growing economic inequality and declining prospects."

There is no such thing, however, as a job in which a worker cannot master skills, develop a sense of craftsmanship, and improve his or her productivity. Several years ago, I was involved in the Dale Carnegie program as both a student and graduate assistant to the instructor. The course offers several excellent lessons in practical charity. For example, how can we say we love our neighbor if we cannot remember his or her name? Dale Carnegie's writings reduce successful personal relationships to two basic components: confidence in one's ability to offer others something of value and a genuine interest in other people. That sounds pretty close to, "Love your neighbor as yourself."

In my case, the Dale Carnegie program had another important side benefit—the opportunity to learn more about the fast-food business, where "dead-end" jobs are said to abound. The class presented an interesting contrast. The largest group of students worked for high-tech Bell Labs. In second place was a company which operates several Burger King restaurants in New York and New Jersey.

During the course, each person gives about 25 short speeches based on personal incidents. After listening to so many of these stories, a Dale Carnegie participant learns a great deal about fellow students' attitudes toward life and work. The fast-food students in our class provided compelling evidence that even the least glamorous job need not be a "dead-end" position. Some of the Burger King crowd had been to college, most had not. All had worked on the counter. In their entry-level work, however, they displayed qualities which signaled potential, and they were attending the Dale Carnegie program as part of their management training.

Two women stood out as shining examples of the way employees can develop, with or without formal education. "Laurie" was a recent high school graduate. She recognized the connection between being a good cheerleader, being a popular student, and being a business leader. She knew that providing cheerful customer service at all hours of the night or day is not an easy chore. She knew that fellow employees need a friend, a booster, an enthusiastic supporter. She started as "one of the gang" but became a guide—first for her shift and later for the entire restaurant.

"Mary" was a mother. After raising her children, she re-entered the work force at the local Burger King. She discovered that her fellow employees—most of them much younger—could use a little "mothering." Her contribution was direction, organization and morale building. Following her instincts of concern, "Mary" too advanced in the company.

My favorite example of skills mastery and craftsmanship in entry-level jobs is drawn from newspaper circulation work, one of the least glamorous occupations imaginable. At the time I was managing the circulation department at *The Asbury Park Press*, we had 165 counselors, who were responsible for supervising and servicing the newspaper's 3,300 youth carriers. According to the recruitment literature we distributed, the part-time counselor position provided a housewife or retiree a way to earn $120 to $150 per week by working less than two hours a day. In truth, the fact that we were able to retain these counselors for more than one day says something about either the state of the economy or the tenacity of the human spirit—or both.

Varying definitions of a counselor's responsibility were a constant source of tension within the circulation department. Yet our failure to develop a precise job description provided the counselor system with its greatest strength. Each person hired adopted a personal conception of the job. Many viewed their duties in very narrow terms: dropping bundles of papers off at carriers' houses and collecting the carriers' bills—nothing more. Others saw themselves as territory managers and carrier advisers—"psyching" carriers up for sales contests, encouraging them to collect one more time from the neighborhood dead beat, and advising them about the value of biting one's tongue when confronted by a chronic complainer. When home computers first became popular, some counselors established elaborate data bases on their carriers. At the other end of the spectrum were counselors who found remembering their 15 carriers' addresses an impossible chore.

All counselors were required to perform certain minimum duties. Had we tried to mandate the exceptional efforts of the best counselors, however, we would have been dealing with a completely different job in a totally different salary range. The service these "super counselors" offered was their gift to the carriers and to the newspaper. Eight years have passed since I was working with newspaper carriers and their counselors, but I have yet to encounter a better example of productivity as uncompensated value than that offered by dedicated circulation employees.

Salaries may not reflect the wide productivity differences among entry-level employees, but job satisfaction and advancement potential certainly do. Fast food and newspaper delivery are only two types of service sector jobs where dedication and craftsmanship are expressions of productivity.

The Marketer

The second business model the productive person should seek to emulate is the marketer. We can enhance our personal productivity by viewing each economic situation as ultimately a customer relationship. Uneasiness with market forces abounds in the social justice literature of the Church. Yet, coming from an institution dedicated to loving, other-directed behavior, this attitude toward the salesperson is surprising. After all, marketing is nothing more than servicing the needs of other people.

The marketing-oriented person or company does not ask: "How much can we get away with?" The marketing-oriented person asks: "How much can we give while still making a profit?" The most innovative, service-oriented companies are always out front of their customers. They give customers more than what they ask for. For example, no customer asked McDonald's to set up drive-through lanes, children's playgrounds, or kids' meals. The company did this because it thought it could provide these services to people and still make a profit. How right it was!

Shortly after I transferred from the newsroom to the marketing side of newspaper publishing, I attended a six-session workshop on copy writing and layout sponsored by the Newspaper Advertising Bureau. I will never be mistaken for an award winning advertising designer, but that course provided me with a powerful insight on the importance of the marketing metaphor to a Catholic understanding of economic life.

The basic rule of advertising copy writing is: "Stress benefits, not features." This was emphasized repeatedly in every session. Benefit language, the instructor explained, is customer-oriented. Feature language, on the other hand, is company- or self-oriented. In the workshop, feature statements such as, "Our umbrellas are large and black," were criticized, while benefit statements such as, "Our umbrellas will keep you dry," were praised.

During that training program, I was struck by the awareness that this most fundamental advertising precept should be the central rule of life. The stress-benefits-not-features principle, which is the key to advertising effectiveness, tells us that other-directed behavior works, while self-centered behavior does not.

Of all segments of the U.S. economy, the advertising industry is probably the least likely to receive praise in religious literature. Yet this industry, at its best, bases its success on the recognition that touting any characteristic of a company other than its ability to satisfy customers is meaningless. Any good advertising executive will tell a client that real service is the only thing that counts in getting and keeping customers. Now, if only that advertising principle—stressing benefits and not features—could become normative for the rest of the economy.

We all know, of course, that realizing the importance of other-directed behavior does not eliminate tricks and fakery. Even companies with strong advertising campaigns can pretend to offer benefits that they do not provide.

Nevertheless, we should derive a certain level of comfort from the fact that our market-oriented economy acknowledges (at least in principle) the goal of placing the customer's interests first. "The customer is always right" is still the accepted wisdom in handling complaints. No company says: "You will feel rotten if you buy our product." All companies that do a substantial amount of advertising and make a concerted effort to market their products and services are committed (at least nominally) to customer service.

All levels of the U.S. economy desperately need workers whose commitment to customer service is real, not just nominal. Followers of the "Son of Man, who came not be served, but to serve" should be in the forefront of a true customer service movement. One way they do this is to become serious students of marketing, the science of detecting and satisfying genuine customer needs.

THE MANAGER

The third model of productivity is the manager, the leader of our economic institutions. By recognizing Holy Orders as one of the seven special sacraments of God's grace, the Church makes a statement about the presence of God in the ordained leaders of the Christian community. In turn, a deeper understanding of the "priesthood of the faithful" requires reflection on the leadership responsibilities demanded of every individual.

Some discussions of leadership dismiss the term "management" with pejorative comments linking it to the status quo. Leadership, on the other hand, is presented as a quality connected to dynamic change. This distinction, however, has little relevance to actual management situations. The best managers are clearly leaders.

Guiding young workers through their transition from employees to managers has been one of the most rewarding aspects of my career. The starting point for this transition can be summarized in a single phrase: group responsibility. The young worker does not become a manager when he or she is promoted into a supervisory position. A worker begins to think like a manager the day he or she accepts responsibility not only for personal actions, but for those of others as well. A worker becomes a manager by exercising leadership among peers.

Incipient managers also identify their personal interests with those of the group. Becoming a good manager is not a selfish process of acquiring power. Rather, true management represents the shift of one's concern away from self and toward the group.

Managers are such valuable members of an organization (and the economy as a whole) because they are willing to step forward and say: "I will be responsible for the performance of my staff. If they do well, I expect to be rewarded. If they fail, I realize I will be held accountable." A good manager, therefore, extends the productivity of his or her people.

Not many managers are asked to lay down their lives for their employees. Each day, though, thousands of managers are asked to lay down their raises, their promotions, their bonuses, and even their jobs because they accepted responsibility for unproductive workers. Extending one's self for one's friends and one's employees is indeed a risky business. But no worker who is unwilling to take that risk should ever complain about being stuck in a "dead-end" job. As "Laurie" and "Mary" showed in the examples above, assuming more responsibility as a manager is an unfailing way to improve personal productivity. It is a model for all who wish to increase their own productivity.

THE INVESTOR

The fourth and final model of productivity is the investor, the person who shows us better than anyone else the importance of risk-taking in all free and loving relationships.

George Gilder, who spent several years writing about sexual relationships (*Sexual Suicide*) and the importance of family (*Naked Nomads*) before focusing his attention on economics and entrepreneurship, is a writer who has influenced greatly my thinking about the economy. His impact has been particularly strong on my growing awareness of what might be called the spiritual dimension of the investment process. Ironically, Michael Novak, the most serious Catholic writer on economic affairs and another of my important intellectual mentors, criticized Gilder's popular treatment of supply-side economics, *Wealth and Poverty*, for being too altruistic. Yet, in this work and later writings, Gilder argues conclusively that investment (implicitly or explicitly) expresses faith and hope. In analyzing poverty he talks about the limited time frame of the poor. The narrow horizon that accompanies economic hopelessness, Gilder notes, often results in an unwillingness to expend effort without certain and immediate reward—in other words, an unwillingness to make long-term investments.

Even among those being paid well above the minimum wage, shortsightedness can be a major factor inhibiting career advancement. Speaking as a manager myself, I personally find constant questions such as: "Will I be paid overtime for this?" or "How big a bonus will I get if I take on this project?" extremely annoying. I am sure I am not alone in preferring employees who are willing to make an act of trust in their managers.

The same people who demand guaranteed rewards often marvel at the high returns paid to investors. They fail to realize, however, that the investor represents pure productivity. Whether recognized or not, the implicit statement an investor makes to an enterprise is this: "Here is my money. If you can use it to make additional money, I expect repayment along with a proportionate share of the gain. But if your use of the money is not productive and does not generate a return, you do not owe me a thing."

As too many stock holders have learned during the record number of bankruptcies in recent years, the rights of equity investors are subordinate to all other claims against the corporation—subordinate to employees, suppliers, government agencies, lending institutions, and bond holders.

What would be the response if we approached our work and all other economic transactions with this same "You don't owe me a thing" attitude? What if all of our economic activity represented an investment? "Here is my work today," we would say to our employer. "If I have added value to the enterprise, I expect to be paid. But, if my work did not make a contribution, you don't owe me a thing." Or to our customer we would say, "Here is the item I am offering you. If the product increases your satisfaction, I expect to be paid. If it does not, you owe me nothing." What would happen if we conditioned all requests for payment on the complete satisfaction of everyone with whom we have an economic relationship?

Most people probably would respond to these questions by saying only fools or saints would try to follow such an unrealistic approach. Throughout the economy, however, millions of investors, commissioned sales people, even some entertainers and professional athletes have their compensation based directly on their performance. In other words, these people are willing to give without a guarantee of getting. The irony of economic life is that these "unrealistic" people are often the wealthiest. Their return far exceeds any "sure thing" arrangement they could structure.

One factor which prevents a full appreciation of the investment process from both an economic and a religious standpoint is the confusion between investing and gambling. Although both involve risk taking, the latter has zero (or perhaps negative) moral significance, while the former is the ultimate key to all economic growth.

As more and more states become dependent upon gambling revenues and pressure builds to expand casino licensing and sports betting, some Catholic leaders are expressing uneasiness about the Church's own dependency on gambling revenue—most notably bingo. The religious case against gambling can be argued along several lines—the economic harm inflicted upon those who lose or the idolatry implicit in submission to the "laws" of chance. One of the most negative impacts of gambling's proliferation is the distortion and misunderstanding it creates about investment, which is the primary way wealth is created.

Investment is the "grain of wheat" which must fall to the ground and die before the economy can enjoy a rich harvest. True investors are motivated by hope—not by chance. They expect a return because of the underlying worth of the enterprise. Their investment represents an endorsement of the endeavor being financed. Accompanying every investment is the statement, "This sounds like a *good* idea." Yet investors also acknowledge the freedom of the marketplace. They accept the reality that not every good idea elicits a favorable response. In a free economy, even worthwhile ventures fail. Thus, the distinguishing feature of true investment is the willingness to place funds at risk. Investment is essentially guided by the hope that goodness begets goodness.

In gambling, on the other hand, there is no underlying worth. The red square is neither better nor worse than the black. Because there is no essential goodness in the process, there is no basis for hope. Once the wheel starts turning, there is no more reason to expect the ball to land in your slot than in mine. The gambler offers others no gift in return. The winner of the game does not make money by providing worthwhile solutions to needs of the other participants, and the winner's gain is linked directly to the loser's pain. While investment can be seen as a metaphor for the risk-taking involved in all loving relationships, gambling is stylized destruction masquerading as economic activity.

The proliferation of gambling is only one of the factors that has fostered misunderstanding about investment in recent years. The junk-bond mentality behind the major financial scandals of the past decade, including insider trading and the collapse of the savings and loan industry, represented an attempt to rewrite the fundamental investment principal: the ratio between risk and reward.

Actually, the early observations of Michael Milken and the other junk-bond proponents were very insightful. They argued correctly that excess caution (fear) can severely limit economic growth. Their innovative approaches to financing created ways for corporations to capitalize on previously undetected sources of value within their organizations and, in this way, they contributed to legitimate economic growth. In the end, however, many of the participants in the financial scandals showed they were not true investors, since they were unwilling, actually, to place their funds at risk. Instead, through intimidation, manipulation, and disregard for the rule of law, they attempted to structure sure-thing situations that would allow them to reap tremendous gains without proportionate risks.

Without profound respect for the freedom of all economic participants, there is little distinction between investing and gambling. But when the true investor pursues prosperity in a spirit of freedom and respect for others, this model provides the definitive lesson on the importance of hope in a productive economy. Even though the investor is motivated by the prospect of a financial reward, his or her motivation has moral significance because it is based on hope rather than certainty. Hope, with its implications of trust, respect and freedom, is the virtue which transforms the investor's self-centered desire into other-serving behavior.

EXPANDING EMPLOYMENT

Despite the obvious connection between the religious no-tion of service and the economic concept of productivity, misun-derstanding about productivity's link to unemployment continues to prevent full appreciation for the effect of increased productiv-ity. This misunderstanding is often stated this way: If everyone works harder, there will be less need for workers. I not only think this belief is wrong but that the opposite is true.

In explaining my position, I turn again to the circulation de-partment at *The Asbury Park Press*. My experience in building a larger staff there highlighted the connection I find between work force performance and job creation. Convincing senior manage-ment that continued circulation expansion required a larger, bet-ter-educated and better-paid administrative team was not easy. The new positions had to be created one by one. Between 1981 and 1986, however, I was permitted to add 12 middle-manage-ment positions to handle the paper's rapid growth.

In a very real sense, each new person hired or promoted into a management slot owed his or her job to the success of the pre-vious manager. One failure could have persuaded top manage-ment that the new positions were more trouble than they were worth. That did not happen. The first person I hired was a truly exceptional employee, Vito Cicero, who went on to become cir-culation director of *The Press* of Atlantic City. With great consis-tency, other new people followed his example of energy and dedi-cation. Since each addition to the management group made a highly visible contribution, the cycle of job creation was allowed to con-tinue.

The most important question a smart company should ask about productive workers is: "Where do we get more like them?" *not* "How do we cut back on them?"

When Catholics recite the Prayer of St. Francis, we do not say: "It would be nice, Lord, if it were better to give than to receive." Instead, we state with conviction: "It is in giving that we receive." We express a reality that is grounded in the Gospel message, not a fantasy based on wishful thinking. The loving way to act is the best way to act, we proclaim. In order to become more productive, therefore, we must shape our economic affairs according to this principle.

For the individual, then, the pursuit of productivity involves the refinement of one's gifts to the economy. Productivity is expressed in many ways—through mastery of one's job and through a recognition that the rewards of love are ever-present but rarely predictable. To the question, "Who is my neighbor?" the productive person answers with the marketer: "My neighbor is my customer." Along with the manager, the productive person says to fellow workers: "You are my brothers and sisters." Finally, the productive person's statement to the economy is that of the investor: "You don't owe me a thing."

INSPIRING PRODUCTIVITY:
THE MANAGEMENT CHALLENGE

As individuals, our Christian faith calls us to lead more productive lives. For those of us in leadership positions—for example, parents, teachers, counselors, managers, administrators, clergy and religious—our faith also is a challenge to motivate others towards productivity. If we regard voluntary productivity as an economic expression of generosity, then we understand that true productivity can never be mandated—it can only be inspired.

Since, as we saw in the previous chapter, hope is the only valid motivation for productivity, management's fostering of productivity is largely a matter of reinforcing hope. For Christians, hope is grounded on the conviction that we are children of a loving God who, as St. Paul tells us, "is able to give you more than you need, so that you will always have all you need for yourselves and more than enough for every good cause." The manager who is willing to give employees more than they need will never have to be concerned about workforce productivity. More specifically, leaders foster productive behavior by reinforcing all the individual aspects of economic generosity.

In his phenomenally successful book, *The Road Less Traveled*, Dr. Scott Peck defined love as the "willingness to extend oneself for the benefit of another." If we look upon productivity as such a loving extension, then an important aspect of managing productivity is to motivate individuals to stretch and expand themselves. For instance, leaders foster mastery, one key expression of productivity, by demanding excellence. The manager is productive (i.e., generates value in excess of cost) only if those being supervised are more productive *with* the manager's involvement than *without* it. The manager is there to inspire sacrifice and effort. The role of the manager is to invite people to be generous.

Most of the managers I have worked for presented this demand without hesitation. One man, Charles Ritscher, however, epitomizes the "good boss" in my career. His history as a marketing manager at *The Asbury Park Press* parallels the story of "The Little Red Hen." Whenever a project at the newspaper needed help, his standard comment was: "Marketing will handle that." Between 1967, when he started with the company, and 1980, when I arrived, he had expanded a one-man promotion department into a large marketing, research and public relations operation. A short time later, he was elected to *The Press'* five-member board of directors and named Vice President of Marketing and Sales, responsible for all of the company's revenue-producing functions.

Ritscher's operating style was promote, promote, promote, and his management style was push, push, push. He often made me angry. He always made me weary. Yet I never resented his direction, since he offered it with affection. He had taken a chance on me when my knowledge of newspaper marketing was still largely theoretical. In him I came to see the essence of what management is all about: bringing forth from people resources they do not know they have or are reluctant to use. Ritscher let me see that the "pusher" often has higher esteem for the "pushee" than the "pushee" himself. He forced me to perform tasks I didn't think could be done. He also showed he knew when to stop pushing and start praising. Words of encouragement were limited, but they always were spoken at the right time.

The inspiring manager always pushes his or her charges toward success. Therefore, requesting someone to venture into new possibilities of success is a loving act. The demand for sacrifice, however, can be extended too far. Requiring someone to take on an assignment that the manager knows cannot be handled and will lead to failure is a "set up" that involves no expression of charity.

Love Is Always "Worth It"

For those attempting to carry out their leadership responsibilities with a Christian perspective, an appropriate step might be to add a phrase from the Lord's Prayer to their management handbooks. "Lead us not into temptation" is a plea all workers should be making to their managers. The task of management is to foster an atmosphere in which generous, productive behavior becomes the norm. The opposite approach, tempting employees with enticements to selfishness, benefits neither the individual nor the organization. When inspiring workers to give more than they get is recognized as management's most important goal, the absurdity of promoting internal rivalries between individuals or departments becomes clear. Any company whose model of inter-departmental relations is a winner-take-all tournament will never develop the generous working relationships that lead to sustained prosperity.

The seminary lesson about the "plus sign" I mentioned earlier bears repeating in this discussion of ways to inspire productivity. To give someone the "plus sign" is to place a positive interpretation on that person's actions. Managers give their employees the "plus sign" when they create an atmosphere of goodwill which encourages innovation and open communication. The employee who knows his or her actions are always looked upon in a favorable light has no reason to withhold important information. On the other hand, management practices designed to keep employees "on edge" or on the defensive destroy goodwill and, therefore, reduce productivity.

Managers intent on inspiring productivity also must reinforce the lesson of "the curve" discussed in the previous chapter by helping their employees cope with life's indeterminate reward system. Underlying all economic behavior is the basic question: "Is it worth it?" Leaders must help their followers answer this question with a resounding "yes" whenever they encounter a situation requiring effort and self-sacrifice. The mark of the Catholic in the economy should be the awareness that love always is "worth it," even though love's immediate payoff may not be clear.

Those who work with young people and the poor have a special responsibility to field the "Is it worth it?" question carefully. Persons seeking to enter the economic system will have difficulty recognizing the value of productive behavior if they are taught that the economy is essentially malign. If Catholics in a position to counsel young people and the economically disadvantaged believe that loving, self-extending behavior is not worth it, if they believe that our culture has become so corrupted that love is never reciprocated, they might need to re-examine their understanding of Christ's redemptive power.

In *Sollicitudo Rei Socialis* (*On Social Concerns*), Pope John Paul II reminds us: "For she (the Church) knows that—in spite of the heritage of sin and the sin which each one is capable of committing—there exists in the human person sufficient qualities and energies, a fundamental goodness, because he or she is the image of the Creator, placed under the redemptive influence of Christ, who united himself in some fashion with every person, and because the efficacious action of the Holy Spirit fills the earth." This Christian conviction that love always is "worth it" must be communicated by those in leadership positions.

On the other hand, promising love's immediate payoff is as false as the cynical view that love is not "worth it." God's love for us and the expressions of this bounty are gifts which cannot be controlled by magic charms, intense prayer, or even hard work. Followers of Christ fail. Followers of Christ experience hardship. In the logic of the cross, however, loving behavior always is "worth it." Creation itself is an invitation to experience what it means to give without any expectation of getting in return. Our existence is a call to a life of eternal happiness within the divine love triangle that sustains itself through love.

KEEP WHAT YOU CREATE

Despite the *gratuitous* aspect of productivity, we must not neglect the proper structuring of economic reward systems, one of the leadership tasks that affects productivity most directly. An *indeterminate* reward system—a system that makes room for free responses and generous behavior—must not deteriorate into a *capricious* one. Financial incentives should reward productive behavior—not discourage it.

Entrepreneurs in our economy distill all incentives to their essence. Their willingness to assume seemingly absurd risks and work loads is based on the most powerful of all economic convictions: You get to keep whatever you create. This belief penetrates to the heart of our paradoxical economic system. Freedom precludes any guarantees, but the generosity freedom allows is the source of all creativity. The hope of enjoying the fruits of one's labor is both a necessary and a sufficient condition to ensure productivity. As long as this hope is present, no other incentive is needed. Once this hope is lost, however, no other incentive can replace it.

Because the "keep what you create" dynamic is so strong, all incentive plans focused on inspiring productivity must be a form of profit sharing. The operative word here is "sharing" since, as we have seen, productivity occurs only in the context of relationships. Not even the entrepreneur, the hero of the individualistic economy, generates new wealth alone. All economic value is created in the marketplace through interaction between buyers and sellers.

More and more managers are discovering that a reliable way to enhance productivity is to measure it precisely and share the benefits with workers. Labor "costs" are basically irrelevant, these managers have learned. Only the *spread* between cost and value is important. Structured properly, profit-sharing plans create a multiplier effect which compounds productivity, widening the *spread* between labor costs and value added.

When the U.S. bishops' economics pastoral appeared several years ago, some commentaries suggested that the section on agriculture policy was inserted merely to satisfy the interests of a few Midwest bishops. The issue of the family farm, however, highlights the motivational value of granting workers an equity interest in their enterprise. The Good Shepherd knew something about the value of "a piece of the action." Hired hands have a habit of bugging out when the wolf arrives, Christ told us. Only the good shepherd, the owner of the flock, stands his ground in the face of adversity.

There are in our economy tasks akin to wrestling wolves—jobs so onerous and so risky that they will only be tackled by good shepherds who are allowed to have a strong sense of "mine." Farming is one of these tasks. (The independent newspaper dealers I worked with for several years make the same argument about their occupation.) Hired hands do fine until danger lurks. Under stress, however, they flee. The bishops' support of the family farm can be seen as a protective measure for the nation. Something as vital as the food supply should not be left entirely to hired hands. The toughest jobs will be tackled only if we give those who undertake them an ownership interest in the endeavor.

Formal profit-sharing plans and stock options, however, are not the only way to inspire employees. In any organization, the most productive competition between management and labor occurs when the two parties try to outdo one another in generosity. The best leaders create an atmosphere where counting the cost no longer makes sense. An incident in 1983 illustrates the way Jules Plangere, Jr., retired publisher of *The Asbury Park Press*, inspired this sentiment in me.

In business, recruiting someone from outside the company at a salary higher than existing managers are paid is not an uncommon occurrence. This was not Plangere's style. He wanted all of his managers to feel part of the team. After calling me into his office to inform me that the newspaper had hired a new production manager, he matter-of-factly told me I would be receiving a $6,000 raise. Until that point in my career—13 years after leaving college—I had worked with the sense of being underpaid. Then, in one quick move, I became "overpaid." Suddenly, I was making more money than I expected. When working for such a generous manager, counting the cost of every effort makes no sense. (As an aside, since leaving *The Press*, getting divorced, and pursuing a career in the Catholic press, my financial situation has declined. Thanks to Plangere, however, I know that the gap between poverty and affluence is not infinitely wide. It can be filled for about $6,000!)

The behavior of managers who inspire their workers suggests that we should abandon our traditional notions of balance and even fairness so that we can make room for the unbalanced idea of generosity. Traditional descriptions of the relationship between workers and employers, such as "full day's work for full day's pay" and "giving employees their just due," are inadequate to explain the dynamics of the productive economy. What is needed is "more."

In asking workers to be more productive, companies are asking them to be generous—to give more than a full day's work for a full day's pay. Such generosity, however, cannot be achieved by force. Threats and coercion are not the tools which will maximize productivity. If companies want their workers to be generous, they must be prepared to reciprocate. They, too, must find a way to offer employees more than they expect.

An example of such generosity can be found in the parable of the laborers in the vineyard, which contains Jesus' description of a very unconventional compensation arrangement. Even the last hired, who gave far less than a full day's work, received a full day's pay. Many of the workers regard the owner of the vineyard's action as grossly unfair. After all, they had worked "a full day in the scorching heat." Still, the owner responds, "I do you no injustice . . . are you envious because I am generous?"

A Living Wage

The doctrine of a "living wage," which has been such an important part of Catholic social teaching in the past century and which flows directly from this parable, offers an extremely effective mechanism for motivating economic generosity. The productive workers so desirable to companies are people willing to do the extras—employees who will take on extra assignments and expend extra efforts to meet important goals. This attitude of willingness and cooperation, however, can only be sustained within a climate of security and trust. In its wisdom, the Church offers employers an excellent piece of management advice: Pay people enough so that they do not have to worry about feeding, housing, and educating their families, and they won't quibble about their work. Once people have a sense of economic security and sufficiency in their lives, they are far less inclined to question whether they are adequately compensated for each specific assignment. Only then can employees afford to be generous in their work.

When viewed in juxtaposition to the "lean and mean" tactics companies are using to extract greater productivity from their workers, the living wage approach looks hopelessly idealistic. Notice, however, that the we-won't-count-the-cost-if-you-don't relationship embodied in the living wage doctrine is the exact type of arrangement successful companies try to structure for their most prized employees. In the bestselling novel, *The Firm,* John Grisham describes the way a corrupt law firm, Bendini, Lambert & Locke, recruited the book's hero, Mitchell McDeere. The senior partners of the firm know that the best way to command an employee's unquestioning loyalty is to give the person more than he or she expects. Bendini, Lambert & Locke was not content to match

Mitch's best offer—the firm topped it by 10 percent and then threw in a black BMW and a low-interest housing loan for extra measure. Like the fictional Bendini, Lambert & Locke, real-life companies offering their senior executives extremely generous compensation packages justify these arrangements by saying they don't want their key employees worrying about making money for themselves. They want their best employees to concentrate on making money for the firm.

As the gospel story suggests, the wisdom of such wily managers should not be ignored. If companies are confident that a $1 million employee will generate value far in excess of cost, why do they doubt that a much more modest living wage for other employees will produce similar returns? One of the major ironies of business life is that the best-paid employees in many organizations are actually the least expensive, since they are the most productive, while the lowest paid workers are often the most expensive, since they generate minimal value beyond their compensation. Too often, this generalization is used to widen the salary gap between those on the top-rung and those on the bottom-rung of the corporate ladder. Companies that follow this approach fail to see generous compensation as an inducement to productivity— not just a reward for it.

What is emerging at some companies after their downsizing is a two-tiered employment structure—an inner cadre of secure, well-paid, highly-motivated managers and an outer group of employees who are viewed as expendable. The productivity of the former group is taken for granted; they get a great deal from the organization but give back even more. The productivity of the latter group, however, is subjected to intense scrutiny. The "expendables" live with the constant fear that as soon as they fail the latest efficiency test they will be replaced by a machine or a "temp." This is not an environment conducive to promoting productivity.

Even managers who forsake the use of blunt terror tactics to prod their employees often miss the real point about low productivity by relying exclusively on training and technology as the solution to their problems. Productive employees are not necessarily equipped with more smarts or better tools than their unproductive counterparts. They are productive primarily because they are willing to *give* more. They have learned the one essential lesson of a prosperous society: On balance, participants must put back into the economy more than they take out of it. Prized employees exhibit the same willingness to surrender that is found in a loving marriage. They stop counting the cost and place their interests in the hands of other people.

Too few of the managers who complain about the absenteeism and inattention of minimum-wage workers recognize that all employees have the same economic needs. If they did accept the similarity between their workers and themselves, managers would see that extending "tier-one" treatment to their entire labor force would boost productivity throughout their companies. The living wage paid to every employee puts all workers in the position of being able to concentrate on generating additional economic value rather than weighing each action on a compensation balancing scale.

Although some managers may question the wisdom of using generous compensation packages as a way of inspiring both blue-collar and white-collar employees to greater productivity, they should appreciate the fact that the link between pay and performance is a complex rather than simple relationship. Once again, we find a situation that would be represented best on a graph by a curve rather than a straight line. Suppose we found that this relationship could be expressed mathematically as $P = C^2$, where "P" is productivity and "C" compensation. In this case, we would discover that productivity was always less than compensation as long as value for compensation was less than one. For instance, the value of $.9^2$ is .81 which is less than .9. On the graph, the curve would be almost flat since each increment of productivity would be less than each increment in compensation. Once compensation went above one (a living wage), however, productivity would jump exponentially. Two squared is four, three squared is nine and so forth. The curve would start shooting straight up.

There is no such magic formula that will help companies optimize the productivity of their employees. Nevertheless, the above theoretical example illustrates a point that people involved in management training know well: The transforming point in the career of a would-be manager often comes with a sudden click. At that moment, the person establishes a bond with the organization and starts to identify the employer's interests with his or her own interests. Inspiring that "click" in every employee is what improving productivity is all about. Until a company's total compensation package (including working conditions and personal respect, as well as wages) reaches "one"—the living wage—the response of "ungrateful" employees to their compensation may be discouraging. Once a company inspires an employee to cross that mysterious threshold, however, a personal loyalty is established. Then each expression of the company's generosity is compounded by the employee and returned in the form of higher performance. From that point on (or until the employee's trust is violated) the veritable magic of productivity occurs. Value exceeds cost by a wide margin.

What the Catholic Church is suggesting through the living wage doctrine is that the un-generous company is wasting its money. Only organizations willing to establish a just relationship with employees by providing them a generous measure of economic sufficiency will be able to inspire true productivity. When one accepts the critical importance of worker generosity to true prosperity, then the conclusion that downsizing and wage cuts are not the answer to the productivity problem becomes apparent.

One final point worth mentioning is that management of older workers in an organization also can be a major contributor to a "don't count the cost" atmosphere. As such, the way older workers are treated can have a direct bearing on the productivity of younger workers. Highly-educated young people, whose energy and innovation are a major source of business productivity, invariably are asked by their employers to give more than they receive. The members of this group are much more likely to respond positively to this request if their employers practice what they preach in regard to their older workers. If, in their treatment of older workers, employers recognize only present contributions—"What have you done for me lately?"—they cannot expect younger workers to heed the "don't count the cost" appeal. Acknowledging the full value of services rendered throughout a career is the soundest way for managers to gain their young employees' trust and to inspire productivity among workers of all ages.

UNSOLICITED FOOTNOTE: MANAGEMENT IN THE CHURCH

Working for Catholic, non-profit publications during the past eight years has presented me with a special opportunity to reflect upon the nature of the management process within a religious context. This experience has at the same time challenged as well as reinforced my conviction that Catholics can play a pivotal role in helping our economy recognize the source of true prosperity. On the one hand, the importance of worker generosity is self-evident in religious organizations, which make no pretense of paying competitive salaries. The difference between what an editor could make at a commercial publication and what he or she is paid at a Catholic publication is clearly a gift—not just to the publication but to the publication's readers as well. Thus, the only way for Catholic publications to recruit and motivate talented workers is to appeal to their sense of dedication.

The Church situation in which worker generosity is most apparent is the Catholic school system. The main reason Catholic schools are able to provide a quality education at lower per-pupil expenditures than most public schools is because Catholic school teachers and administrators are extremely productive. They generate value far in excess of cost, partly because they are willing to donate a portion of their work to their students. This tradition of employee generosity has been the sustaining force not only for the Catholic education system but for the Church's health care and social service systems as well.

Despite this remarkable heritage, many Catholic institutions seem far more intent on importing the management practices of commercial organizations (becoming more "businesslike") than on exporting their own experience of management by inspiration rather than coercion.

In 1989, I was nominated for the board of directors of the Catholic Press Association. Taking a cue from the movie, "The Mission," newly released on video cassette, I said my goal was for Catholic publications to become new "reductions" (the 17th century missions founded by the Jesuits in Paraguay). By this I meant that Catholic publications should strive to become thriving enterprises marketed and managed according to specifically Christian principles. I doubt this campaign statement had any impact on the election, since I was running against the extremely popular and extremely competent Arthur McKenna, general manager of *Catholic New York,* who eventually was elected president of the association. I was disappointed, however, that I did not receive a single comment on my platform from colleagues. Not one person said the development of specifically Christian marketing and management practices was a worthwhile objective. Had I said that my goal was to share the commercial marketing and management techniques I had learned during 16 years in the daily newspaper industry, I feel confident that the reaction would have been more positive. That Catholic institutions, many of whom are struggling financially, have something to learn from business enterprises is accepted without discussion. Yet the idea that the employee and customer relations practiced by Catholic institutions can benefit the wider economy is considered strange and perhaps even a little silly.

Of course, one reason many Catholic institutions do not attempt to export their management practices is that so many of them have little of substance to offer. Although there are notable exceptions, many diocesan newspapers, for instance, evidence weak employee morale. They offer their employees not only low pay but an unpleasant work environment as well. Instead of the atmosphere of magnanimity that should characterize organizations which recognize the importance of employee generosity, preoccupation with insufficient financial resources in Catholic publications often creates an atmosphere of tension, lack of appreciation, and even distrust.

In the Diocese of Trenton where I worked, the newspaper reported to a vicar whose ultimate put-down for an impractical idea was "spoken like a true associate." He was referring to the sharp distinction some priests make between the "pastor" and the "associate priest" mentalities. Because he is concerned with funding and staffing, the job of the pastor is often regarded as something less than spiritual. On the other hand, because he is usually dealing with parishioner service, the associate is regarded as impractical.

In talking with younger priests—who frequently discuss among themselves the less-than-gracious management practices of their pastors and diocesan officials—I once heard the comment that the Church has misinterpreted the priest shortage. There is not a shortage of pastors, these young priests joked, only a shortage of associates. Being an underling in the Church hierarchy, even an ordained male underling, is apparently a less-than-inspiring experience for too many priests. Anyone who thinks this situation exists only in the Diocese of Trenton may want to read J.F. Powers' *Wheat That Springeth Green*, which offers an hilarious description of Church life in an unnamed Midwest archdiocese. I may be jumping to conclusions, but one factual and one fictional encounter with everyday Church management are enough to convince me that Catholic personnel practices could use some refinement.

Inspiring its priests should *not* be a problem for the Church. The Catholic Church is the last institution in the world that should be in need of management consultants. Somewhere within the theology of Holy Orders should be an understanding of leadership and management that priests can share with everyone who directs the lives of others. I have not, unfortunately, met many priests who reflect openly on the link between their priesthood and their management responsibilities.

This is not to say that all priests are poor managers. I have dealt with priests who exhibit an authoritarian management style and others who are reluctant to issue explicit directives. But I also have met many priests who display exceptional administrative abilities. Even these highly competent priest-administrators, however, rarely make a connection between their sacramental charism and their management skills. More common among successful priest-administrators is the feeling that they have sacrificed a specifically priestly ministry to keep the rest of the Church out of debt.

The lack of reflection on priesthood as management is more than a theoretical problem. A very practical result is a work environment within Catholic organizations that can be less pleasant than the atmosphere at even a moderately successful commercial enterprise. If, on the individual level, Church managers—laity as well as priests and religious—are supposedly more prayerful and, presumably, far more charitable than their counterparts in industry, why can they not serve as more of an inspiration to others?

One conclusion I have reached is that the dedication and commitment of Church officials often work against them when they are asked to manage others. Dealing with the fragile egos of thin-skinned subordinates is a time-consuming and energy-draining duty for all managers. But it is a task the best managers in industry willingly perform because they recognize they are dealing with human beings—not saints. Too often, managers in Church offices are tempted to think that they are dealing with people who never experience thoughts of jealousy, resentment, or lack of appreciation. As Dale Carnegie explains so well, appealing to a subordinate's noble instincts is a sound management practice in any organization. Totally ignoring a subordinate's ignoble instincts, however, can precipitate serious personnel problems.

"Why should we have to put up with this pettiness?" is a question I have heard managers in the Church ask with some frequency. "After all, aren't we all committed to the same goal?" The expressed disinterest in "pettiness" can easily become an excuse for management insensitivity. When employees' legitimate (or even irrational) complaints are dismissed with such a comment, the result is lower morale—not higher performance. Not even the best-intentioned managers—not pastors, not bishops, not even the pope—are at liberty to redefine the rules of personal respect. Helping employees stretch their limits is one thing; providing unnecessary opportunities for self-effacement damages productivity in even the most dedicated work groups.

My prayer is that priests will reflect more on their vocations in light of the management process and will reflect more upon the management process in light of the Sacrament of Holy Orders. I hope that priests will come to see themselves as the "managers" of the entire Christian community—not just of Church offices and Church programs. The result of these reflections could be one of the most important contributions of the Catholic Church to economic understanding. Seeing sacramental priesthood as the embodiment of inspirational management—encouraging people to acknowledge, express, and share their personal goodness—will place priests in a special position to inject new vitality into the institutional Church and to bear witness to the world about the management qualities that will foster a more productive and prosperous society.

SECURING PRODUCTIVITY:
THE ROLE OF GOVERNMENT

Even in the most religiously inspired economy, business cycles will conform to the rhythm of the Paschal Mystery. Defeat is as much a part of our economic lives as success. In light of this recognition, we must accept the fact that even companies which treat their employees generously and respectfully may not be able to offer the security of a lifetime contract. In an organic economy, dead branches are pruned so that new shoots can sprout.

Thus, establishing a society's productivity-inducing atmosphere is a responsibility that supersedes the ability of individual managers or even entire companies or industries. If productivity and prosperity are to be abundant, society as a whole must work to establish a pervasive climate of goodwill. In order for people to become productive, they must have the sense that the odds favor the giver—not the taker. Viewed as inducements to productivity, law and justice—which receive such strong emphasis in Catholic social teaching—take on new economic importance. Although voluntary productivity is radically difficult since it involves surrender and self-denial, the moral society has an obligation to facilitate this form of economic generosity—in effect, to make doing good as painless as possible.

Society, through its government, creates this all-important sense of goodwill in at least four ways: (1) by establishing a system of standards and incentives that distinguishes between real and illusory wealth; (2) by offering the economic and political security that diminishes fearful, self-destructive behavior; (3) by promoting the inclusiveness that keeps the economy expanding; and (4)—most importantly—by protecting the freedom that makes voluntary productivity possible.

As we have seen, the prospect that the person who creates new wealth gets to keep it forms the most powerful incentive toward productivity. Once this is understood, society's responsibility in providing economic incentives becomes a matter of reinforcing this most basic conviction. The first step in the development of proper economic incentives is a comprehensive accounting system that distinguishes between productive and unproductive economic activity. A strict standard of profitability is needed to focus society's attention on the formation of true wealth and prosperity. Such a standard would eliminate much of the confusion about what is spurious, what is marginal, and what is legitimate economic activity. Crime, fraud, corruption and environmental destruction are often tolerated in many parts of our society because these activities are associated with economic benefits. Drug dealing provides jobs in the inner city, insider trading expands incomes on Wall Street, and clear cutting provides employment in the logging industry. Unfortunately, the attraction of spurious wealth is often strongest in those places where images of true wealth are least evident. West Virginia is such a place.

REGULATING FRAUD

Shortly after starting my reporting career with the *Charleston Daily Mail*, I was asked to follow up on a story broken by Jim Haught, award-winning investigative reporter for our other-side-of-the-building rival *The Charleston Gazette*. This incident introduced me to a special aspect of the West Virginia economy I would encounter repeatedly in the coming years. Coupled with acceptance of poverty was a great tolerance for corruption and a tremendous susceptibility to fraud on the part of many state residents.

John Smiley, part-time restaurant owner, part-time driving range operator, and part-time con artist, wanted to tell his side of the story, claiming he had been defamed in a *Gazette* account of his activities. Early in our conversation, however, he conceded all the key details in Haught's article. Smiley had developed one of the more original approaches to retailing. He had erected a sign in a large vacant field announcing the future opening of the WEGE City Shopping Center, and then went door-to-door selling coupons offering lifetime discounts at WEGE City stores. The shopping center would never be built, but Smiley, equipped with an attractive presentation folder, was able to sell several of the phony coupons for $1,000 each before the county prosecutor and Haught heard of the scheme.

Smiley's victims were unsophisticated. Yet even prominent West Virginians displayed startling gullibility at times. A few years after the WEGE City episode, our readers were shocked to learn that a former telephone company executive from the city had been accused of fraud in Washington, D.C. They were even more startled when I reported that the victims of Robert Dale Johnson's elaborate Portuguese wine scam included the mayor of Charleston, the state's capitol city, and the presidents of two major West Virginia banks.

The champion of all the schemers I encountered, however, was Theodore R. "Ted" Price, president of Diversified Mountaineer Corporation (DMC). He provided the greatest journalistic challenge of my life. Rumors of improprieties at DMC's Kanawha

City Savings and Loan subsidiary were constant from the time I started at the *Daily Mail*, but the lengthy profile I did on the company in 1973 offered the first public suggestion of the company's pending collapse.

Before DMC filed for bankruptcy in 1974, Price's company had attracted $70 million into uninsured savings accounts and high-risk securities through a strategy that included: (a) aggressive promotion ("This is Roy Clark, pickin' and a grinnin' for Kanawha City Savings and Loan"), (b) glossy financial reports audited by the nationally recognized accounting firm Price Waterhouse & Company, and (c) sheer gall. At one point DMC tried to sell new stock at $3.50 per share when its existing stock was trading for under $2. The bankruptcy hearings disclosed additional details of the DMC shenanigans, and both Jim Haught and I followed the story relentlessly for over two years. Although *The Gazette* and *Daily Mail* pooled their business interests, competition between the two news staffs was intense. Because our journalistic styles and our papers' approach to news were so different, however, Haught and I developed an unusual blend of competition and co-operation on the DMC story. He would come across financial information he didn't need and I would uncover "dirt" I knew the *Daily Mail* would never use. Together, we offered a composite view of the DMC scandal that made very interesting reading.

Haught titillated his readers with hints of seamy sex that accompanied Price's big-time lifestyle. At various times, the allegations had Price linked romantically to a well-known Charleston call girl and one of the financier's male assistants. Meanwhile, I concentrated on tracing the way Price and his staff moved cash among the various DMC subsidiaries one step ahead of the state banking auditors.

Perhaps because I gave full credit to the complexity of their maneuvers, Price and his two senior aides were surprisingly open with DMC financial data. Later I would use the material for my business school thesis that analyzed the company's "growth before profits" development strategy. By the completion of the bankruptcy proceedings, I was truly sorry to see the DMC story and my relationship with Price end.

After he was convicted on federal fraud charges, I wrote to Price in prison with the suggestion that we collaborate on a book about the scandal. He never responded. His prison term was brief, since he was the star witness in an unsuccessful federal prosecution of West Virginia Gov. Arch A. Moore, Jr. (Price said he paid the governor $50,000 to approve a bank charter for DMC, but his outrageous claims had been so well publicized that he had no credibility as a witness. Moore was acquitted on the Price bribery charges but went to prison several years later after being convicted in an unrelated corruption case.) Price was struck by a car and died a short time after his release. At that point, I abandoned my hopes of achieving fame and fortune as his chronicler.

Too bad. Wider exposure of the DMC case, which cost thousands of families a large portion of their savings, may have provided an early warning signal on the all-too-similar savings and loan scandal which erupted nationwide ten years later. Whatever mistakes Price made, he made at least one shrewd decision. He selected West Virginia as his base of operations. The economic climate of the state, where the legacy of poverty has made distinctions between legitimacy and illegitimacy very hazy, was very favorable to Price's get-rich-quick style.

Only in the light of a clear understanding of legitimate profits can the economic damage of such financial crime be exposed. All economic crime is a form of theft which blocks—not enhances—the drive toward prosperity. Through consistent law enforcement, government informs the criminal and fraudulent elements in our society that they have contributed nothing and, thus, deserve nothing in return. In doing this, government can foster a better appreciation for the true wealth-creating process.

REGULATING MARGINAL WEALTH

Comprehensive profitability measurements also apply to marginal, albeit legal, endeavors. The challenge of business is to operate profitably and thereby create new wealth. But business has no innate right to make a profit. Therefore, the government can offer no guarantee of business survival. The company which cannot cover its costs contributes nothing to society and, in fact, has no economic value. Any social theory that makes job creation, rather than wealth creation, the primary goal of economic policy exposes society to business extortion.

Another West Virginia institution, the coal industry, provides a good example of the marginal, albeit legal, wealth problem. In some writings on Appalachia, mine operators are portrayed in almost demonic terms. Actually, they provide a refreshing contrast to the flim-flam characters so prevalent in other parts of the region's economy. There is nothing insubstantial about either a modern coal mine or the people who run them. Nevertheless, after a century of effort, the coal industry has yet to show clear evidence of the black mineral's economic value.

Operating a coal mine is truly profitable only if the price of coal covers the substantial costs of coal extraction and coal consumption. Theoretically, there is no reason why coal cannot be mined in a way that does not damage the terrain, the coal field communities, or the mine workers themselves. The reclamation and production technologies are there. The only thing needed is money. On the other end of the process, there is no theoretical reason why coal cannot be burned without emitting noxious pollutants. Stripped of its impurities, coal is an energy-packed hydrocarbon which can be oxidized (burned) into harmless carbon dioxide and water vapor. The coal treatment and emission control technologies are there, too. Again, the only thing needed is money.

The coal industry stands in the middle of these two enormous sets of costs. The trick the mine operators are asked to perform is to create a spread between coal's value and its costs. The price of coal must be high enough to pay for damage-free extraction and reclamation. At the same time, its price must be low enough to remain competitive with other fuels that do not require the same environmental safeguards. By way of example, let's say utilities can buy coal at $20 per ton, successfully control emissions, and still generate more BTU's for the buck than they would with alternate fuels. On the other side of this hypothetical ledger, let's say the full production and reclamation costs are only $18 per ton. In this example, the operator has earned a $2 per ton profit, which is new wealth created by assembling the mass of concrete, steel, men, women and machinery that goes into operating a modern coal mine.

The coal industry's record of not paying its social bills, however, is legendary. In the early part of the century, the coal barons reported profits when none existed. At the time, the price of coal was too high to be used environmentally and too low to be mined

147

safely. The coal barons' claim to wealth was based solely on inaccurate accounting, which ignored all of the social costs associated with worker health and environmental destruction—incomplete accounting that should not have been permitted by a government intent on fostering real wealth formation. The early mine operators achieved their affluent life styles by inflicting death, dismemberment and disease on their miners and incredible environmental damage on the communities in which they and their allies in the electrical utility industry operated. For many years, the worst of the industry's abuses were accepted because coal mining provided employment for substantial numbers of West Virginians.

Work that produces an item with no added value, however, is not the type of productive activity a prosperity-oriented government should be encouraging.

I started thinking seriously about the coal industry's marginal economic value several years ago. Suggesting the closure of an entire industry then would have been regarded as an outlandish proposition. More recently, however, Great Britain has entertained a serious discussion about eliminating coal mining and burning in that country. This effort to force the coal industry to document its net economic contribution—all benefits minus all costs—should be applauded. To the business which complains that absorbing the costs of worker health, consumer safety, and environmental protection eliminates profits and threatens its existence, society's response should be: "So what!" Prosperous employment can only be provided by a productive enterprise, that is, an enterprise whose positive contribution to society more than offsets any negative stress it inflicts on society. The last thing the economy needs is another endeavor that cannot pay all of its bills.

REGULATING SUCCESS

Spurious and marginal wealth are not the only situations that must be addressed by a comprehensive government incentive system designed to promote productivity. Society also must be prepared to deal with those individuals and businesses who meet even the most rigorous standard of profitability. A government which consistently confiscates the true wealth created through risk taking, exertion and generosity cannot claim to be fostering a benevolent atmosphere for its citizens. Again, "keep what you create" must be at the heart of all incentive plans.

Nevertheless, taxation is completely consistent with government's prosperity-promoting functions, since taxation provides ways to cover the hard-to-account-for social costs of economic activity. In the case of the coal industry, for instance, society as a whole has derived substantial economic benefits from the low-cost electrical power generated by coal-fired turbines. Government financed Black Lung disability payments are one way society is now paying those hidden costs.

Taxation also finances economic security, another extremely important element in government's effort to regulate success. One of the main reasons the rich get richer is that they operate in a climate of security that makes risk taking much less terrifying. Their investing surplus wealth in a new business venture is one level of risk. Poor people investing their rent money is a much different proposition.

The ultimate expression of a society's benevolence is its treatment of the unproductive. By giving to those who cannot be expected to give in return, society establishes the generous atmosphere that encourages all its members to become productive. The very fact that they have nothing to give makes the poor extremely valuable to the productive economy. The poor create an opportunity for society to exercise true charity—to give without the expectation of return. Once assisted, the poor should become the most important communicators of a society's goodwill, without which a society cannot expect to foster productivity and prosperity.

In this context, the Church's concept of a "preferential option for the poor" takes on economic as well as moral significance. The benevolent society intent on productivity is willing to assume obligations where no obligations seem to exist. Such a society acknowledges the economic "rights" of the poor described by the U.S. bishops in *Economic Justice for All*: "life, food, clothing, shelter, rest, medical care and basic education."

At the time the pastoral letter was first drafted in the mid-1980s, the bishops' notion of economic rights met with strong resistance, and the prospect that these rights would be established by law seemed remote. Today, a consensus appears to be emerging that the right to medical care, potentially the most expensive of the bishops' recommended rights, does indeed exist. Business leaders who already offer their employees health benefits are among the strongest advocates of health care reform. They recognize that a system of universal health coverage would introduce a positive measure of fairness and flexibility into the American economy.

By regulating successful enterprises through taxation and other policies, government fosters an atmosphere of fairness and kindness in which productive economic behavior can flourish. Thus, government has a right to expect that the cost of its goodwill maintenance program will be borne by society as a whole and especially by those who benefit most from it—i.e., the *most* successful. Without the security provided by such government programs as Social Security, unemployment insurance, and workmen's compensation insurance, for example, business would have a much more difficult time inspiring the productivity needed to expand the economy. So business must be willing to help pay the costs of those programs.

Regulating success has less chance of going astray if it is linked explicitly to the goal of fostering productivity. Those designing an economic security program face numerous challenges, however. First and foremost, the level of assistance must be high enough so that it can prompt gratitude and generosity among recipients. At the same time, assistance must not be administered in a way that reinforces a negative attitude of selfishness and dependency. Finally, the cost of providing economic security must not be so high that the required levels of taxation on the productive members of society discourage their initiative and effort. Government leaders must remind themselves constantly that the key to a prosperous society is economic generosity on the part of the poor and the affluent alike.

EXPANSION THROUGH INCLUSION

One way government can maintain the necessary balance and keep the cost of its social security systems at positive levels is by promoting economic expansion through increased participation. The emphasis on "overcoming marginalization and powerlessness" in the Catholic Church's social teaching provides an excellent insight into this growth process. Prosperity that is reflective of our triune God's bountifulness can only be developed within an economy open to all participants. Exclusionary practices—whether based on race, gender, sexual orientation, religion, age or even education levels—undermine the goal of full employment that is the key to maximizing prosperity.

In addition to being members of a Church whose faith is centered on the Trinity, Catholics also belong to a religious minority group which has experienced its share of economic discrimination. For these reasons, Catholics have a double obligation to resist all economic barriers that are predicated on the false belief that prosperity is in limited supply. Catholics should be placing their political support behind inclusive programs designed to foster widespread productivity through a climate of compassion and good will. The benevolent society in which such a climate flourishes bases its policies on the conviction that men and women can interact with each other and their environment in creative ways that generate sufficient prosperity for all to have a share.

Although the recommendation that those laden with talents and resources should enter into productive relationships with "less qualified" economic partners may seem to be the ultimate in religious idealism, the Catholic insistence on inclusiveness has a strong underpinning in economics. For nearly two centuries, David Ricardo's insights on international trade have been considered by other economists to be the *Law* of Comparative Advantage. In sharp contrast to the doomsday forecasters of his day who predicted that only the most skilled and efficient would be able to survive in the "new" era of cut-throat global competition then, Ricardo showed how economic relations between highly efficient nations and less efficient ones can be mutually beneficial. Even though Great Britain in his day was the "lowest cost producer" in most manufacturing and agriculture categories, Ricardo successfully argued that importing goods from other countries made sense because this economic strategy allowed the British to concentrate their resources in those areas where they held the *largest comparative* advantage. As a result, Great Britain's reliance on less efficient trading partners benefited both sides of the import-export relationship.

The economic wisdom Ricardo articulated at the start of the 19th century remains valid today and can be applied to individuals as well as nations. Unlike the decathlon athlete who can deliver a superior performance in 10 events, most of us would do well to concentrate on those areas in which are unique talents offer us some form of comparative, productive advantage. We need not be the "best" to succeed. It is only necessary that our talents complement those of our partners.

Thus, a government which promotes economic inclusiveness by such measures as open trade policies and anti-discrimination laws should be supported for both economic and religious reasons. That the emergence of the global economy is causing painful disruptions for some workers in the U.S. and other developed nations cannot be denied. The changing patterns, however, also present a new opportunity for every worker to reflect on the nature of his or her comparative, productive advantage. The willingness of workers in other countries to provide us with a wide variety of goods and services should not be seen as an invitation to unemployment here at home but as a challenge to take our own economic performance to a higher level.

As both Pope John Paul II and the U.S. bishops stress in their economic writings, interdependence is the key to understanding the world economy. Excluding even one potentially productive worker from the world economy lowers the potential level of prosperity available for all.

REGULATION VS. FREEDOM

Discussions about the proper role of the state in economic affairs often are structured as a debate between those who advocate market freedom and those who support government regulation. This approach presents a false dichotomy between regulation and freedom. In reality, the primary justification for government involvement in economic affairs is to *protect* the freedom of economic participants—not to restrict it. The rule of law enforced by government is the way society protects itself from humanity's inexorable tendency toward bondage and thereby preserves the liberty of all citizens. As we saw in the earlier chapter on fear, sin is a force of slavery. The reluctance of humans to accept their status as creatures leads directly to patterns of deceit and control that enslave each of us personally and attempt to enslave all of us collectively as well. Once we accept others as equals, however, the myth of our own omnipotence is shattered. Thus, the only way to keep that myth alive is to keep others in a subservient position.

Government regulations which outlaw treachery and violence do not diminish economic freedom; they enhance it. Antitrust laws which protect companies against the monopolistic practices of their competitors, labor regulations which protect workers against employer control, and product safety and truth-in-advertising laws which protect consumers against the deceits of vendors should be evaluated from the viewpoint of insuring the freedom of all. The role of government in a free society is not to force groups into economic relationships that would not be chosen voluntarily. The role of government is to create a climate of freedom and trust that allows all people to enter into the mutually profitable relationships which are the spawning grounds for true prosperity.

The intent of this analysis of government's role in fostering productivity is to show that a society which fails to enforce a comprehensive and rigid standard of economic justice can never secure the goodwill of its citizens that is so essential to lasting prosperity.

SANCTIFYING PRODUCTIVITY: A SPIRITUALITY FOR ECONOMIC LIFE

Although there are important steps both employers and government can take to inspire and secure productivity, the generation of value in excess of cost is an action which can only be performed by the individual human person. Therefore, the management and politics of productivity must be reinforced by a spirituality of productivity if this type of behavior is to become the norm. Nothing short of a total rethinking of our economic actions will allow us to practice voluntary productivity consciously and consistently. The economy, now regarded as a place where we gain, must become a place where we give.

Motivational writers talk about a "positive mental attitude" as the secret of economic success. The Catholic Church also recognizes the connection between attitude and action, and it provides its faithful with a way of imagining a better life so that they can work to complete the development of the reign of God. The Church's system of signs, saints and sacraments is not idolatrous. Rather, the Church uses these elements to provide concrete images which illumine the fullness of God's love for us and provide specific examples of successful human responses to that love.

Building upon the importance of images in the Catholic tradition, I will attempt, in this final chapter, to fashion a distinctively Catholic "mental attitude" toward the economy. Central to this attitude is an understanding of productivity as an economic expression of holiness. This link between productivity and sanctity will become more evident, I hope, after we reflect upon six key elements in Catholic spirituality (the Eucharist; Marian devotion; the example of St. Joseph; and the theological virtues of faith, hope and love) from an economic perspective. The intended result of this process is an outline for an integrated spirituality of economic life that Catholics can use to energize their relationships—with the Creator as well as with the rest of creation.

THE EUCHARIST AND A SPIRIT OF FULLNESS

When freely rendered, productivity is similar in many ways to Pope John Paul II's concept of solidarity, which has been presented as the economic ideal in contemporary Catholic social teaching. "In the light of faith, solidarity seeks to go beyond itself, to take on the specifically Christian dimensions of total gratuity, forgiveness and reconciliation," the pope writes in *Sollicitudo Rei Socialis (On Social Concerns)*. "One's neighbor is then not only a human being with his or her own rights and a fundamental equality with everyone else, but becomes the living image of God the Father, redeemed by the blood of Jesus Christ and placed under the permanent action of the Holy Spirit."

A spirit of "total gratuity" is the key element in both productivity and solidarity. This seeking "to go beyond" ourselves opens us to a "specifically Christian" dimension of reality, where all of creation can be seen in its relation to the Trinity. As Catholics, we are fortunate that the central ritual of our faith is directly related to this requisite sense of gratuity. Participation in the Eucharist is, in a sense, Catholics' most important economic activity.

The first step in achieving prosperity is not planning or working or sweating or worrying. The first step is experiencing the prosperity we already have. The most basic "chore" that the Church mandates is to assemble regularly as a community, to place ourselves in God's presence, and to remind ourselves of the divine economy that was established through the life, death and resurrection of Jesus Christ. The Catholic community is by definition a eucharistic people. We Catholics do not "go to church." We "gather to celebrate." We adopt the posture of Jesus at the Last Supper— a posture described in the eucharistic prayer of the Mass as one of "thanks and praise."

Once we have activated and reinforced the sense of fullness through our expression of thanks and praise, we are almost *forced* to share. Our sharing is not based on any moralistic compulsion; it is an automatic, almost physical, reaction. Once we are full, we overflow to others.

The Mass celebrates and encourages human sharing by focusing on the ultimate act of divine sharing. We express our faith that Christ not only accepted a "share in our humanity" but also offered the promise of a "share in his divinity." The Eucharist reminds us that the second person of the Trinity has accepted our "otherness"—our apartness from God, our radical imperfection— and in return has offered to share with us his "sameness" with God. In the Mass, our reaction and response to this divine-with-human offer is to enter into deeper "communion" with those around us. We share a meal, we share a sign of peace and fellowship, and we share our common bond with all people—past, present and future—whose lives are marked with the sign of faith.

Many business-motivational programs place a strong emphasis on what is called the "as if" principle. Super salesman Frank Bettinger summarized this approach with a line chanted by generations of Dale Carnegie students: "Act enthusiastic and you'll be enthusiastic."

Catholics have been practicing the "as if" principle for 2,000 years. Celebrating Mass is "acting" thankful, and through this celebration we are to become thankful. "Calling to mind" the reconciling and redemptive work of Jesus Christ, we have only one logical response: "Thanks be to God."

The Mass expresses the realization that the people of God have all we need. Because we have experienced a state of fullness in our lives through our celebration of the Eucharist, Catholics should be leading the way to prosperity. "The rich get richer" is the most basic of all economic truisms. Only those with something to invest can participate fully in economic expansion. "It takes money to make money," we say. The Mass is a celebration of richness. It is a reminder that the most important item we have to share with our human associates is fellowship with Jesus Christ and, through him, fellowship with the Father and the Spirit. No matter what our economic or physical circumstances are, we have something to share. Therefore, we are rich. Approaching our economic situation eucharistically allows us to spot surpluses which can be invested—gifts which can be used to enrich others and, in the process, to enrich ourselves.

The eucharistic attitude activates an electric current essential for economic progress. Like sexuality, economic activity is a reflection of life's pervading polarity. The physical interaction of all particles in the universe can be traced to the balancing of positive and negative charges which create forces such as electromagnetism and gravity. In identical fashion, unifying personal relationships require a double stimulus. All partnerships are sustained through a combination of giving and getting.

Thankfulness energizes the positive pole of the economic development circuit, the sense that we have something useful to contribute. Participation in the Eucharist becomes the foundation of true Christian self-confidence. The posture of thanks and praise provides the strong experience of fullness that must precede all acts of giving. Before we can enrich others, we must acknowledge the blessings we have received.

MARY AND A SPIRIT OF EMPTINESS

Deprived of a counterbalancing force, however, a sense of giftedness or even thankfulness can deteriorate into smugness, which triggers economic isolation—not unifying interaction. An electric current cannot flow through a circuit with only one pole, no matter how strong the positive charge.

The negative charge necessary to complete the circuit and stimulate economic activity is a sense of neediness and dependency equal to the positive charge of eucharistic fullness. "People who need people" are not only the "luckiest people in the world;" they are also the ones most motivated to improve their lot by entering the marketplace.

Just as the Mass provides a powerful experience of thanks and praise, the Catholic spiritual tradition is filled with imagery reinforcing humanity's sense of nothingness, its creaturehood. At the center of this tradition is the figure so important to Catholic spirituality, Mary, the mother of Jesus. Her "Magnificat" recorded in St. Luke's Gospel outlines the inverted logic of God's salvific plan. Mary in her "lowliness" provides an opportunity for God to manifest His "greatness." The "proud" are "confused." The "mighty" are "deposed." The "rich" are "sent empty away," but the "lowly" are "raised . . . to high places" and the "hungry" are "given every good thing."

Mary, the true daughter of Israel, accepts her status as servant. Yet God does not treat her as a slave. "All ages to come will call me blessed," she tells us. "God who is mighty has done great things for me."

Mary's poverty creates the possibility of richness since it opens her to God's grace. Her emptiness creates a vacuum attracting "all good things." The negative charge emitted by her lowliness attracts the positive response of God, whose "mercy is from age to age on those who fear him."

Through her canticle, Mary expresses the reality that the worst thing which can be said of us also is the best. We are creatures, totally other than God. If God is all-perfect, we are all-imperfect. Yet, because each of us is a free individual—separate and distinct from God—we extend God's presence. Like Mary, we by our very existence (independent of any behavior) are an augmentor of God's glory. We magnify "the greatness of the Lord." We who are nothing actually make God's great glory even greater.

The example of Mary and other true saints who "find joy" in their creature status has economic ramifications for both the poor and the wealthy. Poverty represents an essential side of the economic equation. Without a substantial volume of unmet needs, the market cannot exist. Receivers are as important as givers in the economic exchange. Thus, the experience of poverty can prompt a productive relationship when it is coupled with a spirit of openness to the mercy and love of other people. The emptiness of the poor provides a clear channel through which goodness can flow.

On the other hand, the rich will be rebuffed by the market—they will be sent away empty—unless they develop an awareness of their own needs to balance their manifest gifts. The economic participant who refuses to buy eventually runs out of partners to whom he or she can sell. Only the continuous matching of gifts to needs and needs to gifts can sustain a long-term economic relationship.

Both poles of the circuit must be kept clean from corrosion if the current of economic progress is to be sustained. Both the experience of fullness and the experience of emptiness motivate our economic interactions. Through the Eucharist, the celebration of our thankfulness, and through devotion to Mary, the celebration of our lowliness, the Catholic Church provides images which nourish both aspects of economic spirituality.

St. Joseph, Model of Economic Courage and Humility

If fear is evil's primary manifestation in the economy, then the logical solution to the problem is a strong dose of courage. In fact, Pope John Paul II presents courage as the economic virtue for our age: "This path (toward true economic development) is long and complex, and what is more it is constantly threatened because of the intrinsic frailty of human resolutions and achievements and because of the mutability of very unpredictable external circumstances," the pope writes in *Sollicitudo Rei Socialis*. "Nevertheless, one must have the courage to set out on this path and, where some steps have been taken or a part of the journey made, the courage to go to the end."

With its strong tradition of martyrdom and active resistance to all forms of evil, the Catholic Church has never lacked strong images and examples of courage. Yet the figure whose courage has the most relevance to economic problems was neither chewed by lions nor burned at the stake. St. Joseph was the economic provider for Jesus and Mary.

I have often wondered how the Church's attitude toward economic activity would change if Joseph, the carpenter, were pictured as a small business owner rather than a downtrodden handyman. Would Christ's identification with Isaiah's prophecy— "he has sent me to bring glad tidings to the poor"—be weaker if the carpenter's son had bourgeois roots?

Any link between Joseph's sanctity and his business success or failure is pure speculation. The clues about his life, however, suggest he had a lot going for him. "Fear not" was the angel's repeated advice to Joseph, and there is ample biblical evidence that he took this message to heart. He accepted Mary as his wife despite her pregnancy. He packed up the family and moved to Egypt on short notice, and then, when the coast was clear, he quietly moved back to Nazareth.

Is there any reason to suspect that Joseph would not have been courageous in his business affairs? Would he give a misleading cost estimate out of fear of losing a contract? Would he be afraid to suggest unconventional solutions to customers' problems? Would he be nervous about embracing new techniques or technologies? Would he hesitate to "sell" an idea that was in the customer's interests? Would he lack the guts to charge a fair price?

Joseph is doubly important as an economic model since he combined courage with humility, another misunderstood virtue. St. Matthew's Gospel describes Joseph as "an upright man" who lived according to God's agenda, not his own. When only his humility is emphasized, Joseph becomes an economic "sap" surrounded by an image of unrestrained passivity and softness—in other words, the typical image of the "Christian" business person as a wimp. This Joseph can be seen shuffling from job to job, barely lifting his head to mumble, "Got any work today?"

Joseph, however, was both fearless and humble, a unique combination that would have helped him avoid economic trouble. This combination would have sharpened his sense of stewardship and inspired greater attention to craftsmanship; prompted him to delegate work to a talented apprentice and to decline assignments he could not handle; encouraged him to listen to customer concerns rather than offer the same stock answers.

Joseph offers an important lesson to leaders faced with the responsibility of developing persuasiveness without practicing ruthlessness. His display of courage with humility shows that a leader's strength should be a force offering reassurance and security rather than intimidation.

FAITH

As George Gilder explains so clearly in his book, *Wealth and Poverty*, the true focus of economic activity is the future, not the present. Since no form of technological advancement will eliminate uncertainty about the future, Gilder concludes that operating an economy without faith is an impossibility.

Maintaining a posture of generosity in an economy that preaches self-interest certainly requires a strong act of faith. I, for example, strongly believe that productivity—the willingness to generate value in excess of cost—is the creative energy which allows an economy to grow. But my conviction in this matter is influenced greatly by my faith in a loving God who shares the gift of creativity.

As Gilder suggests, however, there is nothing unusual or impractical about functioning with faith in an economy where certainty is unattainable. This, in fact, is the way business operates. Numerous, unverifiable suppositions about people are implicit in the policies which guide corporate relations with customers, employees, stockholders and the public. As a result, similar businesses can exhibit very dissimilar modes of behavior. Even within the same company, different departments can operate with contradictory beliefs. In the tug of war between the sales department and the credit department, for instance, either side can offer evidence supporting the correctness of its view regarding the trustworthiness of customers. Since the issue involved is acceptable risk, however, the debate can only be settled on faith. To trust or not to trust is a continuing business dilemma.

When I was business manager for *The Monitor*, for example, that diocesan newspaper offered parishes free display racks if they would increase the size of their order. Our plan was to give parishes a choice between a floor model rack offered by one company and a table model available from another manufacturer. Both suppliers had done business with me previously when I was working for another newspaper, but neither had sold racks to *The Monitor*.

The order for the floor model went through without a hitch. First came the racks and then the bill. The other order made it past the salesperson, but it was rejected by the factory. No credit has been established, we were told. Payment must accompany the order. Because of this delay, the table model racks arrived too late to be displayed at an important meeting with pastors.

The open-credit company saw losing the order as a greater

risk than not being paid. In dealing with *The Monitor,* that company made the right decision. It received full payment as well as a second order. In dealing with an unscrupulous customer, such a liberal policy may not be as sound. This particular company consistently expects the best of its customers, however, and it is usually rewarded for doing so.

The other vendor saw not getting paid as the greater risk. That company provided the racks once payment was made but offered no trust basis for a long-term relationship. Its policy—however sound from a collection standpoint—did not encourage continued sales. These two companies, like so many others, made decisions based as much on their beliefs about human nature as they did on business realities.

For Christians, faith involves much more than the mere willingness to live with uncertainty. Faith is the ultimate abandonment of control. Faith is the acceptance of our own freedom as well as the freedom of others. Even more, faith is the acceptance of the total otherness of the God revealed to us in Jesus Christ.

In searching for religious images of faith, abandoning the Catholic viewpoint is very tempting. Faith seems such a distinctively Protestant virtue—particularly as it applies to the economy. When Martin Luther decided to take St. Paul's letter to the Romans seriously, the world's political and economic systems changed forever. Democracy and capitalism are a direct result of Luther's focus on "freedom from the law."

The Catholic Church, however, did not revoke St. Paul's canonization when Martin Luther adopted him as a theological hero. Pauline insights into the divine economy are available to all Christians—Catholic as well as Protestant. In fact, American

Catholics should be particularly grateful for the encouragement of their fellow Christians that has helped the Church reactivate insights about the importance of scripture and, thereby, develop a new understanding of both faith and freedom. Catholics participating in the renewal movements that have extended Vatican II's revitalization of the Church have found one of the most important benefits to be awareness that the word of God becomes a power in our lives only when it is taken seriously.

Yet, as the two-part liturgical structure of the Mass shows, the Catholic faith is based on both *word* and *sacrament*. The Catholic tradition has emphasized the totality of Paul's theology of faith and freedom, in which faith tried and faith tested are as important as faith expressed. Paul's understanding of faith not only hinges on freedom from the law but freedom from sin as well. The continued emphasis on faith in action keeps a Catholic vision of the economy from deteriorating into a "believe and grow rich" philosophy. The Catholic insistence that faith must be embodied in the lives of Christians and that faith must be reinforced by visible signs intelligible to the community, as well as to the individual, protects the Church from the drift toward fundamentalism and secularism—two distorted outgrowths of scriptural literalism.

For Catholics intent upon productive involvement in the economy, the full meaning of freedom becomes apparent only in light of their faith. Complete economic freedom involves much more than the absence of government regulations. In the Catholic tradition, only an economy liberated from the economic sins of fear, greed, jealousy and repression—and respectful of each person's distinctive value—can claim to be free.

LOVE

As we near the end of our reflections on the economy, I return to an earlier theme—the link between a Catholic concept of economic success and the fulfillment of our economic responsibilities. Before a goal can be achieved, the goal must be established.

Advocates of self-interest as the only realistic economic motivation would have us believe there is a neutral, "just business," way of relating to others that can lead to success. In this view, if we all look out for ourselves each of us can achieve wealth without helping or hurting other people. This is the same false perspective on personal relationships which glorifies casual sex. That consenting adults can exchange pleasure without having a strong positive or negative impact on their sexual partners is one of the most unrealistic and damaging myths accepted by our society.

In the course of my business career, I have come to realize that there is nothing casual about the sustained creation of new wealth. It requires strong and intense personal relationships. As a result, there appear to be only three approaches to success which offer any significant promise. These are deceit, power or love. We can try to trick the market, we can try to overcome the market, or we can offer the market our generous service. The one thing we cannot do is abandon the market. Only in relationship with other people is economic success obtainable. The most important question to be answered is which of the three ways of relating to the market offers the best prospect for success.

In an economy with increasingly sophisticated consumers and investors and with an increasingly aggressive press, even the most deceitful have achieved only limited success through fraud. Ivan Boesky, Michael Milken, and my West Virginia "hero," Ted Price, may have had the upper hand for a period, but eventually they were punished for their crimes. Despite the grifter's contention that the world is filled with "suckers," the number of people who have been able to retain great wealth through deceit are blessedly few. The human incapacity to invent the perfect scam will not deter some people from pursuing fraudulent ventures but, for the risks involved and the effort required to package a worthwhile "con," the payback is not that great.

This leaves power and love in contention for "best" economic strategy. There is no shortage of people who attempt to achieve economic superiority through force, but I suspect that most of those who choose power as their route to success fail to comprehend the full ugliness of their decision. To intimidate another human through the threat of violence—physical, emotional or economic—is an act of hatred that attempts to blot out the personhood of the victim. To those who define their relationship with others in terms of power, the words of Christ apply: "You have heard the commandment imposed on your forefathers, 'You shall not commit murder; every murderer shall be liable to judgment.' What I say to you is: Everyone who grows angry with his brother shall be liable to judgment; any man who uses abusive language toward his brother shall be answerable to the Sanhedrin, and if he holds him in contempt he risks the fires of Gehenna."

Thus, the selection between power and love as our path to success should not be made without serious consideration.

Rambo: First Blood, Part II, Sylvester Stallone's archetypal action movie of the 1980s, offers an alternate ending to the Christ story that brings the power-love debate into sharp relief. The movie's torture scenes are evocative of the crucifixion agony. Rambo is shown with outstretched arms first hanging over a swamp and later being jolted with an electrical current. Rambo's supplication, however, is not the loving "Father forgive them; they do not know what they are doing." Rambo generates the power to overcome his torturers by harnessing the hatred within himself. His rage is directed not so much at his Vietnamese captors or their Russian advisors. The primary object of his hatred is the father-figure Marshall Murdock, a civilian bureaucrat who devised—then aborted—Rambo's prisoner-of-war rescue mission. The force which sustains Rambo's escape is expressed in the snarling statement, "Murdock, I'm coming to get you!" Once the rage is released, there is no stopping Rambo until he has Murdock by the throat.

This is the way the crucifixion scene could have ended had Christ's love for mankind not been all-powerful. Had Christ not been able to withstand the worst that mankind could throw at him, his rage would not have been limited to his Jewish traitors, his Roman executioners, or even all humanity. His hatred, like Rambo's, would extend to the Father who sent him on a doomed mission.

This, then, is the risk that Father and Son accepted when they first created humanity and then set about reconciling their sinful creatures to themselves. The Father risked losing the love of the Son, and the Son risked losing his love for the Father—all in an effort to demonstrate God's love for creation. God, who is love, risked becoming hate.

Neither the Father nor the Son nor humanity lost that day on

Calvary. Humanity's crucifixion of God was a win-win-win situation. Christ's love was all enduring and all-powerful. He experienced the full depths of abandonment and unrequited love and rose above the pain. He showed the strength of love in the face of even the most hateful force, and in doing so he revealed love's capacity to sustain the drive toward true success. On Calvary, Jesus fulfilled his mission. "It is finished," he said. The everlasting image of love that the Church holds up for our inspection is the tortured body of Christ on the cross. The resurrection, ascension and coming of the Spirit are the explosive results of the love released on Calvary.

The invitation to love our spouse, our parents, our children, and our economic partners is an invitation to join Christ on the cross. That is where we will achieve transcendence. That is where the door to full happiness will be opened to us. Only on Calvary can we recognize that through Christ's death we have the grace to say, "I love you," regardless of the beloved's response. Only on Calvary can we start to experience the full power and freedom that love entails.

Our homes, our offices, our factories, our mines, our shopping malls are constructed on Calvary. Through the economy, we are called to acknowledge the value of another person and to denounce the delusion that we are the center of the universe. The appeal of economic prosperity—like the appeal of sexual pleasure—is a magnetic force drawing us toward unity. Before that unity can be realized, however, we must abandon our selfishness, take up our cross, and follow Jesus.

The reliance on power leads inevitably to hatred and destruction. As such, power is a negative force. It is constrictive and constraining. It cannot provide a foundation for either our own or our nation's economic progress. On the other hand, the love that we learn through contemplation of our crucified savior is a pure positive. Since love is the strongest force, only it can sustain economic expansion. In the economy, our willingness to give out of proportion to what we receive frees us from dependence and opens us to the expansive benefits available from other people.

HOPE

The traditional order of the theological virtues, based on St. Paul's first letter to the Corinthians is faith, hope and love—"and the greatest of these is love." In terms of economic motivation, however, hope is paramount. As we saw in an earlier chapter, the root definition of prosperity is "hopes fulfilled." Hope is the foundation of the Christian reward system. Hope flows from our understanding of love. In fact, it is the reason we love. Therefore, I conclude these reflections with the virtue of hope.

Through the image of the cross we come to see that love can endure under all circumstances—even when love is rebuffed by other people. Yet our hope is that love will not be rejected. Our hope is that others will respond to our love and love us in return.

The Catholic Church, true to the apostolic tradition, preaches Christ crucified. But the story of God's love for us does not end on the cross. The crucifixion was Christ's supreme act of love for us and trust in the Father. The cross is the ultimate expression of the Son's willingness to forsake his equality with the Father. In accepting death, Jesus made himself vulnerable before both man and God.

The balance of the Gospel story after the crucifixion narrative is the account of the Father's response to the Son's love.

Unlike humanity, the Father does not kick the Son when he is down. He raised him up and bestowed on him a name which is above every name. "If Christ was not raised from the dead," St. Paul tells us. "Our faith is a delusion." The resurrection, therefore, provides the overwhelming image of hope which is our trust in the goodness and love of God.

Hope also is trust in the basic goodness of other people—the conviction that people who experience love will love in return. Thus, spreading a message of economic hope requires the constant acknowledgment and affirmation of goodness around us. Christians best tell the good news of Christ's resurrection by presenting examples that show goodness now has the competitive edge. When the stone was rolled back in front of Christ's tomb the balance in the universe was tilted forever. Signs that goodness is snowballing must be spotted and proclaimed.

Unmitigated criticism of economic life mistakes goodness for evil, which is a problem every bit as serious as mistaking evil for good. When two people interact in love and create a baby, the Church rejoices with the couple and helps them celebrate the birth sacramentally. When two people interact in love and create new wealth, however, that act is often viewed with suspicion—if not outright condemnation. An ambivalent moral evaluation of economic life cannot stimulate the hope needed for the "authentic human development" advocated in Catholic social encyclicals.

Christ's resurrection confronts the pervasive sin of every age—that of minimizing God's love for us. For the hopeless, the balance in the universe is tipped toward evil. They perceive any good that occurs to be the result of chance and circumstances. The cynical Christian's identification is with the "loser" Christ who died on the cross.

The challenge of the resurrection is to maximize the evidence that love is supreme. Filled with hope, Christians must spread the good news of Christ's triumph without reservation. The Christian in the economy is prepared to take up a cross daily by accepting the inevitability of failure. Yet, prompted by hope, Christians continue to struggle for success because they see resurrection and new life at the end of the process.

Economically active Christians recognize prosperity as a form of grace—a gift. Nevertheless, because the fullness of life has been promised by Jesus, they expect to be rewarded—not for their sweat, their labor, or their ideas but for their love. They extend love to the economy, respecting the freedom of others but hopeful that love will be returned. Inspired by the resurrection, the Christian communicates a message of both love and hope to every economic partner: "I give you my love, but I respect your freedom and hold you to no obligation. I acknowledge your right not to reciprocate, but I will never do anything to invite your hatred or abuse. Instead, I will constantly encourage you to form a relationship of love. Furthermore, I am convinced that if I am steadfast in my love, the odds are very high that you will love me in return. That is all I can offer. It is my best deal."

For the Christian in the economy, hope is the willingness to settle for love as the only reward.

This book has been about hope. It has attempted to illumine a path of progress which proceeds from love to prosperity and back again. It has been written from the belief that the economy, particularly the American economy with which I am most familiar, is alive. I see the economy as organic, as people planting love and reaping prosperity. I see all economic growth built on productivity, which is nothing more than the loving sacrifice of generous people. These are the signs of the resurrection which stimulate my hope. These are the indicators that Christ's new commandment of love applies as well in the economy as it does in every other part of life.

Afterword
A Theology of Hustle

During my career, I have had the opportunity to attend numerous sales conventions sponsored by major publishing industry trade associations. At many of these meetings, at least one session was devoted to the topic of motivation and, as often as not, the speaker was an overtly religious person. Although I found some of these presentations inspiring, as a Catholic I was struck by the fact that Evangelical Protestantism had pre-empted the task of motivating American business. Where, I would ask myself, is the Catholic vision of economic activity that can energize the Church's followers as they struggle with day-to-day business realities?

THEOLOGY OF HUSTLE

In the fall of 1986, shortly after the U.S. Catholic bishops published the final draft of *Economic Justice for All: Catholic Social Teaching and the U.S. Economy*, I had the opportunity to raise this question in public. With the bishops' document as a back drop, I started writing a weekly column for *The Monitor*, a newspaper serving Catholic families in the dioceses of Trenton and Metuchen, New Jersey. By reflecting and commenting upon economic events, I became increasingly convinced that a Catholic perspective offered an important alternative to the pray-and-grow-rich philosophy found in many "success" books. A truly Catholic "theology of hustle" (my term for the link between spirituality and economic drive) regards the rhythms of success and failure in economic life as an echo of that central theme in Christ's message: "Whoever would save his life will lose it, but whoever loses his life for my sake will find it." In this light, the economy—instead of being an area in which greed is good and selfishness is justified—becomes an important stimulus toward self-transcendence and salvation.

Like my column, this book has drawn on those experiences which sharpened my awareness that "making money" has something to do with "making love." The reflections are not presented as a message from the mountaintop. I am not a Lee Iacocca or a Donald Trump. I have never been anything more than a middle-level manager at a mid-sized company. Yet my career has exposed me to a wide variety of situations that continue to stimulate economic reflections. How many other theorists, for instance, have had the opportunity to field test their ideas about economic motivation while supervising a $14 million circulation department staffed largely by boys and girls?

THE GOOD NEWSPAPER

The most important contributor to my economic views was a 16-year career in the daily newspaper business. Unlike many enterprises, daily newspapers have always recognized a correlation—not a conflict—between public service and profitability. I was fortunate to have matured as a business person in an atmosphere where moral standards and ethical behavior were expected as a matter of course. The values of courtesy and service I first learned as a 12-year-old paper boy were refined and reinforced as my newspaper career developed. My daily newspaper colleagues and I were not saints. Of my own accord, I practiced my share of deceitful, hurtful behavior. Yet I never was ordered to do something that posed even the slightest ethical dilemma.

As a youngster, my images of business people were formed by three men: my father, John Haas, a chemical engineer and manager of a synthetic rubber factory; my maternal grandfather, Charles Varga, a retired banker and business consultant; and John Plummer, the founder of an optics company, who was a close associate of my grandfather and a regular attendee at Varga family gatherings. (Whenever I read the word "entrepreneur," I see Plummer's face.) These were undeniably good men who shared a passion for their work. Naively perhaps, I expected my adult business associates to be thoroughly decent people. That my mentors in the daily newspaper industry lived up to my youthful expectations is one of the most important blessing I have experienced in my career.

The industry I entered in 1970, however, was not an island of economic safety untouched by the issues of profitability, competition and survival. Quite the opposite was true. Newspapers were just starting to ponder their role as commercial enterprises as well as community institutions. When the Gannett Company "went public" on September 24, 1967 and started its unbroken string of quarterly earnings increases, the newspaper industry entered a new era.

The emerging importance of management and marketing within the industry was—and still is—viewed as a threat by many writers and editors. At the best newspapers, however, elitism and isolationism have been replaced by a new spirit of cooperation. The interaction between the news side and the business side has produced substantial benefits for readers, advertisers and employees. These organizations are involved in a serious search for the true meaning of a "good" newspaper.

In the newspaper business, the cost of producing an engaging publication is only slightly higher than the cost of producing a boring one, since both consume tremendous quantities of paper, ink and press time. Yet the financial rewards of publishing a newspaper which commands strong reader loyalty can be enormous, while the pay-back from a weak newspaper is as limited as its following. If some of the observations in this book seem hopelessly idealistic, my defense is that I have seen the economic value of a well-turned phrase. I worked for engaging newspapers.

During my first six years in the newspaper industry, my role was business observer. I started as a political reporter for the *Charleston* (West Virginia) *Daily Mail* and later became that paper's business editor. In this period I also served as a West Virginia "stringer" for national and international news organizations and contributed pieces to *TIME, The Wall Street Journal,* several of McGraw-Hill's business publications, and the Reuters News Service. As a young reporter in that position, avoiding cynicism was difficult. During my stint as a stringer, the very worst aspects of the West Virginia experience—mining disasters, political corruption, labor intrigue, outrageous con artist schemes, and fundamentalist craziness—captured the world's attention and thereby created frequent opportunities for extra income.

After picking up a night-school MBA degree in 1976, I switched from business observer to business practitioner, entering the field of publication marketing during the early years of the newspaper industry's readership movement. I established Charleston Newspapers' first marketing department and then spent several years managing the marketing and circulation functions at *The Asbury Park* (New Jersey) *Press*. My marketing experience, no doubt, is the main reason I view economic activity in terms of the buy-sell paradigm. I also have retained the insights of the industry's Newspaper Readership Project, whose two-fold prescription for success was reader service and inter-departmental cooperation.

During the 1970s, the West Virginia coal industry was my beat. I was in a special position to study that decade's major economic issue, energy, and to observe the distinction between material wealth and enduring prosperity. The mid-70s coal boom, triggered by surging energy prices, provided plenty of journalistic excitement, but a coal-based economy has failed to bring lasting prosperity to West Virginia.

During the 1980s, New Jersey, my new home, was the economic antithesis of West Virginia. Instead of mining hollows like Paint Creek and Cabin Creek, symbols of Appalachian poverty, New Jersey featured the Princeton corridor, the epitome of East Coast affluence. While that state was sitting at the top of the national economic rankings, I tried to analyze differences between New Jersey residents and those in West Virginia. Before I could come up with a satisfactory answer, however, New Jersey's growth industries stopped growing and the state's economy collapsed. Suddenly, New Jersey found itself with a first-place position in the categories of unemployment, bankruptcies and mortgage foreclosures. By the start of the nineties, I knew that the secret of lasting prosperity had eluded the Garden State as well as the Mountain State.

Catholic Influences

I did not set out to be either a journalist or a businessman. My original career goal was to be a Jesuit priest. The four years I spent in the Society of Jesus also have had a strong influence on the way I view business activities. A philosophical perspective may not be the best approach to advertising sales or circulation development but, once started, the quest for ultimate meaning is hard to abandon.

My Jesuit instructors at the philosophate in Shrub Oak, New York, placed particular emphasis on the potential contribution of the American experience to the life of the Catholic Church. The most influential faculty members, such as Robert Johaan and Vincent Potter, did not look to Europe for intellectual guidance. They were part of a distinctively American philosophical tradition developed at Harvard, Yale, Johns Hopkins and Columbia universities. John Dewey and Charles Pearce were cited in lectures as frequently as Thomas Acquinas and Aristotle. My interest in the theoretical underpinnings of the American economic system has remained strong since my seminary days.

My second attempt at a religious career also has molded my economic opinions. Since 1986, I have made my livelihood in the Catholic press—first as marketing coordinator/business manager for *The Monitor*, later as independent consultant to several Catholic publications including *AMERICA*, the Jesuit weekly, and now as business manager for *Commonweal*, a national magazine published by Catholic lay people in New York City. Within the Catholic press, my work has focused on business concerns such as budgets, sales and cash flow rather than on theological issues. Yet employment with a religious organization highlights the essentially religious issues that all work entails. Involvement with the nonprofit sector of the economy also has increased my appreciation for worker generosity, a concept which I have tried to develop through this book.

Catholic publications also provided my first experience with business poverty. Many of them have difficulty paying their people and their suppliers. In trying to strengthen these publications and make them stronger communications channels for the Catholic Church, my colleagues and I have been forced to confront the most fundamental issue facing all Christians in the work place. How does one define and achieve some form of economic success that is in harmony with one's following of Christ?

FAILURE AND SUCCESS

My pondering the meaning of success began at a young age. I have been thinking about the complex variables which affect economic advancement ever since I detected my parents' concern about the pace of my father's career. In late 1985, however, my reflections on success acquired a new intensity when I encountered a double failure. Within a two-month period, my wife asked me for a divorce and my employer asked me to resign. Friends and family commented on the difficulties created by the simultaneous dissolution of a marriage and a career. Their sympathy was greatly appreciated because the emotional turmoil triggered by two such major changes was enormous. Eventually, however, I came to see the convergence of these two events as fortuitous. The search for relief from the double pain led me to the conclusion that there is really only one issue in life. That issue is love.

Most of us are sucked out of our selfishness by an enduring marriage, which allows the magnificent magnetism of sex and intimacy to reach full power. Yet the same force drawing husband and wife toward unity pulsates through the economy as well. Work and family are different stages on which the same basic drama is enacted—the struggle to reconcile our intense experience of individuality and freedom with the equally strong appeal of binding commitments. To achieve success in this struggle we must overcome the limits of our very selves through the transcending power of love.

The economy—the market—is after all nothing more than other people. Our economic partners, no less than our marriage partner, provide us with the opportunity to surrender our selfishness and to enter into fruitful, loving relationships. If we engage in the process with our hearts as well as our hands, economic life forms a crucible in which we can grind away our selfishness and ready our entrance into the bounteous, boundless reign of God.

Acknowledgments

My gratitude at being able to share these observations on the economy extends in a general way to hundreds of people. Yet more specific recognition is in order. Since this is a business book, I would like to pay special tribute to my associates in three job classifications. I want to thank my "managers, mentors and supervisors" for their inspiring direction. This group includes: John McGee, Charles Connor, and the late Howard Salisbury at Charleston Newspapers; Charles Ritscher and Jules Plangere, Jr., at *The Asbury Park Press*; Joseph Glass at *The Monitor*; and Edward Skillin and Margaret O'Brien Steinfels at *Commonweal*. Thanks also to "would-be managers and salepeople" who allowed me to tutor them and expand my own understanding of the management and marketing processes: Tom Martin at Charleston Newspapers; Richard Orloff, Vito Cicero, John Van Pelt, Bill Muller and Nancy Carter at *The Asbury Park Press;* and Tim Moynahan and Debra Giguinto at *The Monitor*. My deepest thanks go to "secretaries and adminitrative assistants," who taught me so many lessons in loving service: the late Jane Barrows at Charleston Newspapers; Mary Alice Renson, Honora Kaye, Lori McGregor, Joan Bougie, Charlotte Ginsburg and Evelyn Johansen at *The Asbury Park Press*; Mary Moynahan, Claire Sanford and Josephine Astore at *The Monitor;* and Sandra Smith and Carmen Alava of *Commonweal.*

The influence of two other persons are more difficult to classify, since their association affected me in so many ways. Al Starr, advertising manager at Charleston Newspapers, introduced me to the wonderful world of selling, and Ron Kennedy, my assistant at

The Asbury Park Press, showed me there can never be a more important business trait than genuine helpfulness toward other people.

The book, however, is about love as much as it is about business. For this aspect of these reflections, I must thank those with whom I have lived on a more intimate level: Jennifer and Beth, who taught me how easy and joyful love can be; Dannan and Erik, who expanded my understanding of fatherhood; and, most especially, Marlene, who has redefined for me the meaning of being in love.

Two authors, whose writings have affected my thinking tremendously, deserve special mention. My hope is that these marketing-based reflections will reinforce Michael Novak's and George Gilder's pioneering work on the moral dimension of capitalism. Gilder's early writings also deepened my understanding that any comprehensive view of relationships must deal with both economics and sexuality.

I would also like to thank John Flanagan, a retired Prudential Insurance Company executive and Catholic deacon, who introduced me to that true business saint, Dale Carnegie. Without Flanagan's encouragement, these reflections would not have become a reality.

Finally, I would like to thank Gregory F. Augustine Pierce, editor and co-publisher of ACTA Publications, who assumed the risk of publishing *We All Have A Share* and guided its editing and production with great skill and encouragement.

Bibliography of Sources

Catholic Social Teaching

Byers, David, editor, *Justice in the Marketplace: Collected Statements of the Vatican and the U.S. Catholic Bishops on Economic Policy, 1891-1984*, U.S. Catholic Conference, Washington, 1985.

Gannon, Thomas M., editor, *The Catholic Challenge to the American Economy: Reflections on the U.S. Bishops' Pastoral Letter on Social Teaching and the U.S. Economy*, Macmillan Publishing Co., New York, 1987.

Novak, Michael, *The Catholic Ethic and the Spirit of Capitalism*, The Free Press, New York, 1993.

   Freedom With Justice: Catholic Social Thought and Liberal Institutions, Harper & Row, San Franciso, 1984.

Pope John Paul II, *Sollicitudo Rei Socialis* (On Social Concerns), *Origins*, Vol. 17, No. 38, March 3, 1988.

Pope John Paul II, *Centesimus Annus* (The 100th Year), *Origins*, Vol. 21, No. 1, May 16, 1991.

U.S. Catholic Conference, *Economic Justice for All: Catholic Social Teaching and the U.S. Economy* (final draft), *Origins*, Vol. 16, No. 24, November 27, 1986.

Economics, Business, Management — Books

Blanchard, Kenneth and Johnson, Spencer, *The One Minute Manager*, Berkeley Publishers, New York, 1987.

Buchholz, Todd G., *New Ideas from Dead Economists*, New American Library, New York, 1989.

Heilbroner, Robert L., *The Wordly Philosophers: The Lives, Times and Ideas of the Great Economic Thinkers* (Third Edition), Simon & Schuster, New York, 1967.

DePree, Max, *Leadership is an Art*, Doubleday, New York, 1989.

Drucker, Peter, *The Practice of Management*, Harper & Row, New York, 1954.

   Management: Tasks—Responsibilities—Practices, Harper & Row, New York, 1974.

Gilder, George, *Wealth and Poverty*, Basic Books, New York, 1981.

   The Spirit of Enterprise, Simon & Schuster, New York, 1984.

Kidder, Tracy, *Soul of a New Machine*, Brown, Little & Co., New York, 1981.

McLellan, David, *Karl Marx: His Life & Thought*, Harper & Row, New York, 1973.

Novak, Michael, *The Spirit of Democratic Capitalism*, Simon & Schuster, New York, 1982.

Peters, Thomas S. and Waterman Jr., Robert H., *In Search of Excellence: Lessons from America's Best Run Companies*, Harper & Row, New York, 1982.

Prichard, Peter, *Making of McPaper: The Inside Story of USA Today*, Andrews & McMeel, Kansas City, Mo., 1987.

Ziglar, Zig, *See You At The Top*, Pelican, New York, 1984.

   Zig Ziglar's Secret of Closing the Sale, Berkeley Publishers, New York, 1987.

Economics, Business, Management — Articles

Loomis, Carol, "The Inside Story of Warren Buffett," *Fortune*, April 11, 1988.

Personal Relationships

Carnegie, Dale, *How to Win Friends and Influence People* (revised edition), Dale Carnegie & Associates, Inc., Garden City, N.Y., 1981.

Carnegie, Dale, *How to Stop Worrying & Start Living* (revised edition), Dale Carnegie & Associates, Inc., Garden City, N.Y., 1984.

Gilder, George, *Naked Nomads: Unmarried Men in America*, Quadrangle/New York Times Book Co., New York, 1974.

Sexual Suicide, Quadrangle/New York Times Book Co., New York, 1973.

Padovani, Martin H., *Healing Wounded Emotions: Overcoming Life's Hurts*, Twenty-Third Publications, Mystic, Ct., 1987.

Peck, M. Scott, *The Road Less Traveled*, Simon & Schuster, New York, 1980.

Spirituality of Economic Life

Haughey, John C., *The Holy Use of Money: Personal Finances in Light of Christian Faith*, Doubleday, New York, 1986.

Converting 9 to 5: A Spirituality of Daily Work, Crossroad, New York, 1989.

Holland, Joe, *Creative Communion: Toward a Sprirituality of Work*, Paulist Press, Mahwah, N.J., 1989.

Droel, William L. and Pierce, Gregory F. Augustine, *Confident & Competent: A Challenge for the Lay Church*, ACTA Publications, Chicago, Il., 1987.

Sherman, Doug and Hendricks, Willam, *Your Work Matters to God*, NavPress, Colorado Springs, Co., 1987.

Theology, Sacraments, Religious Life

Greeley, Andrew, *The Catholic Myth: The Behavior and Beliefs of American Catholics*, Charles Scribner's Sons, New York, 1990.

LaCugna, Catherine Mowry, *God For Us: The Trinity & Christian Life*, Harper San Francisco, 1991.

The New American Bible (Saint Joseph Edition), Catholic Book Publishing Co., New York, 1970.

Martos, Joseph, *Doors to the Sacred: A Historical Introduction to Sacraments in the Catholic Church*, Doubleday, New York, 1982.

U.S. Catholic Conference, *Partners in the Mystery of Redemption: A Pastoral Response to Women's Concerns for Church and Society* (first draft), *Origins*, Vol. 17, No. 45, April 21, 1988.

General

Gallup Jr., George and Castelli, Jim, *The American Catholic People: Their Beliefs, Practices and Values*, Doubleday, New York, 1987.

Greeley, Andrew and McManus, William, *Catholic Contributions*, The Thomas More Press, Chicago, Il., 1987.

The New Jersey Council of Churches, *The Reshaping of New Jersey: The Growing Separation*, The New Jersey Council of Churches, East Orange, N.J., 1988.

Fear of the Open Heart

Fear of the Open Heart

Essays on Contemporary Canadian Writing

Constance Rooke

Coach House Press Toronto

Published with the generous assistance of the Canada Council,
the Ontario Arts Council, and the Ontario Ministry
of Culture and Communications.

Cover photo: Michael Ondaatje.
Typeset and printed at
Coach House Press, Toronto, Canada

Canadian Cataloguing in Publication Data

Rooke, Constance, 1942-
Fear of the open heart

ISBN 0-88910-382-8

1. Canadian fiction (English) – 20th century –
History and criticism.*   I. Title.

PS8199.R66 1989   C813'.54'09   C89-095167-5
PR9192.5.R66 1989

Contents

For Leon
skeptic and true believer
&
for Arthur and P.K.
with love

Fear of the Open Heart

Some time ago I came upon a phrase that magnetized me. It seemed to glow faintly, in exile – to reside where it did (in a passage from Mavis Gallant) whether by chance or perfidious intent, with its true range of implication modestly toned down to suit the context. We might as easily speak of inference, or interference, of the baggage I would bring to it – but in any case I felt that we were right for one another. *Fear of the open heart:* I began to think and even to dream about it. I started, that is to say, romancing the text.

What I saw in this object of my obsessive regard was a chance to deploy three terms – *Canadian, woman,* and *writer* – around that phrase and to see how their interplay might be used to describe patterns found in the works of several English-Canadian women writers. The context told me plainly that 'fear of the open heart' had something to do with *Canada* and with the Scots-Presbyterian repression of feeling that helps to create our notorious garrison mentality. But 'fear of the open heart,' if it means roughly the same thing as 'garrison mentality,' is nevertheless a *female* way of saying it. Gallant's phrase almost trembles in its pink ribbons; the other, brainchild of Northrop Frye, sounds militaristic and true-blue and male. (That opposition struck me as funny, since Gallant is at least as tough if not as gallant as Frye.) One phrase points to the realm of the affections, the other – 'garrison mentality' – to territorial disputes; each is a metaphor grounded in experience that is stereotypically gender-specific. 'Fear of the open heart,' then, may be regarded as a female wording of a basic Canadian mind-set.

And that brings us to my third term: Canadian woman *writer*. 'Fear of the open heart' may also suggest a condition of the writer, the issue of disguise or indirection and of the writer's relationship to her characters or her reader. But to say even this much is to imply a heretical belief in the existence of the author and to necessitate a lengthy digression. Fearfully, but with an open heart, I confess that this is so: for me the author lives. I do not only play with 'texts'; very often I imagine that in the act of reading I am encountering, let us say, Phyllis Webb. And if I as a sophisticated reader believe this (as I know many other readers do), then it contains a truth of some kind, and theory ought to account for it with something other than modish disdain.

Depersonalization does not strike me as altogether a good thing, in literature or elsewhere. I don't believe that the writer is only a sort of neutered monkey pounding a dictionary-machine (and yes, I know what cultural baggage led me to write 'monkey'). I don't make a cult of personality. But I do believe – phenomenologically, if you like – in what I rather too grandly call my theory of intimacy. (I cannot here articulate a larger theory of reading in which to place this idea, nor am I convinced that if in the writing I ran into difficulty I would be obliged to toss out this theory of intimacy – my largest theory of all being that we are ignorant and that 'consistency' in theory, rather like 'unity' in literature, is an important but perilous ideal.)

According to the theory of intimacy, then, *one dimension* of what occurs in the act of reading is the reader's personal encounter with the author. In some cases this sense of an encounter will be so ghostly as to disappear; in other cases it will be overwhelming. The variables are numerous: which reader is in question, which reading, and which passage in the text, whether the author is long dead or freshly dead or living, whether the reader knows (or has read about or knows anyone who knows) the author, whether the reader is familiar with and has been deeply affected by other work of the writer, and so on. But I think the theory holds. I am most forcibly reminded of it when at 'readings' (where the reader / writer dichotomy breaks down) I observe an ordinary reader approaching a flesh-and-blood writer and can see on that reader's face a look (either bold or shy) that will soon blossom into speech: *You don't know me, but I know you.* I am not prepared to call that impulse intrinsically presumptuous or craven, although certainly it can take on either of those qualities. Nor am I willing to dismiss the claim as nonsense.

The reader's knowledge of the writer is of course restricted. But a sample (however atypical) of the writer's sensibility has nonetheless been presented to the reader, who will make of it what she can. And this is rather like what happens in ordinary social contact: we respond to a performance, as when we listen to a dinner companion's story. (The stories I am talking about do not have to be autobiographical or earnest, any more than fiction does.) We choose our friends partly on the basis of how such stories are told. We observe the values implied, the flavour of irony or humour, the choice of apparently peripheral details – and so decide whether we'd like to meet (or read) that person again. There is more to it, naturally. In life, for example, there is also the question of what the other person thinks of oneself. If I observe that my companion has also appreciated my line of chat, or suffered over my painful memories, that will very probably endear her to me.

But is such mutual approbation (or disaffection) possible in a reading encounter? The author cannot know or choose who will read the text and so cannot pass judgement on a particular reader. But as you pursue a course through a text, you may find that an authorial judgement has been ready-made for you and seems to fit precisely or well enough. If, for instance, the reader approves of a character or an idea that is resoundingly mocked by the author, the reader and author will also implicitly judge one another. A disagreement of that kind may affect a relationship that exists in the reader's head no less than one existing in the 'outside' world. Misunderstandings can also occur, and sometimes be resolved. Another thing that is likely to sour a reader / writer relationship is some wide disparity of intelligence: no one likes to feel stupid. (We may or may not choose our writers and our companions accordingly.) But if some readers will allow writers and friends and lovers to be quite a lot smarter than themselves, few are willing to have their noses rubbed in their inferiority.

My theory of intimacy depends upon a recognition that human beings, to a very considerable degree, simultaneously present and create themselves through speech. It contradicts the claim of Roland Barthes that 'the Author, when believed in, is always conceived of as the past of his own book, [... and that] in complete contrast, the modern scriptor is born simultaneously with the text.'[1] The relationship of author to text is not so much that of a father to his child (as Barthes says it must be, if the author is believed in), as that of a speaker to his speech. The speaker of course exists before the speech and presents a part of that anterior self through language; but the speaker is also created through his speech. Each of these statements is true in its own way. The author is father and child; the text is child and father. In another sense they are twins, as Barthes suggests.

This question of the author's priority to or creation by or simultaneity with the text is illuminated by the phenomenon of 'readings' – in which the reader can observe the writer speaking his or her text. All sorts of things are gathered up in that occasion, all kinds of barriers collapsed. Most significant is the fact that a 'reading' dramatizes the relationship between writer and reader – and that, I might add, is surely what attracts the reader to such events. The reader has left her armchair in order to see the once invisible companion and to listen to the sound of that person's voice. But a curious thing happens. What the reader encounters now is also another *reader*, someone cast in the role that she has lately played herself, another recipient and translator of the text, another human being who has been affected by it. The 'authority' of the author (or the other) is at once confirmed and undermined. And that seems to me the egalitarian ideal, both in ordinary human relations and in the attitude we may assume toward writers. Each human being is both creature and creator.

In recent literary theory, the reader has been exalted at the expense of the writer; the author has had to die so that the reader may live. This revolution seems to me unnecessarily bloody in one sense and bloodless in another. In both senses it is too stereotypically male – too close to the garrison, too far from the heart. To begin with, the revolution ought not to be necessary at all; but if the reader does feel trammeled by the authority of the author, she can simply and unilaterally change the terms of their agreement. (She can, in Margaret Atwood's terms, cease to be a victim without becoming an oppressor; this is a context in which that trick is performed with relative ease.) She doesn't have to *kill* the poor bastard. I am aware that this is just a manner of speaking, but it is not a manner I much like. The revolution is also bloodless, as both writer and reader are depersonalized by an excessively mechanistic approach to language. According to Barthes, for instance, 'the scriptor no longer bears within him passions, humours, feelings, impressions, but rather this immense dictionary'; and the reader, who is now the repository and fabricator of the text's unity, is also 'without history, biography, psychology.' Neither party to the relationship can 'any longer be *personal*' [italics mine].[2] Against this claim, I would offer the theory of intimacy: not as a full account of the reading act, but as a reminder of feelings both friendly and hostile that we should not be afraid to admit.

My intention in this essay is to apply the phrase 'fear of the open heart' to three Canadian women writers – Mavis Gallant, Margaret Laurence, and Alice Munro – and so to articulate the quite different kinds of satisfaction I have had in 'knowing' these writers through their work. I will start with the Canadian grounding of that phrase, move through its application to female experience, and end with its significance for the writer. To begin, then, in a respectful mode, I will replace 'the fear of the open heart' in the novella from which I have so blithely extracted it.

Jean Duncan Price, the narrator of Gallant's 'Its Image on the Mirror,' is talking about her Scots-Presbyterian heritage. She refers to her father's belief that 'Scottish blood was the best in the country, responsible for our national character traits of prudence, level-headedness, and self-denial.'[3] Jean's own understanding of this Protestant, Anglo-Scot inheritance is less complimentary: 'The seed of our characters came from another continent. Like the imported daisies and dandelions, it was larger than the parent plant. Flowering in us was the dark bloom of the Old Country – the mistrust of pity, the contempt for weakness, the fear of the open heart' (88-89). This is one explanation of a mind-set that has also been described without recourse to Scots-Presbyterianism. Possibly it was the vast space of Canada that scared us first of all; but, for whatever reason, we are often seen as a frightened or over-cautious people, concerned with external threats and drawing inward to the garrison of a narrowly defined social group, or the garrison of the self.

Jean Price is (somewhat atypically) capable of defining the problem, but not of overcoming it. She is one of a multitude of Gallant characters who imagine that life and happiness are happening elsewhere and that they have been unfairly shut out. Often these characters have a mean-minded and vindictive streak, as a result (or cause) of their exclusion from life, and often they congratulate themselves, smugly and blindly, upon the design of their garrison – so that our concern for their suffering is diminished. Often such characters are paired with another – perhaps another sister, as in the case of 'Its Image on the Mirror' or 'The Cost of Living' – who signifies a more reckless and romantic way of life. But it seems characteristic of Gallant that the focal character or narrator will be the more 'closed' of this pair, and that the happiness even of the more 'open' character will prove illusory.

The pairing of the sisters interests me, especially in relation to the title of 'Its Image on the Mirror,' which Gallant has taken from W.B. Yeats's 'The Shadowy Waters.' Jean's attraction to her sister Isobel is a desire for what Yeats (quoted in the epigraph) calls 'love itself.' The sister is a mirror image both of an idealized self and of the dream of love, which is always on the far side of the looking-glass and unobtainable for either. Jean wants to be united with that romantic image and so is encouraged to see Isobel in the climactic scene wearing 'the dressing gown ... that belonged to both of us years before' (149); all along, she has 'wanted her to say, You and I are alike, and we are not like any other person in this room' (91).

Isobel is cast as a double who enjoys with men an intimacy that is impossible for Jean: 'I had an idea about love, and I thought my sister knew the truth.... They [Isobel and her lover] were the lighted window; I was the watcher on the street' (98-99). Thus, when Jean metaphorically stops 'being the stranger on the dark street' and enters 'the bright rooms of [her] sister's life' (149) – in the mirror of fact, Isobel has entered *her* cold room – Jean believes that she will now learn 'what it is to be Isobel ... and to be loved (150). Ironically, Isobel has come to Jean because she is pregnant and needs 'somebody's whole attention' (152). Uninterested in reciprocity with her besotted sister, in the true intimacy that would return her gaze, Isobel knows exactly where to go to get the attention she wants. We may conclude, then, as Jean implicitly does, that 'to be Isobel' is to be selfish and 'to be loved' is to be in serious trouble.

Love is a risk – especially for woman, as the illicit pregnancy suggests – but paradoxically, at least as it exists on this side of the looking glass, love is also a condition into which we retreat to avoid risk. This is the 'secret' that Isobel calmly passes along to Jean, that love is 'someone between you and the others, blotting out the light' (151). Thus we learn that 'fear of the open heart' can take several forms. Isobel seems reckless, willing to journey into an adulterous affair and later to marry an Italian living in Venezuela; that witty double-dose of *machismo*, however, suggests accurately that if Isobel has escaped Jean's garrison, her propriety and dullness, she has nonetheless landed in a women's prison of her own. Out of fear – 'She might have spent her life being a little weak, a little frightened, if it hadn't been for him' (150-51) –

Isobel has agreed to let a man blot out the light. And Jean, when she hears this, immediately thinks of the 'wall' (151) that defines her own marriage. The two sisters therefore meet in the mirror after all.

What happens next is ambiguous. It may not involve incestuous feeling; it may not matter if it does. If Jean had imagined that through an identification with Isobel she might experience what it is to love and be loved by a man, she realizes now that this is a dead end. Man's claim to be all-sufficing is seen through, permitting Jean to make a claim of her own. The male wall yields to the female mirror and another image floats to the surface of the glass: woman alone, Isobel as the possible object of desire. Wanting to be beautiful for her sister, Jean removes the pins from her hair. Thinking that 'unless we could meet across that landscape we might as well die,' she drags herself forward – 'against the swiftest current, in the fastest river in the world' (153) – and takes Isobel's hand. Jean has left the garrison, risked everything – and is rejected absolutely. Isobel snaps at her, and Jean retreats. She returns at once to an adversarial relationship to Isobel, and will make her 'pay' with a counterfeit of intimacy for the attention she requires. 'It no longer mattered whether my hair was straight or curled' (154).

I do not know whether the love that is extinguished here is sexual. I see a number of reasons for believing that it may be, but will not rehearse those here. What I am interested in is the fact that I have felt afraid to propose this, as if Gallant (in the role of Isobel, to my Jean) would make me feel a fool. But if I were silent, she might laugh at my cowardice. Perhaps I feel imprisoned in the mirror because she declines to take my hand, or to show hers. But somehow the fear of the open heart that begins as a national trait, and develops as a problem specifically for women, ends by determining my sense of the writer herself. A cold wind blows through this novella, and through nearly all the landscape of exile that is Gallant's fiction.

This chill is built into the imagery of Canada's winter climate and of course implies the yearning for something warmer, more 'out-going': 'a climate imagined, a journey never made' (155). But we see in the ambiguous location of that coldness – imaged sometimes as a condition of the world outside, sometimes as the world within – a problem that Gallant reveals also with her mirror-imaging of the two sisters. It would seem perhaps that Gallant's creation (in story after story) of people who suffer from the fear of the open heart, and plots that are determined by it, should cast her in the reader's mind as a champion of open-heartedness. The writer, by that reckoning, would be cast as the 'warm' sister of the 'cold' one caught in the mirror of her text. But it seems to me that Gallant 'is' both sisters – the reckless traveller and the cautious observer – and that the two images converge in the coldness that results from Isobel's denial of Jean.

I cannot properly engage here the vexed question of Gallant's relations to feminism, but I would suggest that the model of sisterhood is an interesting way to approach it. Gallant's female characters are variously imprisoned, and often in ways that are susceptible to a feminist analysis, yet one rarely feels that she is sorry for them, or cheering them on. She seems, therefore, to be denying the sisterly bond. Gallant is the 'exceptional woman,' aloof from, faintly contemptuous of, and possibly fearful of women who are left behind in her chilly texts. (And of course she *is* exceptional. She has written some of the best stories I know, and given me great pleasure.)

'The mistrust of pity, the contempt for weakness, the fear of the open heart' is very precisely Hagar Shipley's problem in *The Stone Angel*. Naturally enough, Margaret Laurence also associates this fear with coldness – and she does so in a way that repeats the inside / outside ambiguity of Gallant's novella. Finding her lonely bed as 'cold as winter,' Hagar thinks her way outside, into an angel imprint made in snow: 'I could drift to sleep in it, like someone caught in a blizzard, and freeze.'[4] That image, casting the great Canadian winter as a killer, also suggests Hagar's complicity in her own living-death. In denying nature, and her own nature, defining self through class, Hagar chooses the garrison: her father's brick house, or Mr. Oatley's stone mansion in Vancouver. And predictably, she finds it a chilly place.

Like Jean Price, Hagar is conceived as heir to a Scots-Presbyterian tradition. That mind-set, crafted abroad yet perfectly attuned (as it must have seemed) to the circumstances of a hostile land, prevents her from achieving an original response. Gender considerations are a significant part of that obstruction. Like Jean, Hagar has been seduced into ladyhood and deprived of her full humanity, including her own genuine sexuality, in the process. (Their brothers have suffered too; symbolically, they are killed by a paternal insistence upon stereotypical masculinity.) But Hagar, in contrast to the mirror-trapped Jean, retains a stubborn inner conviction of her own individuality, and at last she sees in both directions at once. She understands that 'in some far crevice of [her] heart, some cave too deeply buried, too concealed' (292) she has wanted most to rejoice in life. Shackled by a concern for appearance, propriety, she has not allowed herself to 'speak the heart's truth.' Had she ventured to do so, the landscape would have ceased to be hostile. Canada's drought-plagued wilderness would become a garden, watered by the well of love that Hagar (functioning as the angel sent by God to deliver the biblical Hagar) discovers in her own heart.

This opposition *and* identity of Hagar and the angel is signalled first of all by the stone angel that is her mother's monument, which the strong-boned Hagar ironically becomes in order to disclaim the female weakness associated with her mother. It is repeated somewhat less conspicuously in Laurence's handling of her other biblical angel, the one who wrestles with Jacob. The stone angel, in that configuration, wrestles with an external

'other,' with each of her sons in turn; but the most significant arena is internal, Hagar's battle with herself. Inner and outer realms are conflated, as in the
language of Hagar's judgement on herself: 'Pride was my wilderness, and the
demon that led me there was fear' (292). The fortress she makes of her heart
paradoxically causes Hagar to be exiled: fear of the open heart, that is to say,
effectively casts out the heart, as in the case of the 'stone heart' (4) that
another angel holds aloft in the Manawaka cemetery. To bless herself, then,
and to be released from her own demonic fear, Hagar must take a lengthy
journey into 'some far crevice of [her] heart, some cave too deeply buried.'

That journey is the novel itself, in which 'rampant with memory' (5) Hagar
storms the citadel within. She finds there the grace to perform two significant actions, the only 'truly free' acts of her life: 'One was a joke – yet a joke
only as all victories are, the paraphernalia being unequal to the event's reach.
The other was a lie – yet not a lie, for it was spoken at least and at last with
what may perhaps be a kind of love' (307). The first act is to fetch a bedpan for
the young Chinese-Canadian woman who shares her hospital room and then
to laugh both at the absurdity of their shared impotence and at this small
symbolic triumph over it. This is also a victory over Hagar's long condition-
ing, because in laughing at the indignities to which the body may subject us,
and in reaching out to help another person, Hagar is thumbing her nose at
proper appearances. She expresses her freedom from the fear of looking
absurd; and she admits – in strength and weakness – her sisterhood with
other women. Thus, implicitly, she acknowledges her place on the same
false-bottomed boat from which Chinese women were jettisoned by Hagar's
employer. That boat is her female body, which is failing now, and poised to let
go its heavy cargo; it is also her womanhood, the shore to which Hagar is
safely returned at last.

Hagar's second free act – a 'lie – yet not a lie,' is the blessing she bestows on
Marvin: '"You've been good to me, always. A better son than John"' (304).
This is an interesting case of open-heartedness, because in order to give the
faithful, sixty-year-old Marvin his due – the approval that will enable him to
get on with his life – Hagar must conceal her stubborn preference for John,
the son who is still closest to her heart. But Hagar, if she does not entirely
'speak the heart's truth' (292), is getting closer to it. She is yielding, allowing
new truths to assail her and be expressed. In this suddenly contradictory,
exhilarating script, Hagar finds that she is 'strangely cast': long fixed in the
rigid and unforgiving mold of the stone angel, she is now re-cast (out of and
into herself) in a very different angelic role. Thus, the warrior-angel yields at
dawn to the peace of benediction. And while Marvin is explicitly cast as
Jacob, it is plain that he must share this role too with Hagar, for the strangeness of the casting is precisely that Hagar 'can only release [her]self by releasing him' (304).

Contradiction and exhilaration, release accomplished through a joke and a partial truth – that leads us to the heartland of Alice Munro's fiction. Often Munro's heroine tries to guard herself, to stay within the safe, approved parameters of a social group. But she knows very well that an enemy lurks within and has a sneaking fondness for that shadow self, that outlaw or jubilant *saboteur*. She knows her integrity is compromised as she denies a messy, 'vulgar' past for reasons of protective coloration, and she feels bad about her craven ladyhood. She wants to smash the garrison, to say or do the outrageous thing that will acknowledge whatever has been left out. But she is also afraid of appearing ridiculous. Often, it seems to me that Munro (like Gallant and Laurence) regards that self-protectiveness, the fear of appearing ridiculous or incoherent, as an especially Canadian trait.

The quintessential Munro heroine – I am thinking particularly of Rose in *Who Do You Think You Are?* – has three distinct social locations. Her original place is at the lower- or lower-middle-class fringe of a small Ontario town. Vitality is outside the garrison of the town; power and propriety are within. Rose is poised on the brink, desiring more of both. Her second location is marriage to Patrick Blatchford, 'heir to a mercantile empire.'[5] The Blatchfords' chain of department stores (together with their mansion) suggests a garrison, an Anglo-Scots tradition of ownership that is orderly and exclusive. Thus, Rose remarks that Patrick must be ' "a true Scot" ' (84) when she learns of his skill at building stone walls. In becoming Patrick's chatelaine, Rose effectively inverts Hagar's pattern: she moves into the garrison as Hagar had moved out, and away from her father's brick house and general store, to marry a 'bearded Indian' (*Stone*, 45) on the edge of town. But neither woman can live wholly in the second location, since she still identifies herself – in part, or palimpsestically – with the first. Thesis, Rose's assumption that it would feel better to live inside the wall, and antithesis, her discovery that she would rather be outside, yield to a kind of synthesis in her third location, which is the shifting realm of art.

Munro's view of the artist as one who moves through society, and is outside of it as well, is developed in the comic figure of Milton Homer from the story 'Who Do You Think You Are?' That he is a marginal figure is illustrated by the wooden platform at the side of Rose's house and various other yards and porches, where Milton is allowed to perform his antics. That society accords the artist an occasional, quasi-religious centrality is shown by Milton's admission to the parlours of Hanratty when the birth of a child necessitates his rites of naming and invocation. 'Milton Homer's other public function ... was to march in parades' (191), threading his way through the social herd as a sort of gadfly, to mimic all and sundry. He is allowed to do this – an allowed fool – not only because his 'terrible energy' (192) is such that he must be accommodated somehow, but also because the townspeople regard him with 'a particularly obscure sort of pride' (193). He is also, that is to say, the Lord of Misrule and expressive of their energy, their shadow selves.

Whereas Hagar was 'doubly blind' (*Stone*, 3) to inner and outer truths, Milton Homer can *see*, as the names of two blind poets suggest, precisely because he does not see or acknowledge Hagar's 'brake of proper appearances' (*Stone*, 292). In terms of the story's title, he does not care who he is, or what anyone else thinks of him. 'What interests Rose' (*Who*, 194) is the possibility that Milton Homer has *chosen* his blindness, chosen to excise from himself 'a sense of precaution. ... Social inhibition' (193), because she still has that inhibition as well as an artist's interest in discarding it. This is the first thing Munro tells us about her heroine, that Rose 'had a need to picture things, to pursue absurdities, that was stronger than the need to stay out of trouble' (1). We understand, accordingly, that Rose is fated to become an artist.

The third location permits Rose to move around, to indulge in bohemian improprieties, and yet to achieve some measure of power and recognition. As an actress she can break down (or live on both sides of) the wall between self and other, between the one and the many. She moves freely through the human repertoire, all the shapes it can assume, and has the consolation as well of a freemasonry with other artists – a tribe of her own. Yet Rose is also *woman alone*, that oxymoron to end all oxymorons. And sometimes she does want to end it, to come in out of the cold. Thus, we see Rose (rather like Gallant's Jean) gaze hungrily into lighted windows, warm living rooms; and 'it's no good telling herself she wouldn't be long inside ... before she'd wish she was walking the streets' (*Who*, 152).

That leads us to the question of how the fear of the open heart operates for *women*, in these texts by Canadian women writers. The loneliness of Rose, her reactionary and intermittent longing to be coupled, suggests one direction in which this fear can operate. She wants a lover, a '"man for [her] life!"' (164) – someone who will observe, as Simon does in 'Simon's Luck,' that the furnace is inadequate and that what Rose '"needs is some insulation"' (160). She is afraid of the open heart in that sense, the uncommitted heart that lacks a particular, steady companion to provide her with the warmth she needs. But Rose is also very much afraid that if she reveals her need, opens her heart entirely to a particular other, the man will run away. He will react to her then as species-female, whose 'tenderness is greedy, [whose] sensuality is dishonest' (169); her shameful body will be regarded as a trap. And she has a third fear, signalled by the insulation image, that Simon 'is taking her over ... along with the house' (163). This image recalls the wall of love and the blotting out of light in Gallant's novella and seems confirmed later when Rose thinks that 'love removes the world for you, and just as surely when it's going well as when it's going badly' (170).

The 'flaw' in Rose's garrison of the self, the 'danger' of self-abandonment that makes Flo afraid for her in the story 'Privilege,' is her 'headlong hopefulness, readiness, need' (35) for love. Thus, love is conceived as a perilous venturing forth; and it entails the risk of appearing ridiculous, since the beloved may well prove unworthy or unreliable. But love is also an 'enslavement,' a prison in which the woman pines, awaiting her master's pleasure. In 'Simon's Luck,' Rose takes the risk of announcing her love for Simon; and she does this when Simon pretends for a moment to be her servant, just when she had guessed he would assume that role. 'He would say, "I hope I have done it to your satisfaction, mum" and yank a forelock' (164). A sexist norm is playfully reversed, and Rose is catapulted into a vision of equality. Safety and exhilaration seem compatible, so that Rose can open her heart to Simon-the-actor as a kindred spirit. And then he disappears, so that she is left in a familiar brand of female misery. Suddenly she cries *enough!* She gets into her car and drives, halfway across the country, abandoning by this symbolic effort the self that waits and yearns for Simon, to create another self that is out in the world, moving and actually seeing what is there. The turning point comes in a prairie café, where Rose (as artist and free agent) observes some ordinary ice-cream dishes 'in a way that wouldn't be possible to a person in any stage of love. She felt their solidity with a convalescent gratitude' (170). The wall is down; the light – and the right to free passage – is restored. 'The world had stopped being a stage where she might meet him, and gone back to being itself' (170).

It would seem, then, that Rose regards love as impossible for a woman of the world, and that she had made her choice. But the conclusion of 'Simon's Luck,' where Rose learns that Simon has died of cancer – and implicitly, perhaps, vanished for that reason – is a 'disarrangement' (173) that shifts the meaning of the whole. If bad luck had not intervened, Simon might have become '"the man for [her] life"' (164), and Rose might have found that love does not necessarily remove the world. Indeed, the paragraph in which Rose decides that it does ends with a wavering 'So she thought' (170). Now that we know Rose was wrong in her belief that 'His body would not be in question, it never would be' (169), now that Simon's luck, like insulation, has been stripped away, the possibility of love is entertained once more. Munro does not tell us this; she simply requires by her 'disarrangement' that we read the imagery again.

Accordingly, we may see Simon's wish to insulate Rose's house as benevolent. He knew of the cold ahead for both of them; he also badly needed warmth. He desires for them both not a retreat from life, but a nurturing of one another; thus, we may regard his planting of a garden for Rose as equivalent to her purchase of love-foods and flowered sheets for him. And Simon's suggestion that she '"Learn not to be so thin-skinned"' (163) is not an attempt to take 'her over, in a sensible way, along with the house and garden,' not an attempt to place her in the garrison, but a recognition that 'unprotected moments' necessarily lie ahead. Whether Simon is there or not, Rose will be obliged to live in her own skin; and he is advising her to do so courageously, to be less concerned with the risk of 'humiliation,' with the question of who others think she is. In retrospect, then, Simon appears to resolve the contradictions of the open heart. But Simon's death, which removes the world for him, establishing by that ironic parallel that he also 'could seriously lack power' (173), has been required to confirm that Rose and Simon are kindred spirits after all. Equality, we may conclude, in vulnerability as well as strength, is the pre-requisite of love between women and men who would venture out of the garrison. What remains is simply to find it, on this side of the grave.

In *The Diviners*, Margaret Laurence uses the same pattern of social locations – scruffy background, followed by stuffy husband, followed by release into the freemasonry of art – that we have seen in *Who Do You Think You Are?* Like Rose, Morag Gunn thinks she is someone rather remarkable; she has a prodigious appetite for her own life. Thus, Jules Tonnere observes, '"You want it so bad I can just about smell it on you. You'll get it, Morag."'[6] What 'it' is, is not altogether clear. Morag is destined to become a writer, as it turns out; but she also wants social respectability, and she wants love. In short, she wants it all – with an appetite that sounds (and partly is) sexual. She can dispense with respectability easily enough, once she has tasted its ashes, especially since self-respect increases with the demise of her inauthentic marriage and the discovery of her true vocation. And later she is unwilling to give up what she has – Munro's ice-cream dishes, the camaraderie of her unconventional life and her freedom to work – but still she yearns for love and ponders the question of their mutual exclusivity. The right man somehow does not materialize. He is just a little wrong, or (like Simon) out of phase. But the hope of a resolution – at least for other women – remains, and in the meantime Morag *stands for* the open heart.

In the fiction of Mavis Gallant, the hope of chivalric rescue (to which Munro's Rose succumbed in 'The Beggar Maid') is soundly mocked. Thus, we see young women like Veronica in 'Sunday Afternoon' or Jeannie in 'My Heart is Broken' as absurdly helpless. They are already in a garrison defined by passive female roles and cannot conceive of rescuing themselves; each is merely waiting for a man to supply her with a more elegant, more lively cell. In both of these stories, there is some ambiguity as to the appropriate object of derision, the extent to which the woman herself or a patriarchal society should be held responsible for her plight. The appetite for gentility (achieved or not) is also mocked in Gallant's fiction, primarily by the failure of love; but exclusion from gentility is certainly not seen as a benefit-in-disguise.

The ideal would seem to be approached in 'Irina,' which I regard (perhaps not coincidentally) as Gallant's most successful story. Irina is the elderly widow of a famous writer, who wished her to be 'shielded from decisions, [and] allowed to grow in the sun and shade of male protection,'[7] but who, at the same time, failed her in an emotional sense and housed her most uncomfortably. With his death, Irina seized her husband's manuscripts, to decide for herself on the matter of his 'authority'; bought herself an excellent flat – too small, however, to accommodate her clamorous children; and invited a charming, if rather decrepit ex-lover to visit her. It makes an interesting parable, from an historical perspective. Irina has survived the patriarchal era and paid her dues; now she has her independence, 'her' writing, and her lover. There are multiple ironies, of course, mainly having to do with the lateness of the hour, but Irina seems to reflect (and augur forth) her author rather neatly. She has, moreover, the same lady-like ferocity, the same ironic air. You would never catch Irina / Gallant outside in the hurly-burly of a feminist rally, but she has nevertheless accomplished a quite sizable, private palace coup.

There is another issue having to do with women and the open heart that I want to address briefly. And that is the contradictory behaviours which are commonly associated with woman's speech. On the one hand, women are famous for wanting to *talk* about it: to discuss personal relationships, to confront problems, to force communication and agreement. On the other hand, women are said to be evasive, devious, behind-the-scenes manipulators. Feminists, of course, are now pointing out that women have had to operate that way because they lack public power and because they have been trained to walk softly; they have had to move secretly, if they were to move at all. Such metaphors are suggestive in relation to the garrison: when that is regarded as a seat of power, woman moves to its shadowy outskirts, or creeps behind the throne.

The first of these two speech behaviours might be identified with the open heart and the second with the fear of the open heart. The fact that they can often be found in the same woman, according to the time of day or mood or the circumstances in which she finds herself, may help to explain a woman writer's interest in this theme. But there is another way of reconciling the two conflicting traditions: woman may 'tell the truth, but tell it slant' – in Emily Dickinson's phrase, now used by feminist critics in a variety of ways – either because she feels the need of circumspection, or because 'truth,' so-called, is often slant, is full of contradictions and nuances that the patriarchal ideal of clarity (and objectivity) has tended to obscure. Thus, Gallant's Irina remarks that 'whatever she saw and thought and attempted was still fluid and vague.... You looked for clarity, she wrote, and the answer you had was paleness.'[8]

We come, then, to the question of what writing has to do with the fear of the open heart. Writers communicate, by definition, and their perennial subject is the human heart – so that it may seem they ought, again by definition, to be on the side of open-heartedness. But writers often proceed by indirection. Their effects are achieved sideways and they know that. To reveal, moreover, the inconsistencies of the heart may require something very like inconsistency in the writer: a susceptibility to ambiguities and contradictions and not just an itch to straighten them out. And that, of course, is 'openness' of another kind.

The case of the woman writer is particularly interesting in these terms. On the one hand, she may feel that her side of the story has been suppressed so long – and that her need for articulation, and her reader's need, is so great – that she had better approach her subject head-on, announce her opinions without hedging. That impulse has led recently to some very straightforward feminist fiction – 'open-hearted' fiction, if you like. On the other hand, woman's long experience of indirection and introspection and the need to consider the feelings of others has, I suspect, been a significant factor in fiction that tells the truth at a slant. In other words, this sort of writer's experience as a woman may intensify what I think of as the fiction writer's natural attraction to peripheral vision, to the insight which is not yet fixed.

With respect to 'openness' – defined in this case as straightforward expression, or the taking of a firm, clear position – my three writers can be placed along a continuum. At one end is Margaret Laurence, the most 'open' of the three. Though rich in texture, and carefully crafted, her books are not particularly difficult, and their meaning is clear at every level. Alice Munro comes next. Her books seem easy enough, but they are far more complicated and more ambiguous than may at first appear. Mavis Gallant is at the other end. Her work is often so subtle that its meaning, and the author's stand on her themes and characters, may easily escape the reader.

Laurence is a bold and passionate writer. We always sense the steadiness of her respect and her affection for her characters, and that (as opposed to any sense of identification between writer and protagonist) encourages a close connection between protagonist and reader. Laurence's work is characterized by over-determination on obvious thematic levels, while less obvious levels (on close examination) tend to support and repeat the matter of the obvious. If they complicate it, they do so in aid of tolerance – which is a prominent value at all levels of the text. I think, for instance, even of the chick-killing episode in *The Stone Angel*, which seems to me the most complex manipulation of image in Laurence's work. It points in a number of directions at once, but minute examination of that scene still yields a set of ideas that are prominent at the 'obvious' level of the text; and these ideas or meanings, though complex, can be resolved, are at bottom harmonious. In addition, Laurence's insights tend to be focused on large questions which occupy prominent areas of consciousness; she is not a practitioner of peripheral vision to the same degree that Alice Munro and Mavis Gallant are.

Alice Munro is also a 'warm' writer in the sense that a strong feeling of intimacy is generated between reader, character and author. An identification of writer and protagonist allows Munro to be hard on her characters without distancing the reader. Thematically, Munro's fictions are more equivocal than Laurence's. One of Munro's great subjects is embarrassment, or shame; often she will occupy herself with the tension between a character's ambition (her exalted view of self) and her self-criticism, which often relates to over-weening pride. Her eye is on the margin, the point at which something repressed or not seen suddenly materializes in consciousness. Again, she is what I would call a writer of peripheral vision; and when insights do arise from that zone, they remain somehow in suspension or in motion. Although they suggest patterns, they do not immediately make everything else clear and coherent. Munro is always checking and testing: the Munro 'signature' is that moment in the story where she points out that she has missed something, that the full truth of the matter has eluded her. She is open in *that* sense, open to open-endedness, to fresh interpretations.

Structurally, her stories often supply anecdotes which hover round the question that absorbs her – and the links between these will be difficult for the reader to articulate – difficult, but not impossible, except to the degree that they are impossible for Munro. The character in a Munro story who is interpreting her experience, the interpretant, typically has a level of expertise which is close to that of the writer and perhaps the reader. (Munro, however, will often distinguish between a younger version of the interpretant and her present incarnation, who may see more or differently.) In Munro's stories we feel a kind of balance between the open or forthright position and another which is more tentative, which employs something like disguise – silence or deflection – in order not to distort. In Laurence, there is a much stronger sense of resolution, of the central truth coming out loud and clear; and in Gallant, the sense of resolution is generally more muted.

With Mavis Gallant, though we may feel that the full truth of the matter has eluded *us*, we rarely – or so it seems to me – feel that it has eluded Gallant. She seems to claim a larger intelligence than she imputes to the reader. Laurence does not, and Munro does not, even though both of these writers are more open about where they stand than Gallant is. It might seem that Gallant, who does not very often choose to place a platform within the work from which to address the reader or guide her response, therefore *trusts* the reader more ... that she assumes the reader's power to understand the text. But this is not quite the effect achieved. Rather, Gallant is like a harsh mother, who can swim very ably herself, and chooses to instruct her children simply by tossing them into the deep end. If this is an expression of confi dence in the child's (or the reader's) powers, it also feels rather like disdain for ineptitude. There is something rather chilling in Gallant – brilliant and painful as her work is – and it is related (in the way I have just suggested) to this author / reader axis, as well as to the more obvious author / character axis. In Gallant's fiction, the author seems disengaged, her judgement withheld: yet we sense her authority and we feel that her irony has depths that we do not quite plumb. If there are still ambiguities and contradictions in the lower depths – where Mavis Gallant stands alone – she is not telling.

The lure to character / reader identification is much less in Gallant's fiction than in Laurence's or Munro's, partly because the character / author bond is so much weaker. The Gallant protagonist is often not much of a quester; and there is a large gap between the level of expertise of the interpretant and the knowledge implied by the cool, mysterious tone of the narration, the implied author. That knowledge – that authorial clout – also occasionally announces itself very directly. Sometimes her judgement will descend like mercy, as in this authorial comment from her novel *Green Water, Green Sky*: it 'was a test too strong for their powers. It would have been too strong for anyone; they were not magical; they were only human beings.'[9] But what she is talking about here, the test she refers to, is the need for two of her characters to look clearly at themselves and to acknowledge their share of responsibility for what has happened to a third character. It may well seem to the reader that the test should not be too strong for non-magical human beings: that we should not be expected to get first-class marks, but that a fair number of us ought to be able to make a respectable showing. Gallant is not that optimistic; and if she goes mellow on her characters, there is often this barb attached – that not much should be expected of them.

An interesting moment occurs near the end of *Green Water, Green Sky*. George, one of the principal characters, is reflecting on a kind of composite figure (made up of Bonnie and Flor, two members of his family, and a girl he's seen on a Paris street), and we are told this: 'She was a changeable figure, now menacing, now dear; a minute later behaving like a queen in exile, plaintive and haughty, eccentric by birth, unaware, or not caring, that the others were laughing behind their hands.'[10] One thing that is not altogether clear about this passage (in context at least) is whether the *figure* changes or the observer. The complexity of vision in Gallant that makes it possible for her to write a passage like that is quite wonderful and suggests as well the kind of openness I have associated with open-endedness. For Gallant too this everywoman figure observed by George can be both menacing and dear. Human beings generally are that, dangerous or 'menacing' because they are responsible for the mess they perpetrate in their own lives and in the lives of others, *and* 'dear' – capable of appearing in a changing light, quite rightly too, as pitiable and touching and even admirable, given all they have had to bear. So Gallant does activate in her readers both compassion and judgement; but she does not, somehow, allow the reader to feel secure in these responses. Things can change in a minute. The ego of the character – 'behaving like a queen in exile,' pretending not to care about 'the others … laughing behind their hands' – is always vulnerable and that malaise extends to the reader. The perspective can shift at any moment, and we can suddenly feel that some of the laughter behind hands is directed at characters we have lately been admiring, and therefore at us, and that Gallant is herself most particularly amused. One finds a kind of dizzying openness in Gallant, in the sense that there are numerous corridors we might take in our journey through the text, but there is also the risk of encountering Gallant-the-minotaur at any moment, that we will find her laughing behind her hands at us, and then vanishing so that she can spring out at us again. And our sense that she has designed every square centimetre of the maze, and can move within it at will, makes her world – and perhaps her heart – seem closed as well. We may feel in exile there, as her characters do.

The reader's fear that she may mistake the author's intent, or fail to discover some stable meaning in the text, may lead her to behave defensively, to shut the compelling complexities out. That species of the fear of the open heart, I suggest, and discover through my students, happens quite commonly with the work of Mavis Gallant. Her 'coldness,' a function of the mysterious distance from both character and reader, leaves the reader in uneasy proximity to the character – as if both were committed to one of Gallant's many pensions and did not much care for one another's company. Gallant, meanwhile, remains outside of that garrison in a superior sort of exile.

With both Laurence and Munro, the reader feels much closer to the characters, much more comfortable in their society – as if the hostess, in introducing us to other guests, had made a special point of opening the channels to intimacy. Laurence smiles upon us and withdraws; Munro pulls up a chair and tells her stories too. The room is warm. To shift the metaphor, however, one last time, neither writer positions us snugly in a garrison. Margaret Laurence leads us out with a splendid battle cry: *Gainsay Who Dare!* And Alice Munro takes us skilfully, with numerous shifty dodges, through the underbrush of the text.

They are all extraordinary writers who have extended the parameters of our literature. And somehow, each of these three Canadian women writers causes me to believe that our shared topic is the fear of the open heart; each does this not only through her concern with this theme, but through the way she tells her story and where she stands in relation to it. I find, therefore, that I cannot deny my sense of 'knowing' the author through the text, and that a depersonalized account of the reading experience strikes me as a failure of the open heart.

Notes

1. Roland Barthes, 'The Death of the Author,' *Image, Music, Text*, Essays selected and translated by Stephen Heath (Glasgow: Fontana / Collins, 1977), 145.

2. *Ibid.*, 147, 148.

3. Mavis Gallant, *My Heart is Broken* (1957; New York: Random House, 1964), 138. All further references are to this edition and are cited parenthetically in the text (as *Heart*, if clarification is required).

4. Margaret Laurence, *The Stone Angel* (Toronto: McClelland and Stewart, 1968), 81. All further references are to this edition and are cited parenthetically in the text (as *Stone*, if clarification is required).

5. Alice Munro, *Who Do You Think You Are?* (Toronto: Macmillan, 1978), 76. All further references are to this edition and are cited parenthetically in the text (as *Who*, if clarification is required).

6. Margaret Laurence, *The Diviners* (Toronto: McClelland and Stewart, 1974), 134.

7. Mavis Gallant, 'Irina,' *From the Fifteenth District* (Toronto: Macmillan, 1973; rpt. 1979), 228.

8. *Ibid.*, 230.

9. Mavis Gallant, *Green Water, Green Sky* (Toronto: Macmillan, 1983), 69.

10. *Ibid.*, 154.

Waiting for a Final Explanation: Mavis Gallant's 'Irina'

'Irina' is the story of a Christmas day in Irina's old age, a day she passes in the company of Mr. Aiken, for whom at forty Irina had contemplated leaving her husband and children, and of Riri, the grandchild who has been thrust upon her to relieve the supposed depression of a Christmas spent without family. It uses, therefore, two familiar strategies of the short story: the central irony of situation (Riri's intrusion) around which the story can develop, and confinement of the action to a single day to achieve a story-like unity and compression. The day, of course, is designed and peopled in a way that permits the writer to show a whole life – as memory and Mr. Aiken take Irina back, as the idea of death and Riri's future move her forward. Amusingly, the fact that it is Christmas is almost irrelevant. Gallant uses it mainly to show Irina's resistance now to the sanctities of family life – thus does she slyly invert the usual purpose of such ritual days. There is no room for a tree in Irina's apartment, and no excuse made for its absence. Food and drink are supplied in plenty, but nothing of the Christmas ilk. The 'wrapped presents' for Irina that Riri has dutifully transported in his knapsack are never unwrapped or referred to again in our presence – a piece of tact I especially cherished. Instead, Riri (as the family's chief gift) enters and is absorbed and beguiled by the opposed domestic space that Irina occupies with Mr. Aiken: a kind of anti-Christmas, if you like.

And you *do* like it. The writer has made sure of that. Having announced Riri's visit in the first sentence, Gallant backs off to supply an introduction (roughly a third of the story's length) that whets our appetite for the feast ahead. In this space she establishes the conception of Irina maintained by her children: that she is the 'constant reflection' of their revered dead father, Richard Notte. To begin with, Gallant (like Irina's children) attends to *him*, which seems the right way to sketch a reflection. But her description of Notte, filtered through his children's gaze, is wonderfully, subtly barbed and moves us relentlessly into Irina's camp. Even the roll and sweep of Gallant's sentences in this section – so declarative, generalizing, and firm – seems to echo Notte's autocratic personality; but Gallant's ironic rhythm establishes also a counterweight (a female mastery) that *fixes* Notte and prepares us for his wife's ascendancy. Thus, when Gallant permits us finally to enter Irina's apartment, we are eager to confirm our faith that she is by right of

self-assertion the title character 'Irina,' and not the widow Notte (or nothing).
We are ready to delight in the 'anti-Christmas' of a woman who is at last on
her own ground.

We learn near the beginning of Part I that Notte, a Swiss writer, was
characterized in his obituaries as 'the last of a breed, the end of a Tolstoyan
line of moral lightning rods.' That description is instantly sabotaged on two
fronts as Gallant reminds us of the implications both for those writers who
come after him and for his children. Deftly, she makes us see how Notte
would have relished that definition, how the whole of his career was aimed at
that memorial: *après moi, le déluge.* '"What good is money, except to give
away?" he often said' – grandly sweeping aside the question of his family's
comfort, and ensuring that he would be seen as a kind of Tolstoy. He seems in
this posture – as in his 'crack-voiced' pronouncements of doom, his premature assumption of a venerable old age, and his hypochondria – to be clearing
the ground for his own death.

But what of Irina, who is twenty years younger and will surely survive
him? What can he do about that? He leaves what Gallant describes as 'a careful will for such an unworldly person.' In financial terms, Notte's will is
simple enough: 'His wife was to be secure in her lifetime. Upon her death the
residue of income from his work would be shared among the sons and daughters.' His 'careful will,' therefore, seems a reference to the motive of an
accompanying testament, 'which the children had photocopied for the
beauty of the handwriting and the charm of the text. Irina, it began, belonged
to a generation of women shielded from decisions, allowed to grow in the sun
and shade of male protection. This flower, his flower, he wrote, was to be
cherished now as if she were her children's child.' Irina was 'allowed' to grow
in a manner that seems designed to inhibit growth. Now that her protector is
gone, he transfers to his children the task of inhibition – fondly imagining
that what he has conceived as stasis will yield to retrogression.

In his last years, Notte was pampered by Irina as if he were 'a senile child';
the son who observed and despised this behaviour 'at the same time ... felt a
secret between the two, a mystery. He wondered then, but at no other time, if
the secret might not be Irina's invention and property.' We may assume that
Notte's testament – his assertion that *Irina* is a child – is a kind of revenge
against (and denial of) his own decline into second childhood, which Irina
apparently observed with some satisfaction. This last period of Notte's life
was fraught with the drama of encroaching death and his wife's incipient new
life. If the 'secret' of their competition were *his* 'property and invention,' Irina
would be (as the children have supposed her) innocent of any intention to
outlive him. She would simply, metaphorically, 'turn her face to the wall and
die'; she would at the very least accept the definition of Notte's testament
and resign herself to being 'her children's child.'

But she does not. The secret is hers. And it is two-fold: that *Notte* was always the child – because there were '"six children, counting him"' whom she could not leave – and that he has been unsuccessful in containing her potential for independent growth. During all the years of Notte's secret rapacity, his campaign against a world that might survive and forget him, Irina has maintained an identity and an intention her children never saw. She means now to live and do some further thinking of her own. The children would doubt her capacity to do this: they think, for instance, that journalists who refer to the widow's intelligence have been deceived. But they have never looked past Irina's beauty, never cared about 'her origins,' never bothered to think who she might be apart from Notte.

The pivotal moment in Part I comes just after the reading of Notte's will. Irina ignores the charm of his text and turns to the meat: '"In plain words," said Irina, ... "I am the heir."' In preference to the children, Irina now flatly chooses herself. It is a perfectly splendid moment. And our delight is a function of Gallant's previous restraint: only the discussion of a 'secret' has overtly suggested that we might view Irina as something other than Notte's 'constant reflection.' We guessed, of course – but could not reasonably have hoped for such a delicious, *materialistic* lifting of the veil! From this point on, the ironies are less discreet; but as Gallant never quite removes the chance that a reader will see no more than 'the children' do, we can continue to enjoy our perspicacity. The physical description of Irina when she has made her claim ('I am the heir') provides a measure of Gallant's increased willingness to reveal her character. It is really our first personal look at Irina: 'She was wearing dark glasses because her eyes were tired, and a tight hat. She looked tense and foreign.' We can still pass this by, explaining any strangeness by her grief. Or we can recognize that the dark glasses, an emblem of her disguise, shield Irina from the pressure of Notte's will; the glasses work both ways, for she has looked at Notte and been described by him for much too long. Her 'tight hat' and 'tense and foreign' look suggest the pressure of selfhood that is mounting in her head.

As 'Irina' now, she chooses first to subvert Notte's wish in the matter of his papers. He had consigned these to the care of his favourite daughter; but Irina seizes them, refusing to hand authority on to the next generation, and needing to arrive at her own opinion of their merit. We can (like the children) interpret this action as a sign of her continuing devotion, her effort to deny the loss of Notte; but her next action is harder to misread. Whereas Notte had always *rented* 'ramshackle houses,' Irina now *buys* a small apartment in a modern block of the type Notte would despise on principle. This 'tight, neutral flat' signals both her disavowal of Notte's ethic and a wish for privacy; but the children, who cannot imagine that the size of her flat is intentional, take turns at consoling and 'invading' her all the same. (The word 'invading' is another significant departure; Gallant is getting much closer now to Irina's point of view.) Even Irina's furniture, which is of a kind 'usually sold to young couples,' is a sign of her wish for a new independent life.

Yet the children persist in their misconception. When they hear 'a sudden April lightness in her letter,' they *know* that it must be a 'sham happiness' and that 'the crisis would come later.' Three years pass in which Irina works at Notte's journals. A visitor of unspecified gender comes to stay and has 'a depressing effect,' as it seems to the children – since they cannot otherwise account for a letter in which Irina suddenly denies the interest of the journals and the efficacy of all their father's moral warfare. This heresy, together with a letter in which Irina says that 'This Christmas I don't want to go anywhere. I intend to stay here, in my own home,' suggests to the children that the crisis of Irina's grief has come at last.

The reader is by this time attuned to Gallant's irony and convinced that Irina has simply voiced her true opinion of Notte and her exasperation at the supposed necessity of all this familial visiting. But the children, because of a fresh irony yet to be revealed, are also right: this 'person' in Irina's flat has indeed precipitated a crisis. Gallant's ironies proliferate around this figure of whom we know nothing more than the children do; his identity is an extension of Irina's 'secret' and a pleasing, admonitory sign that Mavis Gallant is always well ahead of her reader. Riri's visit is an intrusion especially because of Mr. Aiken's presence – so that the long arm of the family seems to be reaching out (again unconsciously) to place an obstacle between the lovers. And, finally, though it may take us a long time to see this, Riri's visit is (ironically) a good thing. He represents the third factor to be considered in the resolution of Irina's 'crisis,' which is the question of whether her own life has been well spent. Irina's task in this period is to determine if she was right to have stayed with Notte. If his work (the first factor) was necessary to the world, then perhaps she was right to have stayed. The reappearance of her lover (the second factor), just as Irina is winding up her negative assessment of Notte's life-work, suggests that on two counts she was wrong. But Riri, as the token child – who is, moreover (though he does not know it) threatened with the loss of his mother – recalls Irina's third consideration: the need to stay for her children's sake.

As Gallant approaches the end of Part I, she provides us with an important insight and a preparation for the story's close. Irina, we are told – as a sign of her measured fairness – has no favourites among her children; but to one son, because he knew something 'about death and dying,' she confides a longing for her own childhood. This statement apparently runs counter to Irina's resistance of the family's wish to see her as a child, and in fact contributes to their sense of the urgent need for Riri's visit. But it is explained by Irina in her letter: she yearns sometimes for childhood because she wants to 'avoid having to judge herself' and feels that 'now, in old age, she had no excuse for errors.' It is the explanation of a woman who is on the brink of deciding that her life course has been mistaken; who will not flinch from that assessment if it seems correct; who, at the same time, cannot make that judgement because 'whatever she saw and thought and attempted was still fluid and vague.' Irina's quest centres on the meaning of her own experience; but she defines that broadly, to include 'the shape of a table against afternoon light [that] still held a mystery, awaited a final explanation.' Thus she appears more subtle than her dogmatic husband, and thus we understand that an evaluation of Irina's life (and consciousness) cannot be reduced to the question of whether she should have left Notte for Aiken.

Part I concludes with a tricky piece of authorial wit, as the family decides that what Irina craves now is 'a symbol of innocent, continuing life. An animal might do it. Better still, a child.' The implicit hierarchy runs from adult to the intrusive animal to child, in reverse order for the occasion. This sideglancing, witty reduction of the child will be repeated soon in a speech of Irina's: '"If people can be given numbers, like marks in school, ... then children are zero."' Irina's point is not only that children are at the beginning of life, but that so far they are failing to understand it. With Gallant's entire approval, Irina implies also that she is herself working at an advanced level and deserves high marks.

The motif of the child, resounding in various ways through Part I, appropriately comes to rest with this decision by 'the children' to send their childmother a real child for Christmas. Gallant's toughness is wonderfully apparent in the very real child she supplies. Her 'symbol of innocent, continuing life' has, for example, secreted in his pocket 'a Waffen-S.S. emblem' – a symbol of the continuing potential for evil. Riri has learned from experience that he cannot display this publicly, in contrast to the 'R.A.F. badge on his jacket'; but he is still sufficiently indiscriminate (he would hide the R.A.F. badge with equal satisfaction if that were disallowed) and 'innocent' and ignorant of history that we do not really hold him accountable for this sin. He is a child, after all; and for all the self-confidence and spirit of independence that Gallant approves in him, he is still getting his history out of comic books. That he reads *Astérix*, a comic about barbarians for intelligent kids, suggests precisely the mix of mockery and respect that Gallant (like Irina) accords to this 'saviour' who comes for Christmas Day.

Part II of the story begins with the statement that 'Riri did not know that his mother would be in a hospital the minute his back was turned.' We feel both how annoyed he would be by this defection and how threatened; in a single stroke we have Riri's amusingly wary character and his symbolic role as the child who might have been harmed by Irina's departure long ago.

Following a description of the deal struck with his father to recompense Riri for this dull Christmas, and of his accompanying possessions and fiercely independent journey, Riri stands in the lobby of his grandmother's building before a directory which resembles 'the list of names of war dead in his school.' Gallant suggests by this detail that in the child's eyes Irina is already 'fallen,' and she places him in a lift (hinting at Irina's true elevation) to suggest that Riri regards himself as a rising character. In the elevator's mirror, he inspects his own 'dense, thoughtful' reflection with deep approval. With his glasses off, 'the blurred face became even more remarkable' – as the future, of which he is entirely ignorant, seems to bode as well for him as once it did for Irina. We associate them because of Riri's glasses, which recall a reference to Irina's poor eyesight and the dark glasses she wore at the reading of Notte's will. Indeed, we will come to view Riri as Irina's symbolic heir. Even his name, a diminutive of Richard for his grandfather, contains as well an echo of Irina's name. When at last he stands before her door, Riri is poised as we are for a revelation. His 'new sensation [has] to do with a shut, foreign door'; ours concerns a woman in a tight hat who looked 'tense and foreign,' and whom we have long been waiting to meet in *déshabille.*

The door opens a crack, to reveal Irina clutching at the neck of her dressing gown, and then is flung open. The warmth of her flustered greeting is made suspect by the manner in which Irina's fingers dance before her face; Riri has been taught that 'only liars cover their mouths.' But as the story proceeds, Irina and Riri get on remarkably well. There is funny, repeated play on the question of what he is allowed to do at home, with each displaying a characteristic stubbornness as to how these things will be managed in Irina's home. She asks him questions and states principles, but she does not nag; and sometimes, as when Riri supposes that she is anxious to supply him with fresh air, she does not much care (her real concern on that occasion is that Mr. Aiken should have a companion for his icy walk). She has enough distance simply to be amused, for instance, by the quantities of food that Riri can eat. As she observes his sturdy independence, her interest grows; but since it never becomes consuming, and since she carries on with her own life, Riri also becomes interested in her.

In short, their relation is charming and healthy. And there is a fascinating ambiguity in all of this, since we cannot know whether this was Irina's manner as a mother – which might suggest that she had a true vocation for maternity and was right to stay – or whether this is something new. If new, we might regard it simply as an instance of the satisfactory, relaxed relationships that often do occur between children and their grandparents; or we might hypothesize that Irina has repudiated the close mothering which once seemed a moral imperative to her. My own view is that all of these possibilities contain some truth, and that Gallant does not provide us with clear information on this point because she (like Irina) finds that much is 'still fluid and vague.' Gallant is also, I think, concerned to keep moot the general question of whether the Irina we see now is essentially Irina as she has always been. We are confident that she has grown, but less sure of how much growth occurred during her marriage to Notte and how much since his death. There has been some acceleration, of course. But we are left, as Irina is, with the question of whether she would have been better off, would have earned still higher 'marks,' if she had left Notte all those years ago.

We know that we like her now, which makes it equally difficult to regret her decisions and to accept her diminution as Notte's wife. The apartment in which Irina lives has a luminous quality that recalls the mystery of 'the shape of a table against afternoon light.' It seems a representation of Irina herself. What Riri at first regards as 'dark, mound-like objects' suitable for a mausoleum are lit and revealed as the furniture of the self when Irina on Christmas morning opens the draperies and shutters. One object in particular seems to cry out for interpretation: 'a painting of three tulips that must have fallen out of their vase. Behind them was a sky that was all black except for a rainbow.' We recall the image of Irina as Notte's flower, and may speculate that 'three' refers to the present occupants of the flat. Each has been cut off from some nourishment, a deprivation (of mother or lover) that is echoed by the black sky; but the rainbow suggests that a storm is past, and that rewards are here or imminent. For Riri, the shadow of his mother's danger will be removed by the story's close; in the case of Irina and Mr. Aiken, the renewal of friendship is a source of light. But the two stories are related, as these three flowers have fallen from the same vase, as the black sky and rainbow are related, so that still we cannot say whether Irina should have left Richard Notte.

Much of the conversation in Part II centres on Riri's new tape recorder, to which he turns almost immediately in order to practise his English and establish his distance. Gallant uses this to raise the issue of communication, of nationalism and internationalism. We receive the story in English and know that we are in a Swiss apartment; we have previously been informed that Notte wrote in German. But we have not known (or perhaps even considered) in which language the characters are speaking – and that realization jolts us, reminding us of a divisive potential. Now Irina asks Riri, '"What is your best language, by the way?"' and is taken aback by the 'hostility' of his reply: '"I *am* French"' [my italics]. This is the stuff of wars, recalling Riri's two military badges. Irina's sad comment to herself, '"So soon?,"' suggests that the process of discrimination (a choice between the Waffen-S.S. emblem and the R.A.F. badge) has in fact begun – but is revealing itself in a perennially stupid and destructive form. Irina's awareness of such complexity, and her preference for an easy multiplicity of tongues, provides us with a measure of her intelligence and liberal spirit.

Amused by Mr. Aiken's 'stiff French' and oblivious to the linguistic superiority of his elders, Riri proceeds sturdily with his English lesson. 'The swallow flew away with my hopes' is the text that Gallant supplies for Riri to
practise, and for the old people to employ in their coded, private discourse.
Riri takes the phrase through its permutations mechanically, a fact that is
underscored by his use of the machine, whereas Irina and Mr. Aiken are occupied with highly sophisticated levels of meaning. At the first of these levels,
the text suggests a poignancy that we and the aged lovers must associate
with death and the passing of time. The journey through various tenses
enforces this meaning. But a more particular application to their own case
seems probable in the light of information that Gallant withholds until Part
III: the hope of love that Irina dashed in choosing not to fly away with Mr.
Aiken.

That level of meaning is strengthened and complicated when Riri, 'as if
demonstrating to his grandmother how these things should be done,' chants
into his machine this variation: 'The swallows would not fly away if the season is fine.' Mr. Aiken is now provoked to ask, '"Do you know what any of it
means?"' The slight discourtesy of his question may be explained by the
child's mix of pride and ignorance, but a deeper source of irritation is the comment made by this text on Irina's decision to stay with Notte. Mr. Aiken (I
would suggest) is conscious of two possible and very disturbing applications:
either Irina's season with Notte was not 'fine,' in which case her refusal to fly
would seem perverse; or else she stayed because the season was fine enough –
because on balance, and for that season, it was right and natural to stay.
Irina's answer to Mr. Aiken, '"He just needs to know it by heart,"' is a defense
of Riri (and perhaps of herself) that can also be read as an ironic comment on
the rudimentary nature of his education, and perhaps of hers at the time of
the great decision. The word 'heart' is ambiguous. If she is acknowledging an
error, Irina implies that she acted by rote, in accordance with a law that
teaches woman not to abandon her family. If not, Irina implies that in staying
she followed the prompting of her heart. And this ambiguity within the code
suggests again that despite her very advanced level of understanding and
communication now, Irina does not have a single clear answer.

Gallant describes the tape recorder as 'the size of a glasses case' in order to
link the principal means by which we learn (seeing, hearing, speaking) and to
suggest that all our faculties are impaired. Part of the difficulty is that we necessarily approach any 'objective' question from the standpoint of our own
'subjective' experience. All the spectacles and machines in the world cannot
change that. This idea is sustained by three comments from Mr. Aiken.
'"Irina has an odd ear for times and trains,"' he remarks to Riri, apparently in
explanation of her surprise at the child's early arrival. But his covert reference is to the train on which (symbolically) Irina had declined to run away

with him, and to the temporal irony of their reunion now. Similarly, his claim
that '"Irina has an odd ear for English"' may refer to the language in which
his suit was urged and to the peculiarity of her response. But when Irina in
another room, hearing the old man describe to Riri the shakiness of his
hands, calls out that '"When you lift your glass to drink they don't shake,"'
Mr. Aiken is obliged to admit '"She's got an ear like a radar unit."' Irina goes
to the heart of the matter, as perhaps she did in the matter to which all their
discourse circles back. Yet she is poised here, as she was then, between three
aspects of the self: one ironic and oddly apart, another maternal in its concern, and a third attuned to her lover's every word.

Part III of the story gives us at last the story of Irina's decision, the information that we require in order to understand both the lovers' code and Gallant's elaborate and layered ironies. Recalling Mr. Aiken's description of '"an
ear like a radar unit,"' and acknowledging her faulty memory, Irina asserts:
'"But I know *that* day...."' And we know that we are approaching the story's
heart. The scene for this conversation has been carefully laid: 'They were
glassed in on the balcony. The only sound they could hear was of their own
voices.' Nothing will interfere now, it seems. Even the tree that Riri observes
below suggests that a great return, a great unburdening is at hand: 'A large,
spared spruce tree suddenly seemed to retract its branches and allow a great
weight of snow to slip off.' The years of their separation recede, as Riri withdraws: 'They heard him, indoors, starting all over: "Go, went, gone."'

The lovers' talk now is the centrepiece of the story and the most beautifully written part of all. As in a duet, they build a tableau of the day that must
have been their last together. Each corrects or denies details supplied by the
other, but the comedy of this does not diminish the lyricism of the scene.
They proceed as if in a trance, as if they cannot hear that they have disagreed,
for neither is willing to drop a stitch in the cloth they weave. Gallant, of
course, is sounding once more her ground-note: the differing conceptions and
misunderstandings that separate us over time. But in revealing the shared
intensity of the lovers' gaze she also joins them and gives them that day
again. They are 'starting all over,' as Riri is on his machine; and if the tale they
enter turns out to be the perennial one of '"Go, went, gone,"' it is also (for
now) an idyll out of time.

Their differing perceptions assume a pattern:

'The river was so sluggish, I remember. And the willows trailed in
the river.'
'Actually, there was a swift current after the spring rains.'
'But no wind. The clouds were heavy.'

'It was late in the afternoon,' he said. 'We sat on the grass.'

'On a raincoat. You had thought in the morning those clouds meant rain.'

'A young man drowned,' he said. 'Fell out of a boat. Funny, he didn't try to swim. So people kept saying.'

'We saw three firemen in gleaming metal helmets. They fished for him so languidly – the whole day was like that.'

Irina's picture emphasizes the sluggish, heavy, and languid, and so conveys both her wish to postpone the decision and her foreboding of what that decision would be. She wants to stop time, then and now, to shield herself (as with the raincoat) from the knowledge of her choice. Aiken recalls a swift current, the lateness of the hour, as if to urge their journey into the future together. And he ignores entirely Irina's reminder that he had seen that morning 'the clouds' of her refusal.

I think that Irina's answer must have come as they were sitting by the river. We are not told that. Instead, oddly, the image of a drowned man obtrudes in the tranquil scene. And they approach this memory without discord, each supplying details of a similar kind. Now both incline to drift and to postpone their recognition of the dénouement. If the man is drowned, their love is dead – and they do not want to seize its corpse. They proceed in the manner of the firemen with '"a grappling hook,"' hauling it up empty each time, passing the rope back and forth between them: '"They might have been after water-lilies, from the look of them."' As the firemen borrow a '"blue saucepan"' to bail out their boat, so Irina and Mr. Aiken 'borrow' that image, using it to return in memory to their lunch at the restaurant from which the incongruous, pretty saucepan came. It is an earlier and safer point in their day, so that again they may differ, this time in their recollections of the dessert. Aiken seems to imply that Irina left her pudding (left him perhaps) for no good reason, and she corrects him, flatly: '"It was soggy cake."' But if here she implies a defense of her ultimate decision, Irina is also ready to admit that the trout and the wine were '"perfection."' She is no more willing than Aiken to deny their love.

Throughout this scene, Gallant's accuracy and lightness of touch can take our breath away. The parallels are so exact that one cannot help analysis of the kind I have been offering, and at the same time so delicate that one feels (or I do) great reluctance to set them down. That tension in the reader reflects the tension in the scene, the knowledge of the day's outcome (or meaning) and the wish to hold it off. We are now returned from the restaurant to the riverbank and to another image of ineffectual rescue: a fireman on a '"*shaky* bicycle,"' carrying '"*frayed* rope"' [my italics]. The scene is complicated by '"holiday people"' who move from one side of a bridge to the other, just to watch '"the silence"' of the fisherman's boat as it '"slipped off down the river."' Waiting for a train, on which we may imagine Irina having been invited to run away with Aiken, these holiday people are (like the lovers) poised between a future and a death. As they cross over in the lovers' memory to the far side of the bridge, Aiken returns us to '"the silence here."'

The secret has *still* not been revealed; the silence of the glassed-in dream is still inviolate. But this silence, like the mood of holiday associated with their love, is broken as Riri's mechanical, workaday voice is heard again: '"Go, went, gone."' Irina breaks in, to correct an error Riri's mother had also made – and Mr. Aiken begins to weep. Irina has again chosen her family. Only now does Gallant permit Irina briefly to address the issue: '"How could I have left … six children, counting him."'

Part III of the story resumes, moving rapidly over the next few hours, and resuming strong scenic form only when Mr. Aiken has gone out for his walk. Thus, an extended, image-laden scene with Riri balances the scene on the balcony with Aiken. 'As if dreaming,' Irina decides to wash her amber necklaces. In effect, she 'tells' her beads and preserves memory, making the amber shine, as she and Aiken had done on the balcony – only now a part of her intention is to pass something along to Riri. The amber necklaces emerge from a wicker basket, containing two other boxes, a repetition that may cause us to recall the glassed-in balcony as a container of memories. Twice in this scene Riri is jolted – by his senses, the smell of turpentine and the sound of a clinking coin – into homesickness, his own memories. And throughout we feel a tension between Irina's reality and Riri's, moments of convergence and divergence that again recall the balcony scene.

At one point Irina shows Riri 'how to make the beads magnetic by rolling them in his palms.' She is telling him the value of memory, of handling one's past in full sensory detail. And he replies that '"You can do that with plastic, even"' – as if to deny such value. Irina, finding it sad that '"dead matter"' should have this power too, is informed by Riri that amber is also dead. This stops her. Yet her next remark is *à propos*: '"What do you want to be later on? A scientist?"' Irina assumes from Riri's violation of her subjective, poetic reality that he is aimed at relentless objectivity. His reply, however, that he means to be a ski instructor, informs us that Riri is simply committed to a splendid subjectivity of his own.

Irina's wish to pass something along to Riri is conveyed by her two gifts. The first is an amber necklace for his mother, which she permits him to choose. The necklace suggests a continuity between mother and daughter, for Irina tells him that '"Your mother will remember seeing this as I bent down to kiss her goodnight."' As Riri rubs the beads with a soft cloth to bring up their shine, we feel his connection with this female line; later we are told explicitly that 'his mother interested, his grandfather bored him.' The second gift is for Riri, and again Irina knows that he must choose it for himself. Significantly, she does not require that he take something from her past: they will go out to the shops next day if he does not see anything here to please him.

Riri's choice is postponed until the end of the story, but she shows him now two boxes: one containing 'old coins,' the other 'old cancelled stamps.' Both, that is, contain the past in a non-negotiable form that does not interest Riri. His eventual choice of the box that had contained the stamps, including 'A stamp with Hitler and one with an Italian king,' and his refusal of the stamps themselves, seems a clear repudiation of history – and foolish, until we reflect on the evils of that history. We may take this as a sign of hope for a child who treasured an S.S. emblem; we may even suppose that he declines a tradition of specifically *male* misrule.

Because he takes the box itself, a '"beautiful Russian box"' that had belonged to Irina's grandmother, he seems again to connect himself with the female line, and specifically with that Russian past in which Irina's own children (because they are obsessed with their father) have shown no interest. None of this is explicit or conscious; it simply resides in the imagery as a kind of counterweight to another set of details which may incline us to associate Riri with the male line.

Gallant directs our attention to this male line in a story that Irina tells immediately after showing Riri the Russian box. Irina had received at her mother's death-bed a valuable ring, to be preserved in secret since women '"were handed like parcels from their fathers to their husbands"' and then undone by '"the new owner."' Irina goes on to describe the appropriation of all her property by Richard Notte, and her attempt at last to sell the ring when she needed money badly – only to find that the real stones had been replaced by glass, obviously, says Irina, by '"someone's husband – mine or my mother's, or my mother's mother's."' Riri seems implicated in this line of interchangeable perfidious males, partly because he tries to absolve the husbands, partly because the change from jewel to glass recalls Riri's reduction of amber to the value of plastic. Riri, indisputably male, is also the '"new owner"' and despoiler (if you like) of Irina's most valued possession.

But again this is heavy-handed, and contradicted by our sense that Riri in the scene behaves quite pleasantly. We may think back to the balcony scene, the anguish of Irina's containment by Notte which explains part of her anti-male rage in this scene, and so recall that there is another man she has liked much better. Riri cannot easily, then, be cast into outer darkness by reason of his sex. Gallant directs us with great subtlety toward two opposing extremes: an identification of Riri with the male line, so that his appropriation of the box seems a violation of Irina, *and* an identification with the female line, so that it seems a validation of her. Beyond these explanations is the obvious one supplied by Riri himself: that he takes the box because '"the cover fits."'

This play between the infinitely subtle and the resoundingly blunt is *echt*-Gallant. She keeps us reeling, as we see in the case of Riri's ruthlessly deflationary remark. We can take it at face-value, or turn it in the direction of either extreme. He wants the box empty and closed. He means to shut her down, as suggested by the very peculiar (and, of course, entirely childlike) question that he asks just before she shows him the box: '"If you didn't live here, who would?"' We can read this as a kind of death warrant. Or, we may think that his question implies some instinctive concern that she should have a successor and an heir. This reading is supported by Irina's statement that '"after I have died I expect [the box] will be thrown out."' Riri's choice prevents this. Whatever degree of violation or validation may be implied in his choice, and however slight his consciousness of either, I think that we are finally (temporarily) reassured by the feeling that Irina's box is safe. The cover fits because for Riri this visit to his grandmother's flat – the 'box' containing *his* box containing her, at least on the box-rim of consciousness – has (like the child who dreams at the story's close) been laid almost comfortably to rest.

We can move rapidly over the rest of the story: the healing pleasantries of Mr. Aiken's return in Part IV, and the phone call announcing Riri's reprieve (the safety of his mother) in part V. When Riri is wakened in the night by the sound of the telephone, he sees again the 'mound shapes' that had disturbed him in the morning. But the danger passes by without his knowledge. Irina, settling him down again, promises Riri that he will sleep well. She takes him through the dreams that he will have, the container or shape of those dreams rather than their content, which she will not impose: '"short dreams at first, [that] by morning ... will be longer and longer."' In this description we sense again Irina's faith that as life goes on our knowledge must increase, our vision and our 'marks' improve. She has herself glimpsed the final stage: '"The last one of all before you wake up will be like a film"' in its panoramic sweep. But as she turns from the dream's achievement to reality, Irina knows that for now she must rely on daily resolutions. In describing the pleasant sounds that Riri can expect from Mr. Aiken in the morning, she tells herself as well that all three will be safe at least for another day.

Just before he goes off to sleep, Riri tells Irina that he wants the Russian box: 'He had taken, by instinct, the only object she wanted to keep.' Yet she is not shaken by this. She smiles down at Riri, 'knowing how sorry he would be to go and how soon he would leave her behind.' She does not impose herself: 'A doubled-up arm looked uncomfortable but Irina did not interfere; his sunken mind, his unconscious movements, had to be independent, of her or anyone, particularly of her.' I think this last phrase is a signal that Riri *if he is free* can be a spiritual heir for Irina. She will not bribe or bully him by loving Riri 'more or less than any of her grandchildren.' She knows too that the cover (recalled perhaps by the feather quilt in which he sleeps and dreams) will not always fit: 'Anything can be settled for a few days at a time, though not for longer.'

This is the sentence that resolves – so far as it can be resolved – Irina's long debate. She has brought into a kind of harmony her affection for Aiken and her maternal sense; she has been true to herself and the complexity of her experience. She has not answered the question of whether she ought to have left Richard Notte all those years ago, yet she seems content. The measure of her wisdom is that she does not expect in life 'a final explanation.' She can allow the 'mystery' that Mavis Gallant projects – beyond Irina's vision – through the final image of her story.

Gallant ends, lyrically, with a statement that Riri's mind, 'at that moment, in a sunny icicle brightness, was not only skiing but flying.' Riri's flight may recall the swallows that flew away with hope, and his dreamscape may be evocative of death, yet Gallant's final image is clearly and beautifully affirmative. We feel that Riri skis for his elders too, and skis expertly, precisely because he skis alone in a dream of his own choice. The application to Irina is established equally by her awareness of the shape his dreams would take and by her refusal to disturb them. Even Mr. Aiken skis freely through Riri, as on his solitary walk (the journey on which Riri had declined to accompany him) Mr. Aiken's walking stick had looked to the child 'something like a ski pole.' Riri had not expected to find the skiing good, had not even brought his skis. Yet the story ends with this extraordinarily satisfying image of Riri on skis: as if instructed by his spiritual elders, the child travels in a 'sunny icicle brightness' that reconciles his life goal of independence and their journey into the clarity of death.

Munro's Food

I like to read cookbooks (and almost every other kind of book) in bed. I am an enthusiastic eater, and my memory is generally not good. Yet I remember food, countless meals I've prepared or consumed, and countless others whose calorie count was blessedly nil since they were served to me in print. Those textual comestibles I remember best, however, are not from *The Silver Palate* or *The New York Times Cookbook*, but the foods served up in fiction.

Sometimes I am grateful for my poor memory: it means, for instance, that I can read Jane Austen all over again every few years without remembering the plots. Food, though, *sticks*. I will get the strangest presentiments, as I'm reading along in a novel or short story I've read before: I will know that when I turn the page, tuna-fish sandwiches, let us say – with dubious relish, but plentiful mayonnaise – will be there on the page, the bread still fresh (or stale, if that was the writer's point). Mrs. Ramsay's *boeuf en daube* will of course still be warm; I'm sure that most of us remember that, from Virginia Woolf's *To the Lighthouse*. But the bay leaves lurking in her sauce? I would hazard a guess that not everyone remembers that culinary detail.

I rehearse these pecadillos here in order to give fair warning. You may conclude when I've had my say that the claims I am making for a language of food in the fiction of Alice Munro – a kind of gustatory, alimentary discourse – proceed unreasonably from the critic's idiosyncratic vision or her unruly appetite. I wouldn't say so myself. I think that most of what I shall be saying will be obvious, honest meat-and-potatoes fare – which is not to say that Alice Munro does not herself cook up some very fancy stuff.

Virginia Woolf remarks in *A Room of One's Own* that novelists 'seldom spare a word for what was eaten. It is part of the novelist's convention not to mention soup and salmon and ducklings, as if soup and salmon and ducklings were of no importance ...' (16). It is a convention that Woolf herself delights in violating, as she goes about the business of establishing a female tradition. I'm not sure that she is right, incidentally: it seems to me (disqualified as I may be by the avidity of my gaze) that there is quite a lot of food in fiction, even male fiction, and that it has been there for some time. Certainly it is abundant in French fiction, with the rise of the bourgeois novel in the nineteenth century – and it is there with manifest purpose. It is there because

41

food *meant* so much, and so many different things, in the society depicted by those novels. Similarly, food is especially prevalent in fiction by women because it figures so prominently, and with such a vast range of implication, in what Munro calls the lives of girls and women.

Females, that is to say, do much more than their share of the world's cooking. That circumstance, though it may keep her too long in the kitchen, is wonderfully useful to the woman writer when she enters a room of her own and takes up fiction. She is likely to have available for use considerable expertise in the *language* of food. I mean, of course, a symbolic language rather than a simply referential, esoteric list of terms like *roux* or bundt pan. She knows that a plate of scrambled eggs, presented in a particular way – under, over, or perfectly done, in concert with or long before the toast – can express quite eloquently (whether the message is read or not) the cook's own disposition, perhaps especially *vis à vis* the recipient of the eggs. This is an enormously complex language, and particularly well-suited for use in fiction because it often *looks* so innocent. Assume, for example, that it's breakfast time: lots of other things are going on, and the eggs on the table or on the page are simply eggs. So it seems. The beauty of the thing is that these fictional / factual eggs *look* so natural; you can offer them up with a straight face, and let the reader get on with the process of decoding the message, or not – just as he likes. If he wants to, or if that's all he's capable of doing, the dullard can simply bolt your eggs and run.

Writers – particularly writers like Alice Munro – love this kind of thing and rely on it. They are infamously sneaky and always on the lookout for ways to say a thing without *seeming* to say it. Thus do they escape the ignominy of the obvious. Occasionally, of course, they may want to run naked through the streets (for variety's sake), and the language of food allows that too. It can scream as well as whisper. It can do anything. Consider, for instance, how conspicuous that platter of scrambled eggs would seem if it were served as *dessert* at an embassy dinner.

The language of food, like any other sort of language, I suppose, has what might be described as two levels: one that we hold in common, and another that is particular to the user. We might call that a personal dialect. Before I turn to Munro's particular case, though – her dialect within food's mother tongue – I want to sketch some of the obvious symbolic potential of food for anybody's fiction. All of this and a good deal more is actualized in Munro's fictional practice.

I begin with the idea of hunger or appetite – desire for something, caused by the lack of it. This I take to be an instance of the *gap* which has attracted the interest of so many contemporary theorists. The desire for food translates with ease to other appetites, most notably perhaps the sexual and metaphysical. As in the case of these other appetites, the gap may seem to close temporarily; always, it reasserts itself. The wrong foods may be desired and consumed, or the right ones sought and never found. Excess may lead to revulsion, so that desire shoots off in another direction. Persistent, absolute frustration of desire will cause the organism to starve.

Food is to varying degrees frivolous *and* a dire necessity; the writer may emphasize either end of this spectrum, or make use of persistent ambiguity. Food can speak to the bliss of elaboration, luxury, decoration, novelty, entertainment, and so on – or to the guilt associated with decadence. It has gustatory and alimentary dimensions. We live to eat, or eat to live. We eat in order to have strength to work, or work in order to purchase pleasure. In any case, our pleasures pass – both in the short view and in the long. Food is fuel for a dying animal; food includes animals already dead. It decays, as we do. Food speaks of death, therefore, as eloquently as it speaks of life.

Eating is sacred, because it signifies the incorporation of the other – which must be hallowed where it is not taboo. I invite you to think of Holy Communion and of cannibalism, or to consider Eve. She eats the apple in order to gain knowledge of the world; this can be either a very bad or a very good thing – paradise lost in the orthodox version, power very laudably (if perilously) assumed in the feminist revision of the tale. To eat is also to converse, to engage in a dialogue with the world; thus Satan is positioned at the human creature's ear.

The act of eating is for Freud an archetype of intercourse, understandably enough; contact between self and other, orality and sexuality begin with the infant sucking at its mother's breast. I'm not going to pursue that line of inquiry, except to note the obvious fact that eating is an intimate bodily practice, a transaction carried out (most often) in the company of other people. It is in the first instance a trope for *social* intercourse. Eating is useful to the writer because in life it brings people together, both literally and symbolically. Tension between individuals or the easing of tension can be dramatized round a table, where it is measured implicitly against an ideal of communion. To show a character eating *alone* is to shadow forth that same ideal.

Food has to *get* to the table, of course. Someone has to grow or catch or buy it; someone has to prepare it. Issues of power and gender relations are clamouring here, for articulation through the language of food; but I shall set them aside – together with much else of latent symbolic value in the mother tongue – in order to leave room on the plate for Alice Munro's actual stories. In those stories, of course, Munro also uses food to perform a thousand local feats of characterization – as, for example, when she has Kimberly carry the vegetables to the table in 'Labor Day Dinner' (Kimberly is sternly Christian, a discordant presence at this pagan feast), or when Peter in 'White Dump' carries his own breakfast to the table (dry cereal with honey) instead of some part of the hot breakfast everyone else will share.

I'm going to start with a crudely coloured account of what I take to be Munro's most accustomed psychological terrain. The young Munro heroine has a voracious appetite for life: she wants it all. She wants to *be* it all. Yet she is restrained in her outlandish ambitions by a number of factors, including fear of exposure as a vain and greedy girl. All around her are warnings. If she 'eats' too much, or too pretentiously, if she claims a preference for exotic foods (like half a grapefruit), if she expands too far into knowledge of the world – she'll get killed for her presumption. The body grows at its peril, because anti-life forces are at work in our society, and because we die in any case. She is torn between a fondness for the body and a fear that it will betray her, partly by distracting her from other serious business (like her art), partly because love is unreliable. As the heroine grows older, she learns to cope with the alternating rhythms of her life – the demands of body and mind, for instance, or the need to take care and the need to take risks. She holds on to a wry but still essentially heroic conception of the self. She eats and is eaten by the world; her *job* is to watch what she's doing, and to answer as honestly as she can the ubiquitous question 'Who do you think you are?'

Interestingly, the relationship between food and death is suggested most powerfully in stories about children. Initiation involves a recognition that death is the final stage of life, of biological processes that begin with birth and are maintained through feeding, digestion and excretion. In the face of death, however, what the children observe is a remarkable rush for *more food*. In 'Heirs of the Living Body,' Del sees food everywhere she looks; this altogether customary funereal abundance marks a reliance upon convention, through which Del's aunts have always kept dangerous emotions at bay. Behind that convention, as Aunt Moira remarks, is the knowledge that 'they all bring their appetites to funerals' (*Lives* 44). People come together and eat in order to affirm their own enduring vitality, the on-goingness of their lives. Yet food – the language through which they affirm life – carries a strong counter-message of the drift toward death. Del's mother, with her brave, unwelcome news about a future in which body parts may become exchangeable, insists upon the physicality of life; unwittingly, Del's conventional aunts (the genteel antagonists of her mother) signal the same truth with the feast prepared for Uncle Craig's funeral.

Del is afraid to view the body. Her cousin Mary Agnes also frightens Del, and in a parallel way; her arrested mental development is another kind of cautionary tale. When Mary Agnes tries to force Del to see Uncle Craig, and so effectively to admit her own limitations, Del bites her arm. Tasting the blood of her kin seems to Del so unforgivable as to offer her a way out of the human family. But there *is* no way out; and soon Del is sitting like an invalid with a blanket over her knees, with strangely adult tea and cake – her share of the funereal communion. She has a kind of vision then of physical shame: 'to be made of flesh,' she thinks, is 'humiliation' (48). Helplessness is revealed to Del 'as the most obscene thing there could be.' Earlier, hearing of a sexual exposure suffered by Mary Agnes, she had thought of naked buttocks as 'the most shameful, helpless-looking part of anybody's body' (36). Later, she recalls her aunts' strategy for masking bathroom smells. But now she sees the larger picture; the body, 'anybody's body,' for all our artful dodges, ends in waste. Death cannot be avoided, so Del goes forth to view the body after all.

'Heirs of the Living Body' concludes with the aunts giving Del her uncle's manuscript – a colourless, repetitive history of the county – which they hope she will complete, since she has a talent for composition; and they give it to her in a black metal box, as if to protect Uncle Craig's brain-child from decay. Brains, however, are not exchangeable parts. She will obviously not complete the history; she will not even risk the contagion of Uncle Craig's dullness. And so when she wants to put her own manuscripts in the black box for safe-keeping, she takes his to a cardboard box in the cellar – where, like Uncle Craig himself, eventually it dissolves. The point I am making here is that Del means to beat death with her own inimitable brain; with reckless *fiction*, she will oppose the history of her race – a history like Uncle Craig's of death and interchangeable parts.

Thus, 'Heirs of the Living Body' ends on a defiant note after all, and points beyond the text to the 'living body' of Munro's own work. Ironically, that work reflects the gift that Del's aunts ascribe to Craig: 'He could get everything in and still make it read smooth' (52). Equally, it rises to Del's own fierce standard: 'They were talking to somebody who believed that the only duty of the writer is to produce a masterpiece.' The two sides of the Alice Munro persona are clearly articulated here: the *exceptional* death-defying Alice, and the modest all-inclusive one. (I have, admittedly, drifted away from *food* in this discussion. My excuse is that food is just one part of the living body of the text and that, as Del's mother says, the *combination* of elements is what's remarkable.)

In 'Princess Ida' – which is the next story or chapter in *Lives of Girls and Women* – Del is exposed to the death of another uncle. Again we see the rush for food, as Uncle Bill (dying of cancer) buys a carload of treats, ostensibly for the family, in fact to stuff himself with life. (In the same spirit, he has bought a shiny, death-glittering young wife called Nile; sex and food point to the same grim conclusion.) Her uncle's 'idiot largesse' (72) in the bake shop reminds Del of a story 'in which a little girl manages to get her wishes granted ... and they all turn out, of course, to make her miserable' (71). One of the girl's wishes is to have 'everything she had ever wanted to eat' – and Del (I was pleased to discover) has read the description of the food over and over again, 'for pure pleasure.' Now Uncle Bill's cancer makes her wary; it seems a fairytale punishment 'inflicted by supernatural powers always on the lookout for greed.' Even Del's mother remarks that 'maybe with less eating he would have lived to be old' (75) – and Del reflects that 'too much might really be too much' (71).

Uncle Bill claims that his 'sweet tooth has never gone sour' (72) – but the stink of death and a mistaken life is all around him. Del calls him, with an irony he does not hear, her 'fairy godfather'; and the question, obviously, is whether the life of sweets he would thrust upon her can be trusted. Del is attracted to a vision of plenty, but she lives in a society which has taught her to be suspicious of it. One of her essential tasks will be to sort out how much of appetite-regulation is grudging and puritanical, and how much is really necessary.

The figure of Uncle Bill as fairy-godfather calls up a number of other Munro stories in which adults offering food to children are regarded as potential killers. In 'Half a Grapefruit,' for example, Flo tells Rose a story from her own childhood, about a woman reputed to have psychic powers who had offered Flo what she believed was poisoned cake. That she feels obliged to eat the cake suggests both the awesome power of adult figures and the inescapability of death. But the threat is romantic, as Flo waits 'in a gradually reduced state of terror, it must have been, and exultation, and desire, to see how death would slice the day' (Who, 53). In something of the same state of curiosity, Del's mother had as a child eaten cucumbers and milk because she believed the combination was poisonous and would get her into heaven.

In a story called 'Images,' this motif becomes more complex – as the narrator, who compares herself to 'the children in fairy tales' (Dance, 43), discovers a less glamorous kind of poison in food prepared by a nurse who has seemed to 'let her power loose in the house' (32); the taste of death, however, merging with the taste of helplessness, is now described as 'something foreign, gritty, depressing.' In 'Images,' death becomes real; and the witch is revealed as an ordinary mortal who lacks control over the operations of life and death. Adults, once seen as all-powerful and reliable caretakers, become magically wicked when news of death is first considered by the child; the poisoner is then demystified, his power gone. When the adult is seen as helpless in the face of death, the child moves closer to an understanding of her own mortality.

In 'Providence,' Rose's daughter invents a more promising fairy story. Anna endows each of her princesses with a particular colour, and then gives them foods of the same colour; thus, for example, the white princess gets 'mashed potatoes, vanilla ice cream, shredded coconut and meringue off the tops of pies' (Who, 144), while the blue princess dines on 'grapes and ink.' (This, of course, is a clear instance of characterization through food, indicative of Anna's grasp of the fictional principle that we are what we eat.) But it is the brown princess who interests me most especially: 'though drably dressed

[she] feasted better than anybody; she has roast beef and gravy and chocolate cake with icing, also chocolate ice cream with chocolate fudge sauce.' Moreover, while the brown princess is not assigned a colour-coded flower, she is allowed to shit; the '"rude things"' in her garden may therefore serve as fertilizer for the lilies, narcissi, and roses of the other princesses. The diet Anna gives to each princess is comically unbalanced, but the brown princess suggests that Anna is moving toward a common, very realistic ground.

The white princess, by the way, reminds me of Char in 'Something I've Been Meaning to Tell You' – who would be appalled by the hearty calorie-load and world-view of the brown princess. Char's ideal world is bathed in a white light; her lover, Blaikie Noble, has hair 'bleached by the sun' (Something, 6), wears 'a creamy suit' (4), and is compared by Char's sister to 'a vanilla ice cream cone.' When the real world disappoints her, Char turns to blueing and bleach, whiteners and purgatives; she wants to remove herself from a gross physical world. Yet because she is human, after all, lovely, ethereal Char is described as having 'inherited the tendency' (15) to become heavy. Her ambivalence (desire and revulsion) is reflected in the eating binges which alternate with her violent fasts. But this is only a mockery of the regulated appetite. In the end, Char loses all colour and effectively poisons herself through abstinence; her life-denying asceticism is as debilitating to body and spirit as was the gluttony of Del's Uncle Bill.

Food is often used as a bribe in Munro's fiction, to ensnare rebellious characters, and lure them into compromising behaviours sanctioned by the family and the community. In their duplicity, such foods are poisonous; they function like Eve's apple in reverse, to keep her safely in the garden. Rose, for example, in 'Royal Beatings,' is determined not to forgive the offense she has suffered; then, insidiously, Flo slips her a tray of good things to eat. And Rose is 'roused and troubled and drawn back ... [into family life] by the smell of salmon, the anticipation of crisp chocolate' (Who, 19). In 'Who Do You Think You Are?', Miss Hattie recalls converting Chinese heathens by feeding them what she regards as 'a better diet.' In a similar way, she and her sister curb the equally heathen, 'ferocious gifts and terrible energy' (192) of their antic nephew Milton Homer by stuffing his mouth full of candy.

Food is associated with home, and the feeling of being cared for or neglected, as we might expect. Literal starvation is no more chilling than the emotional sort. And homes can fail. Thus, the two daughters in 'The Peace of Utrecht' offer cold comfort to their ailing mother and take 'all [genuine] emotion away from ... [their] dealings with her, as you might take meat away from a prisoner to weaken him, till he died' (Dance, 199). Significantly, the mother is depleted by their lack of anger no less than by an absence of tenderness; she is made unreal when deprived of any kind of emotional food. In 'The Beggar Maid,' Rose finds that 'there was never enough to eat' (Who, 67) in Dr.

Henshawe's house, and the young boarders in 'The Moon in the Orange Street Skating Rink' are always ravenous; in both stories, Munro is establishing the sense of alienation and anxiety that attends removal from the family home. Now they are just boarders; now, perhaps, the supply of food will fail. These young people are eating madly, furtively – in order not to disappear.

In the last two stories I have named – 'The Beggar Maid' and 'The Moon in the Orange Street Skating Rink' – the ferocious appetites of the young people point in another direction as well: toward sex, of course. Like Del in 'Baptizing,' they are hungry for it. Thus, in 'Baptizing,' when Del is stirred physically by the 'throbbing glory' (*Lives*, 153) of opera, she converts her lust to another appetite. 'Opera made me hungry,' Del says. And so she eats 'fried egg sandwiches, stacks of soda crackers held together with honey and peanut butter,' and compares this to masturbating; both activities make her feel 'gloomy.' I would ask you, however, to consider *what* she eats: the wishful two-ness of a sandwich, or soda crackers held together with sweet and sticky fillings.

Rose, in 'The Beggar Maid,' does acquire a lover – the inappropriate Patrick. As the time of their first lovemaking draws near, Rose finds herself overwhelmed by a craving for sweets: 'Often in class or in the middle of a movie she started thinking about fudge cupcakes, brownies, some kind of cake Dr. Henshawe bought at the European Bakery; it was filled with dollops of rich bitter chocolate, that ran out on the plate. Whenever she tried to think about herself and Patrick, whenever she made up her mind to decide what she really felt, these cravings intervened' (*Who*, 80). This unremittingly chocolate list of foods may suggest that Rose is kin to the brown princess. It suggests too that what she's getting into will eventually make her sick; *and* it allows us to suppose that Patrick, whom she has called the 'White God' (78), is not really 'chocolate' enough for the earthy Rose.

As the Munro heroine ages, she continues to be very much interested in sexual pleasure and to think of it in terms of food. In 'Bardon Bus,' for example, we are told that 'the room is brimming with gratitude and pleasure, a rich broth of love, a golden twilight of life … you can drink the air' (*Moons*, 124). In 'Providence' and 'Simon's Luck,' Rose prepares for the arrival of her lover by laying in such luxurious provisions as 'that good bitter marmelade in the stone jar' (*Who*, 145) or real cream and crabmeat. This is the language of what she hopes will be shared gifts. But she is often disappointed. When Simon fails to reappear, Rose takes off – and leaves the Camembert she had bought 'still weeping on the kitchen counter' (168). Interestingly, the images that inform Rose of her recovery from obsessive love are 'coffee-pots and the bright, probably stale pieces of lemon and raspberry pie, the thick glass dishes they put ice-cream or jello in' (170). She can *see* these things again, these ordinary things, with a writer's eye; she has returned, that is to say, to her other primary form of nourishment – her other way of communing with the other.

The poet Lydia, in a story called 'Dulse,' is also trying to cope with the pain of a lost love. Rather than 'committing suicide' (*Moons*, 42), she makes 'efforts, one after the other' (36). She sets 'little blocks on top of one another and she [has] a day.' Each ordinary chore, such as remembering that 'she had to buy some food' (41), becomes a battle against inertia and despair in which she is only partly victorious. It amazes her 'to think that she had chosen the loaf of bread and the cheese, which were now lying on the floor in the hall. How had she imagined that she was going to chew and swallow them?' (42). Lydia too takes off, for a New Brunswick guest house – and there encounters other people, who are also trying to proceed with their lives: the proprietor, who might spend eighteen hours a day in an endless round of cooking and baking, or the elderly guest who eats 'in a very deliberate way, giving the impression that the order in which he lifted forkfuls of food to his lips was not haphazard, there was a reason for the turnip to follow the potatoes, and for the deep-fried scallops, which were not large, to be cut neatly in half' (38). Food here expresses the courage – even the gallantry – of human beings; it takes them through.

The most interesting image of food in this story, however, is the title image. There are three labourers at the guest house, and Lydia has fantasies about the probable flavours of sex with each. Vincent, one of these men, supplies the group with dulse, 'a kind of seaweed, greenish-brown, salty and fishy-tasting' (47), which he claims is 'good for you.' This dulse, I would suggest, tastes of sex. As the story nears its close, the men are gone and Lydia has not in fact slept with any of them. She appears almost to have sworn off men, whom she must propitiate and by whom she is repeatedly let down. She has reacted with anger to the old man's doting story about Willa Cather, who would return a dinner if she was not pleased by it; Lydia thinks that Cather (a writer, of course, and a lesbian) can be 'imperious' (57) because 'she never lived with a man.'

But the story ends with the proprietor – who has herself moved on to a new, more satisfactory man – telling Lydia that Vincent has left her a present of dulse. And we are told that 'this present slyly warmed her, from a distance' (59); thus we know that in time another man bearing strange gifts will appear on Lydia's horizon. Despite herself, and whether it is good for her or not, she has learned to like the taste of dulse. How this taste will combine with the requirements of her art is another question, one that the story addresses briefly through Lydia's musings on the case of Willa Cather. She wonders if sex would be any easier with a woman; she wonders too if the old man would say that Willa Cather 'did not have to find a way to live, as other people did, that she was Willa Cather' (58). In any case, Lydia knows that her own taste is for men – and that writers, like other people, do have to find a way to live. Like other people, they are 'up and down' (59); like others, they are dependent on the tides.

Love is work. As Lydia says, 'you have to invent it, and re-invent it, and

never know if these efforts are enough' (52). 'Lichen' is another story that
reveals partly through images of food preparation the efforts women make to
have a significant life in the face of disappointments. Stella is a divorced
woman whose former husband, David, is now preparing to cast off yet
another woman. All of Stella's efforts with David were not enough, and now
she has reinvented a life – of meals and friends and work – into which David
periodically descends, as if to remind her of sexual failure.

David is embarrassed by Stella's corpulence, which seems even now to
reflect poorly on his sexual taste. At the same time, he idealizes her in a
favourite image from their marriage: Stella with 'sunlit hair' (*Progress*, 53)
carrying a casserole, and looking 'not half so fat as now.' She cries out 'greet-
ings to her neighbors, laughing, protesting about some cooking misadven-
ture. Of course the food she brought would be wonderful, and she brought not
only the food but the whole longed-for spirit of the neighborhood party.'
David, however, has chosen to forsake this wholesome guiding light – who,
incidentally, is currently doing research on an old lighthouse.

He shows Stella a picture of the girl he is salivating over now – the focal
point of which is her pubic hair; and Stella pretends it's lichen, thinking to
herself that really it looks more like the 'dark silky pelt of some unlucky
rodent' (42). At a seemly distance from this image, we learn that the woman
in the picture had once – squeamishly, as she thought – lost a part in a movie
because she didn't want 'a tame rat between her legs' (49). Now, of course, she
has taken on the rat and been immortalized as dead meat by the camera after
all.

The woman David has brought on this occasion to Stella's house, to whom
he will soon give the '"big chop"' (43), is beginning to sense her doom. '"You
know, there's a smell women get"' (40), David remarks complacently, as
Stella prepares the roast. '"It's when they know you don't want them
anymore. Stale."' Stella's response to this is signalled when she 'slaps the
meat over,' and begins to speak of '"groins [that] are going to have to be
rewired entirely"' because the forces of nature have '"worn them to cob-
webs."' Worn-out meat, particularly meat that has aged too visibly: this is
exactly what David (who has taken to dyeing his own hair) wants to avoid in
women. He'll give them the '"big chop"' – turn flesh into meat – rather than
acknowledge his own aging.

Despite the order of her life, the pleasure she takes in such things as 'a
good fish soup ... simmering on the stove' (55), Stella is revealed as vulnerable
to despair; she is threatened by 'the old cavity opening up in her' – appetite,
grief at the loss of love, her coming death – and experiences 'a pause, a lost
heartbeat, a harsh little break in the flow of days and nights as she keeps
them going.' Stella herself is in fact very like the 'lichen' in the photograph,
which has gone gray in the harsh sunlight to which David has exposed it; like

the lichen, she is 'a plant mysteriously nourished on the rocks.' Stella feeds herself, as she feeds others – gallantly holding on, dealing as well as she can with the 'old cavity' that continues to open and in which finally she too will dissolve.

The feeding of others is a common event in Munro's female-centred fiction. Often it suggests the woman's sense of obligation and her feelings of guilt. Thus, Rose in 'Providence' 'would think there was something disastrously wrong, when she saw Anna in front of the television set eating Captain Crunch, at the very hour when families everywhere were gathered at kitchen or dining-room tables, preparing to eat and quarrel and amuse and torment each other. So she got a chicken, she made a thick golden soup with vegetables and barley. Anna wanted Captain Crunch instead' (Who, 140-141). Good nutrition stands for ideal functioning in family life, and woman's traditional responsibility for that feat; Munro typically manipulates such images with a mix of irony and nostalgia.

'Labor Day Dinner' is a story concerned largely with the desperate attempts women make to please men, their endless accommodation, and delicate maneuverings. All that labour occasionally succeeds; the cloud of discord, perhaps by miracle, will sometimes lift – and a group of human beings will feel secure; remote from 'this and that disaster … they [will] sit, all healthy, relatively sane, with a lovely dinner and lovely wine inside them, in the beautiful, undestroyed countryside' (Moons, 157). Such moments of reprieve, however, occur in the context of habitual effort, as even the title of this story – 'Labor Day Dinner' – suggests. As in the famous dinner-party scene in To the Lighthouse, harmony will sometimes be achieved; it may appear – even to those who have knocked themselves out to make it possible – a kind of happy accident, for it can always fail; and in time, of course, it will.

Munro signals this at her story's close, when several of the characters, driving home from the candle-lit dinner, are nearly wiped out by a black car with its lights out. These characters are threatened by the abiding fact of their mortality, but they are threatened also by discord within the family. At the beginning of the story this double threat is imaged by a raspberry bombe, the 'pretentious concoction' (138) – a dream of bliss – that Roberta brings to the feast: 'She has packed it in ice cubes and wrapped it in dish towels, but she is eager to get it into the freezer.' The bombe could melt; we can almost hear it ticking away.

'White Dump' is another story structured by meals in which the family is at risk. The unreliable family stove is an image of the threat which hovers over the family. At first, the stove is associated with Sophie, who is considered by her grown son to be an unsatisfactory cook and an unsatisfactory mother. Because she refuses to fix the oven, she turns out 'hard roast potatoes, cakes raw in the middle, chicken bloody at the bone' (Progress, 279). Her womb (it would seem) is from the male perspective faulty, and her breasts have also come up short; Laurence has had to 'push and pull at Sophie, and no matter what he got out of her it would never be enough' (290). The essence of her fault is that Sophie, an Old Norse scholar and a socialist, has cared too much about other things. Her daughter-in-law Isabel fails Laurence in another way.

Although she has worked hard to become a good cook and has cared for Laurence 'by clever and constant exertions' (304), Isabel too betrays him with her body. She strives on the top of the stove to devise a satisfactory dinner for Laurence's birthday; underneath (as it were) she sets in motion an affair that will end the marriage. One of Laurence's presents is an airplane ride; the pilot is the man with whom Isabel will have her affair, and the pilot's wife is coincidentally the 'caterer' who makes the birthday cake. As caterer, this woman – who likewise caters to her pilot husband, in the sense that she tolerates his infidelity – must compensate for Isabel's inadequate stove. (Another woman makes Laurence's *birthday* cake in her oven, as Isabel prepares to take her unsatisfactory *womb* – her oven, if you will – elsewhere.)

The title image of 'White Dump' returns us to the notion of poisonous sweets. From the plane, Laurence had seen a silica quarry, which Sophie identifies as the source of that tacky, '"pretentious stuff"' (306) called '"white marble"' that is used on paths in Aubreyville; earlier, in fact, we have seen this ersatz stuff in the Aubreyville neighborhood of the catering woman. This is also, of course, the pilot's home – so that on two counts we may identify the white dump with the pilot. Isabel herself introduces the term white dump, recalling how when she was a child the local biscuit factory would occasionally dump a mountain of white icing in the yard, and how it seemed to Isabel and the other children who swarmed there '"the most wonderful promising thing"' (306). Isabel points out in an aside that it must have been terrible for their teeth. In a particularly tricky piece of business, Alice Munro has Isabel offer the dentist in Aubrey ville as an excuse for one of her meetings with the pilot. We are not surprised, therefore, that the affair – like the white sugar dump of Isabel's childhood – leads to decay. (It ends Isabel's marriage and becomes sordid in itself; '"the only pure part"' (308) of an affair, Isabel remarks much later to her daughter, is '"at the beginning ... just when it flashes on you what's possible."')

I want to conclude with one more helping of dessert, from the story called 'Spelling.' Rose has come back to Hanratty, to preside over Flo's removal to the County Home. And Flo is resistant. When Rose describes to her the meals that are served in the Home, Flo asks – suspiciously, but with a hint of weakening – '"What was for dessert?"' (*Who*, 182). Rose tells her that there was ice cream with a choice of sauce: '"Chocolate. Butterscotch. Walnut."' Rose also has a dream, however, in which Flo appears 'radiant [and] satisfied' (184) as she is offered a more impressive choice of 'chocolate mousse, trifle, Black Forest Cake.' Dessert here figures as a reward, something that comes at the end of a hard and bitter and galling life, in which choices were scarce. The Home – which Flo at one point confuses with the hospital in which long ago she'd had a gallstone operation – is an ironic image of that reward.

Rose wishes it were otherwise, wishes that she could devote herself now to nurturing her stepmother in Flo's own home. But she cannot. Like most of Munro's women, she cannot fit herself for long into the self-sacrificial mold. She can, however, do two other things for Flo. One of these is imaged with great subtlety at the story's close, when she tells Flo a lovely lie – that she has taken the gallstone home with her, for safekeeping. I read this as an echo of what Del did with Uncle Craig's black box; Rose and Del, as avatars of Munro herself, are artist figures who may seem (even to themselves) to betray their family histories. In fact, through imagination such women transform, redeem, and preserve; they make a *lasting* feast, from the ingredients of their lives.

The other thing that Rose does for Flo – and 'Rose thought that she had never done anything in her life that came near pleasing Flo as this did' (181) – is to make her a heavenly trifle. It pleases her, I would suggest, because it is luscious – a moment of ungrudging luxury, after a life of gall – and also because it marks a point of identification with Rose. I will close with a list of ingredients, in which the soul of Rose reaches out to Flo's soul in the language of food, language of the body that Flo herself can understand: 'The suave dreamy custard, the nipping berries, robust peaches, luxury of sherry-soaked cake, munificence of whipped cream.'

('"Lovely," said Flo and sat remembering, appreciating, belching a little.')

Works Cited

Munro, Alice. *Dance of the Happy Shades.* Toronto: McGraw-Hill, 1968. (Abbreviated *Dance.*)

———. *Lives of Girls and Women.* Scarborough: Signet, 1974. Soft-cover reprint. (Abbreviated *Lives.*)

———. *The Moons of Jupiter.* Toronto: Penguin, 1987. Soft-cover reprint. (Abbreviated *Moons.*)

———. *The Progress of Love.* Toronto: McClelland and Stewart, 1986. (Abbreviated *Progress.*)

———. *Something I've Been Meaning to Tell You.* Scarborough: Signet, 1975. Soft-cover reprint. (Abbreviated *Something.*)

———. *Who Do You Think You Are?* Toronto: Macmillan of Canada, 1978. (Abbreviated *Who.*)

Woolf, Virginia. *A Room of One's Own.* London: The Hogarth Press, 1959.

A Feminist Reading of *The Stone Angel*

The Stone Angel is a carefully organized novel which operates on two obvious levels: the present time of the novel which takes us through Hagar's last days on earth, and the past time of memory which moves us in strict chronological order through the major events of her life to explain the old woman whom we see now. In support of this structure, we are made to sense the physically decrepit Hagar as a mask behind which the true Hagar continues to reside. The novel is also elaborately based upon the biblical stories of Hagar and Jacob and upon sacramental patterns of confession and communion, so that the reader may well arrive at yet another sense of the novel's two dimensions: in the foreground (both past and present) we have the realistic tale of a woman's pride, and in the background (where confirmations or hidden meanings are supposed to lie) a Christian context within which we are to measure the significance of that pride. Thus, we might suppose that Hagar's pride is something like Eve's and that it is seen by the author as reprehensible, the cause of her fall from the garden. Yet here we falter. In the realistic foreground we feel that Hagar's pride is not merely her downfall, but also her salvation – and we may question what sense to make of that within the religious context. Our difficulty is compounded by Hagar's refusal to capitulate finally to that insistent religious dimension. While she does clearly make certain accommodations, it is equally apparent that Hagar approaches her death still in the spirit of those lines from Dylan Thomas which Laurence employs as epigraph: 'Do not go gentle into that good night. / Rage, rage against the dying of the light.'

The difficulty which has been described here comes from our expectation that background and foreground should cohere, and perhaps from an assumption that any extensive use of the Bible and sacraments will very probably signal belief. Some of this difficulty can be resolved if we approach *The Stone Angel* from a feminist perspective. If we consider the role of Christianity in Hagar's life as a woman, we may find another justification for the weight which is given to Christianity in this novel and a partial explanation for Hagar's resistance to it. We will also discover another significant area of backgrounding, an area of feminist concern which explains or corrects our vision of the foreground in which a woman is chastized for her mistreatment

54

of men. These various backgrounds – the past time of the novel, the religious and feminist dimensions – must be considered together if we are to understand *The Stone Angel* as a whole. They cohere as an historical explanation of how Hagar came to be the woman she is at the point of death.

The feminist dimension of *The Stone Angel* can be described as a kind of backgrounding because there is almost no overt consideration of these themes, and because the foreground may seem to be occupied with antithetical ideas. If Hagar is Everywoman, she is apparently a woman on trial for her crimes against men. Indeed, Hagar sees in the woods of Shadow Point the imaginary props and players for a jury trial in which she will summarily be found guilty; her sense of guilt is also indicated when she finds an old scale with its weights missing. But if the trial were a fair one and her attorney as eloquent as Margaret Laurence, there is little question that Hagar would be let off on compassionate grounds. *The Stone Angel* is told in the first person, by Hagar Shipley – so that Laurence must do all her pleading behind the scenes. In that background she prepares a devastating brief, a full-scale feminist analysis which operates as counter-weight to the crime of pride. While she admits Hagar's share of responsibility, Laurence also cites patriarchal society as a kind of instigating culprit; and she argues that men and women alike have been injured by the forces which lead to Hagar's intractable, compensatory pride. The novel avoids polemic by this fortunate circumstance, that Hagar cannot herself articulate (because historically she does not know) the feminist view of her case. Thus, Laurence is compelled to embody these ideas rather than to discuss them, and she does so ultimately in defense of her heroine.

Hagar is consistently identified with the stone angel which is the central image of the novel, indicative obviously of her pride and blindness. But the angel is in fact a monument to Hagar's mother, 'who relinquished her feeble ghost as [Hagar] gained [her] stubborn one' (3). The association of angel and mother will require our careful attention, for it is obscured by Jason Currie's evident lack of interest in his dead wife and by our knowledge that the stone angel is essentially a monument to his own pride. Indeed, so thoroughly has she been obliterated that even her name is missing from the text. Hagar has supplanted her mother, rejected her image and chosen instead to mirror her father's pride. But in the shadow of that stone angel which she becomes is another angel, ministering and mild – the kind of woman we take her mother to have been.

This stone angel is an imported creature, not anything original to the Canadian soil. The would-be pharaoh Jason Currie has purchased it from Italy, presumably because he thinks he can establish his pre-eminence in Manawaka only through an image crafted abroad. Clearly his is the colonial sensibility which looks to the old world for its values and for a continuation of class privilege. By the time Hagar is an old woman, Jason's pretensions (like those of Ozymandias) will have turned to dust: the Currie-Shipley stone will be recognized by a new generation as simply Canadian, marking the graves of two pioneering families with little to choose between them. The angel itself is 'askew and tilted' (305); and even marble does not last forever, as we know from the description of Hagar's aged skin: 'too white ... too dry, powdery as blown dust when the rains failed, flaking with dryness as an old bone will flake and chalk, left out in a sun that grinds bone and flesh and earth to dust as though in a mortar of fire with a pestle of crushing light' (54). In the light of truth, which is partly the recognition of our common mortality, the proud marble angel will finally be dissolved. But there is another angel which also must be laid to rest. And that is the image which Jason Currie seems to have imported from Britain: the Victorian image of woman as 'The Angel in the House,' a seminal conception of the Victorian era which is celebrated in Coventry Patmore's poem of the same name. This angel is soft, but it is ironically as rigid in conception as the marble image which Jason Currie erects over the corpse of a wife driven to an early grave – a woman puzzled, we may suppose, that her accommodation to the feminine ideal has served her no better than this. The stone angel in this sense expresses Jason Currie's privilege as a *man*, as well as the privilege he enjoys as a man of substance. Jason had little use for women, and little reverence for those feminine virtues which inspired men like John Ruskin or Coventry Patmore to such absurd heights of idolatry; but he shared their more significant belief in male superiority, and he accepted their notions of what behaviour and what education were appropriate for a lady.

Hagar very naturally wishes to exhibit whatever qualities are consistent with her pride and are admired by others. Her nearest judge is Jason, who encourages the male virtues in her and neglects certain of the feminine virtues which he will expect her eventually to display. Proud of her refusal to cry in the scene where he beats her with a ruler, Jason remarks that she has a 'backbone' (10) and takes after him. He is proud also of her intelligence, but wishes it had been granted to his sons instead. So Hagar is courageous, proud, brainy – everything that her father admires; and she is also female, so that these virtues are perceived as useless. Morever, they prevent the subservience which Jason ultimately expects of her. The tender virtues are not developed in Hagar: she perceives them only as weakness, a malleability which is unacceptable to her sense of self. She repudiates the silliness of other girls, dislikes anything flimsy or gutless. Only when she becomes aware of the standard which holds Lottie Dreiser's china-doll prettiness superior to her own strong-boned handsomeness does Hagar begin to share her father's view that a genetic irony has transpired in the Currie family: *she* should have inherited her mother's 'daintiness' (59), and the 'graceful unspirited boys' (7) should have had their father's ox-like strength. Symbolically, however, Hagar's backbone and other insistent bones preserve her from the repulsive formlessness which is stereotypically assigned to women, even as they condemn her in another sense to the rigidity of a stone angel.

In particular, Hagar loathes the vulnerability which she associates with the image of her mother, and which she perceives is equally despised by her father. Jason Currie would occasionally squeeze out a tear at the thought of his late wife, for the edification of 'the matrons of the town, who found a tear for the female dead a reassuring tribute to thankless motherhood' (59). Margaret Laurence reminds us here of the perils which attended childbirth in the days before antibiotics, and which required that women be rather forcibly locked into a conception of themselves as mothers to the race. Hagar has no wish to be a martyr; thus, she approaches the birth of her first son reluctantly, convinced it will be the death of her. Often in the novel, images of the birth process seem repulsive – as when Hagar observes the 'mammoth matriarchal fly ... labouring obscenely to squeeze out of herself her white and clustered eggs' (170). As a child Hagar refuses to be lulled by her father's crocodile tears; she knows that her mother was 'the brood mare who lay beneath [the monument] because she'd proved no match for his stud' (43). So Jason Currie pays his token dues to womankind in pretending to honour his wife for her status as victim, but Hagar – instead of feeling compassion or anger on her mother's behalf – merely shares in his contempt for the biological slavery of women.

Jason's wife, in the daguerrotype which Hagar keeps of her, is 'a spindly and anxious girl ... [who] peers perplexed out of her little frame, wondering how on earth to please' (59). That little frame is, of course, the straitjacket which Hagar wishes to avoid in her own life. It requires of women that they live to please others, and it is clearly pernicious. But Hagar reacts too extremely, becoming hidebound in pride – so that only at the point of death can she engage in 'truly free' (307) acts of maternal tenderness. The first of these, involving the pursuit of a bedpan for her young roommate in the hospital, is possible only because Hagar has been liberated from an actual straitjacket. The second of her free acts also signifies a release from constriction and a motherly reaching out to others, as Hagar breaks the death-hold of her wrestling match with Marvin (in the role of Jacob) to give her son the angel's blessing. Although she does not remember her mother in these last hours of life, Hagar as she approaches her own grave has achieved something like a reconciliation with that other angel. So it is that Hagar's last thought, as she holds the glass of water triumphantly in her own hands, taking what there is to be had, is 'There. There' (308). These are the mother words, which she has failed to supply for others in their deepest need – and which should have been as free as water. Three times before in the novel these words have appeared, once when she thought but could not say them to Bram (85), once when she was trying to calm herself into remembering the name of Shadow Point (146), and once when she congratulated herself for standing upright in the woods: 'There. There' (191). Motherless, Hagar has for nearly all her life been unable to give a mother's love and consolation to the people who needed her. In these last words, she appears as a mother to herself: it is a beautiful resolution of her independence and her need.

As the woman who was not there, Hagar's mother figures powerfully also in the lives of her two sons. Their sexual identity is uncertain. Dan is described in terms which may suggest effeminacy, and Matt is childless for reasons which are bitterly apparent to his wife (the suggestion is that they did not make love, or not often). Although either or both of the brothers might be considered homosexual, Laurence does not give us information to conclude that – nor does it matter in the least. What does matter is that the Currie brothers have been made deeply miserable in two ways: they have not been allowed to experience or to express feminine tenderness, and they have failed to achieve an imposed standard of masculinity. These sons are a considerable disappointment to Jason Currie, whose expectations about what a man ought to be and what a woman ought to be have damaged the lives of all his children.

The extent of that psychological damage to his sons is indicated symboli-cally in their early deaths. Particularly in Matt's case, death seems a release from an impossibly blighted existence; Dan presumably escaped before the bars of his cage were altogether apparent to him. At the moment of Dan's death we see clearly what has been missing from their lives: Matt wraps around himself the plaid shawl of their mother, and so becomes her in order to console Dan. We realize in this poignant tableau that both boys have been sorely deprived by their mother's death, occasioned by the birth of Hagar – and this is one reason for their resentment of Hagar. But that feeling might have been avoided if Hagar had supplied anything of the mother's tenderness which they missed on her account, or if their father had done so. As it hap-pens, Jason Currie prefers his daughter. Thus it would seem to the boys that Hagar has deprived them of both parents, and they express their resentment by taking a switch to Hagar whenever their father has beaten them. The harshness of the father is in this way communicated to the surviving female, who has refused to embody the gentleness of their mother.

The plaid shawl is first offered to Hagar, who refuses to wear it despite Matt's pleading. It is easier for Matt, a boy, to assume this maternal guise than it is for Hagar – who is unwilling to relinquish even for this occasion her own identity, and particularly unwilling to associate herself with what she takes to be the mother's frailty. When Hagar marries, Matt thinks of sending her the shawl as a wedding gift, either to mock her lack of womanliness, or to invest her with those qualities which the shawl represents and which she will need as wife and mother. For whatever reason, Matt changes his mind. And Hagar goes into marriage without the talismanic shawl, unable still to express the tenderness she mistakes for weakness. Repeatedly we see Hagar on the point of relenting, of acknowledging despised feminine sentiments in herself – feelings which *are* there, and which are needed badly; repeatedly, she retreats into that pride which is based on her rejection of the mother image.

Another face of the angel is mistaken by Hagar as belonging solely to the stone angel of her father's pride, and this is the image of herself as a lady which she embraces gladly. What she forgets is that a lady is first of all a woman. Essentially, Hagar falls victim to the lure which is held out by John Ruskin in *Sesame and Lilies*: much as Jason Currie would produce a tear in payment to thankless motherhood, so Ruskin sugar-coats the pill of servitude to men by describing woman as queen of her own household. Ruskin appeals covertly to a sense of class in his audience, an eminence which women achieve through the standing of their fathers and husbands. In this way women are to be compensated for the inferior position they hold in relation to men; with this pride of class in their hearts, women who were less than wholly convinced by Ruskin's arguments about a woman's special powers (of gentleness, piety, and so on) might still be reconciled to the subservience which is in fact allocated to them as a sex. We may suppose that some women were so daunted by male authority that they neglected to take refuge in this bounty of Ruskin's; thus, Hagar's mother in the daguerrotype 'looks so worried that she will not know what to do, although she came of good family and ought not to have had a moment's hesitation about the propriety of her ways' (59). Hagar would not be so intimidated, but it takes her some time to realize that behind the lady she becomes is a woman in harness.

As her mother was a brood mare, so Hagar when she is sent by Jason to the young ladies' academy in Toronto is described as 'the dark-maned colt off to the training ring' (42). Jason *wants* the angel of his house to be proud, requires her social arrogance as an extension of his own – although he naturally expects obedience within doors. It was his wife's failure to embody both halves of this paradoxical ideal which made him feel that her death for Hagar's life was 'a fair exchange' (59). He would rather have a thoroughbred who acts like one, so long as he can keep possession of the reins. Hagar is sent east because ' "there's no woman here to teach you how to dress and behave like a lady" ' (42), and she returns two years later to confront her father's evaluation of the expense. Always the canny Scots merchant, Jason examines his daughter's lady-like attire and nods approval, 'as though I were a thing and his' (43). Hagar does rebel momentarily when she discovers her father's opposition to her plan to become a teacher, but she yields and walks upstairs to begin her duties as Jason's chatelaine. She pauses there on the landing to stare rather enigmatically at an engraving of cattle. Hagar is on her way to discovering that the distance from chatelaine to chattel, from dark-maned colt to brood mare to cow, is not so very impressive after all.

Hagar's education has been as close as possible to that of a Victorian young lady: 'I knew embroidery, and French, and menu-planning for a five-course meal, and poetry, and how to take a firm hand with servants, and the most becoming way of dressing my hair' (42-43). Thus superfluously equipped, she returns to grace Jason's transplanted haven of Victoriana, his 'square brick palace so oddly antimacassared in the wilderness' (43). Like certain of his brother merchants abroad, Jason requires such aristocratic trappings in his chatelaine as proof to the world (in this case, Manawaka) that he is a rising man. Very little of what Hagar learns in Toronto would have served her in a career as a teacher, still less in the life she chooses after three years as Jason's hostess. In each instance, we see the irrelevance of imported concepts of gentility to life on the Canadian prairie. We see also that an education which aims at making woman decorative will keep her dependent upon men. Later Hagar will envy young women like the nurse (284) who have been better equipped for autonomous survival.

When Hagar has had enough of her father's rule, she marries Bram Shipley – because he offers an opportunity for rebellion, and because she is attracted to him physically. Since the erotic component in the masculine image has been carefully obscured in Jason Currie's household, Hagar's response to this in Bram is rebellious; but since Jason's own stereotypical view of masculinity has been communicated to Hagar, he is peculiarly responsible for the fact that she prefers Bram with his exaggerated masculinity to 'the pliable boys of good family whom [Jason] trotted home' (48) for Hagar's inspection. Mare-like and malleable, they must have seemed like women to her – and singularly unappetizing, as most things female are to Hagar. There ought to have been other alternatives, but Hagar has reached the point where it is necessary for her to leave Jason: the harness is chafing beyond endurance. Bram looks like freedom because he would look so unsatisfactory to her father. But again, her rebellion is not so thorough as she supposes, for Hagar intends to reform Bram into something more like what her father has in mind. Thus, she luxuriates in his savagery – 'he looked like a bearded Indian' – and in the next instant imagines him 'rigged out in a suit of gray soft as a dove's feathers' (45). Her laundered, fairy-tale vision of the life she would lead with Bram is similarly inspired by the poetry she has read in Toronto, so that Bram is cast in her imagination as the primitive who would miraculously prove to be a gentleman. The lady is still in harness, blind to the rough plebian life outside her sphere.

Then Hagar marries and the veil is lifted. She finds that one of the identities envisioned for her husband is impossible: Bram Shipley is obviously not going to improve his grammar, or prosper, or take to wearing the clothes of a gentleman. He is not going to do any of those things because he never wanted them enough, and because the contempt which his new wife shows for what he is makes him resist any of her efforts to remodel him. Yet Bram had been attracted to Hagar largely because of her lady-like ways; like the Victorian male, he aimed at procuring an angel for his house – some gentle female refinement as a compensation for the roughness which the male endures in his role as provider. Bram's roughness is more literal, his provision scantier by far – but he is not so different from Jason as Hagar thinks. Thus, he gives her the elegant decanter as a wedding gift, and so like Jason he wants sons (not daughters) to create a dynasty. Hagar's response to this ambition in Bram is *'the nerve of him'* (101), anger both at his absurd social presumption and at this new proof of masculine arrogance. Bram could not have supposed that the angel would find his manner so disgusting, or that her pride of class (based irrevocably on her father rather than on him) would so thoroughly obstruct her wifely subservience and love. Bram's genteel ambitions (never very strong) wither in the stone angel's gaze. But there is another Bram, corresponding to Hagar's more genuinely rebellious image of the man she married – and this is the sexual, laughing Bram, the one who seemed to promise joy.

We come now to one of the most insistent themes of the novel. Hagar is unable to let Bram know the satisfaction she feels in their lovemaking; her pride as a lady forbids any admission of that kind, so that ironically she cannot profit fully from her choice of a virile man. Immediately following her memory of this forced coldness in Bram's bed, Hagar is seen as an old woman lying flat on her back and 'cold as winter' in another bed, remembering how children lie down in snow to make 'the outline of an angel with spread wings' (81). Significantly crafted in childhood, this snow angel recalls obviously the whiteness and chill of marble as well as the chastity of the Victorian angel. The root cause of Hagar's dilemma is religion, by way of Jason – for her father's dour presbyterianism holds that sexuality is evil. Accordingly, his affair with 'No-Name Lottie Dreiser's mother' is perceived as dirty, something to be concealed from decent folk. Jason's partner in crime is a Victorian stereotype, abused and dwelling in shadows: 'her face soft and blank as though she expected nothing out of life ... she began to trudge up the hill' (18). Because women like this exist, others may remain pure – so absurdly pure in fact, that Hagar is condemned to enter marriage with absolutely no information about what will happen on her wedding night. The sum of Jason's teaching is that '"Men have terrible thoughts"' (46), a notion which explains in part (for there are also economic motives) the Victorian allocation of chastity to women: as angels they must compensate for the bestiality of men, keeping humanity as far as possible out of Satan's grasp. Particularly was the lady to be unimpassioned, while women of a lower order (harlots and half-breeds) might be lascivious in the service of any man who chose to risk perdition. Hagar is not devout, but she is Presbyterian and Victorian enough to associate sex with stable beasts and the lower classes, with men who cannot help themselves, and with ladies least of all. In this way is her body victimized – not that she must endure her husband's embrace, but that she may not labour in love for their mutual satisfaction. She is paid for her sacrifice in being known as a lady. Again and again, Hagar relinquishes her claim to a full humanity – always in order that she may remain a lady, always failing to perceive that this apparent superiority is a ruse.

Hagar's exposure to genteel poetry and art have also contributed to her view of love as asexual: 'Love, I fancied, must consist of words and deeds as delicate as lavender sachets, not like things he did sprawled on the high white bedstead that rattled like a train' (80). Bram has proven more rough Indian than Hagar had any reason to suspect. She brings to his house a print by Holman Hunt which she had acquired in the East (always the avenue for Victoriana): 'I did so much admire the knight and lady's swooning adoration, until one day I saw the coyness of the pair, playing at passion, and in a fury I dropped the picture, gilt frame and all, into the slough, feeling it had betrayed me' (82-83). Significantly, this picture is juxtaposed against another of horses – which Bram dislikes, despite his passion for horses, because he is annoyed that Hagar prefers the picture of the thing to the reality. The horses here (recalling Jason as stud to his wife's broodmare) obviously signify the truth of sexuality, in contrast to the myth which is perpetrated in Holman Hunt's picture. But Hagar knows that she has been betrayed, is angered not by the harsh reality of love so much as by the fact that lies such as these pale images of Holman Hunt have cut her off from authentic passion.

Hagar enters in her marriage to Bram a new kind of subjugation. She has escaped the destiny of Victorian females who sacrifice everything to their parents, a fate like that of the poor Manawaka spinster whose tomb inscription reads: 'Rest in peace. From toil, surcease. Regina Weese' (4). But sexual experience is not liberating for her, and the work she must perform for a houseful of men is still drudgery. That ox-like strength she would once have exchanged for daintiness takes her through twenty-four years of hard labour in which she becomes increasingly like Bram's first wife. Clara Shipley, 'inarticulate as a stabled beast' (46), was fat, her voice gruff as a man's; likewise, Hagar gains bulk (for lack, she believes, of a proper lady's corset) and wears a man's overcoat without remembering to object. But internally she remains Hagar Currie. She is contemptuous of Bram's daughters by Clara, coarse women who cannot in any way transcend their condition. At the same time she is reduced in the fashion of all such farm wives to cheating her husband on the egg money and never questions that what little Bram's farm makes is not his own entirely. She is Hagar the Egyptian bondwoman of Genesis, no happier in her servitude than was that other Hagar. Always she rejects the satisfaction of martyrdom, the support which Clara Shipley received from what Hagar calls her 'morbid motto': *No Cross No Crown'* (193). Even as an old woman, Hagar will recoil from the martyrish attitudes of her daughter-in-law, despising that slavish Christianity which looks for its reward in another world. Hagar is too proud to grovel for profit, and we may honour her for that, even as we deplore her failure to appreciate the labours of Doris, and of those other women with whom she denies kinship.

Finally, Hagar decides to leave Bram. The offense to her pride has become unendurable, and she is anxious to provide another sort of environment for John, the favoured son in whom she believes the Currie heritage will flower. Ironically, she must become a servant in earnest – a woman in uniform, no longer veiled as daughter or wife – in order to earn money and to live in the sort of house she thinks is appropriate for a Currie. Also ironically, her new position echoes that of Auntie Doll, housekeeper to the Curries, in relation to whom Hagar had supposed herself 'quite different ... a different sort entirely' (34). That she has gone from bad to worse is suggested by the peculiarly unsavoury manner in which Mr. Oatley, her employer, has made his fortune: he has shipped Oriental wives into Canada, allowing them to plummet through the false bottom of the vessel whenever Immigration men become suspicious. This grisly practice obtrudes oddly in the book, until we realize that it announces the author's concern with the wrongs which have been perpetrated against women by male society.

In a male fortress, then, a house founded on the death of women, Hagar lives quietly with John and at night (but only then) yearns for the body of her husband. She has resumed a version of the place she held in Jason Currie's house, and in her retreat to such spurious prestige has re-created for John the prison of her own childhood. John is deprived of Bram, as the Currie brothers were deprived of their father's love; and he is raised to hold himself aloof in pride, in circumstances which reveal the foolishness of pride. When the Depression strikes and his prospects are reduced to zero, John returns to Manawaka. There he presides over the death of Bram, caring for him as Matt had for Dan – again as a substitute for Hagar, who comes finally but is not recognized. This is a kind of retribution for her unwillingness at Dan's death to bend and assume another's role: now Bram, the one person who called her Hagar, mistakes her for 'his fat and cow-like first wife' (173), Clara.

During this and a subsequent visit to Manawaka, Hagar observes the love which is growing up between John and Arlene Simmons, who is Lottie Dreiser's daughter. Arlene's position in Manawaka society is superior to John's, a neat reversal of the time when Hagar could hold herself superior to Lottie. Thus, John thinks at first that he is Bram-like for Arlene, illicit and therefore attractive as an opportunity for rebellion. But Arlene is free of such considerations. She has abandoned the sense of class superiority and with it the sense of sex as something a woman cannot enjoy without demeaning herself. She loves John and is capable of redeeming him for a life of joy – not of changing him exactly, as Hagar (thinking of Bram) warns her that she cannot, but of being open to him in such a way that John will change and grow of his own volition. That 'stiff black seed on the page' of her *Sweet Pea Reader*, at which Hagar had stared as a child, hoping it would 'swell and blossom into something different, something rare' (13), shows signs of doing just that in the relationship of Arlene and Hagar's son. Seeing how freely Arlene can show her passion to John, Hagar finds it 'incredible that such a spate of unapologetic life should flourish in this mean and crabbed world' (208) – incredible perhaps, but for an instant she believes in this new, miraculous life for men and women.

Then she conspires with Lottie to separate their children, symbolically to stamp out their life, just as once before she stood by as Lottie trampled on the chicks emerging from their shells; in both cases death is accomplished presumably for the good of its victims. In the same punishing spirit, Jason Currie had claimed that he beat his daughter for her own good; thus he forbade her marriage to Bram. In fact his motive was self-interested, and the motive is what counts. Hagar, in need of water (her well in the wilderness) at Shadow Point, will quote Coleridge and ask 'What albatross did I slay, for mercy's sake?' (186). She will wound a gull (the spirit of love) and think 'I'd gladly kill it, but I can't bring myself to go near enough' (217). The significance of this seems to be that Hagar's fastidious pride keeps her from an act of mercy, as it had when she refused to wear the plaid shawl to ease Dan's death. In causing the separation of John and Arlene, however, their mothers do not kill 'for mercy's sake,' but for their own. John (whose mother will not allow him independent life) regresses to the recklessness of an embittered child and kills both himself and Arlene in a car crash. Their life is coolly stamped out. And Hagar's albatross, the guilt she feels for John's death, will be appeased only when Hagar in the role of the ancient mariner can look into her heart and admit the failure of love.

The circumstances surrounding John's death are repressed by Hagar (and kept from the reader) until the turning and gathering point of the novel, which occurs at Shadow Point. Hagar has run away from her house in Vancouver because Marvin and Doris intend to put her in the nursing home which Hagar the Egyptian thinks of as 'a mausoleum' (96): she is running still from incarceration, from any imposed image of herself as feeble or subject to another's will. Twice before Hagar had fled from her father's mausoleum to Bram's house, and from there to Mr. Oatley's death-like mansion in Vancouver. Her destination now repeats the flight to Bram's house. The abandoned house in which she first seeks shelter is unpainted, as the Shipley place had been; but now Hagar takes satisfaction in its weathered state, thinking how Marvin (the proper son, who sells house paint) would disapprove as once she relished Jason Currie's disapproval. Her second shelter, the cannery, with its 'rusted and unrecognizable machinery' and the 'skeleton' (215) of a fishboat, also recalls the Shipley place, where 'rusty machinery stood like aged bodies gradually expiring from exposure, ribs turned to the sun' (169). These connections are important, because at Shadow Point Hagar will confront the deaths associated with the drought-plagued Shipley place – Bram's death, and finally John's. Hagar, we may remember, is herself a figure of the drought: her aged skin is 'powdery as blown dust when the rains failed ... left out in a sun that grinds bone and flesh and earth to dust as though in a mortar of fire with a pestle of light' (54). But she will also, when she has suffered enough of such fiery enlightenment, be granted the mercy of water before her own death comes in fact.

Significantly, she must descend a stairway to arrive at the place where her genuine freedom will begin. There may be echoes here of that staircase she climbed up in Jason's house to begin her tenure as his chatelaine. Now, as the stone angel topples, as a lady would come down from her pedestal, so Hagar laboriously descends the half-rotted steps which lead to the beach. 'It's not a proper stairway, actually' (151) – it is returning to its natural condition, just as Hagar, 'feeling slightly dizzy,' abandons propriety to enter the depths of her own nature. On the way down these steps she feels the 'goatsbeard brush satyr-like' against her, as Bram had done when they met; and she sees a kind of wildflower called the Star of Bethlehem, which (together with the Pan images) implies the spiritual rebirth which is waiting for her at Shadow Point. She delights in thinking of herself as Meg Merrilies, from the poem by Keats – an old gypsy woman (common, by the world's reckoning) whose house was 'out of doors,' whose 'book' (like Hagar's) was 'a churchyard tomb' (152). It is as Meg *Merrilies* that she will encounter *Murray Lees*, her spiritual double, and drink the wine which is referred to in Keats's poem. They will exhibit toward one another something of that ease-giving generosity which is also contained in the poem: 'She plaited mats o' rushes, / And gave them to the cottagers / She met among the bushes.' Old Meg is compassionate; she sings and decks her hair with garlands (as Hagar does with June bugs); she rejoices in nature; and she dies. The model of womanhood she offers to Hagar on the eve of her own death is also one of independence and undiminished pride: 'Old Meg was brave as Margaret Queen / and tall as Amazon.' This is the resolution of compassion and pride which Hagar seeks.

On the beach, Hagar sees a small boy and girl playing house. These children are later compared to John and Arlene, and there is also a connection with Hagar and Murray Lees, who take up residence together in the cannery. The girl is nagging at the boy, fussing about appearances; and Hagar wants to warn her that she will lose him if she continues to be so critical, so niggardly of praise. Again, the drought metaphor is employed: *The branches will wither, the roots they will die, / You'll be all forsaken and you'll never know why'* (188). When she intervenes, however, the children cling to one another; and this show of unity makes Hagar think that she has underestimated them, as clearly she does in the case of John and Arlene. Rather strangely, Hagar has claimed that she was herself forsaken: 'I never left them. It was the other way around, I swear it' (164). In any case, she is at last beginning to know why. She acknowledges here that love is the water required for growth, and that false pride can kill as surely as the drought. When love fails, each partner is forsaken; both lose, and blame is not the crucial issue.

The turning point comes with the arrival of Murray F. Lees. Almost her first remark to him is '"I hope you'll excuse my appearance"' (220), but soon Hagar relaxes enough to share his wine and listen to his tale. What she hears is essentially her own story: a tale in which religion plays an important role, where the chief villains are a concern for appearances and the denial of sexuality, and where the catastrophe involves the loss of a son. Murray's story is about two women, his mother and his wife. Rose Ferney was his mother's name, '"A delicate name, she used to say"' (224), but Rose was in fact as tough as a morning glory vine. Ironically, Hagar fails to see herself in Rose: '"Fancy spending your life worrying what people were thinking. She must have had a rather weak character"' (227). The point, of course, is that the proverbial clinging vine takes many forms, both strong and weak; the frailty of women can be deceptive (as in the case of Rose or Lottie), and the tenacity which is shown in an obsessive regard for appearances is also weakness.

Murray's grandfather was a circuit rider, an evangelist who greatly embarrassed his Anglican daughter-in-law; yet Murray preferred '"hellfire to [his mother's] lavender talcum"' (234), and became himself a Redeemer's Advocate. The passion of that sect became still more attractive when he met Lou at Bible Camp, for here it seemed was a religion in which '"prayer and *that*"' were not the '"odd combination"' (227) that Hagar thinks they are. Then Lou got pregnant and began to worry (as Murray's mother always had) about her reputation. They married, but her concern grew with the arrival of a child too big to be premature – and her heart went out of sex. She thought that God was punishing her, and her religion became (like Jason's Presbyterianism) a denial of the flesh. But the real punishment came for Lou and Murray, as it had for Hagar, in the *death* of their son – and not his birth, which was the fruit of love. Thus, the child is killed in a fire while Lou is in the tabernacle with Murray, '"begging for the keys of heaven"' (233). They are punished symbolically, as Hagar is throughout her life and especially in John's death, for the denial of sexuality which Laurence opposes so vehemently in this novel. In Lou's original sensuality and its demise, we see clearly what Laurence believes has

been done to women in the name of religion and propriety; in Murray's deprivation at the change in his wife, we see how this process has worked also to
the disadvantage of the male.

Hagar does not come to any conscious realization of her error in listening
to Murray's story. But it works on her subconsciously, as in a sort of dream
she admits the guilt which is parallel to Murray's, and he assumes the role of
John in order to forgive her. She also exhibits forgiveness toward Murray, first
in trying to assuage his guilt over the fire, and second in pardoning him for
the broken promise which brings Marvin and Doris to the cannery. Strictly
speaking, Hagar is wrong when she tells Murray that '"No one's to blame"'
(234) for his son's death. Yet there are times when compassion requires us to
act and speak not strictly in accordance with some ideal of truth, but with a
clear sense of the other's plight. That same generosity in which Hagar has
failed so often, and which she is learning with such difficulty now, must in
the end be applied to her. We judge her less harshly than we might because we
acknowledge the power of those forces which have worked against her. At
the same time, we admire Hagar's pride precisely because it is a form (however twisted) of resistance to those forces – a statement, in fact, that Hagar
Shipley is her own woman. She will not beg at heaven's gate, or cite excuses;
if there is a God, he must take her as we do – for better or worse.

With the arrival of Marvin and Doris at the cannery, we learn that Hagar is
dying. She is taken to a hospital, where her pride seems to be thriving still as
she insists that Marvin get her a private room. A ward full of helpless women,
where you sleep 'as you would in a barracks or a potter's field, cheek-by-jowl
with heaven knows who all' (255), is not the place for Hagar. Although she has
just been comforted by a night in the proximity of Murray Lees, 'Nothing is
ever changed at a single stroke' (88). In fact, the ward is exactly what Hagar
needs, and she is kept there long enough to make friends with Elva Jardine, a
common *woman* – as if to repeat in another key her experience of comrade-
ship with Murray Lees. It is at this point in the novel that the theme of sisterhood becomes apparent. After a lifetime of despising women, Hagar is at last
compelled to join the ranks of her own sex. Her democratization (the lessen-
ing of class pride) takes the form of a movement toward her fellow women in
order to suggest that Hagar has turned to pride of class partly as an escape
from the humiliations of her sex.

Elva Jardine recalls Mrs. Steiner, the woman at Silverthreads Nursing
Home who had seemed briefly to hold out the promise of friendship for
Hagar. It was she who spoke of the comfort to be had from daughters (a point
also made by Lottie), and who articulated Hagar's own astonishment at the
way a woman's body can travel from puberty through childbirth to meno-
pause with such harrowing speed that the *mind* seems left behind at every
stage, aghast and wondering. Hagar liked Mrs. Steiner immediately, but saw

her as a trap designed to make Silverthreads and resignation seem attractive. She ran from that 'oriental shrug' which accompanied Mrs. Steiner's ironic question: '"Where will you go? You got someplace to go?"' (104). Having run from 'oriental' (or submissive) womanhood as far as she was able, Hagar at last can run no more; the body is insistent, and now what it insists upon is death. Thus, she confronts her *human* fate simultaneously with her identity as woman, which she recognizes through Elva and other women in the hospital. It is important for Laurence that Hagar should make this connection before she dies.

Hagar doesn't like Elva immediately, for her pride interferes, and she recoils as usual from the sort of woman who seems 'flimsy as moth wings' (269). But Elva is tough in spirit, as well as compassionate toward other women and tender in the love she exhibits toward her husband. All of this is a lesson for Hagar, one that strikes to her roots because Elva (by a fortunate coincidence) is from Manawaka. Thus, Hagar can return in imagination to claim Bram instead of Jason (whom she might have used to impress Elva) and to admit through Elva her kinship with those common women of Manawaka she had once denied. Like Mrs. Steiner, Elva Jardine faces her own imminent death as a woman and with courage, revealing to Hagar that the two are not at odds. And she offers another lesson in the way she handles the indignities of bowel and bladder which have been so oppressive to Hagar in her infirmity. She struggles to the bathroom on her '"own two pins"' (268), but will accept help when she needs it – as well as *offer* help, in the shape of a bedpan for Mrs. Dobereiner. Hagar proves that she has learned what Elva has to teach when (valiantly, but with an appreciation of absurdity) she gets the bedpan for Sandra Wong, her final roommate. Those bedsheets which Doris washed so frequently, without complaining to Hagar until the end, are recalled by these events – so that we have a sense of many women joining together to admit the realities of the body, and to deal with the indignities that oppose them.

In Sandra Wong, Hagar confronts the changes which have occurred in women's lives. Laurence makes her Chinese so that Hagar can imagine her as 'the granddaughter of one of the small foot-bound women whom Mr. Oatley smuggled in, when Oriental wives were frowned upon' (286). But Sandra 'speaks just like Tina' (286), Hagar's own liberated granddaughter – which places Hagar squarely in that generation of women whose feet were bound. The corset of a lady was more appealing to Hagar, and would seem more natural; but it is not dissimilar in function, as both forms of binding work to restrict the movements of women and reduce their size. And all of this occurs for the delectation of the male, whose vanity is flattered by an implicit comparison to his own superior mobility and stature, while ironically the vanity of women is provoked to make her collaborate in the process of diminution. In effect, woman turns to self-love in order to avoid self-hatred; she defeats

no
Freehold
(p.271)

herself in order to save herself when she embraces pride of class or personal vanity as her defense. This image of constriction (the footbinding) connects with that straitjacket of pride from which Hagar must be released in order to get the bedpan for Sandra and to bless Marvin – her two 'truly free' (307) acts – and so reveals the deep interpenetration of these themes in the novel. Hagar's own complicity is further implied when she thinks, 'Maybe I owe my house to her grandmother's passage money. There's a thought' (286-287). She does not pursue that thought, but we may – and realize that Hagar's mistake has been to join forces with the oppressor (all that Jason Currie has represented in the way of patriarchal, Victorian arrogance), and that she has done so for her own profit, although that profit has been illusory. In fact, she has been deformed as badly as those other women from whom she had hoped to dissociate herself. As their feet were crippled, so in her compensatory pride Hagar has been kept from the natural, healthy development of feeling which was her birthright as a woman and as a human being.

Hagar welcomes the changes which have come about for women, that the young nurse has training which allows her independence and that Sandra Wong can refer knowledgeably to hysterectomies, but she knows that nothing changes all at once: 'The plagues go on from generation to generation' (284). With Tina, however, it seems that progress has been made, for contrary to her grandmother's expectation Tina has found 'a man who'll bear her independence' (62), and Hagar sends her a sapphire ring as a wedding present. With this ring, the novel comes full circle. It had belonged to Hagar's despised mother, and should have gone (as Hagar tells Doris in a gesture of reconciliation) to her despised daughter-in-law first of all. It might also have gone to Arlene, of course, if Hagar had possessed the wisdom then that she shows now in sending the ring to Tina. Hagar does not envision here a future for women without men, but a situation in which men and women will be free to love one another and to respect each other's needs. She cannot undo the past. She will not deny the person she has been. But in the act of ring-giving, Hagar succeeds in linking four generations of women with some faith that whatever plagues continue, of pride or other oppression, there will also be increasing joy.

Work Cited

Laurence, Margaret. *The Stone Angel.* Toronto: McClelland and Stewart, 1964. All references are to this edition, and are cited parenthetically in the text.

Hagar's Old Age:
The Stone Angel as *Vollendungsroman*

'And then –' *The Stone Angel* closes, signalling the instant of Hagar's death, and the conundrum of its sequel, and one further pressing question – which is whether (in fictional terms) Hagar will live on. *The Stone Angel*, an act of imagination performed by Margaret Laurence, is completed with those words; 'and then –' it's up to us, her readers and heirs, to say whether Laurence has pulled it off, her own implicit goal, which is to confer immortality upon a thing made out of words. And I refer here to Hagar, rather than to the novel which contains and shapes her. Immortality is paradoxically achieved if we are made to see the character as something *more* than words; the trick that Laurence attempts (with words that last) is to make her seem like flesh and blood, perishable and poignant beyond words for just that reason.

Clearly, the trick has worked. In Canadian literature, Hagar is reigning still as Queen of all the characters. Even critics who are theoretically bound to recall that any character is really only a linguistic content – a series of characters, in the alphabetical sense – may slip and fall into the heresy of the real where Hagar is concerned. What I shall be arguing in this essay is that Hagar's peculiarly strong 'reality' quotient is a function of her pressing *need* for some version of continuance, some species of immortality. We find ourselves compelled – by language, for how else can any case be argued? – to grant her what we can. Further, I would suggest that Hagar's need is a function of her old age, as the proximity of death and the spectacle of ninety misspent years demand *riposte*.

In an essay called 'Gadgetry or Growing: Form and Voice in the Novel,' Margaret Laurence defined herself as a writer whose fate or task or vocation was the creation of character. And Laurence was inclined, always, to speak of her characters as if they were real, as if they were people to whom she owed something, as if they had rights that could be violated by a careless author. That authorial stance is familiar enough. But Laurence – as if intoning Hagar's famous battle-cry, 'Gainsay Who Dare!' – stood her ground with remarkable firmness: 'Form for its own sake is an abstraction which carries no allure for me' (55). What she sought was 'a form which would allow the characters to come through' (54), 'a form through which the characters can breathe' (55). Laurence's job, as she construed it, was to listen well to their voices and to devise a structure in which her characters would appear to 'breathe,' a kind of hospitable, open-air auditorium in which their stories might be told and heard.

I am interested in the visual metaphor that Laurence found when she tried to describe her ideal form: 'a forest, through which one can see outward, in which the shapes of trees do not prevent air and sun, and in which the trees themselves are growing structures, something alive' (55). What seems to be at work here is the revision and reversal of an old cliché. We should not be prevented by the trees from seeing out of the forest; that is, the elements of form must not obscure our vision of that reality which lies beyond art – and animates it. And we should not be prevented from seeing the trees by the forest; that is, the form as a whole (a finished abstraction, the book or forest) must not obscure our vision of that reality which continues to grow and change within it.

But I am also interested in the metaphors of form that Laurence excluded in the essay called 'Gadgetry or Growing': 'I see it not like a house or a cathedral or any enclosing edifice, but rather as a forest.' Her concern, it seems, is to discover a form in which characters can breathe fresh air. And I think this follows from her interest in the dialectic between fixed or rooted elements of the human personality and the winds of change. She wants her characters to breathe not only in the sense of coming to life, and transcending the 'gadgetry' of form, but also in the sense of 'growing.' Her exclusion of the metaphor of the house has a special bearing on the topic of Hagar's old age, because Hagar has throughout her life made the mistake of identifying herself with that 'enclosing edifice.' In old age, and in the 'growing' form of the novel that Laurence discovers for her, Hagar is able at last to emerge from the carapace of her 'house.' It is only in this departure from her accustomed form that Hagar can achieve the immortality of characters who are 'growing' still in the last chapter.

'Gadgetry or Growing' is also the essay in which Laurence spoke of her uncertainty over the chronological ordering of Hagar's memory and the 'poetic' quality of her voice. Laurence's question was whether the methods she had chosen 'diminish[ed] the novel's resemblance to life' (56). On the memory issue, she defended her choice by suggesting that a more apparently haphazard arrangement might have confused the reader, and that in any case 'writing – however consciously unordered its method – is never as disorderly as life. Art, in fact, is never life. It is never as paradoxical, chaotic, complex or alive as life' (56-57). I think, in fact, that Laurence was right in her assessment that 'the novel is probably too orderly.' But there is another argument that can be made, one that proceeds from her reminder that art is never life, one that seizes upon the difference – not to excuse the gap, but to exploit it.

The Stone Angel is a novel. We know that as we read, and we know absolutely that it is an attempt by Margaret Laurence to redeem or perform a salvage operation on a character who means a great deal to her. The text is an
arena in which Laurence exercises both her skill and her love – for this imagined person, for whatever real persons may have contributed to the invention
of Hagar, and for the human enterprise. I would argue that a significant factor
in our admiration or love for this novel is the *presence* of Laurence, accom-
plishing through art the feat of human salvage; the river flows both ways, and
we associate Margaret Laurence's triumph (the struggle and reach of her
imagination) with Hagar's own emancipation, so that each extends a kind of
grace or power to the other.

So Hagar's memories are invoked in chronological order; moreover, each
memory is interrupted by a present event only when the past segment has
yielded its relevant content. The effect of all this is to remind us of artifice, for
good or ill. The threat to realism is contained by various artful dodges, including the credible triggers for memory which propel Hagar from the present
into the past. A notable and complex example occurs in the woods at Shadow
Point, where Hagar sees the sparrows as 'jurors [who would] condemn [her]
quick as a wink, no doubt' (192), and then remembers the locus of her 'crime,'
the scene in which she and Lottie had plotted to separate their children.
Because this is a particularly long segment, Laurence also gives us a clump of
moss and a blind slug which are sounded fore and aft to frame the memory;
these are natural, probable signposts, to be sure – but they are also mutedly
symbolic, and artful. (We feel the slowness of time, the long repression of dangerous psychic material.)

I have chosen this example – rather than, say, the paintings in the doctor's
office that cause Hagar to recall pictures hung at the Shipley place – because,
while the trigger here is not straightforward, it is credible in spite of the artfulness imputed to Hagar herself. We might say that the moss and slug are
Laurence's doing, and that the judgement parallel is Hagar's. But in fact some
slippage occurs in both directions, and we understand that Hagar is not
unlike her author in the need to tease out and shape the meanings of her
material. Memory *is* an art. It becomes more potent as Hagar becomes more
skilled in the integration of past and present, as she learns from each how to
learn from the other; and she educates herself, with the assistance of her
author, partly through the manipulation of symbol.

Therefore I would argue that the gap between art and life which is revealed
to Laurence by the necessarily greater disorder of life is a dynamic gap; from
the energy that crosses to and fro both are enriched. If *The Stone Angel* can be
criticized for an excessive orderliness – and I would extend the charge beyond
the matter of chronological memory, to include an excessively orderly (or
over-resolved) handling of image – this is clearly not a fatal flaw. The novel is

splendid in any case. And it is splendid partly because art and life, or the author and the character, are allowed to reflect each other passionately across that gap.

I have been dealing here surreptitiously with the question of Hagar's 'poetic' voice, which Laurence also addresses in 'Gadgetry or Growing' as a possible lapse in verisimilitude. On this point, however, she is more confident. Laurence begins by recalling her anxiety when she read over certain of Hagar's more elaborate or 'poetic' descriptions: 'Were these in fact Hagar or were they me? I worried about this quite a lot, because I did not want Hagar to think out of character' (57). But she justifies her decision to let this voice stand by appealing to her sense of conviction in the writing – 'I could not really believe those descriptions *were* out of character' – and to the notion that rescinding them 'would be a kind of insult' to Hagar. She argues further that 'even people who are relatively inarticulate ... are perfectly capable within themselves of perceiving the world in more poetic terms ... than their outer voices might indicate.'

This defense suggests Laurence's fervent advocacy of her character, her need to take Hagar's side and to arm her as fully as their shared humanity permits. I would accept the spirit of her contention that the inner voice can be more articulate or 'poetic' than the outer, but Hagar's voice – with its high degree of rhetorical polish, even in the vernacular – is nonetheless very clearly a literary construct. I am not troubled by this fact, however; I *like* it. The effect of Hagar's very literary panache is not of self-consciousness on her author's part, but rather of a desire (shared by author and character) that Hagar should express herself as well and as fully as possible before the lights go out.

W.H. New, in an essay called 'Every Now and Then: Voice and Language in Laurence's *The Stone Angel*,' discusses 'the *writerly* quality of the language with which Hagar constructs the world' (81) and suggests (what is clearly so) that the tension between her formal and vernacular styles of speech reflects a social tension within both Hagar and her world. Where I differ from New is in his suggestion that Hagar's formal or 'finishing school' voice is reducible to the enemy within, which has protected and distracted her from the truths of the body and ordinary life that 'come during the passages of uncontrolled utterance, when the *natural* Hagar can be heard' (92). New recognizes that the 'natural,' anti-hierarchical Hagar is also posited in the abundant natural imagery of even her most formal speech; but I think he romanticizes the 'natural' and the inarticulate, and dismisses too much of what is valuable in Hagar's character, when he suggests that the elaborate *style* of such passages is simply Hagar's way of 'distanc[ing] herself from life' (90). To pursue the evident social tensions in her language this far is to run the risk of despising Hagar's eloquence.

I am reminded of Margaret Laurence's fear that to censor Hagar's 'poetic' voice 'would be a kind of insult to her. And that, I wasn't willing to risk – indeed I did not dare' (Gadgetry, 57). In deciding to trust that voice as Hagar's own, Laurence appealed to the truth of the subconscious – from which all writing partly comes, and in which the character is born; it would seem, then, that Laurence herself believed in the spiritual authenticity of Hagar's educated voice. The mistake that New makes, in my opinion, is to accept too literally or too purely the fictional proposition that Hagar's voice is that of a 'real' person. Its modulations are therefore regarded precisely as if they had been transcribed from life, and Hagar is held strictly accountable for them all. This credulity leads the critic astray, whereas the novelist's brand of poetic faith in the 'reality' of her character allows Margaret Laurence to speak for Hagar with conviction – and to negotiate with impunity the gap between life and art.

§

My concern here with the interplay of life and art, and of the character with her author, is a necessary approach to the main topic of this essay, which is *The Stone Angel* as a novel 'about' old age. I have been studying such novels for several years now, and I have coined a term by which to refer to them: the *Vollendungsroman*, the novel of 'completion' or 'winding up.' *The Stone Angel* has become my central or prototypical example of the genre, for a number of reasons that I shall be sketching here. The least provable of these is also one of the most compelling: that I sense generally in the *Vollendungsroman*, and with great force in *The Stone Angel*, a kind of alliance between the elderly character and the author – as language itself becomes the agent of affirmation.

A special intensity (resulting from the proximity to darkness) characterizes the *Vollendungsroman*. The writer's imagination, I would suggest, is challenged by the prospect of the character's demise, and by the need to 'capture' a life before it vanishes. Behind this, and quite apart from the question of the author's own age, is undoubtedly the spectre of the writer's own age and prospective death. Writing is always an act directed against death; it may become that more specifically and more urgently when the writer's subject is old age. Thus, we feel strongly the need Laurence feels to let her elderly protagonist *speak* 'before [her] mouth is stopped with dark' (139).

The act of speech operates in the *Vollendungsroman* in several ways. Broadly or metaphorically speaking, it is all of the *writing* performed on the protagonist's behalf by the novelist; more literally, it includes the inner (silent) discourse of the protagonist; finally, of course, it is all speech performed out loud by the elderly protagonist. Speech of this most literal kind may be divided further. Often, there is something that must be said to other characters, in order to free them for their own lives; this is illustrated by Hagar's statement to Marvin that he has been 'good to [her], always. A better son than John' (304). And it is typical of the *Vollendungsroman* that the truth of this crucial speech act should be in question; what matters is that the thing be said, the gist of it, before the power of speech is gone. An imprecise formulation – even a lie, though Hagar speaks more truly than she knows – is not only preferable to silence, but all that can be hoped for. If Hagar fails 'to speak the heart's truth' (292), she fails in part because we all necessarily fail – and because language fails, always.

Still it is what we have. Through language, we communicate some portion or version of 'the heart's truth' and so become visible, assuming a more or less reliable shape in one another's eyes – so that Marvin, in his turn, can remark to the nurse that his mother is 'a holy terror' (304), and Hagar can feel this accolade as 'more than [she] could ... reasonably have expected out of life, for he has spoken with such anger and such tenderness' (305). However imperfectly, Hagar and Marvin connect *in time* through language. Such moments have a heightened importance in the *Vollendungsroman*, where time is running out.

It is also characteristic of the *Vollendungsroman* that the elderly protagonist is tormented by the memory of characters who have died before some vital message could be delivered or received. Thus, Hagar wants Bram to know she loved him and wants John to know that she regrets the plot to separate him from Arlene. And it is too late. But *The Stone Angel*, like other *Vollendungsromans*, supplies amelioration through delayed and displaced speech, as figures like Murray Lees appear to take the words that Hagar needs to give. None of this can change the damage she has done to others in the past; 'Nothing can take away those years' (292), as Hagar knows full well, unleashing the savage irony that she hears in the minister's words of comfort. Yet language can begin to repair the damage Hagar has done to herself. Speech acts, exchanged with surrogate figures, help her to see what might have been and what she is capable of being even now. They collapse time even as they enforce its tragic necessity, and reveal to Hagar her continuing potential for connectedness in the human family. They point both to the past in which she might have spoken thus, and to the present in which she does.

Hagar thinks that she is 'unchangeable, unregenerate. I go on speaking in the same way, always' (293); thus, her problem with speech is as much with what she says as what she fails to say; and her problem is that in both ways she separates herself from others. Following this self-accusation, however, Hagar withdraws her dismissive remark about the minister – '"We didn't have a single solitary thing to say to one another"' – and admits to Doris that '"He sang for me, and it did me good."' Interestingly, the hymn that Hagar had requested of Mr. Troy is the one '"that starts out *All people that on earth do dwell"'* (291); thus, the 'single solitary' state of alienation and failed speech is pierced by chords addressing all. Song here – as often in the *Vollendungsroman* – seems to leap the gap between silence and speech, bringing into consciousness the individual's yearning for community. It propels Hagar into the kind of recognition which occurs most frequently for the elderly protagonist, a need to shake off the 'chains within' and welcome joy.

Words that are delivered to surviving characters, messages that are routed to the dead through intermediaries (so that the elderly character may be delivered from the burden of silence or mistaken speech), talk in which the aged protagonist may exercise a freer version of the self – these are some of the speech acts that point toward affirmation in the *Vollendungsroman*. Always, they are imperfect or imprecise. But that is necessarily the case, since the *Vollendungsroman* negotiates between speech and silence, between the lived and unlived life – and since desire is never satisfied. What seems to matter is that it be expressed.

Hagar's life has been more mistaken than most – her story more unspoken and misspoken – but the distance she feels between what her life has been and what it should have been is entirely typical of the *Vollendungsroman*. I have connected this German neologism for the novel of old age, of 'completion' or 'winding up,' with a certain measure of irony, since a characteristic of these texts is the recognition that human projects are never completed. Time runs out, as pages do. Only rarely does such a text conclude with a ringing endorsement of what the developmental psychologist Erik Erikson refers to as the old person's 'one and only life.' An exception of this kind is Willa Cather's 'Neighbor Rosicky,' which ends with the statement that 'Rosicky's life seemed to [the doctor] complete and beautiful'; in Cather's novella, the life itself is regarded as a finished work of art, and closure comes without a pang. But *The Stone Angel*, in which Hagar is struggling desperately to change and grow, in which categorically she refuses to gloss over her mistakes and deprivation, is a far more typical case. Art here reflects *and* seeks to compensate for the incompletion of a human life.

For reasons I shall continue to explore, I would argue that the elderly protagonist has pronounced fictional clout. Simone de Beauvoir, however, in *The Coming of Age*, takes a very different view of the uses of the elderly in fiction: 'If an old man is dealt with in his subjective aspect he is not a good hero for a novel; he is finished, set, with no hope, no development to be looked for.... Nothing that can happen to him is of any importance' (210). Novels like *The Stone Angel* prove her wrong, resoundingly. But what is particularly striking in this statement is the notion that elderly protagonists cannot engage our interest if 'dealt with in [their] subjective aspect.' For this is exactly the 'aspect' of old age that contemporary fiction chooses to reveal. When the closed subject becomes an open book, when the mask of stereotypical old age is torn away and the icon stirs, when the elderly character in fiction is allowed to reveal herself as *subject*, we discover that indeed there is 'development to be looked for.' In the case of *The Stone Angel*, that development is 'looked for' – by author, character, and reader – all the more urgently because of the constraints that operate against it.

The Stone Angel gives us the elderly protagonist from the inside. A cantankerous old woman, Hagar Shipley is an obstacle and a problem for her family; but we take her side to a remarkable degree, because we are given access to it. (Consider, in contrast, the figure of the 'old lady' in Sheila Watson's *The Double Hook*: deprived of access to Mrs. Potter's voice, readers typically accept the desirability of her removal and may even approve her murder.) So we see what Hagar says and does and the effect she has on others – and much of that we would judge harshly; but because Hagar is allowed to tell her own story, because we enter her consciousness and live there, we can respond to her more fairly. We learn to value her rich sensuality and the free play of her wit; we see the other side of the coin, the capacity for joy, all the positive qualities that have been so tragically denied in Hagar's presentation of self to the world. We come to understand as well the social forces – familial, patriarchal, and puritanical – which have led her to this distortion. And that very pride which we deplore in its outer workings, as well as for Hagar's sake, is revealed to us as a means of survival.

The subject of old age is a powerful one for other reasons too. The invisibility or marginalization of old people, their reduction to stereotype, their occupation of a zone behind the mask – all of this may provide special impetus to one of the writer's most crucial drives, which is to *see* other human beings clearly. The indignities suffered by the elderly – as their bodies betray them, as memory fails, as social power is stripped away and condescension mounts – may also stimulate the writer's need to proffer dignity through art. Any reader of *The Stone Angel* will recall how Laurence moves us inexorably (detail by scathing detail) from a puerile assumption of the 'we' – '"Well, how are we today?" he inquires' (277) – to a truer sense of the tribulations of old people.

Questions such as these relate to the elderly person's claim upon a writer's empathy or compassion. But the elderly character is also attractive for a number of more technical literary reasons. To begin with, she makes available to the writer nearly the whole span of a life history – as opposed to just that truncated, glibly predictive bit before the heroine decides whom to marry. She picks up the human story at a pivotal and richly dramatic point, when the evaluation of life seems most urgent, and when the old dramatic question of what comes next is most especially poignant. She may also function for the writer as a touchstone (and victim or champion) of social attitudes that have shaped our past and that operate still even in a climate of radical revision. All of this, Hagar clearly does.

The Stone Angel is a prototypical example of the *Vollendungsroman* also in its extensive use of the most characteristic imagery of old age. Consider (for instance) the image of the house, with which Laurence plays so elaborately in using 'Stonehouse' as Aunt Doll's surname (to forecast Hagar's tenure as housekeeper in Mr. Oatley's stone house) and in having Marvin sell housepaint (to imply an interest in appearances, which Hagar forswears when she claims the weatherbeaten house at Shadow Point as her own). Laurence begins her manipulation of this image with the old woman's characteristic fear of dispossession. The house is then developed as an image of the self, the societal construct and the body. What Hagar must do in preparation for her death is what Saul Bellow's elderly heroine in 'Leaving the Yellow House' and countless others must do. She must wean herself from that cocoon, that carapace of appearances, that entrenched idea of the self, and 'admit' the forces of nature. Understandably, she is afraid. Her fear of intruders in the house is the fear of death that Laurence explores in many strands of the novel's imagery.

Other images that are typical of the *Vollendungsroman* include the sea (which is opposed to the house, as the site of dissolution and rebirth) and the transitional identification of Hagar as a gypsy (who makes her home in nature). Angels – as figures posed between two worlds, as messengers and mediators – are also surprisingly common. The last example I will offer here is the mirror, which Laurence uses (again, typically) in two opposing ways. On the one hand, she holds the mirror up to a literal and appalling truth – as Hagar sees in it 'a puffed face purpled with veins as though someone had scribbled over the skin with an indelible pencil' (79) – and on the other hand, she permits Hagar to 'feel that if [she] were to walk carefully up to [her] room, approach the mirror softly, take it by surprise, [she] would see there again that Hagar with the shining hair ...' (42). In these examples (and others I might have chosen), the power of the image is unleashed by a sense of rich particularity – as if the image had been minted just for Hagar – and by a sense of universality.

Perhaps the most common form of the *Vollendungsroman* is the life review, in which narrative time is divided between past and present. The past – in which the characteristic matter of the *Bildungsroman* is recapitulated – is typically approached and controlled through the operation of the elderly protagonist's memory. The present 'mirrors' the past in a number of complex ways, as the protagonist's most basic identity themes are both reasserted and deconstructed in the final phases of life. Very often – as happens at the point of John's death – the narrative of the past will break off sharply, leaving a gap between that period and the narrative present. At such junctures the possibilities of life appear to close down, the seal of failure is imprinted, and a desirable version of the self seems unattainable. The elderly protagonist will often repress this juncture at which vitality was lost; its eventual approach, however, will be another kind of turning point, a courageous breaking of the seal, releasing her into a new sense of possibility.

If the character's old age is purely a framing device – if little or no attention is paid to development in the present or to the experience of being old – then the novel is not by my definition a *Vollendungsroman*. There are also a number of contemporary novels that focus primarily on the present time of elderly protagonists. Thus, a *Vollendungsroman* like Muriel Spark's *Memento Mori* or Paul Scott's *Staying On* will contain elements of the life review without being structured by this process in the way that *The Stone Angel* clearly is. Generally, however, a considerable portion of the narrative time is spent in the past. In this respect as in many others, Laurence's novel is a kind of template for the genre.

The life review is more than a structural device. It has philosophical implications that take us to the heart of the *Vollendungsroman* and the lives of elderly people. In 1963 (one year prior to the appearance of *The Stone Angel*), Robert N. Butler published an essay called 'The Life Review: An Interpretation of Reminiscence in the Aged,' in which he posited 'the universal occurrence in older people of an inner experience or mental process of reviewing one's life' (65). He was arguing against the custom prevailing at that time, which was 'to identify reminiscence in the aged with psychological dysfunction.' Butler suggests that 'the life review, Janus-like, involves facing death as well as looking back' (67) and that 'potentially [it] proceeds towards personality reorganization. Thus, the life review is not synonymous with, but includes reminiscence.' It includes also, that is to say, as *The Stone Angel* does, a vital concern with the possibility of change.

Many of Butler's insights and clinical observations are relevant to the case of Hagar, and to the process of the life review as it is depicted in fiction. He remarks, for instance, that 'imagery of past events and symbols of death seem frequent in waking life as well as in dreams, suggesting that the life review is a highly visual process' (68). Inherently, then, the life review is a kind of *literary* process as well; and Butler may be cited as supplying evidence for the interpenetration of life and art that helps to characterize the *Vollendungsroman*. The verisimilitude of Hagar's 'poetic' voice, as a register of visually proliferating images – birds and eggs, for example, images that we associate with death and captivity and rebirth – is vindicated by Butler's work.

His essay is also concerned with the question of therapeutic value in the process of the life review. Butler rejects the position of certain psychotherapists that old people should not be encouraged to engage in life review, since they will only be devastated by their failures and their incapacity to repair them. He argues instead for the inherent value of 'truth' and for the possibility of change at any point in the life cycle; he believes, in any case, in the inevitability of the life review. Yet Butler acknowledges the risk for three kinds of

people: 'those who always tended to avoid the present and put great emphasis
on the future ... those who have consciously exercised the human capacity to
injure others ... [and those who are] characterologically arrogant and prideful'
(70). Although harsh and incomplete, this might serve a wary therapist as a
thumbnail sketch of Hagar Shipley.

Margaret Laurence, however, would not be dissuaded – any more than
Hagar is herself. At risk in all these ways, Hagar profits nonetheless (and we
profit) from her life review. She 'proceeds *toward* personality reorganization'
(Butler 67, italics mine). To suggest also how we profit, I shall turn to the work
of two other gerontologists. Kathleen Woodward, in her critique of Butler's
famous essay, argues that 'his notion of plot is Aristotelian; that is, it ...
possesses 'wholeness' ... and thus unity' (146). Butler is charged with assuming that the life story will be 'resolved' in an out-moded literary way; indeed,
in Woodward's view, he *uses* such literature to construct his pleasing, but fal-
lacious, sense of completion in life. But *The Stone Angel* does not actually
'affirm' Hagar's life in terms of unity or wholeness. Indeed, it seizes upon the
open ending and upon filaments launched into the future; it discovers hope
paradoxically, through the recognition of failure. Certainly it does not ask us
to regard Hagar's life as anything like that of Cather's 'Neighbor Rosicky.'

Laurence in fact directs us toward what Harry R. Moody calls 'the public
world' (158). First Hagar must go there; dramatically, this is signalled by
Hagar's residence in the public ward, where she begins to think of others and
to consider the possibility of social change. Thus, she contemplates (for
example) a world in which her granddaughter's husband could accept her
sturdy independence, a world in which women are acquiring knowledge of
their bodies as well as knowledge that might lead to jobs that use their minds.
She gets there, however – to Moody's 'public world' – only because she has
the courage to persist in the life review. From that story she learns how other
stories might be written *better*.

Moody's idea is that the story should be told out loud. The life review process should transport the elderly person from a private and solipsistic space
into a public one, in which the story can be heard. In fact, Moody is concerned
less with the therapeutic value of the life review than with its importance for
society at large; his interest is focussed on the loss to society that is entailed
by our narcissistic denial of the experience of the aged. Reminiscence,
Moody suggests, is not – as Aristotle thought – opposed to hope: 'It is the
other way around' (160), since 'old people live and remember for the sake of
the future' (161). But Moody recognizes as well the benefit that accrues to the
old person whose story is heard: 'The singing of the song and the telling of the
tale *must* become public in order to shine through the natural ruin of time.'

The public story is never finished. And neither is the private one, though
it needs to be told (however partially) before the story is cut off: 'And then –' It

needs telling for its contribution to the public story, and because the elderly person must know that the communal realm is somehow real, if she is not to feel that her annihilation is complete. She can stand – Hagar can – the knowledge that 'the plagues go on from generation to generation' (284) and that 'nothing is ever changed at a single stroke' (88); she can stand to know (and *needs* to know) that her own life has been a failure, in most of the ways that count. But she needs to speak. Hagar has only begun to speak 'the heart's truth' when her time runs out; and she has little chance to review her life for others, although she makes a crucial start with Murray Lees.

Happily – for Hagar's sake, I'd like to say, as well as for ours – her insistent voice was heard in the 'Shadow Point' of Margaret Laurence's subconscious. There, it grew, by nature and by art. It became at last the 'forest' of Laurence's text, where the voice of Hagar Shipley speaks. It became 'a forest, through which one can see outward, in which the shapes of trees do not prevent air and sun, and in which the trees themselves are growing structures, something alive.' And it became that through the force of Margaret Laurence's compassionate imagination. I knew Margaret Laurence only slightly – I spent no more than a dozen hours in her company – but I think I learned this much: that Laurence was moved above all by a need to fight, for herself and others, a need to lend her womanly strength. She had a lot of Hagar in her – and as Hagar would have wished, she wrote with her own life a better story.

Works Cited

Butler, Robert N. 'The Life Review: An Interpretation of Reminiscence in the Aged.' *Psychiatry* 26.1 (1963): 65-76.

de Beauvoir, Simone. *The Coming of Age.* New York: Putnam's, 1972.

Laurence, Margaret. 'Gadgetry or Growing: Form and Voice in the Novel.' *Journal of Canadian Fiction* 27.1 (1980): 54-62.

———. *The Stone Angel.* Toronto: McClelland and Stewart, New Canadian Library, 1982.

Moody, Harry R. 'Reminiscence and the Recovery of the Public World.' *Journal of Gerontological Social Work* 7.1 / 2 (1984): 157-66.

New. W.H. 'Every Now and Then: Voice and Language in Laurence's *The Stone Angel.' Canadian Literature* 93 (1982): 79-96.

Woodward, Kathleen. 'Reminiscence and the Life Review: Prospects and Retrospects.' *What Does It Mean to Grow Old?: Reflections from the Humanities.* Ed. Thomas R. Cole and Sally Gadow. Durham, N.C.: Duke University Press, 1986. 135-61.

Women of *The Double Hook*

Sheila Watson has said very little about *The Double Hook*. The little she has said, however, is – like her single, tiny novel – vast. Her only published remarks, the transcript of a talk she gave in Edmonton, are to be found in the special issue of *Open Letter* devoted to her work, in a piece called 'What I'm Going To Do.' Watson refers there to her publisher's decision to put a photograph on the cover of her novel – 'which seemed to [Watson] completely wrong' (181). A photograph, we may suppose, would be too literal and too restrictive. She supplied them instead with a 'double hook' she'd found in Paris. Some learned man had told Watson that double hooks do not exist 'in nature' (182); and it's especially pleasing that this woman who achieved what the received Canadian wisdom of the day had told her was impossible – a novel reconciling the 'regional' and the 'international' – should have found her double hook in bookish Paris, the very hook *she* knew was embedded in the flesh and ground of British Columbia.

What's more, the hook was *hand-made*. The photographer had to enlarge it to fill the cover, 'and as he enlarged it, all the imperfections, the beautiful imperfections of hand work began to show. It looked like quite a smooth hook when you held it in your hand, but as it grew larger and larger you could see all these ... perfections? Imperfections? I don't know.' So it is with this dangerous, lovely novel. It grows larger and larger, the more closely we examine it; and the more closely we look, the more we see the 'imperfections' in our hand-made, human knowledge – 'imperfections' which might, in the last analysis, be indistinguishable from 'perfections.' They *might* be, if there were a last analysis. 'I don't know,' says Sheila Watson, defying closure.

She is a writer who welcomes collaboration – multiple, imperfect readings of her text – just as she delighted in the imperfections of the hand-made double hook, and in the work of the photographer: 'It gave me an enormous pleasure when I saw the book in this cover, because it seemed like a co-creation. It was the first thing that happened after the writing of the book, that is, it had caused someone else to make something else which I thought was in itself very lovely.' All of this makes a handy metaphor for the work of critics, examining and enlarging the text, exposing the 'imperfections' of its knowledge and their own; it invites the co-creator / critic to be faithful to the text *and* to make 'something else.'

Another passage in the Edmonton talk draws attention to itself more forcibly. It's a statement of theme, in which Sheila Watson tells us what she 'wanted to say' in *The Double Hook*: '[something] about how people are driven, how if they have no art, how if they have no tradition, how if they have no ritual, they are driven in one of two ways, either towards violence or towards insensibility – if they have no mediating rituals which manifest themselves in what I suppose we call art forms' (183). I would comment here that ritual itself is a 'response to ambivalence' (Turner, 72), that mediation does not mean perfect resolution, and that the art forms preferred by Watson are those which can accommodate and make lovely the 'imperfections' of the double hook. I would comment further that the middle ground between violence and insensibility is life, made possible by art. And it is wide and various enough; it is not – like the grave from which James Potter turns away – a place 'too short for a man to stretch himself in' (99). The middle ground is also the realm of art; critics can move there, avoiding the two extremes of torpor and violence against the text. But first of all it is *life*, defined most crucially in terms of our response to co-inhabitants, our need to avoid both destruction (or vindictive rage) and solipsistic denial. Art helps us to do this because it teaches empathy. Watson's stated theme invites us to consider art in terms of its consequences for human life.

This leads me to the third and last of the passages I would excerpt from the Edmonton talk. In this, Watson speaks of her concern with 'figures in a ground, from which they could not be separated' (183). This passage has been widely and profitably interpreted as asserting the primacy of a linguistic context, and as a kind of warning to any critic who would treat these 'figures' as people – or, indeed, as characters in any ordinary sense. But the emphasis of the passage is otherwise: 'I didn't think of them as people in a place, in a stage set, in a place which had to be described for itself, as it existed outside the interaction of the people with the objects, with the things, with the other existences with which they came into contact. So that the people are entwined, they're interacting with the landscape, and the landscape is interacting with them ... not the landscape, the things about them, the other things which exist.' Watson's concern here is not primarily to deny that the 'figures' are people – indeed, she refers to them as such. She is interested rather in their relationship to the ground, 'the other things which exist'; she is arguing for a kind of textual ecology and (I think) for an *ethic* of attention to the workings of a whole, which again has consequences for both art and life.

I labour this point because the passage has been used to deflect critical attention from one of the issues I will be addressing today: the murder of Mrs. Potter, as a bad thing. It has been argued, by John Grube and others, that Mrs. Potter is a 'symbol'; it seems to follow, for too many of Watson's readers, that it's pretty well okay to kill a symbol, if what she symbolizes is death. She is, after all, just a thing made out of words. (So, of course, are the other figures;

but in Mrs. Potter's case the signals of humanity have been tuned out.) We can then cite other writing – T.S. Eliot and Jessie Weston's *From Ritual to Romance* – in order to regard her killer as a questing knight, and saviour of the Wasteland. But I think the old lady's murder is wrong, and I am troubled by the willingness to call language and art as exonerating witnesses – especially when, as Watson suggests in the statement of her theme, the particular use of 'art forms' is to establish a place of mediation, a middle ground that dissuades us from the extremes of violence and insensibility.

§

My subject is the women of *The Double Hook*. Both collectively and as individuals, these women (or figures, if you like) have been under-valued, under-read. The privileging of male characters is evident, for instance, in this influential statement by John Grube: 'The hero, James, comes to represent suffering humanity as well as its deliverer, Felix Prosper the priestly, William Potter the rational aspect of man and society' (10). In that composite figure of the human animal, I find the exclusion of females most disturbing. With at least as much justice, one could devise another trinity made up of their *wives*: Ara representing the visionary, and Angel the practical, with Lenchen cast as the deliverer and emancipated mother of us all. My point, however, is that the marginalization of female characters has weakened critical discourse on *The Double Hook*: it leaves us dangling – as if on a single hook – and blinds us to much of what is happening in Watson's entwined and interactive text.

This marginalization occurs also within the text, in the sense that Sheila Watson depicts there a sexist society. Amply she baits the female half of her double hook, to suggest that the male / female opposition is one of the most problematic of the novel's binary pairs. (It's not her fault, I'm saying, that so few have taken the bait.) Watson signals her concern with the marginalization of females through the repetition – in the mouths of nearly all her characters – of aphoristic statements beginning with the words 'a man.' William, for example, says 'a man gets used to things being as they are from day to day' (52) and 'A man does what he can' (53). The novel offers nearly a hundred examples of this verbal tic, and clusters them so that periodically we are required to take notice. Most often, there is room for doubt as to the referent – whether human beings in general, or only men are at issue. Moreover, at critical points, Watson varies her usage, so that we hear occasionally about 'a person'; thus she draws attention to the problematic reference of 'a man' and the possibility that women are being left out of too many of the aphoristic characterizations of humankind.

This issue comes to a head in an exchange between William and James and Heinrich, following James's return to the community. James says 'I ran away ... but I circled and ended here the way a man does when he's lost' (132). And

William comments that 'a person only escapes in circles no matter how far the rope spins' – whereupon Heinrich (a rather androgynous figure, a boy who can't figure out why man's talk and woman's talk cannot overlap) reminds us that 'There was Greta as well as James.' Women, that is to say, must be taken into account. Then, thinking of his sister Lenchen, but reacting (it seems to me) as well to all these endless pronouncements and speculations about 'a man,' Heinrich turns to James and asks a ringing, splendidly disruptive question: 'Tell me, he said, what would a girl do?' And there is no reply.

Let me turn then to the particular women of *The Double Hook*, and attempt to fill in some of the silence. I begin most particularly with Mrs. Potter, a figure struck to the ground on the novel's first page – and resurrected by the author on the second page. For what purpose? Partly, I think, in order to insist (as the old lady herself insists) that she not be effaced, that certain pressing questions must be posed and answers sought. Mrs. Potter's continuing presence can be thought of as a kind of trick, black comedy inspired by Coyote (with whom she is closely aligned) or by Watson as Coyote. It's a trick on the reader, upsetting expectations about the powers appropriate to a dead old woman. It places us in the position of the valley people, who are outraged by her stubborn adherence to life – so that we may be seduced into taking James's part; at the same time, it denies the efficacy of the murder. But it is a trick, and finally a benevolent one – a fictional dispensation, postponing the full reality of death, and giving us a chance to rescind approval of the matricide.

Mrs. Potter is a figure marginalized thrice over: *dead, old, woman*. She is denied a voice, deprived of her status as a human subject – and she resists. A literary gerontologist would be interested in her case, because it illustrates very clearly the pressure that is exerted against the elderly, an insistence upon what sociologists refer to as disengagement. The task of old age is sometimes given as the transcendence of ego, which may be translated as a willingness to let go of social power. It is easy to detect a vested interest in the allocation of this task; the process may be recommended as spiritually advantageous for the old, when its egotistical motive (on the part of the young) is simply to reduce clutter or competition within the circle. Mrs. Potter is killed because she refuses disengagement. She is asked to die to make room for her children, and because her children (it seems) cannot pursue their own development as individuals in the face of Mrs. Potter's monumental discontent. And she refuses to die, precisely because she is discontent.

Another way of saying all this is that Mrs. Potter is killed because she is old, because others want to take the story away from her. In the hotel, James offers this explanation of his mother's death: 'She was old, James said, speaking to the parrot. It was the heat that took her and climbing round in the creek bottom' (101). Three causes of death, or justifications of her murder, are given here – old age, God's anger (the heat, or what is referred to on the second page of the novel as the 'fire of righteousness' 20), and the persistence of her quest. On that second page, we are introduced to the same trinity of explanation. James kills her on the first page: she is pushed 'into the shadow of death … by James's will. By James's hand. By James's words: This is my day. You'll not fish today.' But we turn the page to find that 'Still the old lady fished' (20). And then we hear someone – the author, presumably; an authoritative voice – moved to outrage by the old woman's persistence. If there were no water in the creek (if nature, that is, made fishing absurd), or if God himself came to rebuke her, still Mrs. Potter would persist in her folly. Thus, the author as well as God and nature would seem to take sides with James against his mother.

Why is this God who is summoned by the authorial imagination so angry at Mrs. Potter? We note that his benevolence and suffering are signalled *before* his anger: he comes 'holding out the long finger of salvation, moaning in the darkness.' But the finger is accusatory now, and the moan turns into thunder as God comes to confront the woman rebel. To signal both displeasure and his control of nature, on which previously (we may assume) God's finger had written his own name, he comes 'skimming across the water, drying up the blue signature like blotting paper.' God is angry, no doubt, because Mrs. Potter has failed in the task of reading his text; she has resisted his authorial clout, his intention, both in the story of salvation through Christ and in the tradition of nature as God's book, which is supposed to make him manifest to a loving heart.

In drying up the waters of salvation and his signature, God cites the destructive power which is half of his double hook. 'Defying an answer,' he considers that surely now his point – his power to create and destroy – is irrefutable. But Mrs. Potter is not impressed. She 'would have thrown her line against the rebuke; she would have caught a piece of mud and looked it over.' She casts her own line. She reads this mud, instead of God's intent; as if to assert her own authority and to deny her creaturely status, she takes 'the barb' and *writes* on the creek bottom. Mrs. Potter has assumed the prerogatives of the Author and of the Fisherman – of Christ, that is – and she has failed to read his name upon the waters; her own soul is therefore the fish she cannot catch. But God's wrath, it seems, is provoked also by her shameless refusal to die. This refusal subverts his text in a particularly outrageous manner; his whole story is dependent upon the mortality of his creatures, and upon his exclusive authorial power to confer immortality (or supply another ending).

I am not suggesting that Watson opposes God in this scene; it is she, after all, who invokes him. But I do think there is something tricky at work here. Watson is author too, and it is she who permits the old woman to continue fishing. In the end, Mrs. Potter seems to accept her death with grace; both she and God might be said to win out, because the dispensation of the text gives the old lady some extra time, and what transpires in the interval of her ghostly persistence is enough to save Mrs. Potter's soul. That dispensation is Sheila Watson's gift to the woman who is both victim and victimizer, both fish and Fisherwoman.

This double vision of the old lady is implied by the story of the rat that Felix pokes down from the rafters. We associate Mrs. Potter with the rat because she dies in the rafters, and because James connects his mother's intrusive eyes with 'rats' eyes on the barn rafters' (43). Felix pokes at his rat with a pole that recalls the fishing rod; and the rat ('mad with dread') runs down the pole to attack him – as if moving from the position of fish to that of Fisherwoman, from object to subject. At this point, Felix's terrier attacks (she is suggestive of Coyote, in whose mouth the old lady is once seen), and the sight of 'White foam on the brown swirl' on the rat's bitten neck recalls to Felix a vision of 'The old lady fishing in the brown water for fish she'd never eat. The old lady year after year' (39). Our sense that the rat and the old woman have been attacked unreasonably is strengthened by Watson's juxtaposition of this scene with Felix's memory of Angel and the bear that isn't a bear – so that the threat she feels is overblown.

The rat scene may be recalled once more at the end of the novel, when Kip confesses to Felix that he 'kept at' James like a dog with a porcupine, until the porcupine turned on him. In this configuration, the rat's pole spins and James becomes the porcupine (or rat) provoked by the dog (or Kip or his Coyote mother). Felix, however, declines the analogical excuse: 'James's got more than a porcupine has to answer for' (133). And William makes a similar distinction between man and beast just a few pages before, when he asserts that 'A man ... [is] not just a lone bull who ... can charge at anything that takes his fancy' (129).

Mrs. Potter's subtle and complex association with animals ('other things which exist') works to extend our moral awareness, and helps us not to judge her too harshly. This is true even of her association with the 'great cow' who refuses to nourish or cast a shadow for the protection of her young, because (as William points out) 'The most unaccountable thing ... is the way the sun falls' (22). The fault is not necessarily or entirely with the cow.

One final animal I would discuss – perhaps the most enigmatic in the book, next to Coyote – can also be linked to Mrs. Potter. I mean the parrot, to whom James addresses his remarks in the hotel bar. In a muted way, Watson uses this parrot to effect a reconciliation between mother and son. Recalling Flaubert's parrot in *Un Coeur Simple*, the parrot suggests the Holy Ghost – or the unholy ghost (for the town is a place of theological inversion, where whores are named Lily, Felicia, and Christine). Like Mrs. Potter's ghost, it is a creature suspended between two worlds. James 'confesses' to the parrot in the bar, and responds to a familiar 'note of authority' (103) in the parrot's raised voice. It's funny too that the parrot requires him to buy 'drinks all round' (100), given Mrs. Potter's refusal to share her fish; though bossy, this parroted phrase may even be a sign that the old lady's spirit is moving toward generosity. James orders beer for the parrot too, suggesting a shadow of compassion for the woman's loneliness and her hard life: 'It's little enough he must have to live for. One parrot in this whole bloody universe of men' (103). Then James loses his money at the brothel, willingly, so that his return to the settlement is sealed – and at this point he sees 'the lights of the hotel where the parrot who lived between two worlds was probably asleep now, stupid with beer and age' (109). Thus we may suppose that his mother's spirit too is finding rest.

Throughout the novel, Watson's other figures think and speak ill of Mrs. Potter. She is impugned for seeing too much, for failures of her maternal function, for not eating or sharing her fish, for trespass, and for disturbing the peace. She is also *silenced*, so that she has no chance to reveal herself to us more fully. I think of another old woman, Hagar in *The Stone Angel*, and of how harshly we would judge that 'holy terror' if Margaret Laurence had not allowed us to construct her as a subject, if we had not had access to her consciousness. The comparison is interesting as well in light of the feminist subtext that helps us in each novel to look more kindly at the old woman's pride.

Occasionally, it is possible to interpret an observation by Henrich or Kip or Ara – who remarks that 'She was the one who noticed' (75) – as a defence of Mrs. Potter's persistent 'seeing.' But there is only one character who supports Mrs. Potter directly. Greta is complaining about her mother's Diogenes-like obsession with the lamp: 'Holding it up in broad daylight ... looking where there's nothing to be found. Nothing but dust. No person's got a right to keep looking. To keep looking and blackening lamp globes for others to clean' (31). And Angel Prosper, who is ironically scrubbing Greta's floor at the time, cannot accept this: 'Angel sat back on her heels.... You mean you're not going to let her do it anymore, Angel said. One person's got as much right as another. Maybe she don't ask you to clean those globes. There's things people want to see.' Greta's own vision has been 'blackened' – by her mother, as she thinks – but Angel points out that Greta's servitude to darkness is finally her own doing. Angel defends Mrs. Potter's right to see, and implicitly requires her killers (for Greta is complicit with James) to accept responsibility for their own decision not to 'let her do it anymore.'

Angel's name suggests that she too is a creature between two worlds; she moves between two men, and she is a messenger and a mediator. Thus, it seems appropriate that she is poised between 'the wall shadow [and] ... the window light' when she concludes her defense of Mrs. Potter with the compassionate recognition that 'there's things get lost.' Angel is a wonderful character. She is tough, as when she challenges Greta in this scene: 'Why didn't you take your own lamp and go looking for something? Angel said. You've never in all your life burned anything but a little oil to finish doing in the house' (31-32). Her speech is prophetic, since Greta will end by burning up both herself and the house; but Angel's intent is not unkindly (any more than Mrs. Potter's is, in her one recorded speech, the warning to Greta not to play with matches: 'A person has to know how to play with fire' 85). Angel knows that this bitter, sexually frustrated woman has 'a whole case of dynamite under her skirt' (73), and suspects that it is too late for Greta to save herself. But she also believes in taking responsibility for one's own life: 'Who says where a woman shall lie but that very woman herself. Who keeps chawing at a man but a man's own self?' (60).

Angel has had trouble over men. Greta says, in fact, that she has 'burned and spilled enough oil to light up the whole country' (32) – a reference to Angel's having left Felix Prosper to live with Theophil. But the oil that Angel burns is not destructive; and the lamp that Felix recalls her lighting – if it is not 'a wax candle to the Virgin' (38) – is nevertheless used for life, 'against the mist that brought death.' When Felix neglects her, Angel takes her many children and moves on to another man. When Theophil turns out to be worse – even more self-enclosed, and determined to stifle and 'break' her, as Felix 'never tried to' (40) – she simply packs up her children again and returns to Felix. (The cast of characters in the valley, including the supply of available men, is sorely limited.) Felix, however, happily, has learned something from Lenchen about female pain. Although he thinks of Angel as 'tough and rooted as a thistle. He'd never heard her cry' (125), he now understands 'the pain of a growing root' and will be able to respond to Angel's needs more fully. As a sort of reward for this insight, Sheila Watson allows her born-again bridegroom to lose a great deal of weight in a hurry.

'A woman sharpens herself to endure,' Angel tells Lenchen. 'Since she can be trod on like an egg, she grows herself to stone' (123). This speech recalls William's claim that 'Ma was hard on [Greta].... She thought grief was what a woman was born to' (113) – and may cause us to glimpse some benevolence in Mrs. Potter's harsh mothering. Though Greta complains that she 'was never let run loose' (66), the context of that remark is sexual; and William recalls her girlhood as a time of 'sliding down stacks and falling into creeks' (131). The suggestion is that for a time at least she did run free – like Angel's children, or as Lenchen did before her 'female' troubles began. Greta herself says of the female plight that 'A woman can stand what a man can't stand. To be scorned by others ...' (66). And Lenchen tells Kip, 'Girls don't have things to give' (62). These are women living under patriarchy. But as Angel tells Lenchen, there is no use 'snivelling' (117) about it. The thing to do is the best you

can – and take a little pride in yourself as well. That is largely the message
that Angel bears.

Lenchen is an interesting case. Early in the novel, we see her with 'heavy
heeled boots beating impatience' (25), walking 'as a man might walk' (40); she
talks of wanting to 'get away' because 'It's time [she] learned something else,'
though she claims to 'know even as much as ... James Potter' (25), and doesn't
at all like James's demonstrably false assumption that she is incompetent
with animals. But as things get worse – her mother kicks her out because she
is pregnant, and James ignores her and strikes her with a whip and finally
abandons her – Lenchen's pride is broken. 'She's been rid on the curb, Felix
thought. And felt the prick of steel' (40). Lenchen is marginalized, outcast;
she begins to pity herself and finally to blame herself. But Angel stops her,
pointing out that 'the whole world is a big lot for one girl to wreck' (117).

When the baby starts to come, Angel leaves the midwifery to Felix – and
goes to bring the Widow Wagner to her daughter's bedside. The Widow is a
kind of ironic double for Mrs. Potter; her fear of God's judgement, for
example, is the other hook of the other old matriarch's defiance, as her willed
blindness is the counterfoil of Mrs. Potter's willful seeing. They are linked
also through the imagery of cows. A comic echo of Mrs. Potter's maternal
failure comes in the scene where the Widow speaks to her cow, urging her to
shake off the suckling calf: 'We're old women both of us' (118). But 'The cow
and the calf paid no attention to her,' and the Widow blames herself for 'wasting' the milk: 'There will be none for the children' (119), she says – forgetting
about the calf. The point is that not all needs can be satisfied at once, by any
old woman.

The Widow Wagner has made progress, however. She is trying to help.
Thus, for example, she takes scissors and cuts some hoarded 'cloth of her
own spinning' (115) in order to make a singlet for her grandchild. By this
action, she moves from past to future. And Watson recalls the ubiquitous
imagery of thread, found (for example) in Williams's story of the woman who
used thread 'to sew up her man after he was throwed on a barbed-wire fence'
(21). The implication of that tale is that although we live under more or less
desperate constraints and are bound by mortality, many woes and rifts *can* be
repaired. Thread unravels, to be sure, but it 'has a hundred uses.' Few are
more auspicious than this making of the baby's singlet; most, in this patriarchal valley, require the labour of women.

I would argue, nevertheless, that Sheila Watson implies some restoration
of matriarchal power at the end of *The Double Hook*. Her women have ral-
lied, under Angel's banner; Lenchen, for instance, calmly informs James that
their son will be called Felix. Another mother-son relationship begins; and
another Potter matriarch is created by Felix's birth.

I want to close with a few words about Ara, the barren woman who has extraordinary, fruitful visions of both death and life, and through whom we hear Coyote's final cry: 'I have set his feet on soft ground; / I have set his feet on the sloping shoulders / of the world' (134). In this valley, no one's happiness is assured. Ara herself has a tenuous purchase on the earth, for she was 'made to beat her hands against rock faces and to set her foot on sliding shale' (81). Whereas 'Lenchen was part of any animal she rode,' Ara rides 'stiff as a clothes peg'; William defends her though, as he recalls a dog 'that could ride a horse as well as a man. When the going got rough.' Thus, Ara (under Angel's tutelage) is able to drive the team that carries the Widow back to Lenchen. This movement toward community and toward integration with 'the other things which exist' is significant, to be sure. But we are impressed equally by Ara's expression of wonder at this unaccustomed success with horses: 'Wherever I go I most often go by my own strength' (128). For this is still the valley of *The Double Hook*, in which the hook of community is opposed by reminders of our solitude – as in Angel's statement that 'One man is one man and two men or ten men aren't something else,' or that 'There's no word to tell that when [a man and a woman] get together in bed they're still anything but two people' (86).

Ara will do what she can; and there are signs that William, her unquenchable, stolid husband, will be more responsive to Ara's pain. She may even learn from him that, on balance, 'It's best to be trusting and loving' (75). But many of Ara's desires are unfulfilled. We see, for instance, the ache of her childlessness in Ara's relationship to Heinrich, who treats her as a kind of surrogate mother: 'I don't know what to do' (83), he says on one occasion, and Ara replies bitterly, 'You have your own Ma.' In the novel's final scene, we are told that 'Ara didn't want to look at James' (134). I can think of a couple of explanations of this enigmatic and therefore peculiarly prominent line. Perhaps it signifies a continuing hostility to James for his ill treatment of Lenchen and his mother. It may also suggest that Ara is attracted to the valley's most potent male, for the novel supplies other hints of that possibility. But in any case, we know through Ara – perhaps more than through any other figure – that pain is real. The miraculous, healing baby we are given at the end of *The Double Hook* cannot change that: 'I never see baby-clothes, [Ara] said, that I don't think how a child puts on suffering with them' (119).

Life in the valley of *The Double Hook* is imperfect. People make it by hand, working at what is given with whatever equipment comes to hand, trying to live with one another and with the other things which exist. They fail, and descend into violence or insensibility, when they can no longer see the reality of others; that's when they kill or become stupefied. But they fail in any case. Vision fails, and must be found again: so that they can see to thread the needle, so that they can see where the fabric has been torn. Vision *means* seeing the darkness too. Women are specialists at this: working in the dark, on the margins – under duress, as we all are. And I think it is important to *see* the women of *The Double Hook*, both their undervaluing and their value, as these female figures go about their Mother's business of making babies, making up visions, making do.

Works Cited

Grube, John, introd. *The Double Hook*. New Canadian Library, No. 54. Toronto: McClelland and Stewart, 1966. 5-14.

Turner, Margaret E. 'Fiction, Break, Silence: Language. Sheila Watson's "The Double Hook."' *Ariel*, 18.2 (April 1984): 65-78.

Watson, Sheila. 'What I'm Going To Do.' *Sheila Watson: A Collection* [*Open Letter* 3.1 (Winter 1974-75)].

———. *The Double Hook*. New Canadian Library, No. 54. Toronto: McClelland and Stewart, 1966.

Dog in a Grey Room: The Happy Ending of *Coming Through Slaughter*

I know that many readers have found *Coming Through Slaughter*, and especially its conclusion, extraordinarily bleak. The more I read the book, the more convinced I am that *Slaughter* has a happy ending. And I think you have to do that: really enter the book, travel in a visceral way through the images, to see the affirmation that lies on the other side of *Slaughter*. If you stay on this side, the story is undeniably grim. But if you can go far enough with Ondaatje, follow through the immensely complex and proliferating images, his yearnings, as Ondaatje followed Bolden's, then a *bouleversement* will occur for you as well. It is the motive force of the book, why it was written at all, and why I love it.

I take Buddy Bolden to be the hero of the novel, indeed an exemplary case of the artist as hero. Sam Solecki, in a footnote to his essay 'Making and Destroying: Michael Ondaatje's *Coming Through Slaughter* and Extremist Art,' quotes Ondaatje as having said that '"the problems Bolden has are the problems any artist has at some time,"' and then says that Ondaatje 'overstates the point' (25). Solecki argues that there are two kinds of artist, the 'ordinary' or 'normal' artist and the 'extremist.' The difference, he says, 'begins as one of degree but leads ultimately to almost one of kind' (26). Stephen Scobie, in '*Coming Through Slaughter*: Fictional Magnets and Spider's Webbs,' also regards the novel as a portrait of the artist – 'or more precisely a certain kind of artist' (6). Both critics are therefore concerned with splitting off the self-destructive Buddy Bolden from Ondaatje as articulate survivor. And both read *Coming Through Slaughter* as, in Solecki's words, 'announcing the bankruptcy of extremist art' (44).

I would not deny the usefulness of Solecki's distinction between two kinds of artists, but I think that it can lead to a mistaken emphasis in the interpretation of *Coming Through Slaughter*. It seems to me wrong to divorce author and character at the end, to suggest that one (Ondaatje, like Conrad's Marlowe in *Heart of Darkness*) is saved by caution and the other (Bolden, like Kurtz) is doomed by excess. Imaginatively – and again I would claim that this is the *reason* for the book – Ondaatje goes with Bolden all the way. If in actuality he does not, that is beside the point. If at the end we sense a part of him moving away, that is only because the book is over now. Bolden the extremist knows what Ondaatje knows: that the need to break through 'certainties,' to find new ways of thinking and seeing and being, is the very essence of creativity. Extremist art is that which in its style and subject matter takes that 'breaking through' somehow more literally than the normal artist may do. And particularly because such a visceral or extreme response to the imperative of breaking through may find expression in the artist's life as well as in his work, there will always be a natural attraction to and fear of the extremist.

Take marriage now, as a synecdoche for life: the task there is not, I think, to make a seemly, stable artifact. You don't want to figure out a reasonably good way of being, and then stick to that – any more than you would want to write *The Rape of the Lock* over again, or a verbatim repeat of your own last novel. Or if you do, you're not an artist. It may be argued that artists in particular are tempted by domestic certainty – to balance the risk-taking of their art, to get their work *done*. But surely the best thing is to keep both life and art on the move. And that is partly the explanation of the peculiar attraction we may feel to those extremist artists who live out the extremes, as well as write about them. In some way it *is* a validation of their art. Both Solecki and Ondaatje are concerned with the grotesquerie of the audience which cries out for blood, 'the peanut-crunching crowd' of Sylvia Plath's 'Lady Lazarus' that 'Shoves in to see / The big strip tease.' But there is also an honourable motive for our fascination with the extreme, and from the perspective of that motive the suffering extremist is observed not as scapegoat but as hero. I say this because I believe it's only accident, or only history, that makes us associate extremism with madness, stereotypically 'wild' living, suicide and the like: I think other forms of extremism are there for the making, in life as in art. However literally the usual modes of extremism are lived out, they are still primarily metaphors for breaking through. As such, they have an evolutionary thrust. And 'self-destruction' is a loaded term, hiding – it may be – the chance of growth.

I do not intend this argument as a hymn to the wife-battering genius. Nor do I think I'm romanticizing the suicide or the lunatic. Margarethe von Trotta's film *Marianne and Juliane* may help to make my point. In that film, however profoundly we may deplore the actions of the sister who becomes a terrorist, we come to understand that she is motivated at least in part by something purely admirable: she has *looked*, harder than most of us have, at the intolerable misery, the inadequacy of the given world. She strikes out at that. And we make a bad mistake if we concern ourselves only with psychoanalysis or politics, the question of why and how she went wrong. Lessons of moderation are not the only lessons to be learned. Only by understanding the point at which she is right, that extremity of vision, will we discover the right response to what she sees. Solecki uses as an epigraph for his essay two lines from Adrienne Rich: 'Madness. Suicide. Murder. / Is there no way out but these?' The answer must eventually be yes. In the meantime, such extremism may land the artist in a still more wretched part of hell; or it may yield him peace through nothingness, a mere cessation of life's pain and contradictions. But there is also a chance of imaginative transcendence, entry into a state of being which is prophetic of our goal on *this* side of Slaughter. This last, I think, is what happens to Buddy Bolden.

The position elaborated in this essay may seem to place me in opposition to Stephen Scobie and Sam Solecki, whose essays on *Coming Through Slaughter* I admire. In fact, my own essay will assume much of the ground covered by Scobie and Solecki. I shall be filling in their map, looking at images and thinking about characters partly in ways they have not, arriving at a different place with their help. In terms of theme, I shall be concerned with issues of love and power, with egoism and the transcendence of ego, with old questions about the self and the other, the one and the many. Among the image patterns I shall examine, high roads and by-ways on Michael Ondaatje's own map, are the following: landscape, rooms and wallpaper, clouds, veins, the polarity of black and white, the colour blue, dogs, the mattress whores, and the dolphin sonographs. *Coming Through Slaughter* is intensely poetic; its logic – its argument if you like – is that of poetry. But it is also a novel, whose characters (and their deployment) must not recede from view; and so I have chosen to place Bolden's journey in the foreground, to deal with the images as they arise, rather than to pursue each pattern separately. For reasons of economy, and with great reluctance, I shall have to ignore to a considerable degree Ondaatje's brilliant juxtapositions, the temporal dislocations and orchestration of voices in his text, and will move through Bolden's journey in chronological order.

As the title may suggest, the most pervasive kind of imagery in *Coming Through Slaughter* is spatial: the idea of a landscape (the life journey) through which Bolden moves, the parade (of display to others) which he enters and exits, and the rooms (the psychic space) in which he lives alone and with others. Of his first life phase we know nothing, for 'Bolden had never spoken of his past.... Landscape suicide.' At fifteen he meets Webb, telling nothing, and at seventeen they take an apartment together: we enter his landscape at that point.

They live in a neutral, 'brown painted apartment' (42) where they 'gradually paste their characters [like wallpaper] onto each other.' They spend a week alone 'building up the apartment in Pontchartrain,' establishing their relationship, the space they occupy together. Their activities are parallel: Webb's play with the magnets and Bolden's with the cornet. Each of these activities is a performance, and each involves opposing forces in the air – 'the precision of the forces' that Webb must explain to Bolden. At first, Webb is the dominant partner, 'Webb who was the public figure, Bolden the side-kick.' When they emerge from that week in the room, however, their relationship seems equal, their friendship 'a public act of repartee' as they bounce 'jokes off each other in female company' (35), performing for women they trade back and forth, their taste in whom, 'diverse at first, becomes embarrassingly similar' (42). This is the language of exchange, and it connects with Buddy's later account of the usual pattern of relationship between the sexes: 'the slow true intimacy, disintegration after they exchanged personalities and mannerisms, the growing tired of each other's speed' (88).

Now they begin to move apart. More precisely, Bolden moves ahead: 'It was Bolden who had jumped up, who had swallowed everything Webb was' (36). Buddy's persona is launched upon the world with his 'very famous entrance' (38) into the New Orleans parade. And Bolden's success as an artist is torment to Webb, because it is proof of his superior magnetism; it is torment also because Webb has been 'swallowed' by Bolden and cannot let him go. But this does not mean that Webb is powerless. If Bolden has 'swallowed' Webb, he has also internalized him. The Bolden who 'jumped up' did so at the internal behest of Webb, responding automatically to his magnets – the pull of audience.

Webb's behaviour throughout the novel needs to be understood in these terms. Like Buddy, he is 'drawn to opposites.... In terror we lean in the direction that is most unlike us. Running past your own character into pain' (96). As audience, Webb is attracted to Buddy the artist; as detective, to Buddy of the criminal silence, the mysterious 'landscape suicide.' He draws him out of nothingness, until he 'jumps up' as Bolden's photographic image will do in Bellocq's darkroom, again at the insistence of Webb. Only by returning the Bolden who contains him to the artist's path can Webb convince himself of his own continuing existence. Recalling their shared space in the apartment, he attempts (rather like Ondaatje) to enter imaginatively into Bolden's body and brain and so to track him down. Ultimately he fails. Bolden's return to the parade turns out to be the act which propels him successfully into another space, beyond Webb's reach or power of explanation. Bolden 'breaks through' the window and lands in a room in which there is no further need to shatter the glass. Webb, to whom Buddy had said, 'You come too. Put your hand through this window' (91), cannot follow. Attempting to escape the room in which he learns of that other room in the asylum where Bolden lives on, Webb's 'unknown flesh' (the Bolden in him that he cannot know) tries to 'break through the wall' and crashes over the 'hands and glasses' that Bolden breaks to achieve his goal. But Webb-the-spider's brain, 'puffed ... up with poison' (150) by the news of Bolden's incarceration, cannot work itself free of the asylum room; his body too fails to expel the poison. He cannot vomit (cannot express the feeling that pours through Bolden's horn in the parade), and so Webb ends a ruined and imprisoned man. His sweat, as Bella Cornish observes, has 'driven itself onto the wall' (151). (Ondaatje fares better: without explanation, he can enter Bolden's last room and know it for something different from the horror that is all Webb sees.)

Leaving Webb and the Pontchartrain apartment Bolden goes to New Orleans. 'His life at this time had a fine and precise balance to it, with a careful allotment of hours. A barber, publisher of *The Cricket*, a cornet player, good husband and father, and an infamous man about town' (13). These activities – 'labels' (106) he derisively calls them on his later return to this terrain – balance one another to comprise Bolden's persona and to fill out his day. Still Bolden's complex persona does not satisfy him, for it does not include *enough*; he is 'tormented by order, what was outside it' (37). It is for this reason that diverse stories about Bolden 'were like spokes on a rimless wheel ending in air' (63); Bolden's hunger for more kept the rim at bay.

Each role in turn involves its own balance, a principle of exchange and of risk. As a barber, he ministers to 'the vanity of others,' and the work seems a kind of 'slavery' (48); at the same time he is a skilled performer and occupies a central position, as the others come to him. 'Offering visions of new styles' (12), he lures them toward something perceived as dangerous: 'Men hate to see themselves change.... This is the power I live in. I manipulate their looks' (48). Thus Bolden's razor supplies to others the chance of beauty or disfigurement (the two possible conclusions of the novel). And all of this occurs within a room, the perimeter of which reinforces this issue of the instability of a personality or image. To reflect and multiply the image there are mirrors, including the one Pickett breaks when he is disfigured by Buddy; 'against the window' through which Pickett and Bolden will later crash there is 'ice [that] changed shape all day before your eyes'; on the wall against which Bolden's figure is defined there is 'the wallpaper of Louisiana birds,' recalling the paranoid and self-destructive birds drawn by Audubon; and, finally, on the ceiling is another image of that rimless wheel, the fan 'turning like a giant knife' (47) that hovers over all the book.

As publisher of *The Cricket*, Bolden practises the art of exchange by taking in the multitudinous, chaotic life of the street and expelling it 'unedited' (13). In the barber shop he copes with 'thick facts' (24) in the same way that he breathes in the 'hair flecks' he must then 'blow ... cough ... and spit out' (47) again. The news comes to him from customers and from '"spiders"' (13) who are extensions of Bolden-the-spider, as Bolden himself is an extension of Webb. Relationship nearly always works this way in *Coming Through Slaughter*, the other becoming somehow identified with the self as 'exchanged personalities' (88). *The Cricket* is Bolden's diary 'and everybody else's.' Its 'intricacy' is a history of exchange, involving 'details of the children and the ladies changing hands like coins or a cigarette travelling at mouth level around the room.' This picture comes to Buddy, however, only when he can look back at *The Cricket* and realize that its structure (significantly male-dominated) does not make the inclusive 'sense' he had supposed it did: 'that was the craziness I left. Cricket noises and Cricket music for that is what we are when watched by people bigger than us' (113-114). The self is larger when its ego is less.

With its 'excessive references to death,' *The Cricket* is also informed by a principle of risk. It is important to see that the half-dozen examples cited are all of one kind: as in the case of 'referees slashed to death by fighting cocks,' the death results from what one does (profession or deed). 'The possibilities [of chaos, extinction] were terrifying to Bolden and he hunted out examples obsessively as if building a wall. A boy with a fear of heights climbing slowly up a tree.' Buddy's actions, that is, take him always closer to the edge. The deaths of others, lived out imaginatively by Bolden, are prophetic of his own collapse: the *Cricket* stories, the 'dreams of his children dying,' and the death of his wife's mother, which is 'saved by its fictional quality and nothing else' (24). The 'wall' of print or dream or 'fictional quality' cannot hold forever; the self must ultimately cross over to the other's fate. The 'dreams of his children dying' are Buddy's dreams, his responsibility (as glimpsed in the previously cited passage about 'children ... changing hands like coins'); and so in one dream the news of his child's death leads Buddy to pick up 'the wood handled knife with the serrated edge and [push] it again and again into his left wrist' (29). The death of Nora's mother (who tells Bolden about the self-destructive birds) similarly connects with Bolden's own end. According to Webb, she is strangled in her car by her pet python as Isadora Duncan was by her own scarf; she is killed, that is, by what she does and by a linear, turning thing (snake or scarf, like the spoke of a rimless wheel) that connects her with the other. Also, her body disappears, and Bolden is suspected of her murder; but he is innocent of that, just as I believe he is innocent of his own. Past Audubon's country, they simply disappear from view.

It is as a musician that Bolden practises exchange and risk most vividly. 'Unconcerned with the crack of the lip ... he was obsessed with the magic of air, those smells that turned neuter as they revolved in his lung then spat out in the chosen key.' Although Bolden's music is drawn from 'those smells' within a room, and though he sees it as 'animals fighting in the room,' his music also seems to reach for a purer space: 'his mouth would drag a net of air in and dress it in notes and make it last and last, yearning to leave it up there in the sky like air transformed into cloud. He could see the air, could tell where it was freshest in a room by the colour' (14). The cloud cycle is parallel to the circulation of air; the cloud itself suggests that point where the cycle achieves tangible, but still evanescent form. This helps to explain Bolden's preference for music that shows 'all the possibilities in the middle of the story.' He could 'dive into the stories found in the barbershop' (43), as into a river, and come up with cloud. The cycle begins with the audience or with Bolden *as* audience: 'the perfect audience' reacting 'excessively to the stories his clients in the chair told him, throwing himself into the situation' (42). Bolden's famed loudness is necessary to balance the weight of all he takes in, but it is also a function of his extremism or excess, his yearning for more than a room contains: '"the patrons in the front rows of the theatre always got up after the first number and moved back"' (44).

'Bolden broke the path' precisely because he wanted to keep the pattern of his music open – 'As if, when he was playing, he was lost and hunting for the right accidental notes' (37). Again, the landscape metaphor suggests Bolden's wish not to be subject to an order imposed by himself or others. To find where he wants to go, Bolden must eschew conventional 'wisdom' – the orderliness of music like Robichaux's, of putting 'emotions into patterns which a listening crowd had to follow.' He avoids it because 'it is not real' (93). Instead, he plays 'a music that had so little wisdom you wanted to clean nearly every note he passed, passed it seemed along the way as if travelling in a car, passed before he had even approached it and saw it clearly.' Bolden is driven by the wish to include it all – 'pain and gentleness and everything jammed into each number' (37) – and by the need to keep all of these strands flying so that one day he might arrive at a place of 'real' order, 'real' wisdom. Vision and peace at last.

Bolden is also a family man and 'famous fucker' (106). The relationship with his children begins his day (as they are at the start of theirs) and is enacted on 'washed, empty streets' as Bolden walks them to school – 'giv[ing] himself completely to them during the walk, no barriers.' Again, he practises exchange, tells them 'all he knew at the moment ... in turn learn[ing] the new street songs from them' (13). The relationship with Nora, however, is troubled by the past. She brings to their union a history of the street, her time as a whore and the original hope – 'the roads she imagined she could take as a child' (54) – that Bellocq tries to capture in his photographs of the whores. In Nora's case, this is imaged in slightly tarnished form by her lovely street child's fantasy of the sandman who is late because he 'just stopped to get a drink' (15). Nora's life now takes place primarily in a room. There she lives with Buddy, 'good husband and ... infamous man about town' (13), and there she waits for him (as for the sandman) to drag 'his bone home' (17).

'She had played Bolden's game, knew his extra sex. When they were alone together it was still a crowded room' (110). This association of the Nora-Bolden relationship with a 'crowded room' is enforced by Webb's visit in pursuit of Bolden, and the elaborate attention paid to the apartment at that point. Now that it is empty of Bolden, Nora gestures toward 'its old wallpaper and few chairs like a tired showman.' Webb hovers at her doorstep before Nora's

arrival and again as he leaves, walking backward down the steps: 'Nora closing the door more, narrow, just to the width of her face' (21). Webb's insistence, his need to get into Bolden's psychic space, is also revealed in his mim-
icry of Bolden's role in that room: 'He has covered her against the window,
leaning very close to her, like a lover' (20).

An important image of the period before the collapse of Bolden's equilib-
rium comes in the scene where an angry Bolden strikes out at the window of
their marriage, and brakes just in time. The window is 'starred' (recalling the
fan) and 'his hand miraculously uncut.' Nora's ability to contain the chaos of
their crowded room, so long as he will contain it, is clear: 'She was delighted
by the performance' (16). She seems in fact a very good mate for Bolden. 'She
had never been a shadow' (110) and even as a whore was able 'to save delicate
rules and ceremonies for herself.' She is like him and not like him: 'her body a
system of emotions and triggers he got lost in.' Nora is right for him equally
because of that 'system' and because he cannot explain it: 'He was lost in the
details, he could find no exact focus towards her. And so he drew her power
over himself' (15).

Although his love for Nora develops from this perception of a complexity
(form and chaos) that is compatible with his own and with his music, Bolden
begins to focus on just the 'certainties' of Nora. Because he loves her, certainty there 'went to the spine' (15); because of his own mounting chaos, and
greater need for that 'spine,' Bolden assigns to her 'the certainties he loathed
and needed' (78). Her power narrows to those 'certain answers' (16) and 'short
cuts to his arguments [that] at times cleared away the chaos he embraced'
(110). It narrows still further to the certainty that Bolden begins to equate
with sexual fidelity – her fidelity. Both this sexual inequity and his reduction
of her are painful to Nora; she knows 'what he owed her and hadn't given her'
(121). But the relationship holds until Bolden decides she has been unfaithful
with Pickett. Then it seems the spine is broken, then certainty is 'liquid at
the root' (78), then Bolden goes crashing through the window.

Part One of the novel ends with Buddy at Robin's doorstep. It does not
include any discussion of Bellocq or Pickett, the two figures who provide
some explanation of how Bolden happened to leave one woman's room for
the other. Part Two takes Buddy through his time with Robin and Jaelin,
through the discovery by Webb and interval at Webb's cabin, and ends at the
point of Bolden's strange return to the New Orleans parade. Part Two, the
outer voice of which is Buddy's 'explanation' of himself to Webb, is also concerned with Webb's visits to those two figures missing from Part One – first
Bellocq, and then Pickett. This order is significant, I think, for it is essentially
what happens with Bellocq that drives Buddy to the fight with Pickett.
Nora's infidelity, if real, is not the primary cause of Bolden's departure. And
Nora recognizes this. Accounting later for her hatred of Bellocq, she tells
Buddy: 'Look at you. Look at what he did to you' (127).

As Scobie has shown, Bellocq is Webb's opposite – 'the friend who scorned all the giraffes of fame' (91). His relationship to Bolden seems to begin at reversed poles, with Bolden as public figure 'the patronizing one' (64). Bellocq learns, however, that it is he who patronizes and instructs Bolden – as Webb did initially. In the end, Bolden eludes and surpasses both of his mentors; both strive to enter his space, both feel guilt over what they have done to Bolden, and both fail to achieve his success in coming through slaughter. So Webb and Bellocq are parallel figures as well. In his role as Webb's opposite, Bellocq urges Bolden 'to step back into [his] body as if into a black room.... Unable then to be watched by others ... blind to everything but the owned pain in [him]self' (91). In Bellocq's darkroom there is a chance for Buddy to develop the self which he is in danger of losing to the audience. He must retreat into this 'black room' of self in part because his ego (as distinct from the self) has grown unruly in the light of all the adulation he has received. Thus, Bellocq appeals to Bolden as the 'first person I met who had absolutely no interest in my music. That sounds vain don't it!' (59). And Bolden has reason to worry about his vanity. But he also needs to retreat into Bellocq's darkroom for the sake of his music, which has not yet achieved the transcendence of the last parade (a perfect blend of self and other). Thus, when Bolden says to Bellocq, 'You don't think much of this music do you,' his answer is 'Not yet' (91).

The Bellocq-Bolden relationship is a study in black and white. Bellocq is primarily associated with 'the narrow dark focus of the eye' (the self) as against Buddy and 'the crazy chaos of white' (68). He offers the self imaged by a 'black shape' arising out of the 'pregnant white paper' (52) when Webb comes in search of Buddy. But like Bolden's, the photographer's art requires black *and* white. And Bellocq learns more about the value of white from Bolden. Whiteness signifies chaos, anonymity, and the other – all that is outside the black specificity of self. In the botched photo of his own death, Bellocq finds himself 'surrounded by whiteness' as if 'a cloud has stuffed itself into his room' (67). That cloud suggests to me the presence of Bolden; it is linked to the whiteness into which Bolden has 'already half-receded' in the photo given to Webb. And Bellocq is half-glad that Bolden has eluded them, that he has 'reversed the process and gone back into white' (53). So Bellocq is torn between black and white, the self he is and the other he yearns for. In Bellocq's photos, this misery comes out grey: the 'light grey' (123) of the whorehouse wallpaper and the 'grey light which must have been the yellow shining off' (117) the walls of the opium dens. But in Bolden's final room, a scene only apparently of misery, grey becomes the colour of a perfect blend.

The opposition of black and white is only one metaphor for the difference between Bellocq and Bolden. Whereas Bolden is 'a social dog' who roams 'through conversations as if they were the countryside not listening carefully just picking up moments,' Bellocq in his lonely room is 'self-sufficient, complete as a perpetual motion machine.' Bolden's spontaneity and lack of focus are balanced by the 'slow convolution' of Bellocq's 'brain' (56). Because it is the 'interfering' (31) brain Buddy watches for as Robin cuts carrots that drives Bolden's hand through the fan at last, the reader (like Nora) may blame the influence of Bellocq for Bolden's end. I do not only because I consider that end triumphant. Bellocq's end, however, is tragic because he cannot include the other in his construction of the self. Bellocq's failure in this regard is scarcely his fault. Lacking utterly Bolden's power to attract, Bellocq in his photographs of the whores does his best to recognize the value and beauty of others – but they will have nothing to do with him, so that he can only 'romance them later with a knife' (55).

Bellocq's difference from Bolden yields at many points to likeness. Even the knife Bellocq uses in his effort 'to enter the photographs' recalls the knives associated with Bolden. Within the scarred photographs is a willed reciprocity, a principle of exchange, that recalls Bolden's art – as the 'genuine scars' on the bodies of the whores and the gouges made by Bellocq 'reflect each other.' For Bolden as for Bellocq, 'the making and destroying [come] from the same source, same lust, same surgery his brain was capable of' (55). For both, that source is the lure of the other; it is the will to include or incorporate the other in the construction of the self. When that effort of inclusion fails, the self lashes out – and particular others will be hurt. Increasingly disgusted, the self at last turns its destruction inward. Bolden finds at that moment an all-inclusive other, as Bellocq does not, and so can destroy one version of the self to make another.

But there are other points of likeness. Each man insists upon the essential kindness of the other. Both are artists, and although neither considers himself professional, both carry their professions 'with [them] always, like a wife' – Bolden 'his mouthpiece even in exile' (57) and Bellocq the camera gear that also seems a part of his own body. In the subject matter of Bellocq's work, the whores, of course, and the 'sections of boats' that he photographed 'to help ship designers' (56), there is further evidence of his link to Bolden; he serves 'to help' Bolden design a journey (often imagined as a river journey) that Bolden with his fear of water could not have taken without the aid of his crippled friend.

What Bolden loved in Bellocq, he says, 'were the possibilities in his silence' (91). He despises the clamour of his own art, the inflated ego – posing as self, posing as generous to the other – that is only 'stealing chickens, nailing things to the wall.' Always taking, he finds that 'reputation made the room narrower and narrower, till you were ... full of your own echoes, till you were drinking in only your own recycled air' (86). This is the 'furnished room' he occupies and contrasts with Bellocq as 'a window looking out' (59). He sees in Bellocq's 'silence' a chance to construct the self which might truly regard the other. Bellocq, however, fears that his talk and silence have done Bolden a disservice, 'tempt[ing] Buddy on. Buddy who was once enviably public.' In the suicide room he risks going over the edge himself because it was their talk that moved Bolden 'gradually off the edge of the social world.' While Bellocq was at ease there – 'he lived on the edge in any case' – Bolden was not, and to Bellocq's surprise, 'he moved past him like a naive explorer looking for footholds.' And so Bellocq regrets also his silence: 'he could so easily have explained the ironies,' his bitter knowledge that 'the mystic privacy one can be so proud of has no alphabet of noise or meaning to the people outside' (64). The real irony, however, is that unknown to Bellocq his naive friend has found other 'possibilities' in the silence: 'the mystic privacy' Bolden finds at last is different from Bellocq's embittered pride in its successful inclusion of the other, and so it does not matter that it has no 'meaning to the people outside.'

Bellocq's death scene is a mocking self-portrait. As a hydrocephalic, Bellocq knows that 'his blood and water circulation' dooms him to an early death; that fact serves as another link to Bolden, who also has difficulty with a build-up of pressure in his brain, but cures himself and lives on. Both Bellocq's 'circulation and walk' are impaired, and each is a metaphor for the other – leading him to stage his first and last performance in a room which is also an image of his brain. 'He did not walk that much ... never shot landscapes, mostly portraits' (57). The final portrait, revealing the influence of Bolden, features a man alone surrounded by a circular (fan-like) 'balcony' of empty chairs. His audience is ghostly, brought in to observe the psychodrama of an utterly solitary man. Calmly, Bellocq sets fire to the wallpaper (his self-image or brain's rim) and 'formally' breathes in the smoke. Although he must know that he has embarked upon a suicide, part of Bellocq expects this extreme act to provoke the 'other' for whom he performs into a miraculous feat of rescue. Or perhaps the force of his irony is such that Bellocq expects to triumph in this way over his need of the other. In either case, he is surprised when the design breaks down. Vomiting out smoke, he goes crashing through the chairs and hopes still to find the wall intact – the wall of 'certainty' (of others miraculously there or definitely gone) that would either 'catch or hide him.' But the wall itself is gone. At this last moment, Bellocq seems to choose life – but without the other there is no life, no opposite and balancing force 'to clasp him into a certainty.' And so Bellocq 'falls, dissolving out of his pose' (67).

Bellocq's influence provokes the assault upon Pickett first in the sense that it brings Bolden to the point where he too must release an intolerable pressure. More particularly, Bolden attacks Pickett because he is suffering from the ego's last-ditch conflict with the emergent self's distaste for the way Bolden has been dealing with the other. Details of the fight itself – the broken mirrors, the weapons that join Bolden and Pickett as if they were the same creature, the broken window through which Pickett crashes and Bolden 'come[s] ... too' (74) – all suggest that Bolden's rampage is essentially directed against himself. Bolden and the voice of Ondaatje, cutting their own faces, are later described as 'defiling the people they did not wish to be' (134). Now Pickett the handsome pimp, who mirrors obscenely Buddy's own strutting ego, is a displaced version of that enemy within. The attack on Pickett's beauty might also be regarded as vengeance for Bellocq, an attempt to deprive this alter-ego of the physical advantage they both possess. Pickett, when he becomes the Fly King in an opium den, is reduced from the lofty stature of pimp to the condition of the mattress whores, photographed and wept over by Bellocq. Like them, and like Bolden when he reaches that state, Pickett no longer protests. His face is cut as the whores are cut in Bellocq's photos. The scars are 'roads on his face' (71), a landscape of suffering that has brought him to one of the grey rooms photographed by Bellocq.

Bolden does not quite know what he is doing in the assault on Pickett. 'What the hell is wrong with me?' (73), he asks. He is, of course, crazed by the belief that Nora has been unfaithful; the failure of that one 'certainty' upsets his whole precarious balance. But beneath his sexual jealousy is a horror at his lust for possession and power, as Bolden nearly sees: 'You know ... in spite of everything that happens, we still think a helluva lot of ourselves!' That recognition causes Bolden in a fit of self-loathing to bite his wrist and feel 'his vein tingling at the near chance it had of almost going free' (79). It is not yet time, however, for Buddy's release. The wish to escape ego continues to clash with crazy expressions of ego in the paranoid behaviour that Bolden exhibits after the fight with Pickett and before his disappearance.

Bolden goes to Shell Beach by boat, a mode of travel that signals both a radical departure and a parallel to his asylum journey; this is the second, as that will be the last, of his landscape suicides. In Shell Beach he meets the Brewitts, who will give him refuge. But as his band boards the train for their return to New Orleans, Buddy is 'frozen,' incapable of bearing his pain or of choosing between past and future; and then he wakes 'to see the train disappearing away from his body like a vein.' It is time to go to the Brewitts – 'the silent ones. Post music. After ambition.' But he is 'scared of everybody' (39) and cannot present to them or to anyone the self he now loathes. For two days he wanders in a landscape full of whores and music, a 'spider perfect[ing] in silence' all that he hears, absorbing the noises and smells of his old life. 'He took it in and locked it.' This is Bolden's preparation for the time he will spend in Robin's room, when his music stops. As prey and predator, he absorbs the 'luscious poison ... until he couldn't be entered anymore. A fat full king. The hawk its locked claws full of salmon going under greedy with it for the final time' (40-41). Bolden is trying blindly to lower himself, sinking 'through the pavement into the music,' resting on its 'grid' (41) like a fly (or

Fly King) against the web; still he shares in the power of spider, king, and hawk. At last Bolden arrives at Robin's doorstep, 'shaking' and pleading for 'help,' wearing a coat he wants to burn because 'it stank so much' (45).

Bolden's entry into a kind of waterscape with the Brewitts is confirmed by his immersion in their bathtub. There his 'armour of dirt' explodes, and he rises out of the water feeling 'everything drain off him' (58) like a dissolved skin. He can now enter Robin's 'white room' (86). Bolden has fled from Bellocq's darkroom, 'diving through a wave' (67) as his friend did, because he cannot yet reconcile the black and the white. His movement now toward whiteness is a retreat from the 'owned pain' (91) that was too much for him to bear. Unable to find a true order in that world, he wants to recover the 'fear of certainties.' His sojourn here is nevertheless proof of Bellocq's ascendancy over Webb, for he will live silent, 'anonymous and alone in a white room with no history and no parading' (86).

In another sense, Bolden's stay in the white room is an attempt to replay his New Orleans story and to redress its wrongs. His attraction to Robin Brewitt makes sense for Bolden at this time because there is also a Jaelin Brewitt, so that when Bolden uses 'his cornet as jewelry' he can make 'music for the three of them' (33). His relationship with the Brewitts will give Bolden a chance to explore the possibility of a love that is not possessive, from which ego may retire. This is the meaning of the 'Wolf-Ryat star,' named for two men who found the star (Robin); it is a 'new star' (65), an effort to achieve in the triangular relationship a love that is not ego-bound. Its critical importance for Bolden's quest is revealed in the image of the star that recalls the 'starred' (16) window of his marriage to Nora. He hopes this time to live in peace, and counts on reflecting Jaelin's kindness instead of Pickett's ego. Thus, when he and Robin make love for the first time Bolden seems to request the triangle: 'I wouldn't feel different if I was [Jaelin]' (58).

Love with Robin takes place in a room, but 'it could have been a sky not a ceiling above him' (59). Expressing that sense of freedom, and framing his time with Robin, is this line: 'Passing wet chicory that lies in the field like the sky' (60, 85). Because chicory is blue it reflects the sky, as Bolden and Robin reflect one another. This line indicates as well that Bolden's time in the peaceful white room is a prelude to his grey room on the far side of Slaughter, as the chicory field is passed on the way to that last asylum. In the white room, as in the grey, Bolden is 'King of Corners'; he can 'make something unknown in the shape of this room' (86). When they first lock themselves into the room – 'the snap of the lock is the last word [they] speak' – there are other 'bodies in the air' (61); but as Bolden presses Robin into the corners, and as their bodies practise the art of exchange, the room is suddenly 'empty of other histories.' In the making of 'something unknown,' they are like 'animals meeting an unknown breed.' They can take 'a step past the territory' (62) of all that was known before.

Still the relationship does not achieve what Buddy needs. 'Everybody's love in the air' does not keep Jaelin from being shut out or Bolden's ego shut down. 'As dogs wait for their masters to go to sleep' (92), so Jaelin waits each night to assume Bolden's former position – aiming his music at the lovers in their bed. The question of power arises again, and with it the conflict of black and white. Bolden quarrels with Robin, throwing the whiteness of milk in her 'lost beautiful brown face' (68) – as if to charge her with the failure of all she had seemed to promise. But this is Bolden's construction, his fantasy. When he asks only whiteness of Robin, and blames her for the intrusion of 'dark … complications' (69), he repeats the error that he made with Nora. He shuts out a part of her reality. The displacement of his own guilt also reminds us of his time with Nora. He believes now in a choice: 'There can be either the narrow dark focus of the eye or the crazy chaos of white, … wishing to burn them out till they are stones' (68). But he is wrong. He must still bring them together. And he is wrong to imply that Robin has introduced the darkness to their waterscape: he sees it too. He is only 'wishing' for blindness, trying not to see that he does necessarily inflict pain through his affair with Robin. To escape their quarrel, Robin and Buddy go swimming. Diving like loons, they find in the water both darkness and a 'dull star of white water.' Because the 'evil dark … creatures' of ego and sexual possession are present now, the Wolf-Ryat star is fading. Still it draws him. And when Robin says, 'I'm Jaelin's wife and I'm in love with you, there's nothing simple,' Buddy's reply that 'it should be' (69) can mean *both* that Robin must choose between them and that there should be no necessity of choice.

Thus, even before Webb arrives to ply his magnets, there is a renewed disturbance in the room. Webb finds Bolden in the bath that frames his time with Robin. Veering away from Webb's insistent 'noise,' reacting as well to the news of Bellocq's suicide, Buddy attempts like Audubon's water turkey to drown himself. His 'eyes staring up aching' (83) recall both his aversion to 'eyes clogged with people' (when Robin's 'white' house became treacherously 'dark') and his attraction to 'the crazy chaos of white, that is the eyes wide, wishing to burn them out till they are stones' (68). Since Bolden is still not ready to unify the black and the white, since whiteness now would mean the end of his quest, he is obliged to come up for air. Webb is seen as the trainer of Buddy the 'social dog' (56), who 'set out to breed [him] into something better' and did. But he went too far, becoming 'like those breeders of bull terriers in the Storyville pits' who train their dogs to keep on killing even as they are cut 'in half' (89) themselves. In this image and in the other which has Webb-the-trainer compelling him toward 'the worthless taste of worthless rabbit' (84), it is clear that Bolden deplores not only his own suicidal bifurcation and the worthlessness of the prize, but also the killer instinct that is being awakened in him once more. Also, he is in agony over what this means to the 'unknown breed' (62) of his love with Robin – so that as he is about to tell her of Webb's victory, Bolden is 'like a huge, wild animal going round and round the bathroom' (84).

Bolden's last sexual encounter with Robin suggests this vicious pull of audience, as in the white room once empty of parading they 'give each other a performance, the wound of ice' (87). Now that Webb has 'placed [his] past and future on this table like a road,' Robin's 'landscape' out of time is 'alien' to Bolden. There is history again in the white room, and 'barrier glass' (86) between them. Time is the tragedy that has them 'already travelling on the morning bus' (87) – a fatality in relationship that Bolden contemplates when he is really on the bus, imagining the whole doomed course of an affair with the woman who sits beside him. What he wants, Bolden decides, is 'cruel, pure relationship' (88). The syntax is ambiguous, but I think 'cruel' is not primarily a co-ordinate adjective; that is, Bolden wants 'pure relationship' and knows that this departure from troublesome particularity is 'cruel' both to Robin and Nora and to himself. Thus, his hand goes 'crashing' down on Robin's empty 'half of the bed' when he sees her 'blue cloud light in the room' (87). 'Blue' marks the point at which the visible and invisible meet, as the gas when Bolden lit Nora's stove 'popped up blue, something invisible finding a form' (124). But now it goes the other way: 'she's gone' (87). Bolden too, when he has achieved his 'real' (93) form, will retreat into invisibility.

Honeymoon cabin, training ground, darkroom – Webb's cabin at Lake Ponchartrain is the place where Bolden does the painful brainwork on love, music and selfhood that is needed to bring his life together. Always torn between solitude and the need for people (hating whatever 'I am doing and want[ing] the other'), he feels now cut 'in half' by Webb – for ironically his trainer has 'point[ed]' (89) him in the direction of blackness urged by Bellocq. In this prolonged and nearly absolute solitude, Buddy cannot seek the other in his customary ways. As the self develops, therefore, so does the intensity of Bolden's desire for the other.

His one companion is a black dog. Bolden's progress with Robin toward an 'unknown breed' (62) advances now to 'a major breakthrough in the spread of hound civilization' – as Bolden scratches earth over the dog's piss, 'return[ing] the compliment' paid first by the dog, showing that he knows the dog's 'system' (90). Each performs with and for the other in perfect equality; and the dog 'not used to softness' becomes an avatar of woman, as Bolden is 'snuggled against his warmth' (98). Bolden is weaning himself from the need for particular others, moving with the dog toward 'pure relationship' (88): at last he will *become* the dog.

His desire for the other, though acute, is now generalized; 'I am alone. I desire every woman I remember.' Robin 'has become anonymous as cloud,' blurring 'into Nora and everybody else' (100); and then 'even her cloud' is gone, as the 'lake and sky [that] will be light blue' (102) suggest both the integration of her 'blue cloud light' (87) and the 'wet chicory that lies in the field like the sky' (60). The light of the other is also imaged by the cabin Buddy sees across the lake: 'Everyone I know lives there and when the light is on it means they are there' (98). This abstraction is comforting; it frees him both from fear and hope of others arriving at the dark cabin of the self. When Crawley does arrive with the 'girl fan' (a figure of audience and woman in one), Bolden is tormented by the desire 'to start a fight,' to thrust his 'horn in her skirt' (99). Still he is torn between the particular and the general; and 'terrified now of their lost love,' the 'soft private sentiment' for Nora and his children that he 'forgot to explode,' Bolden pushes his tongue into the mouth of his friend's girl, whose name he 'cannot even remember' (102).

In thinking about his music, Bolden retains the ideal of an open form: music that 'swallowed moods and kept three or four going at the same time which was what I wanted' (95), music played for an audience that could 'come in where they pleased and leave when they please' (94). But there is also a new strength of self in his music, coming from the 'owned pain,' the 'blackness' he tells Webb 'there is a need to come home' (91) with, to wed at last with the other. Buddy does not mean to fail. All his 'fathers' in music, 'those who put their bodies over barbed wire' (95), have failed in one way or another – each becoming 'a remnant, a ladder for others' (102). Bolden will not. And so he returns to New Orleans 'thinking along a stone path' (102), 'knowing it is just stone' (101), but firm in his purpose. Bolden's return to the parade is very different from his first entry, following the time with Webb in the Pontchartrain apartment. This time his talk with Webb has been imaginary; this time it is all in his own head – he knows he is going into 'nightmare' (106) and has hardened himself against the fear as well as the lure of particularity. What he intends is a kind of suicide, an exit from the known world. 'All suicides all acts of privacy are romantic,' Webb says, and Bolden acknowledges that he 'may be right' (101). Still it is Bolden's only chance of success. He must face and resolve once and for all 'the dream of the wheel over his hand' (40). All he needs for that now are self-discipline and then 'the right audience' (89).

Bolden is experiencing the pain of separation from the known world, the hardness and coldness that will achieve it, as on the bus he rubs his 'brain against the cold window' (106). He passes the test of Cornish and Nora, whom he regards as 'statues of personality,' no longer occupying the 'landscape' of time in which passion destroys. Bolden has repudiated his possessive love, and the gentle Cornish seems another version of Jaelin whom this time he will not displace. 'Hunger[ing] to be as still as them,' Bolden is locking the last of his passion in – 'boiled down in love and anger into dynamo that cannot move except on itself' (112). The hardness remains even in his ghostly intimacy with Nora: 'The diamond had to love the earth it passed along the way, every speck and angle of the other's history, for the diamond had been earth too' (111). And he is able to sit back 'with just his face laughing at the jokes,' surviving 'the people in a house watching him,' because essentially he 'wasn't even in the room' (120). Bolden is pointed relentlessly toward a new psychic space.

On the second evening of his return, Buddy goes 'parading' (118) in the domain of the diseased mattress whores. Because of his 'fast rich walk' they fear he is a pimp, come to break their ankles so they cannot return to Story-ville. Bolden's old horror at the pimp in himself (the exploiter of others) and his identification with the whores – 'my brain tonight has a mattress strapped to its back' – come together, as other opposites will do in his immi-nent release. Bolden compares himself to the mattress whores, 'their bodies murdered and my brain suicided,' to acknowledge that the stick-wielding pimp is in his own case internalized. There are two kinds of mattress whores, between whom Bolden is poised: the 'gypsy feet' with broken ankles, who are 'immune from the swinging stick' (119), and those who still have something to fear, who retreat into the white mist, 'the shallows of the river where the pimps with good shoes won't follow' (118). The second type suggests Bolden retreating into his waterscape from Webb, sick at the prostitution of his art. The gypsy-foot whores suggest Bolden as he will be in the asylum, when the 'swinging stick' has delivered him from any further pain. That connection is strengthened when Bolden declines a fellow inmate's suggestion first of escape and then (when Lord comes back limping) of the sharpened glass with which, to protest their lot, the older inmates cut the tendons of their ankles. Bolden is a 'gypsy' in his prison and has no need of protest or escape. Now he sees that 'there is no horror in the way they run their lives,' and knows that these 'grey angels' (119) are pointing the way, 'sentries' (118) on his own path.

At last comes the parade, with Bolden's 'note like a bird flying out of the shit' (129). Recalling Crawley with his 'tail of shit' (30) and the gypsy-foot whores with their 'driblets of manure' (119), Bolden's transcendent music is founded on shit, on suffering and deprivation, unlike the music of a 'techni-cian – which went gliding down river and missed all the shit on the bottom' (95-96). Here the fan or star, representing the opposed influences that have tormented Buddy's life, comes after one last and glorious 'spinning' to a stop. Buddy's passion is released in the 'parade of ego,' as 'like a spaniel strutting' (129) he plays to attract the right 'bitch,' the perfect audience 'testing me taunting me to make it past her, old hero, old ego tested against one as cold and pure as himself.' As 'Robin, Nora, Crawley's girl's tongue' (130) she is the all-inclusive other, offering pure relationship; and she has a male companion, 'a beautiful dancer too' (129), so that the triangular relationship is echoed in this final spinning of the star. Self and other merge as Bolden becomes 'the dancer' and she throws him 'in the direction and the speed she wishes like an angry shadow'; Bolden has what he 'wanted, always, loss of privacy in the playing' (130). His 'last long squawk' simultaneously 'spear[s] her' and goes 'like a javelin' through Buddy's brain. 'The blood that is real' brings 'fresh energy in its suitcase,' the vein bursting free so that Bolden has finally 'what [he] wanted' (131). A *bouleversement* has occurred; he has entered another space.

Bolden's successful wedding of self and other in his last parade is forecast in the dolphin sonographs that are pictured (in black, white, and grey) and described in the novel's epigraph. The left-hand sonograph shows a squawk, 'common emotional expressions that have many frequencies or pitches, which are vocalized simultaneously': this represents the other. The right-hand sonograph shows the 'signature whistle,' a 'pure' sound that identifies a particular dolphin and its location: this represents the self. 'The middle sonograph shows a dolphin making two kinds of signals simultaneously,' as Bolden does in the parade with his squawks and the pure notes that he trained himself to play in Webb's cabin. As 'no one knows how a dolphin makes both' sounds simultaneously, so Bolden's achievement takes him beyond our understanding to an unknown world – where we would need 'a machine more sensitive than the human ear' to hear the music playing in his head.

To get to the asylum, which he refers to as 'a pound' (139), Bolden passes '*through* the country that Audubon drew' and '*through* Sunshine ... and Slaughter' (italics mine). Slaughter and Sunshine – like pain and joy, self and other, the one and the many, ego and the loss of ego – have come together in the 'river' (131) of the parade. On the other side of Sunshine and Slaughter, beyond the changing landscape of water and cloud and ice, what looks like an eternal repetition of Slaughter is for Bolden a sun-blessed, heavenly new life. The Mississippi River is 'a friend travelling with him, like an audience watching Huck Finn going by train to hell' (155), but the audience is wrong. The reference to Huck Finn suggests (to me at least) the 'territory ahead' that Huck sought and Bolden has found – in what looks to the audience like hell, but is really a mysterious heaven. Because the water has been gone *through*, Ondaatje can say that Bolden is buried not in Holtz Cemetery where 'the high water table conveniently takes the flesh away in six months' (134), but in First Street where dogs are buried. He has evolved, that is, to an unknown breed; he has become like Bellocq's dog, whom Bolden had watched closely enough to see that although 'all day it would seem to be doing nothing ... it would be *busy*' (59). The significance of Bolden's activity in that territory ahead cannot be rationally understood. 'As you try to explain me I will spit you, yellow, out of my mouth' (140), Bolden says – recalling the dog in the cabin who 'moves his body into perfect manoeuvering position [as Bolden has done] so he can get his tongue between the yellow [leaves] and reach the invisible water' (90).

The room in which he lives is entirely satisfactory. Bolden can fulfill in this new psychic space the potential of the white room, making 'something unknown in the shape of this room' (86). Throughout the novel corners have been a principal locale of sexual activity, because in sex we approach the boundary of the self to press ourselves against the other (whom we 'corner' if the approach is aggressive). That need is no longer relevant to Bolden. The reference to corners in the asylum – 'there is the corner and there is the corner ...' (146) – seems ominous, for there we know he will be raped again and again by the 'ladies in blue pajamas' (148); but Buddy thinks that 'everybody who touches [him] must be beautiful' (135), and he doesn't mind. The attendants in blue pajamas, like the 'blue necklace' of his handcuffs, have been imaginatively transformed. Bolden in his 'white dress' and the 'breastless woman in blue' (139) are beyond gender conflict, and violence is unreal.

Best of all, he has friendship. At night he is alone; but in the day the sun (the light of the other) comes to his room, and Bolden is 'blessed by the visit of his friend.' The 'yellow' of explanation yields to the 'warm yellow' of his friend's hand 'magically' and 'simultaneously' (148) joined to Bolden's hand in tender understanding. Time is no longer destructive, as Buddy measures the sun's progress through his room with a system of strings – a contrast to the frenzy of Webb's magnets which nevertheless reveals Bolden's continuing engagement with the other. The 'last movement' into the fan that 'happens forever and ever in his memory' (136) suggests not eternal agony, but a transcendence which (beyond explanation) repeats harmoniously the play of opposites – as in 'the travelling spokes of light' Buddy can bathe his face *and* dry it. Regarding 'work as his duty to the sun' (148), Bolden unites stillness and motion; he 'goes around touching things' (149), the 'unimportant objects' (86) that are now the reliable furnishings of his psychic space. And in the world outside the room, his friend has 'bleached everything' (133) so that we cannot pin Buddy down.

Back in New Orleans, his other friends regard Bolden's fate with horror. They think of the asylum as hell, though their speech is studded with exclamations – 'heaven' (149) and '*jesus*' (145) – that should reveal to us the ultimate success of Bolden's effort to play 'the devil's music and hymns at the same time' (134). 'Lord' uses 'his silence as an oracle' (141), knowing that 'salvation' has been performed on the 'throat' (139) of this man who knew the devil and the shit; but in New Orleans they ask: 'What good is all that [suffering] if we can't learn or know?' (145). They will only know if they 'come too.' They want to learn from his *failure*, making him 'a remnant, a ladder for others' (102); and Buddy eludes them. He escapes the fate of Freddie Amacker, for instance, who is happy to be a 'remnant' for 'a really good [white, dreadful] singer like Perry Como.' Amacker's song, furthermore, gives a precise summary of the world that revealed its full horror to Buddy Bolden: 'The name of the song is "All the boys got to love me, that's all"' (154), and it recounts the tale of a man who kills his girl out of jealousy. Neither the compulsion of the audience's love nor the sexual violence of the song bothers Amacker in the least. We know then that Bolden is well out of his game.

The last paragraph of the novel is for many readers a portrait of misery, signalling enclosure, terror, failure – in short, the bankruptcy of extremist art. But it is the right ending, as Bolden has forewarned us: 'The right ending is an open door you can't see too far out of. It can mean exactly the opposite of what you are thinking' (94). For me, 'the grey walls that darken into corner' and the 'window with teeth in it' no longer threaten; there seems no need to look out the window for 'clouds and other things,' as everything is there in the grey room already. 'There are no prizes' (156), Ondaatje concludes. And I can understand how one might read that as a statement of defeat. But say that 'You come too. Put your hand through this window' (91), and I think that you would find a place in which the whole, pernicious issue of 'prizes' and the contentious ego has simply gone away. The black knight doesn't win, and neither does the white. Another way of saying that is that the dog in a grey room *does*. I should close with an admission that the right ending – 'There are no prizes' – can mean 'exactly the opposite' of what I'm thinking too. It is the risk an extremist critic has to take.

Works Cited

1. *Essays on Canadian Writing*, No. 12 (Fall 1978), 25.
2. *Ibid.*, 26.
3. *Essays on Canadian Writing*, No. 12 (Fall 1978), 6.
4. *Op. cit.*, 44.

P.K. Page:
The Chameleon and the Centre

P.K. Page is Canada's finest poet. I begin here on dangerous ground, without any illusion that the mere surveyor's report which is to follow can prove it safe. But it has seemed to me this judgement ought to appear in print. The work itself is secure in any case; though not extensive by a literal measurement of books placed end to end, it has earned for P.K. Page a high reputation amongst Canadian poets and the Order of Canada, a recent tribute to her achievement. By another sort of measure the expanse of her poetry is overwhelming. Once inside her garden we feel it to be a precisely articulated and teeming universe; we have only to count how much is in it and how thoroughly each element is seen in order to have a sense of almost infinite duration in this richly compacted poetic world. The sun and the moon and the stars extend its space. Water and air are abundant. The animal, vegetable, and mineral kingdoms are all contained within its boundaries. Human beings of all ages and levels of consciousness are there: people who can recognize those other kingdoms of being, or connect with one another, or know an angel when they see one, as well as those who cannot. The climate in P.K. Page's garden is variable, but the factor which determines it is always the intensity of vision. Another word for this is love.

§

In 1944 *The Sun and the Moon* was published under the pseudonym Judith Cape, with considerable reluctance on the part of the author who had finished with it several years before and who was now making another sort of name for herself in the Montreal *Preview* group of poets. In 1973 the novel was reissued by Anansi with P.K. Page's name up front. *The Sun and the Moon* is intensely romantic and sometimes overwritten, a kind of girl's secret garden which it might understandably have seemed reckless to unlock for public viewing. But it is also an extraordinarily powerful book. The key turned reveals her secret to be essentially the same as that of the mature poet; at least it provides us with her authentic starting place.

Born during a lunar eclipse, the heroine has an empathic gift which allows her to be still and attend and to penetrate in deepening waves of ecstatic identification the being of a rock or chair or tree. The passages in which she does

113

so are utterly convincing both as Kristin's reality and as evidence of the author's own empathic knowledge. Kristin had always been strangely distant from the other children whose bodies moved perpetually, and from the adults who talked so long and senselessly; only in her grandmother had the child found another human being who was sufficiently still for her empathic approach. The failure to attend separated these people not only from Kristin but from the world which had really been given to them as well as to her. Her mother had once possessed a touch of Kristin's magic, but suppressed it so far that she became almost entirely the sad and conventional creature whose most reiterated concern was that Kristin should remember to wear a hat. As an article of faith, *The Sun and the Moon* proposes that Kristin's gift is crucially necessary to the fulfillment of human life. It is no accidental perversity that Grace (Kristin's mother, fallen from the grace of her true identity) should lose her husband's love precisely at the moment when she has achieved the superficiality of his habitual world, for even this dimly sighted man could connect in a vital way only with what is real. Essentially this is encouraging news. It means that all human beings have the capacity for vision, although a social climate such as this one of money and cocktail parties will create multiple barriers to impede and distort our vision. At this juncture *The Sun and the Moon* connects obviously with the poetry of regret for social constraints that Page was writing at the time of the novel's publication.

When a talented painter named Carl Bridges enters the book, he seems a figure of dreams conjured there by his youthful creator. Carl is the splendid, solar male – a counterpart for the lunar Kristin, so that empathy can be explored under the banner of romantic love; and he is an artist whose powers can be revealed as essentially empathic. Thus, he extends the thematic content of the novel. Carl Bridges is encountered first at a cocktail party where in contrast to Kristin he is adept at making the appropriate social gestures without capitulation; they fall in love instantly and between them construct a *bridge* which Kristin discovers can connect her with the rest of humanity. Each is attracted by the other's stillness. Magnetically their courtship leads these lovers into nature, away from noisy restaurants and the trivial world. Then disaster comes in a profoundly disturbing shape. Kristin learns that her empathic knowledge of Carl acts as a kind of succubus, annihilating his identity and his talent; she decides finally to release him by diverting her attention and assuming the identity of a tree. We may ask where truth inhabits such a nightmare. In the first place, the distortions of authorial inexperience must be set aside: just as Carl is himself the figment of a girl's yearning, so the lethal quality of Kristin's love is only a supposition based on fear. Love itself is never repudiated, as Kristin's ultimate act of self-sacrifice should make clear. The catastrophe of this novel is not a metaphor for the poisonous effect of love on the individual identity of its participants. Rather it stems from an experience of empathy so literal and profound that we can understand the author's fear.

Keats in his discussion of negative capability and the Chameleon Poet suggests that the true poet must be able to enter the life even of a billiard ball, and he describes another experience of empathy in terms that are precursory of *The Sun and the Moon*: 'When I am in a room with People if I ever am free from speculating on creatures of my own brain, then not myself goes home to myself: but the identity of every one in the room [so] begins to press upon me that, I am in a very little time an[ni]hilated.'[1] An additional form of the risk considered by Page in her novel about empathy is self-annihilation. The fear expressed in her poetry as well is that one might enter (which is the same thing as being assaulted by) another form of being and never be released. Either one other scrap of being or a world full of marauding images might seem a threat to the identity of the empathizer; and not only identity in the usual sense, but access to reality would then be destroyed. Yet without empathy such access is impossible; it must not be rejected either by the poet or by any human being. The solution for the Chameleon Poet is to find her centre in being, a process which involves moving beyond images to their symbols. What is meant by this should subsequently become more clear.

§

The best possible guide to an understanding of the poetry is an astonishingly transparent and beautiful essay called 'Questions and Images' (*Canadian Literature*, Summer 1969), in which Page describes the inner events of her time in Brazil and Mexico and their consequences for her return to Canada. Suddenly 'devoid of words' in the foreign culture of Brazil, 'pelted ... with images,' and wondering 'where wordlessness [could] lead' (17), Page found that entirely of their own accord her writing had ceased and drawing had begun. She saw 'churches, golden as the eye of God ... so miraculously proportioned that one wondered if proportion alone might actually alter consciousness'; 'Moorish designs in tiles and lattices [which] created infinities of intricate repetition' (17); and the 'infinitely dilatable eye' of the macaw, a vortex leading her 'into a minute cosmos which contained all the staggering dimensions of outer space' (18). This was precisely the food her imagination craved. Its first nourishment was for P.K. Irwin, the artist newly born in Brazil with more than another language now to make her own. She proceeded to trace with a neophyte's diffident pen 'all things bright and beautiful,' and then 'the pen began dreaming. It began a life of its own' (18). Yet it was the same pen, insisting upon its own authentic direction: from this beautiful, intricately latticed world through the vortex of the golden eye into the miraculous proportions of space that is at once inner and outer. The illuminations of Brazil (and later, of Mexico) were also to affect her poetry.

Brazil had renewed her sense of the infinitely reverberating richness of
this world and had intensified her experience of the *bouleversement* which
propels us into another space. The sense of design in that other realm was
confirmed for P.K. Page in the next phase of her travel: 'If Brazil was day, then
Mexico was night.... Objects dissolved into their symbols' (19). Her understanding of the poet as a conduit for truth had deepened, so that 'poetry was
more than ever now in the perceiving. My only access to it was through the
dream and the drawing' (20). She also began to read with a special urgency: 'As
if pursued by the Hound of Heaven I raced back and forth among the Collected Works of Jung, The Perennial Philosophy, The Doors of Perception,
Zen, C.S. Lewis, St. John of the Cross' (20). Questions were now more pressing than images. And she was led eventually into the mystical literature of
the Sufis, where she found particular help.

The woman who returned to Canada was turned around, strangely preoccupied: 'I began to sense another realm – interrelated – the high doh of a scale
in which we are the low. And in a sudden and momentary bouleversement, I
realize that I have been upside down in life – like a tree on its head, roots exposed to the air' (21). In another crucially revealing metaphor of this remarkable
essay, Page recalls to us the stereotypic toys of childhood: 'The picture,
viewed alone, was of a boy with an umbrella and a dog. Seen through the
green filter, the umbrella disappeared. The red filter demolished the dog' (21).
She concludes that for the time being her 'primary concern is to remove the
filters' (22), which means to see the picture whole and undistorted. What
those filters are, P.K. Page (who was once Judith Cape and who became P.K.
Irwin) had found a more *conscious* way of understanding, but 'my subconscious evidently knew something about the tyranny of subjectivity years ago
when it desired to go "through to the area behind the eyes / where silent,
unrefracted whiteness lies"' (21). This is the area which is approached by the
transmutation of image into symbol, and from which all the distorting filters
have been removed. In finding consciousness altered, we become aware of
the previous consciousness as a refractive or distorting filter – a tissue of
entrenched attitudes – and of the former self as a kind of mask. We acknowledge both the past tyranny of subjectivity and its continuing assaults, the
multiple filters of our mundane existence. We might then translate our
yearning into the work which the Sufis describe as *making a new head*.

We aim at 'the area behind the eyes / where silent, unrefractive whiteness
lies.' Page tells us that when she wrote 'Stories of Snow'[2] she hadn't yet
understood this image, 'but it arrived complete' ('Questions and Images,' 21).
The poem is an account of the yearning to be other than we are, expressed
also as the desire to be in another place: 'Those in the vegetable rain retain /
an area behind their sprouting eyes / held soft and rounded with the dream of
snow.' In aggressively tropical countries, 'an imaginary snowstorm some-

times falls'; thus do we escape in dreams from what Page later called the tyranny of subjectivity, and 'lie back weeping' to find the daylight, mul-
ticoloured world unchanged. Presumably these landscapes could be turned
around, since the basic strategy of the poem seems to be one of contrast: the
imagination seeks an opposite reality and suffers anguish when the bridge to
that other country fails. Why then does Page avoid the choice which the
introduction of Holland's snowscape would seem to admit? Why (for
instance) do those Dutch hunters not rise sorrowing from the loss of dreams
laden with great red and blue flowers? This seems to me part of the genius of
the poem, that our attention is not directed to a reductive turnabout. The
human imagination wants not simply an opposite reality (an escape as such)
but *truth*, which is here intuitively conveyed to us as 'silent, unrefractive
whiteness.' Noisy, insistent colour is also a better image for the sensual
world from which all dreamers begin.

§

Before proceeding with the poetry, I want to provide a glimpse of the Sufi philosophy in which P.K. Page has found illuminated so much of the truth that
had been working for expression in her art even from its beginning. Both her
empathic gift (which gives us the Chameleon Poet) and the sense of having
been 'upside down in life' (which leads to her mystical centre) are precisely
accounted for in the Sufi's understanding of reality. What follows is taken
from a book called *The Sufis*, by Idries Shah.[3] 'Mankind, according to the
Sufis, is infinitely perfectable. The perfection comes about through attune-
ment with the whole of existence' (24). But to approach this integration we
must somehow get free 'from the adhesion of rigid thinking' (46); here poetry
can be of some assistance, because 'Sufis say that an idea will enter the conditioned (veiled) mind only if it is so phrased as to be able to bypass the screen of
conditionings' (121). For all our efforts to arrive at 'the end product, the Completed Man' (29) there is only one beginning; in all of our true work 'the
dynamic force is love' (x).

   There is a Sufi fable about the human situation according to which an
ideal community of the El Ar people (their name is an anagram of *real*) were
expatriated to an island refuge 'whose features were only roughly similar to
those of the original homeland' (2). Retaining only a shadowy collection of
their original state, this island people declined into the practice of a rationally constructed gospel known as 'Please' (anagram of *asleep*); they were
increasingly *dis*pleased by the activities of those among them who
attempted the arts of shipbuilding and swimming in order to regain a homeland in which the majority no longer believed. Boats were considered imaginary vehicles, absurd and unnecessary since 'there was nowhere to go' (5). It
seems to me that any student of P.K. Page must respond to this fable with a

shock of recognition, for displayed there according to their proper functions in her work are the insistent images of travel, vision, sleep, and water. The poet's sense of community *vs.* isolation can be understood in the homeland of the El Ar people. Gardens and landscapes and homecoming. Expulsion and entrapment. Efforts to penetrate rock, to move through reconstructed air, to enter the sea. Memory and imagination, the language of the eye. Dreaming as superior to the sleep of day. Wherever we go in her poetry, the same archetypal signposts may be discovered.

'Leather Jacket' (141-142) is a comparatively recent poem which illustrates the Sufi influence. We can imagine the poet's satisfaction in finding the quotation from Suhrawardi which she employs as epigraph: *'One day the King laid hold on one of the peacocks and gave orders that he should be sewn up in a leather jacket.'* In the poem she mourns for 'that many-eyed bird / blind' and wandering through the garden in its leather jacket, a metaphor for human entrapment which obviously does not require special knowledge from the reader. But for P.K. Page there must have been a marvellous sensation of *déjà vu* in the discovery of a Sufic cult which joins the peacock and the angel in a fashion so perfectly attuned to the shapings of her own imagination: 'angels are the higher faculties in man' and the peacock is associated with a homophone meaning *verdant land,* so that the Peacock Angel cult is concerned with 'the expansion of the "land," the mind, through the higher faculties' (*The Sufis,* 386). Not only do two of the most important figures in her poetry come together, but they do so to express visionary intensity (as she does) in terms of the mind expanding and becoming integrated with the landscape. Its tail of many eyes spread and open to the beauty of the land, the peacock is angelic; the mind has access to and can become the garden. But with the descent of the leather jacket the poet asks us to 'Cry, cry for the peacock' – reminding us of the bird's harsh cry and placing it in the human heart.

> The peacock sees nothing
> smells nothing
> hears nothing at all
> remembers nothing
> but a terrible yearning
> a hurt beyond bearing
> an almost memory
> of a fan of feathers
> a growing garden ...

The yearning which is expressed here and throughout Page's work is a basic element of our experience, a source of energy which converts to love. It can join us with the peacock, with one another; it can make us angelic and cause the leather jacket to disappear. The garden would be ours again.

§

The socialist perspective in the early work of P.K. Page might easily be seen as a false start, a deflection from the true course of her mystical sensibility. Thus, we might regret the historic accident of the 1940s which placed her in Montreal among the *Preview* group of poets. But in fact this sort of grounding was entirely natural and auspicious. Page looked first at the given world: the particular terrain which she encountered during this period matters less than her desire that it should be inhabitable (that obstacles should be removed) for others as well as for herself. Because social justice was not a matter of indifference to the poet, a kind of anchor in ordinary reality was supplied. The mysticism which has obviously increased in time has always required that she practise an alternate detachment and identification in relation to ordinary life. She has never ceased to care for the fates of other people. We can always hear the practical woman in the aspiring mystic – a voice which is properly disturbed by such things as sexism or office slavery, and which is concerned with both halves of any metaphor.

The title poem of her first collection (*As Ten As Twenty*, 1946) states the poet's belief that political consciousness is liberating. 'For we can live now, love: / a million in us breathe' (34). This internalization, this sense of a common cause, removes the distorting filter of isolation: it can 'tear off the patent gloves / and atrophy our myths.' The *bouleversement* which occurs so frequently in the work of P.K. Page takes on a political colour. As the million funnel through to populate her mind, the poet can move – enlarged and still proliferating – in an opposite direction:

> As ten, as twenty, now
> we break from single thought
> and rid of being two
> receive them and walk out.

Romantic love is understood as having doubled the sum, an addition to the self which is nevertheless inadequate to break the barrier of 'single thought.' Only when the lovers open themselves to humanity at large do they begin to live, walking out together into 'lands our own and theirs.' The approach to numerical infinity and the journey into the world are implied metaphors for the perfection of the self through love. Political consciousness becomes mystical, yet both matter: the particular occasion (perhaps the Spanish Civil War) which provoked the author's sympathy, and the effect of this on spiritual growth.

An early group of poems concerned with stenographers and other office workers reflects the author's political consciousness in another way. A single story of mundane and metaphysical dimensions emerges as central to the experience of these poems. It's wartime and the office girls are lonely. They mark time by assiduously prettying their 'mirror-worn faces' ('The Stenographers,' 18); but mainly they go about their office chores in a kind of daze – unknowing and pitiable creatures whose lives are tracked by the empathizing poet. She follows them round the treadmill 'from their moist sleep arising' ('Morning, Noon, and Night,' 16) through the anguished calm of noon and into the waters of night. She pursues them also on 'the forced march of Monday to Saturday' ('The Stenographers,' 17) and even during the yearly brief vacation of 'Summer Resort,' where they up periscope to 'scan the scene for love' (3).

Nearly always they are under water. In 'Shipbuilding Office,' the jargon of their work 'floats very lightly, like flotsam / in heads stormily holding the perilous oceans of love' (5). This is the only poem in which an office is permitted to reveal its ultimate function. Because this office is like all the others, we may conclude that shipbuilding is a metaphor for all of the work from which the girls are alienated and ought not to be. Obviously, shipbuilding is a task with the potential of meaning for these water-logged dreamers. But so far the sense of communal effort in a valuable enterprise is missing; ships are remote and imaginary vehicles, just as they were for the islanders in the Sufi fable recounted earlier. The bosses are culpable to the extent that they have contributed to an inhuman environment. We are made to remember in these poems that society should be organized in such a way that labour is not deadening; the daily labour for which we are paid ought to harmonize with our larger work as human beings. But the women with whom Page sympathizes are also at fault. They suffer acutely from the disjunction between their need for love and the barren reality of their daily lives, yet 'hardly guess / themselves as more than surface indolence' ('Morning, Noon, and Night,' 16). Submerged in fuzzy dreams of love, they fail to exercise their own imaginative faculties; the dim hope of chivalric rescue contributes to their paralysis. By such passivity they collaborate with the bosses, separating themselves from the work of shipbuilding (both mundane and metaphysical) and so remaining uninstructed by the truth contained within their dreams of love.

Yet 'they without message,' for whom the words in which they traffic are utterly meaningless, can sometimes 'seem to sense / each other's anguish with the swift / sympathy of the deaf and dumb' ('Typists,' 7). Although inarticulate, this sense of a common predicament could be the beginning of change. Together with dreams and briefly liberating memories of a better time and place – as when 'they glimpse the smooth hours when they were children' ('The Stenographers,' 17) – the sense of shared anguish could point the way to 'a future more like life.' But 'some – if you speak to them of a different world, / a future more like life – become sharp, / give you their whittled face / and turn away like offended starlings from a wind' ('Offices,' 6). They refuse consciousness, reject angrily the suggestion of a different world. At the end of 'The Stenographers,' P.K. Page indicates the cost of such refusal with a brilliant image: 'In their eyes I have seen / the pin men of madness in marathon trim / race round the track of the stadium pupil.' We respond with shock to the intrusion of what seems a foreign element in the poem. This is a wind to offend starlings, the voice of the poet who looks deeply into the 'mirror-worn faces' of the stenographers and pronounces a metaphorical warning. They have glimpsed with their own eyes and then denied what the poet understands: that madness can result from their treadmill pace and that the 'marathon trim' which they assess anxiously in their mirrors is unlikely to end in victory. Some change is necessary – perhaps first a recognition that others are running with them, and next that all of them need to get out of 'the stadium pupil' of self-absorption.

§

The poet's generosity of spirit is apparent in the many poems concerned with people who are inarticulate, outcast, imprisoned, freakish, psychologically enslaved, or ill. One such poem is 'The Condemned' (14-15). It will serve here to illustrate the fashion in which Page moves from a sympathy for the literally construed plight of unfortunate people toward a universalizing of their experience in her own terms. 'The Condemned' is an improbable love poem about escaping prisoners. To emphasize its genre, I shall venture an odd comparison with Keats's 'The Eve of St. Agnes.' The dream of escape from prison is at first a dream of love. It begins in the dark as two convicts chip away at what separates them from one another, 'feeling the walls would dissolve with love.' The task they perform has a meaning beyond itself:

> In an area a cigarette could light, everything lived.
> The intricate machinery of the head
> stopped, and the heart's attention
> increased the circumference of what they loved.

Finally their hands touch:

> it was so suddenly tender in that prison
> birds might have sung from water – just as if
> two mouths meeting and melting had become each other.

This is the mystical moment at which the lovers converge, the 'solution sweet' of Keats's famous poem. Natural imagery celebrates the occasion in both poems, as practical and metaphysical victories are simultaneously won. Like the youthful Madeline and Porphyro on their way out of the foemen's castle, these convicts leave the prison miraculously: 'plunging through velvet to an earth so stiff / their footfall left no mark.' Clearly the problem for Page is the same as it was for Keats. The lovers are challenged to sustain the

fluidity of spiritual communion, the protective magic of vision, in the stiff-
ness of the real and often deathly world. At first the outside world is a continuation of what they have achieved within:

> Their lungs, in all that air, filled like balloons,
> pastel and luminous against the dark:
> no angels could have had more grace
> in a children's heaven full of suns and moons.

> But light destroyed their splendour, all their soft
> movements jerked to woodcuts and the lace
> of their imagination atrophied.

The 'heart's attention' has been identified with 'imagination,' which spins
out 'lace' in an increasing circumference. But now the spiritual magnitude
they had attained in prison shrinks, so that by an ironic and retrogressive
bouleversement 'everywhere they went was nowhere at all.' What was soft
and lovely as lace becomes hard, ceases to extend itself, and is 'jerked to
woodcuts.' Keats also uses the imagery of stasis (a decline into the immobility of an arras, jerking motions prior to a hard freeze) to suggest the 'imagination atrophied' which is P.K. Page's recurrent nightmare. His lovers are
ambiguously saved, while hers are not – but an interesting similarity remains
in the fact that for both poets love and imagination become equivalent terms
and operate as the only adequate protection against death-in-life.

A recurrent pattern in many of the author's poems traces the return of a
character to some homeland about which he has been dreaming and which
turns out not to be the locus of his heart's desire. Often, this failure is marked
by a confrontation with some reductive image of the self when the character
has arrived at what ought to be his home. Wanted posters function in this
way for the escaping prisoners of 'The Condemned,' as they find 'their stark
identities – all they had left – / were mirrored upon fence and parish hall / and
plastered on the staring countryside.' 'Unable to Hate or Love' (26-27) concerns the return of a soldier from overseas, and this time (as in several other
poems) crowds of people are out to applaud and welcome the traveller. But
the occasion fails:

> It was almost as if there were figures behind his eyes
> that he couldn't completely see around or through;
> as if in front of him there were others who
> partially blocked his view, who might even speak
> gibberish or cry if he opened his mouth.

This proliferation of selves is also common in Page's work, a frightening dissolution which means that the individual is unable to place himself in the

surrounding world. The returning soldier (like the prisoners in 'The Condemned') is suddenly afraid of 'the too-big spaces' and 'knew, at last, that most of his dreams were lies / and himself a prisoner still behind his face, / unable to be free in any place.' Disorientation is a sufficiently familiar occurrence in the circumstances which the poem records, so that we can read the poem quite simply in political terms: the soldier is confused about the meaning of his recent captivity and is unable 'to hate the enemy as they wished him to / or love his countrymen as he would like to do.' But the pattern which is repeated through so many poems suggests that behind any given journey back, the author sees an experience of archetypal significance: radical disappointment or dislocation occurs because another sort of homecoming was prefigured in the dreams of the traveller. Either the dream must be considered a lie when ordinary reality is confronted, or the traveller must continue the quest until he finds himself at home in being. He will never be free or properly himself until that journey has been accomplished.

People with obvious psychological troubles inhabit many of the poems. Distortions of personality are lamentable in proportion to the degree by which they obscure vision; thus each case study of an acutely disturbed person serves in part to dramatize the condition of us all. But vision is not a dogmatic obsession which supplants all other concerns or eliminates the interest of individual differences. Instead, it works as the measure of a liberal imagination: human pain (which matters for itself) is considered as a consequence of obstruction and human fulfillment as the attainment of complete access to reality. Often with anger, Page will indicate how one person can damage the well-being or clear-sightedness of another. 'Paranoid' (45) is an account of a boy whose problem is that 'he loved himself too much' and whose eventually complete solipsism was set in motion by a mother who conceived of him as a god, allowing that 'Thunder stemmed from his whims.' Nothing but self is judged holy: 'Crouching in his own torso as in a chapel / the stained glass of his blood / glowed in the light.' The poem is a kind of parody of growth in which the integration of self and world happens by denial, by the failure to detect anything real for the nourishment of the self, so that finally the paranoid protagonist who has consumed as vacancies the earth and 'the heavens too' is left as a dead and sightless moon 'reflecting light.'

In a poem called 'Only Child' (46-48) another boy seeks to rebel against his mother's manipulation of the natural world he loves. She intrudes upon his privacy, placing his own concepts and terms before him so insistently that the continuum of reality is nearly destroyed for her son. '"Observe, / the canvas back's a diver,' and her words / stuccoed the slatey water of the lake.' Repeatedly in the author's work, hardness marks the end of sight. Again, 'When she said, "Look!" / he let his eyeballs harden / and when the two birds came and nested in the garden / he felt their softness, gentle, near his heart.'

The boy chooses his own way of vision. But a dream (brilliantly written)
warns of the mother's encroaching victory, his defeat:

> Dozens of flying things surrounded him
> on a green terrace in the sun
> and one by one
> as if he held caresses in his palm
> he caught them all and snapped and wrung their necks
> brittle as little sticks.
> Then through the bald, unfeathered air
> and coldly as a man would walk
> against a metal backdrop, he
> bore down on her
> and placed them in her wide maternal lap
> and accurately said their names aloud:
> woodpecker, sparrow, meadowlark, nuthatch.

'Portrait of Marina' (51-53) concerns another person damaged by a parent
who imposes on the child his own favoured version of reality. Interestingly,
both here and in 'Only Child' the obstruction of parental insistence is placed
before some part of reality which is especially beloved by the poet so that the
child's loss is passionately underscored. The father had named his daughter
Marina to 'make her a water woman, rich with bells,' an eventuality which
would have been lovely and possible had she been left free to discover such an
identity for herself. Thus, 'his call / fretted her more than waves.' Another
symbol of her father's tyranny is Marina's life-work, an embroidered picture
of the sea: 'To her the name Marina simply meant / he held his furious needle
for her thin / fingers to thread again with more blue wool / to sew the ocean of
his memory.' In a fashion reminiscent of the Lady of Shalott, Marina has been
imprisoned and separated from reality:

> The salt upon the panes, the grains of sand
> that crunched beneath her heel
> her father's voice, 'Marina!' – all these broke
> her trembling edifice. The needle shook
> like ice between her fingers.
> In her head
> too many mirrors dizzied her and broke.

Marina is destroyed, however, by reflections rather than by an immediate
experience of reality.

Physical illness is the subject of another group of remarkable poems in
which the author's rage and sympathy seem to be coursing through every
line. Some of the images and a general impression of tautness or emotional

strain recall Sylvia Plath (especially in her poem 'Tulips') with the signal difference that Page's feeling is for other people. Indeed, a comparison of these
equally passionate poets (which unfortunately cannot be undertaken here)
would illuminate the extraordinary empathic power of P.K. Page. In 'The
Sick' (94-95) Page examines the varying responses to hospitalization, concluding with an image that embraces all and establishes the undercurrent of
community in an alien world. 'The Sentimental Surgeon' (96-97) is an angry,
beautifully crafted poem which tells of a dying patient, the genuinely sympathetic nurse 'who is pledged to serve and make no sound / ... while her rebellious lungs / are bright with anger,' and the preening, autocratic surgeon who
only pretends to care:

> Diagnosis proclaims the operation urgent,
> yet flowers float sadly in his salon face
> where tense and straining at their tendon traces
> should crouch the whippets of love.

'The Probationer' (98-99) traces the character of a fledgling nurse from the
metamorphosing point of view of an improving patient who finally departs
the hospital like 'a present she has made.' Relationships are strangely
coloured in the unnatural light of hospitals. But certainly the most powerful
poem of this group is 'Nursing Home' (100-2) in which the poet first particu-
larizes the suffering of the old inmates with consummate artistic authority,
and next quite rightly claims 'There are no words for it / there are no words.'
In the last lines she asks, 'Where are they going / these voyagers? / Who
steers?' At best a detour with an occasional friendly guide, illness is generally
seen in these poems as a terrible interruption of human life; at worst the
poet's empathic sense of disorientation is so extreme that she seems to
despair of the journey ending well.

§

P.K. Page often writes about children. Many poems are specifically devoted to
the subject of childhood, while others refer to it as a kind of touchstone for
wonder. The poet taps our childhood memories in order to recall a pre-condi-
tioned state of being. She allows for the exceptional case history, but generally she seems to think of childhood as a period of inchoate dreams – something like a condition of free-fall before ordinary adult consciousness takes
over and demands that the cord be pulled. 'Shipbuilding Office' speaks of a
young woman whose face has 'hardly emerged / from the dive of childhood'
(5). In growing up, we take on shape; but Page customarily sees this process as
rigidification, a closing of the waters of vision rather than the location on dry
land of an authentic identity. Her 'Little Girls' (41) invite comparison with
the Wordsworthian child who, trailing clouds of glory, was father to the man:

'More than discovery – rediscovery. / They renew / acquaintanceship with all things / as with flowers in dreams.' These children move easily in their flowing world, like artists at peace: 'And delicate as a sketch made by being, / they merge in a singular way with their own thoughts.' When anger does come, it 'blows into them and through their muslin / easily as sand or wind.' But with the onset of adult consciousness they assume an externally imposed identity and 'for a time' lose their place in being:

> Older, they become round and hard, demand
> shapes that are real, castles on the shore
> and all the lines and angles of tradition
> are mustered for them in their eagerness
> to become whole, fit themselves to the thing
> they see outside them,
> while the thing they left
> lies like a caul in some abandoned place,
> unremembered by fingers or the incredibly bright
> stones, which for a time replace their eyes.

The thing left behind is a 'caul,' suggesting that childhood continues a prenatal insulation; yet the world contained within the caul was visionary, as we know from its being 'unremembered by ... stones, which for a time replace their eyes.'

'Young Girls' (43) marks a transitional stage, in which the water imagery that was implied by the sand and shore of the previous poem becomes crucial to our understanding of adolescence. In school the girls are 'like porpoises'; some leap,'But most, deep in their daze, dawdle and roll, / their little breasts like wounds beneath their clothes.' The waters of a dreaming childhood are complicated by tides of menstrual blood which relentlessly bring the mermaids into shore:

> Too much weeping in them and unfamiliar blood
> has set them perilously afloat.
> Not divers these – but as if the waters rose in flood –
> making them partially amphibious
> and always drowning a little and hearing bells;
> until the day the shore line wavers less
> and caught and swung on the bright hooks of their sex,
> earth becomes home, their natural element.

A feminist perspective is apparent here. The 'bright hooks of their sex' are like the 'lines and angles of tradition' in 'Little Girls'; in both poems the amphibious mermaids are caught, answering the pull of bells – which sound for death or weddings – and moving toward 'castles on shore' in order to assume what is now ironically called 'their natural element,' the traditional female role.

'Blowing Boy' (44) uses air and water in a similar fashion to explore the transition period for an adolescent male. 'Generation' (28) speaks of 'the dreadful opacity of adolescence,' another sort of caul which separates maturing children from the understanding of an adult world:

> We were an ignored
> and undeclared ultimatum
> of solid children;
> moving behind our flesh
> like tumblers on the lawn
> of an unknown future,
> taking no definite shape –
> shifting and merging
> with an agenda
> of unanswerable questions
> growing like roots.

The shape has not yet been assumed, but roots have begun to grow. In this poem, rigidification is circumvented by a liberating political consciousness: 'love roll[s] from a bolt / long as the soil,' and this particular generation of children find an authentic home in the world.

In 'The Bands and the Beautiful Children' (40) Page writes out of the spatial sense which is always so remarkable in her work. The inner / outer world of children is celebrated as the 'auditorium of light' or the 'building of sound' which is constructed in their imaginations when a marching band 'makes a tunnel of the open street.' This is an important moment, childhood's version of the altered consciousness that Page experienced again through the miraculous proportions of a Brazilian church. When the band stops playing, the castle in the air crumbles:

> And the children, lost, lost,
> in an open space,
> remember the certainty of the anchored home
> and cry on the unknown edge of their own city
> their lips stiff from an imaginary trumpet.

This is another form of the mermaids' lament. The children's real home was in open space; so long as imagination's anchor held, that space was familiarly constructed as 'their own city.' But with the collapse of vision, open air became alien just as the sea had become fearful to its own beautiful inhabitants. Tears mark the transition. Hope for a recovery of the homeland – even

now they 'cry on the unknown edge' – is to be found in the prelapsarian memory, the sense of 'lips stiff from an imaginary trumpet.'

One of the author's finest poems offers as the last of its 'Images of Angels'
(61-63) the picture of a child walking in innocence 'along an avenue hand in
hand' with his 'milk-white playmates.' Suddenly he takes a step and finds
himself listening to the music of the spheres:

> take a step
> and all the telephone wires would become taut
> as the high strings of a harp
> and space be merely the spaces between strings
> and the world mute, except for a thin singing,
> as if a sphere – big enough to be in it
> and yet small
> so that a glance through the lashes
> would show it whole –
> were fashioned very finely out of wire
> and turning in a wind.

This is musical architecture, the homeland lost in 'The Bands and the Beautiful Children.' Telephone wires on an ordinary street become the strings of an
angel's harp and make a sphere seen through the also constructive, also
rounded lashes of a child's eye. Centred in the eye-sized, child-sized, cosmic
sphere, he sees it whole; and we may recall in passing how through the vortex
of the macaw's eye, Page had been led 'into a minute cosmos which contained
all the staggering dimensions of outer space.' But the child will lose his place
if the rational faculty insists too far upon any literal measurement:

> But say the angelic word
> and *this* innocent
> with his almost-unicorn
> would let it go –
> (even a child would know
> that angels should be flying in the sky!)
> and feeling implicated in a lie,
> his flesh would grow
> cold
> and snow
> would cover the warm and sunny avenue.

Again and again, Page mourns the collapse of vision.

But she keeps on building. Her children grow up, and she gives us poems
about love – a whole series of poems in which lovers try to renew Eden. 'Love
Poem' (79) tells of the possible resurrection, affirming the creative power of

memory: 'Remembering you and reviewing / our structural love / the past rearises alive / from its smothering dust.' In 'T-Bar' (80-81) the poet carries a procession of somnambulist lovers up the mountain, providing an awesome context for those occasional moments when the human pair become 'wards of eternity.' Such moments pass; the lovers wake, cannot maintain their unity – and so decline from grace as 'spastic T-bars pivot and descend.' 'The Glass Air' (69-70) concerns a dream in which the speaker's heroic lover has 'come to share' her 'prairie childhood.' He traps a gopher, who turns upon them with a vengeance so that both lovers are covered with blood. It seems the enigmatic gopher is a kind of talisman for the lady's past which her lover attempts to possess. The dream of a return to childhood can be interpreted as a test of the lovers' relationship, a trial uncovering their failure as adults: 'And we two, dots upon that endless plain, Leviathan became / and filled and broke / the glass air like twin figures, vast, in stone.' Thus do the nightmarish qualities of the dream solidify, like the lovers themselves to destroy the visionary world through ego. Often the poems about love's difficulty are themselves especially hard to understand, as if to mirror the peculiarity of division where union has been the aim. Often the male is associated with something closed and hard like stone, marble, or metal. But the poet is aware of this imagery as deriving from her own perspective as woman, and she seeks always to extend her vision beyond it rather than to congratulate herself for an identification with the softness of flowers or water. 'Vegetable Island' (86-87) is illuminating in this respect. Excellent poems like 'The Flower and the Rock' (72), 'Water and Marble' (73), and 'The Metal and the Flower' (74) compel our belief partly by the intensity of such effort.

Her people travel and grow old. Some pursue their journey like 'The Permanent Tourists' (110) who see nothing: 'Classic in their anxiety they call / all sculptured immemorial stone / into their passive eyes, as rivers / draw ruined columns to their placid glass.' But there are also poems like 'Brazilian Fazenda' (112) in which the field of vision is radiant and alive. In 'Journey Home' (116-17) we find a literal homecoming that comes close to satisfying the demands of the spirit, as the traveller races by train across the Canadian winter landscape and merges with it in a series of empathic transformations. The poem ends as he walks off in the approximate direction of home, his shoulders 'light and white' as though 'wings were growing' with angelic, expansive consciousness. Another group of poems stems from the recognitions of advancing age. 'The Murder' (138) repudiates a belief in one's own death, begs forgiveness for a time when the lack of faith had operated as 'attempted murder / of a body existing outside time / and indestructible, being endless.' In 'Masqueraders' (140), the poet sees through the symptoms of age to recall not only youth but the splendour that transcends any temporal phase – as human beings 'in reality, are / dark, fair, and shinier / than the masks we wear or wore.' This sense of the ideal hovers behind all of the poet's human characterizations.

§

A surprising number of the author's most important poems are located in a garden. The lost city and homeland are other archetypes of the same desire for a return to one's place in being, but for Page the garden has always been especially productive. 'Now This Cold Man ...' (109) is a lyrical account of spring coming to a garden, warming the heart of the man who works there and is cold from the stoppage of vision. The garden and the man are simultaneously reborn:

> Now this cold man in his garden feels the ice
> thawing from branches of his lungs and brain:
> the blood thins in artery and vein,
> the stiff eyes slip again.

Gradually he becomes the garden: 'jonquils blossom from his skull ... and something rare and perfect, yet unknown, / stirs like a foetus just behind his eyes.' The integration of a human being with the land is always achieved by love, the heart's attention – as in the glad eroticism of 'Personal Landscape' (67) where the poet describes a Blakean sort of intermingling with the land's body. Vision is accomplished not only by the eye, but through a collaboration of all our organs and faculties: 'A lung-born land, this / a breath spilling, / scanned by the valvular heart's / field glasses.'

'After Rain' (135-36) begins with the voice of a woman celebrating her own responsiveness to the natural world. She is self-consciously the poet, one who is so much the mistress of her own garden (her own craft) that she can cause images to grow there and to proliferate as if from a magical deluge. What she makes out of this garden is impressive poetry:

> I none too sober slipping in the mud
> where rigged with guys of rain
> the clothes-reel gauche
> as the rangey skeleton of some
> gaunt delicate spidery mute
> is pitched as if
> listening;
> while hung from one thin rib
> a silver web –
> its infant, skeletal, diminutive,
> now sagged with sequins, pulled ellipsoid,
> glistening.

Then comes the extraordinary line: 'I suffer shame in all these images.' And the poem is on its way to something much better than brilliant description. She has just noticed Giovanni, her companion in the garden who 'shakes a doleful head' over the ruin of his work: 'I find his ache exists beyond my rim / and almost weep to see a broken man / made subject to my whim.' The poet remembers that 'the garden is primeval,' and she sees in her gardener Giovanni two aspects of Adam – one 'so beautiful and diademmed,' the other 'broken.' She regrets that Giovanni cannot see the present beauty of the garden (or his own related beauty) and that she in her exuberance had forgotten the pain of Eden's ruin:

> O choir him, birds, and let him come to rest
> within this beauty as one rests in love,
> till pears upon the boughs
> encrusted with
> small snails as pale as pearls
> hang golden in
> a heart that knows tears are a part of love.

To understand the next and final stanza of the poem, we must recognize that she does not abandon her previous vision. She only corrects it, expands it to 'a size / larger than seeing'; and therefore she allows the snails from the first line of her rhapsody to enter her prayer for Giovanni. Are the snails also a version of the serpent, and the pears of the apple, in a reconciliation of the two Edens? In any event, the final stanza in which she prays for herself must also be read as a criticism of her own work:

> And choir me too to keep my heart a size
> larger than seeing, unseduced by each
> bright glimpse of beauty striking like a bell,
> so that the whole may toll,
> its meaning shine
> clear of the myriad images that still –
> do what I will – encumber its pure line.

The poet for whom empathy has been a gift so powerful as to be threatening must also find the power to be 'unseduced by each / bright glimpse of beauty' in her garden. To remain in Eden she must convert image to symbol; and paradoxically her source of power must still be empathy, 'a heart that knows tears are a part of love.' Eve was seduced by self-love or pride; in another sense she falls through susceptibility to image. Page recognizes that for her garden to be ordered and radiant, it will be necessary to defeat what she has elsewhere called 'the tyranny of subjectivity.' Thus, the woman must bring Giovanni (the ordering principle) within her 'rim' – not as one who is subject to her whim, but as himself. His pain cannot be left out of the account while a talented poet pursues the delights of a private imagistic world. When he is remembered their common world becomes a symbolic Eden.

'If It Were You' (91-93) and 'Arras' (104-5) are two of P.K. Page's most disturbing and beautiful poems. Again the personae find themselves in a garden. In the first of these poems she makes it 'you, bewildered – not me this time' who experiences the pain of vision gone astray. This strategy has the effectiveness of a nightmare in broad day. It lets us know thoroughly the terror of dissolution; the terror of losing one's place in a familiarly structured world; and the appalling isolation of a garden in which no one answers, where birds brushing one's coat are 'angels of deliverance / for a moment only.' Madness or self-murder could result from watching 'the great sun, stampeding through the sky' and seeing it drop:

> a football in your hands
> and shrink as you watched it
> to a small dark dot
> forever escaping focus
> like the injury to the cornea which darts
> hard as a cinder across the sight but dims
> fading into the air like a hocus-pocus
> the minute that you are aware
> and stare at it.

This is another *bouleversement* in the wrong direction. Nothing but self remains after such devastation. One could 'become Ishmael,' the poet says – for how could one help being outcast and alone if 'all the exquisite unborns of your dreams / deserted you to snigger behind their hands.' But the poet *can* help it and does in her other visionary poems.

In 'Arras' the poet is transported to a garden tapestry where she sees again the exquisite, perfected human beings of her dreams; and again she finds them aloof, 'motionless, / folding slow eyes on nothing.' They refuse to recognize her. We might suppose that she has trespassed, perhaps that her ego is at fault. For a moment she seems to be at the heart of nightmare: 'The spinning world is stuck upon its poles, / the stillness points a bone at me.' Silently accused and cursed, she confesses it was her eye that permitted a peacock to enter the arras. But in fact this is not a confession of guilt; her answer defies the hex, supplying proof of her visionary capacity and of her right to a place in the garden. The bird belongs on such a tapestry. He is like an ace or a trump card dealt to the poet from a tarot pack in which 'The cards, all suits, are royal when I look.' Her 'future on this arras' is in truth assured. The poet's confession becomes a cry of intended victory, heard by the reader only if he can love as she can the peacock's beauty. 'Does no one care?' This interpretation is supported when the poet repeats her audacious feat of vision at the end of the poem: 'another line has trolled the encircling air, / another bird assumes its furled disguise.' To suggest that the flat and alien nature of this garden is itself a disguise, the bone of accusation is shaped like an arrow aimed at her centre and like the peacock as it enters the arras: 'Voluptuous it came. / Its head the ferrule and its lovely tail folded.' That the shape is also phallic suggests an equation of vision with love; the peacock 'was strangely slim / to fit the retina.' Following their linear insinuation into the tapestry's design, the peacock proudly spreads its 'eye-bright' tail and the poet walks on 'sandalled feet' through space that less visionary mortals (those with an overwhelming fear of death, the bone pointing) would dismiss as impenetrable. Still the fear in this poem belongs to the author also – the fear of enclosure. It is occasioned by her sense that others cannot see what she does, or by a sense that her own visionary powers need further exercise. But the fear is overcome to the extent that she refuses to surrender vision. Page will solicit from 'the encircling air' as many peacocks as it takes to establish free access in the garden.

'Cry Ararat!' (144–47) is a poem describing the evanescence of vision. Its title alludes to the mountain from which the Biblical dove had brought proof of life's continuance, a second chance at Eden for survivors of the flood. The poem begins in a watery dream with a sighting 'through binoculars' of Mount Ararat. Swiftly the dreamer's 'fingers seek accurate focus,' knowing that 'the bird / has vanished so often / before the sharp lens / could deliver it.' At this moment focus is achieved and the mountain appears: 'The faraway, here.' But if the dreamer were to reach out for it with her hands, Ararat would vanish. Page is making here a crucial distinction between two kinds of effort: 'the focus of the total I' which is required for vision, and aggression which always fails. She issues a warning:

> Remember the statue,
> that space in the air
> which with nothing to hold
> what the minute is giving
> *is* through each point
> where its marble touches air.

She chooses the statue for its stillness, its lack of any capacity to reach out for 'what the minute is giving.' This very lack, however, means that the statue receives 'through each point / where its marble touches air' all that the moment can give. It makes the moment eternal, just as the statue itself exists permanently in the surround of being. In the same way, children live in the radiant embrace of a 'quick landscape' whose every flower or bird is real and perfect. This is the condition of the dream:

> when dreaming, you desire
> and ask for nothing more
> than stillness to receive
> the I-am animal,
> the We-are leaf and flower,
> the distant mountain near.

But the child grows up and the dreamer wakes, declines painfully into 'the unreality of bright day,' and is haunted by the memory of beautiful Ararat. We all know this loss. But some who are like the poet spend their lives in an effort of vision:

> I, a bird,
> landed that very instant
> and complete –
> as if I had drawn a circle in my flight
> and filled its shape –
> find air a perfect fit.

So far this is visionary effort of the right kind; the air surrounds her ('Remember the statue') and like the innocent dove who 'believed / in her sweet wings and in the rising peak' she attains Ararat. But the moment passes when she reaches out for more:

> ... with the next tentative lift
> of my indescribable wings
> the ceiling looms
> heavy as the tomb.

She returns to the world of ceilings, enclosure, and death. She asks if the material world must seem inert, if the freedom of air must always be lost: '"Must my most exquisite and private dream / remain unleavened?"' In the final couplet, however, Page captures the two sides of her 'spinning coin' and ends with the visionary: 'A single leaf can block a mountainside; / all Ararat be conjured by a leaf.'

'Another Space' (148-49) records a dream so powerful and satisfying that the poet seems able to awake from it with continuing faith in the dream's reality. She dreams of marvellous people dancing on a beach, of being reeled lovingly into their human circle – which becomes spherical, connected by an invisible axis to a 'starry spool.' The dream is full of metamorphoses as she approaches nearer to the heart of vision, but is still puzzling: 'I see them there in three dimensions yet / their height implies another space / ... I speculate on some dimension I can barely guess.' She sees Chagall figures, 'each fiddling on an instrument,' and the bow of each cosmic musician becomes 'an arrow almost. Arrow *is*.' Page uses the word *almost* frequently in her poems, as a sign that she will claim nothing more than what she knows. Here finally she can abandon it. 'Arrow *is*.' The headman's arrow is let fly:

> to strike the absolute centre of my skull
> *my* absolute centre somehow
> with such skill
> such staggering lightness
> that the blow is love.

The Chameleon Poet has found her centre in being. Love (reciprocated now) is the dynamic force of the Sufis. The beach is Ararat, or the homeland of the El Ar people. The arrow is a further transformation of the bone in 'Arras,' but now a single insinuation suffices to end enclosure and to remove the last of the obstacles to vision:

> And something in me melts.
> It is as if a glass partition melts –
> or something I had always thought was glass –
> some pane that halved my heart
> is proved, in its melting, ice.

> And to-fro all the atoms pass
> in bright osmosis
> hitherto
> in stasis locked
> where now a new
> direction opens like an eye.

This extraordinarily beautiful poem is placed at the end of *Poems Selected and New*. It embraces all of the author's most passionate concerns, brings all of her most insistent images together, and provides us with assurance that her *eye* (the last word in the book) will never be closed.

Notes

1. Letter to Richard Woodhouse, 27 October 1818. *Letters of John Keats, A New Selection*, edited by Robert Gittings (London: Oxford University Press, 1975), 158.

2. *Poems Selected and New* (Toronto: Anansi Press, 1974), 88-89. All further citations from the poetry of P.K. Page refer to this edition and are indicated parenthetically in the text.

3. (London: Jonathan Cape, 1969).

Approaching P.K. Page's 'Arras'

'Arras' is masterful, an awesome visionary poem which has sometimes (by my reckoning) been misunderstood. Page contends here with giant forces, and she will triumph, but if we are to follow her toward that victory, we must not be deceived as to the nature of our common enemy. The mistake which has been made is to suppose that the peacock or the royal denizens of the arras are finally sinister.[1] In fact, I would suggest, they represent the glory (the perfection of human life) which is sought by the poet in 'Arras' and throughout her work. Her struggle is to join them, to attain their stature, not to escape or defeat them; and her enemy is any impediment to that goal. The imperviousness of those royal figures should not mislead us, for the perceived obstruction is not really of their making.

Perhaps the difficulty begins with the question of where we are: inside a dream, or looking at a tapestry, or perhaps (especially if we know this much about the poet) at a garden party surrounded by such elegant figures as Page would have encountered in her role as the wife of a diplomat. Indeed these multiple settings coalesce, to account in part for the sense of dislocation. Or the difficulty may begin with the first two lines: 'Consider a new habit – classical, / and trees espaliered on the wall like candelabra.'[2] We are jarred by this opening, I think – deprived of an easy orientation; presumably we are being asked to enter the arras of the title, an impression which is soon confirmed. But why *consider*? This may suggest something tentative, possibly an experience which is to be approached cautiously. Yet the original meaning of 'consider' is to look closely, so that the first word of the poem can be read as an imperative. Look deeply and come in, the poet says. We consider a 'habit' – the fabric of the arras and a habit of mind, which is 'new' in the sense of being revolutionary or consciousness-altering, but also 'classical' and so antique, formal, and enduring. We shall enter, accordingly, a world which is always there for us and seldom known.

Still on the verge of the arras, we see 'trees espaliered on the wall like candelabra.' The flatness of the arras is changing as the tree tendrils (branches of the candelabra) reach out into our space and draw us forth. In the next line we are magically within the arras: 'How still upon that lawn our sandalled feet.' We feel the cushion of grass, and tread lightly – for we are spirits and unsure of our welcome. So far it has been *our* feet – the poet seemingly had *us* consider – but for the rest of the poem she forgets us, having other and more urgent claims on her attention. We are with her or not, in soft focus. It is also possible that she summons only herself to the arras world and that 'our sandalled feet' belong to dissociated halves of the poet's self, one from the realm of here and one from there. Or she may approach with other guests, if we conceive of the primary setting as a garden which is seen as two-dimensional like an arras.

An impression of stillness is suddenly dispersed by the raucous cry of an intruder who is considerably less circumspect than the poet:

> But a peacock rattling his rattan tail and screaming
> has found a point of entry. Through whose eye
> did it insinuate in furled disguise
> to shake its jewels and silk upon that grass?

In one sense, this peacock (who enters almost simultaneously with the poet) is another version of herself; thus we discover later that it was her eye which summoned him. This dissociation is characteristic of dreams and a function of the dreamer's anxiety. She fears that the peacock's noise will rouse the legitimate inhabitants of the arras and cause them to eject her, so she denies this royal and rampaging alter-ego. Soon the poet will discover that her strategy is a mistake, her fear misdirected. The peacock's mode of entry is correct; she needs more rather than less of the peacock in herself, and so she will end the poem with summoning more birds to the arras.

This king of birds who heralds their mutual arrival is described by the poet with a scarcely concealed sense of jubilation. Two contexts merge: the natural behaviour of the peacock, whose tail is linear when folded, who shakes himself violently in order to unfurl that sudden splendour; and the method of tapestry-making, whereby a linear needle pierces the fabric at 'a point of entry' to insert the sinuous coloured thread which is in the needle's 'eye.' Just as suddenly as we have entered the two-dimensional arras, so miraculously does one stitch suffice to create the entire peacock – an echo of his transformation when the tail lifts. The peacock is *disguised* and *insinuates* himself into the garden; this diction has understandably had satanic associations for some readers, but the real splendour of the peacock and the total meaning of the poem should contradict that reading. The garden is 'classical,' after all – not biblical. The language of deception (which clashes with the peacock's self-insistent scream) comes mainly from the speaker's own insecurity, and it is therefore significant that she will re-describe the peacock's entry in very different terms somewhat later in the poem. A further meaning of this disguise relates to the subtlety not of devils, but of poets. It is enough for now that we should note how very appropriately this peacock (with 'its jewels and silk') is dressed for the occasion. He is precisely the sort of being (like a unicorn or hart) whom we might expect in this tapestried world; he is also a monarch returning from exile, a guest handsomely attired.

The shifts in 'Arras' are abrupt, as in dreams or dream-like movies. The peacock who had so troubled the poet is not mentioned again for some time. She backs up from (represses and denies) this too-strong image, and looks for safety: 'The peaches hang like lanterns. No one joins / those figures on the arras.' The stillness has returned, and the poet is separate from 'those figures' who are mentioned now for the first time. Peaches are often espaliered, trained to grow against a flat surface; for that reason and because they 'hang like lanterns,' they remind us of the candelabra and make us feel the poet has retraced her steps. The peaches are heavy, softly glowing lamps which cast a portentous light – but they are not, except inconsequentially, I think, the apples of a fallen Eden. And who is this no one? Neither the temporarily banished peacock nor any part of the poet's self nor any other guests who may be present have joined 'those figures on the arras' – who seem inviolate, another race of beings. But they are *figures*, while the others are *no one*, invisible and unrealized.

In the next lines, the poet moves again within her aura of invisibility:

> Who am I
> or who am I become that walking here
> I am observer, other, Gemini,
> starred for a green garden of cinema?

As in the passage through a dream one's identity may be fluid, so here the poet questions who she is and feels herself becoming 'other.' This division can be seen as a process of growth as well as of alienation. The 'other' which she becomes is 'Gemini,' the sign of the zodiac which is opposite to Sagittarius, Page's own sign; but fortunately that information is not vital, for 'Gemini' itself conveys the sense of a divided person – divided and also doubled, so that the poet can move beyond the limits of a single subjectivity. The sense of division as alienation is enforced by the words 'observer' and 'other,' which should be recalled when we come to assess the aloof quality of 'those figures' and to determine who is responsible for their distance from the poet. She is not yet at home within the arras world. She is uncertain of her role, though in the language of astrology she is 'starred' (fated) to come here. Dream-like, the co-ordinates shift to the language of film as the poet thinks she is 'starred for a green garden of cinema.' The controlling analogy is between dreams and movies, in which roles and scenes may shift as the camera or the dreamer's eye moves on. The dreamer may be reduced from star to hanger-on if her courage fails; she may be cast as extra or as victim or as heroine at different times, for she is partly the author or director of her dream and partly an actor without contract or knowledge of the script.

If this analogy has been understood, the next lines will be less puzzling to the reader:

> I ask, what did they deal me in this pack?
> The cards, all suits, are royal when I look.
> My fingers slipping on a monarch's face
> twitch and grow slack.
> I want a hand to clutch, a heart to crack.

There is a submerged link here between astrology and the tarot pack, although 'this pack' is essentially the ordinary one which runs from deuce to ace – with the crucial, dream-induced difference that 'the cards, all suits, are royal when I look.' We may also begin to feel that 'Arras' is a looking-glass world, with the poet cast as Alice encountering the fearful Queen of Hearts. The dreamer's plot, in any case, has taken what is also for her a disconcerting turn: 'I ask, what did they deal me in this pack?' Contained in this line is a sense of powerlessness, of there being someone else in charge of the poet's fate – the deck has been stacked, and perhaps against her. Yet surely a hand composed entirely of face cards would be a winning hand?

The appropriate response to all this royalty can be gauged if one looks at an essay called 'The Sense of Angels,' in which P.K. Page writes about her friend A.M. Klein. There she recalls a poem of Klein's which 'remind[ed her] that man is royal even when he forgets he is in the unreality (unroyality – it is the same word) of day to day.'[3] All suits, all kinds of human beings, are royal when we look deeply enough. And the world of 'Arras' is precisely the real or royal world which underlies the ordinary, which abides on the other side of the looking-glass. It is a fascinating coincidence that Page's essay about Klein begins with the elaborate description of a garden party in Brazil, where her husband was the Canadian ambassador and where Page first heard the news of Klein's grave illness. Her memories of Klein talking in a Montreal kitchen and wearing an ordinary dark suit are juxtaposed against the 'colored silks and satins, diamonds, pearls' which surround her in the Brazilian garden; but the opposition between two worlds is less meaningful than the fact that these present images, 'straight out of the Arabian nights, [are] worthy of Klein's most elaborate metaphors.'[4] Klein's liberal imagination, that is, led him with P.K. Page to perceive the world of our forgotten royalty.

So the hand which the poet has been dealt in 'Arras' is indeed a winning hand, although she has yet to understand fully the design of her dream or the nature of 'those figures' or herself. The cards, she finds, are 'royal when I look.' These last three words do more than fill the line. Only when she *looks* do they become royal; previously the fact of royalty was beyond the range of her perception, but now the camera or the dreamer's eye has fastened on the essential truth. Yet the figures which were remote on the arras are still remote, even as she holds them card-like in her hand: they are flat as cards are, two-dimensional like the arras before that is penetrated. The perception of royalty has nevertheless had a powerful effect on the poet, causing her to come this much closer to the figures and to wish that she might come closer still, and at the time making her afraid of so much majesty. Thus, her fingers slip, 'twitch and grow slack' as the poet loses faith in her ability to connect with (to become herself) this ideal image of humanity. We note that it is *her* fingers which lose their grip on the royal figures, although what she feels is more nearly a lack of cooperation on their part: 'I want a hand to clutch, a heart to crack.' She wants reciprocity, help from the figures whom *she* perceives as flat and who are therefore unable to reach out to her. Their heartlessness is only an appearance which it is the poet's task to penetrate, but the reason for this appearance needs further investigation.

It is at this juncture that the poet's experience with formal occasions such as the one she described in 'The Sense of Angels' may become relevant. In the garden of 'Arras' we find the perfected human beings of our dreams, figures so truly exalted that the poet will need to spend her life in the effort of understanding them and attaining their stature. Yet because her vision of them is still imperfect and because dreams *are* fashioned of such strange comminglings, these figures have been confused with their opposites: fallen beings whom we find in everyday (albeit expensive) gardens, pretending to an exalted condition although their exercise of vision has been so slight that they are unaffected by what the *poet* sees even now. The poet's everyday frustration with unseeing others becomes in the dream world of 'Arras' frustration at her own limited capacity for vision, which she projects on 'those figures' so that they become as heartless and unseeing as the pretentious hosts of a garden party. But the truest explanation of their imperviousness is simply that these figures represent the poet's ideal self, from which she will remain distant (and who will remain distant from her) until the journey is complete.

In the next lines, we are again returned to stillness. There has been another dissolve of a threatening image, another retreat to the verge of the arras:

> No one is moving now, the stillness is
> infinite. If I should make a break....
> take to my springy heels ...? But nothing moves.
> The spinning world is stuck upon its poles,
> the stillness points a bone at me. I fear
> the future on this arras.

At this nadir the poet is afraid not of being expelled from the garden, but of dying there. She contemplates withdrawal of vision, recalling in the reference to her 'springy heels' the transitional moment when on 'sandalled feet' she had stepped into the arras. She despairs at having come thus far, and then no farther in her journey; at such a stopping place 'the spinning world is stuck upon its poles.' Without the recognition she requires from those royal figures, the poet feels condemned to a living death; it seems less horrible to retreat into the ordinary world than to stay here and be mocked eternally by the evidence of her presumption. But the possibility of an exit seems blocked by the infinite stillness. There is a loss of dimension as 'the spinning world is stuck upon its poles,' reduced to the flat surface of an imprisoning arras. And now 'the stillness points a bone' at the poet, accusing her of trespass (because she has not established her right to a place in the garden) and of presumptuous vision (because paradoxically her vision did not reach far enough). The pointing of a bone is an aboriginal hex which brings death to the accused. Significantly it is 'the stillness' which condemns her, the stillness which is what she fears as her 'future on this arras.'

But here the world begins to spin again, as the poet speaks to defy the hex: 'I confess: / It was my eye.' Faced with the alternative of a spiritual death, she finds new courage and rises phoenix-like to claim the peacock as her own creation. This is less a confession than a cry of intended victory, a return to the ordeal of vision. She describes again the arrival of the peacock, but in nakedly impassioned language now, acknowledging her eye's complicity and love:

> Voluptuous it came.
> Its head the ferrule and its lovely tail
> folded so sweetly; it was strangely slim
> to fit the retina. And then it shook
> and was a peacock – living patina,
> eye-bright, maculate!
> Does no one care?

In the spinning world, the bone of death has been magically transformed into a phallus of love – as if it had boomeranged through the air from her accuser to the poet. Everything here is erotically charged, as if the poet would reply unashamedly (and unlike Eve) and with all the energy at her command to the accusation which has been made against her. Thus, the peacock's coming is 'voluptuous,' its head is the 'ferrule' or the penis tip, and its lovely, sweetly folded tail is 'strangely slim' to enter the poet's body. Vision and love are equated, so that the peacock (gloriously male) enters both arras and woman through the poet's eye: 'it was strangely slim / to fit the retina.' At the moment of orgasm or transformation, the lovers are realized: 'it shook / and was a peacock.' And they are royalized. The poet has seen and loved and been and made the peacock; this is her answer to the stillness, her proof that she is a legitimate inhabitant of this realm where all 'are royal when I look.'

The peacock is now fully displayed: 'living patina / eye-bright, maculate!' Art springs to life in the wonder of 'living patina,' as if to claim the durability of the poet's vision. The many eyes of the peacock's tail connect him with the poet's eye and indicate the cosmic plenitude at which always she directs her gaze. The word 'maculate,' meaning spotted, refers again to the many eyes – but recalls also its opposite, *immaculate,* in the spinning world of which this bird is justly king. Surely this triumph will be acknowledged? In the next line we come to the poet's heart-cry, her astonishment that such splendour does not revolutionize the world: 'Does no one care?' Again we must ask who this 'no one' is, for on at least one previous occasion 'no one' was clearly not 'those figures.' I would argue that the poet's cry resounds throughout the arras world like the peacock's scream to shatter our composure first of all, and that it is directed to the royal figures only secondarily. For them it means something rather different: not that these perfected beings are incapable (as we may seem) of appreciating the peacock, but that she had hoped this image would be enough to close the gap between herself and them. Perhaps also her cry returns the poet briefly to a fallen world outside the arras, so that the royal figures have become for the duration of her cry their shadow selves – the denizens of an ordinary garden.

In the final lines of the poem we hear the poet's sorrow that her journey is unfinished and her renewed, passionate determination to reach that goal:

> I thought their hands might hold me if I spoke.
> I dreamed the bite of fingers in my flesh,
> their poke smashed by an image, but they stand
> as if within a treacle, motionless,
> folding slow eyes on nothing. While they stare
> another line has trolled the encircling air,
> another bird assumed its furled disguise.

Her strategy is now explained. If she *spoke,* in a poem summoned up an image like this miraculous and hex-defying peacock as a proof of vision, she thought 'their hands might hold me.' The peacock was her claim on them, her way of getting 'a hand to clutch, a heart to crack.' But it was not enough, as no single poem or feat of vision can be enough to satisfy us finally. We may *dream* of that ultimate attainment, as the poet here 'dreamed the bite of fingers' in her flesh and dreamed that she could smash 'their poke' (dissolve that last barrier) with an image, but the rhythm of our lives is such that we awake from dreams and must repeat their labour. Progress can be made, however; and so the violence of the poet's imagery in these lines suggests both the momentum of her desire and the frustration which comes from her proximity to the object of that desire. She sees them, maddeningly close – but 'as if within a treacle, motionless / folding slow eyes on nothing.' They see nothing without because all is within, the whole spinning world. The poet's determination to persevere and at last to enter that perfect sphere is revealed when she solicits from 'the encircling air' another secret agent. She summons another line, another bird. She will not quit that arras. It is a splendid ending, a statement that there will be no ending but success.

The reading of 'Arras' which has been offered here is consistent with the rest of the poet's work, as any reading which sees her beloved peacock or the royal figures as sinister I think is not. But if any doubt remains concerning the nature of those impervious beings, perhaps the best way of dispelling it is to look briefly at 'Another Space' – a less difficult, equally brilliant poem which resembles 'Arras' in several ways and confirms its meaning. Here again the poet encounters a circle of strange beings who extend (still further now) her sense of space: 'I see them there in three dimensions yet / their height implies another space.'[5] She is drawn always closer to them, for this poem describes a dream of joy and is not subject to the withdrawals we have known in daylight and in 'Arras.' These beings are not hostile to the poet, yet the moment of their union with her is accomplished by an arrow (related to the peacock and the aboriginal bone of 'Arras') which is shot by 'the headman':

> to strike the absolute centre of my skull
> *my* absolute centre somehow
> with such skill
> such staggering lightness
> that the blow is love.

As in 'Arras' the poet's desire to 'smash' and 'crack' the figures with her peacock-arrow in fact expressed her will to love them, as the bone became a phallus, so here 'the blow is love.' It suffices now to dissolve the last barrier, which is correctly perceived as surrounding not those figures but ourselves:

> And something in me melts.
> It is as if a glass partition melts –
> or something I had always thought was glass –
> some pane that halved my heart
> is proved, in its melting, ice.
> And to-fro all the atoms pass
> in bright osmosis
> hitherto
> in stasis locked
> where now a new
> direction opens like an eye.

P.K. Page arrives at the 'bright' reciprocity, the end of 'stasis locked,' and the triumph of vision for which she worked so valiantly in 'Arras.' Heart-whole, no longer 'Gemini', she has left for now the pain of subjectivity behind. For now, but not forever yet. When the dreamer wakes, she will be glad of peacocks waiting for the next attempt.

Notes

1. See A.J.M. Smith, 'The Poetry of P.K. Page,' *Canadian Literature* 50 (Autumn 1971): 26; S. Namjoshi, 'Double Landscape,' *Canadian Literature* 67 (Winter 1976): 27; and D.G. Jones, *Butterfly on Rock* (Toronto: University of Toronto Press, 1970), 17.

2. P.K. Page, 'Arras,' *Poems Selected and New* (Toronto: Anansi, 1974), 104.

3. P.K. Page, 'The Sense of Angels,' *Dialog* (Passover, 1973): 19.

4. *Ibid.*, 18.

5. 'Another Space,' *Poems Selected and New*, 148.

Pastoral Restraint:
John Metcalf's *The Lady Who Sold Furniture*

One of the most delicious features of *The Lady Who Sold Furniture* is its title. Nothing illicit or odd is conveyed by the title itself, and no practitioner of that trade is introduced, and so the reader conveniently forgets the title. Metcalf bides his time. He gets on with the creation of a world in which Jeanne, the fascinating housekeeper, is our focal point; and he makes this world through Peter's eyes, using in a third-person narration the perspective of the man who loves her. Only when we have been thoroughly charmed does Metcalf unleash his title, establishing its legitimacy – Jeanne is, after all, the title character – and collapsing our unwary, passive assumptions about work in a single leap. A lady who sells furniture needn't own it, or be employed by others for that purpose; a housekeeper may choose to *keep*, or appropriate for ready cash, the furniture entrusted to her care. Jeanne simply, and rather splendidly, assumes her right to turn things down-side-up.

All through that richly comic scene in which Mr. Arkle and his lads dismantle the first house, the title (without any explicit verbal signal) keeps resounding. It's exhilarating, as if Metcalf's nerve and Jeanne's had coalesced. But our renewed consciousness of the title also directs attention to Peter, who must now come to terms with Jeanne's profession. The title signifies the object of Peter's regard: both the woman herself and the astonishing fact of what she does. What to think about Jeanne, how to accommodate or judge her larceny, that is the question that carries us (via Peter) through to the novella's close. Metcalf, however, places one stringent limitation upon his access – and therefore our access – to Peter's consciousness. Neither in his memories nor in his present observation of Jeanne does Peter engage in any recorded judgement of her or any explication of his ambiguous feelings. And so the reader must work, attending carefully to the selection and deployment of physical detail – for that is how Metcalf constructs a social context and the portrait of a sensibility, and how he guides us to an understanding of Peter's response to Jeanne.

In a curious way, this decision of Metcalf's echoes and extends his trick with the title, his faith that in time all will be made clear. Our excitement in the art of the novella is maintained by this new form of narrative tact. We keep waiting for Peter's moral discomfiture to be made explicit; we keep on

being pleased when it is not. On another level, this strategy of restraint works
to suggest Peter's deep resistance to any condemnation of Jeanne. We are
unsure of the extent to which Peter (as opposed to Metcalf) is avoiding the
activity of explicit judgement, but we sense that they have somehow become
allies. Once Metcalf kept Jeanne's secret; now he keeps Peter's.

This conspiracy of silence makes the novella feel *friendly*. The reader who
does her job will not feel left out; on the contrary, she will unite with writer
and protagonist in the wish not to be hard on Jeanne, and not to lose her. She
is our 'love-object,' our friend and comrade and fellow-wit, our purveyor of
excitement in a grey place. In short, Jeanne gives the parties – she does this
literally, on several occasions – and we don't want the party to end. We fear
the CID who seem poised to take Jeanne away to prison again, and equally we
fear the cops in ourselves who would call her guilty. Thus, our friendly conspiracy is insecure on two fronts, and we grow closer to Jeanne in elegiac
desire as the threat of disclosure mounts.

With lovely tact, Jeanne saves Peter – and indeed the whole cabal of Peter,
Metcalf, and ourselves – from having to witness her collapse into judgement.
She suggests that she is leaving him because the CID are on her trail, but it is
clear that she also knows about the 'undercover cop' (the criticism of her)
that lurks within Peter himself. What she *says* is that she is unwilling to iron
'"five years of shirts"' (93) for him. This is a reference to the prison term she
anticipates if caught, and recalls her earlier description of the '"twelve
months"' when she was obliged to make her bed to the matron's specifica-
tions and to spend her '"days working in the laundry"' (16). Metcalf doesn't
tell us flatly that Jeanne has been in prison, and again his motive seems a
gentlemanly restraint. But the laundry language in which this information is
conveyed has at least two additional uses. First, it proclaims Jeanne's anger at
domestic servitude. It underscores the ironic appropriateness of her chosen
crime (in effect, she steals the shirts off the backs of the employers who had
compelled her to launder them), and the darker irony of the job that is
assigned to her in prison (a return to the ironing board, the spring board of further bitterness and further crime). And secondly, it implies Jeanne's awareness of what I am calling the 'undercover cop' in Peter. She won't launder
shirts *for him*, and her overt meaning (that she declines prison as the price of
continuing their affair) works easily with the covert (that prison would be *for
him* in the sense that it follows naturally from the belief system to which
Peter still in part adheres). If the reader does not see that in her two 'laundry'
speeches Jeanne is alluding to prison, she will suppose that Jeanne is expressing a horror of domestic subjugation by the male. And in any case, as a result
of Metcalf's policy of restraint, a ghost of that meaning remains: Jeanne is
always vigilant on this point, even if her lover is innocent of any wish to use
her as his servant. On all levels of meaning, then, Jeanne resists a threat to her

freedom; and on all levels, Peter (against his will and Jeanne's) is associated with that threat.

The final irony, of course, is that Jeanne's decision denies them both the freedom to love. As they part, each pursues what seems a pre-destined course; neither seems really free. Yet Jeanne, with the tact referred to earlier, has done her best to end things well. She has revealed to Peter the impossibility of his full support of her, without challenging him to deny it. She has allowed his judgement against her, and her own awareness of that judgement, to remain implicit. And she has let him see her last when she is still uncaught, still the free-wheeling lady who charmed the pants off Peter Hendricks. In each of these ways, Jeanne eases the guilt that he must feel for judging her, and preserves her self-respect.

Jeanne's parting gift to Peter is a leather document case, an emblem of the profession he has chosen, and an echo of the time when she had proposed this gift to mock his teaching: '"You could put all your little report cards in it"' (56). But Jeanne trusts him now to understand the complex tone of both her gift and her jaunty, plaintive exit line: '"It's executive styling,"' she says. And he, after a lengthy pause, replies in kind: '"It's best quality hide"' (100). Tongue-in-cheek, the superlatives mock a world they both despise; tongue-out-of-cheek, they imply approval of the first-class time they've had together.

Any surviving mockery of Peter's career is balanced by a mockery of Jeanne, who has been mistaken in thinking that when she gets something like this case by redeeming coupons from a vile-tasting brand of cigarettes, she gets it free. Peter had explained this in the original 'document case' scene, where the sub-text was an attack by each (in Peter's case perhaps an unconscious attack) upon the other's line of work: '"You pay for all that with the price of the cigarettes"' (55). Peter was reacting on that occasion not to the cliché of a housekeeper clipping coupons, but to a thief who had paid and would continue to pay a terrible price for what she clips.

Another meaning of the gift, then, is that both lovers will pay (and now understand that they will pay) the vile-tasting, hidden costs of their two careers. And a principal cost for each is the necessity of their separation. The gift marks their divergent paths – for Jeanne has extracted Peter's badge of respectability from her own purloined suitcase – and allows them at the same time one last stroke of intimacy, the chance to show a lover's multi-layered understanding.

So the lady who sold furniture walks away; and the novella that doesn't quite bear her name – Jeanne is, after all, a woman of many aliases – comes to an end. But the title achieves, at least for me, a new resonance at this point. I think of 'lady,' how it carries the dark issue of class and of privileges denied to Jeanne, and how it suggests a lover's tenderness, Jeanne as Peter's lady. And

I think of 'sold,' its ominous past tense. (Is she rotting in prison now?) In any case, she recedes; she is lost to our whole doting, doubting cabal. But one thing more. Sometimes I feel that Jeanne (because of her intense fictional reality) has simply been translated beyond our reach, like the lovers at the end of *The Eve of St. Agnes*: 'ay, ages long ago / These lovers fled away into the storm.' And I, of course, wish then that Peter could have gone away with her. (The remaining parts of this essay will explain why he cannot.)

§

The Lady Who Sold Furniture reflects in its structure a concern with the worlds of holiday and everyday, a movement between rural and urban scenes. In Jeanne herself the pattern is laid down: the alternation of housekeeping jobs with periods of holiday. But in robbing everyday to pay for holiday, Jeanne cynically disposes of or inverts a tradition that in Peter's case remains (although tenuously) persuasive. This is a tradition which holds that 'everyday' is to be enriched by values that are sincerely held in 'holiday.' It is essentially a *literary* tradition – Peter, we remember, is a student and teacher of literature – in which pastoral interludes are followed by responsible, heroic action in such 'real' places as the battlefield or the throne room. Typically, the hero is refreshed and enlightened by his passage through the wood; he is made compassionate by spending time with social inferiors, and comes out a better ruler than he would otherwise have been. Metcalf uses this tradition, and announces that he is using it when Jim (the RAF type who employs Jeanne) misquotes Prince Hal: 'If all the year were playing holidays / To sport would be as tedious as to work' (*Henry IV, Part I*: I.ii.227-28; the mangled version occurs on p. 27 of Metcalf's text).

Peter has recently finished university, what Jim calls his '"halcyon days"' (27) and Jeanne his '"teacher-training lark"' (30). That period was succeeded by 'long weeks of [farm] labour in the Channel Islands' (9), from which he has just returned as the novella opens. Now he can look forward to 'three weeks of idleness' (9) before his 'real' work starts up at Gartree Comprehensive School. Phases one ('sport' at the university') and two ('work' in the Channel Islands) establish the pastoral and heroic rhythm that repeats itself in phases three (idleness) and four (Gartree). But the pastoral setting of the Channel Islands and the fact that farm labour is not Peter's 'real' work suggest that the first three phases also represent *versions* of the pastoral: a time and place of contemplation, a retreat to the more natural world of simple folk, and a period of revelry and 'misrule.' The latter, of course, is the domain of Falstaff and of Jeanne. In all of these it is supposed that the hero will learn something useful for his return from holiday to everyday. But he must move on, and so must Peter Hendricks.

Metcalf uses this tradition both seriously and ironically. For all his reluctance, and his abhorrence of what education has come down to in a place like Gartree, Peter (like Metcalf behind him) really does believe that '"teaching's an important job"' (56). And he takes with him from the 'pastoral' world certain banners: a love of true learning from the university, an understanding of the relationship between nature and art (how each is an aspect of life, which must be revered), and a concern for the lives of 'ordinary' people. The second of these principles takes us into the very heart of pastoral, which is paradoxically the most 'artificial' of literary genres. The first in combination with the third points us toward that curious mix of elitism and egalitarianism which again is characteristic of the pastoral – and of Metcalf's sensibility. It explains why Peter works at Gartree, where his students spell the word for the story of their lives '*Atobagifry. Autobiogriphy. Attobagioph*' (72): he is *needed* there. So the social, transformative function of his pastoral values is taken seriously by Peter. But there is an irony too, in the recognition that Peter's chance of transforming the world is very slight. He is not given the authority that is typically held in reserve for the arrival of the pastoral hero. Hero threatens to become anti-hero in these circumstances. And so when Jeanne calls to summon him back to the world of holiday, Peter departs with enormous glee, leaving his autobiography assignments (and the lives of his students) still unmarked.

As Metcalf teaches us through images the moral necessity of Peter's eventual separation from Jeanne, so he uses images (the physical detail of an environment) to reveal that his hero's pastoral values stand little chance of successful implantation in the 'real' world of Gartree. The first image confronting Peter as he enters Gartree Comprehensive is 'a reproduction of some pastoral scene' (58), an indication of how remote his values will seem to the inhabitants of this place. Immediately after seeing 'another reproduction of a pastoral scene. Sheep. A lady in a straw hat' (63), Peter looks at a clock – one of the many clocks strategically placed by Metcalf to suggest that something important (and related to the timeless world of pastoral) has been lost to us. Part of the loss is timelessness itself, the sense of eternal youth that exists in pastoral (although in tension with the necessity to mature into the heroic phase). As a place established for youth and for their successful maturation, Gartree should reflect both of these dimensions of the pastoral. Instead, ironically, the clock that controls life (that keeps everyone moving on) does so in an atmosphere which is hostile to any true growth. It's eight-thirty, on Peter's first day of work – and already it seems too late.

We feel this because Peter has just met the headmaster, the wildly ineffectual and eccentric Mr. Stine who is pre-occupied with his plant and his toy watering can. The numerous young human plants in Gartree's garden are

clearly getting very little help from him. This image (like the pastoral repro-
ductions) suggests that the institution retains some faint, vestigial memory
of its purpose; but Mr. Stine cannot focus on this, any more than he can complete a sentence or a train of thought, or recall the purpose of what he is staring at as Peter leaves – the broken-off lead of a mechanical pencil. In the staff
room which Peter enters after looking at the clock, we discover that his fel-
low-teachers are scarcely more promising. Indeed, it seems that their goal is
to *become* Mr. Stine. Certainly they share his complete lack of interest in any
contribution that Peter might wish to make. There is no pigeon-hole
assigned to Peter yet, no tea mug for him. And two of his colleagues are
engaged in a deeply peculiar discussion of *directions*: how to get from a pointless point A to a pointless point B as cagily as possible. It is a clear metaphor of
their passage through this school.

That image and many others were prepared for in a journey that Peter
takes in his period of idleness, before the job at Gartree has begun. Instead of
going on what he knows is a '"nicer"' (20) trip to the zoo with Jeanne and her
daughter, Peter chooses to practise and clock the route to Gartree. Everything he sees on that trip suggests the demise of nature and the futility of his
pastoral intentions. All the streets around Gartree are *named* for trees, but
'there was not a tree in sight' (22). The sense of death in time – a fading of the
pastoral vision that is carried also by Jeanne's fear of aging – is conveyed in
the image of 'an old man in a black overcoat ... sitting on a concrete bench
staring at the floral clock' (23). On the 'padlocked gates' of the school itself he
sees the Gartree crest – with its traditional motto, *Virtue and Knowledge,*'
and the traditional oak tree, but also with 'three black birds' positioned omi-
nously 'underneath the roots of the tree' (23). The tree of knowledge seems an
endangered species, therefore, even before we have encountered the
pathetic, deflationary image of Mr. Stine's toy watering can.

§

A full response to the images (and therefore the meaning) of *The Lady Who
Sold Furniture* can only occur if the reader moves in a complex way back and
forth within the fiction. This is always necessary in reading, but is especially
so in a fiction that is largely concerned with the operation of time. Metcalf
chooses to reveal the principal events of his novella in chronological order,
but he also ensures that his reader will become accustomed to a back-and-
forth rhythm by enacting that in the play of Peter's consciousness. I can give
only a few small examples of this: how Peter in the classroom projects himself into the lunchtime spectacle of a colleague chewing 'with his mouth
open' (73), or how at the seaside with Jeanne's small daughter he closes his
eyes in order to savour images just past.

Another example may suggest how such temporal dislocation points us toward Metcalf's elaborate play with images. As Peter is shaving on the morning of his visit to Gartree environs, he projects himself forward through 'the Valley' and sees in imagination numerous images of decay and decline and destruction that will haunt the novella as a whole. These include indications that life stopped somehow at the time of the war – 'a sign from 1945, *Welcome Home Our Bill*' or 'the hoardings which masked the bomb-sites' (21) – and include 'the wreckers' who will be coming soon to 'raze the Valley to an uneven field of rubble – broken brick and plaster, splintered laths' (22). We should remember this when the plaster starts 'flaking off the ceiling' (40) as a result of the labours of Mr. Arkle and his 'wreckers.' And we should remember the Valley when Peter at Gartree, staring out at the playground, recalls a fragment from a serial comic of his own childhood: 'It had been set in Canada. Engineers were going to flood a valley ...' (66). That destruction had been endorsed by society, just as 'the wreckers' of the Valley will be licensed to do their work, even if Mr. Arkle's men are not. In the comic world of Peter's childhood an elaborate scheme had killed the engineers in the nick of time; but in his present world the Valley cannot be saved.

We should also remember the engineer who wanted to flood a Valley when Peter (as another sort of social engineer) makes a dam with the help of Jeanne and her daughter Anna. This occurs during their holiday by the sea, following Jeanne's devastation of the first house. Peter's symbolic intention (here and at Gartree) is to stop 'progress,' to save what he can from being destroyed by the barbarian hordes. At this point we may also recall (and understand the purpose of) Metcalf's curious description of schoolchildren riding in circles on bicycles 'without mudguards' (23). Jeanne's participation in the damming (despite her complicity with the barbarians) makes sense for her because she fears the operation of time – the loss of youth, the end of holiday, the return to prison. But Anna, too young to understand the destructive nature of time, quickly loses interest in the project. Art fails in this effort to contain or civilize nature; the dam breaks, or begins to do so, as Jeanne and Peter look back. Similarly, their idyllic interlude is breaking down. Jeanne has not been particularly peaceful or well on this afternoon which ends with swallows gathering for their evening feed; and that night the lovers quarrel (though they make it up in bed, relying upon nature still); and the next thing we know, the time has come for Peter to leave for Gartree.

Metcalf's delicate attention to the nuances of afternoon and evening may be recalled in an exchange that occurs as Peter waits in a pub near Gartree for the bus that will take him back to Jeanne. He is luxuriating in the sense of time seized from work (by Jeanne's phone call, her pretense of his mother's illness) when he overhears two old soldiers talking about the Great War. They reminisce about the horses that were commandeered to pull the gun carriages, and complain about being led senselessly from pillar to post by the welfare bureaucracy, and when Peter leaves and bids them '"Afternoon!"' they implicitly correct him: '"Goodnight, boy, goodnight"' (78). This scene should also recall the war images from the Valley, because again we have a strong sense of society's failure, a sense that progress is largely an illusion. One war gives way to the next; horses if attached to gun carriages will shortly turn into mechanical horses, the engines of yet another war. Structurally, this scene works to cast its shadow forward over the last time that Peter will spend with Jeanne – a time that begins with the departure of party guests, 'their voices calling again, "Goodnight"' (79).

§

The question of pastoral and its relationship to Peter's profession, together with the images of destruction in time that we have just examined, may lead us now to the figure of Anna. Again, Metcalf operates with great subtlety. He permits our understanding of Anna's importance for the novella to grow naturally out of the image structure of the text. She is not the subject of any dispute, and Peter does not engage in any recorded concerns about her fate, but Peter is a teacher and Anna is a child – and the question of her education (especially her moral education) is all the more powerful for remaining unasked. Ironically, his profession also means that Peter must abandon Anna to the sole care of a criminal (if loving) mother.

With her youth and charm, her love of play and conspicuous appearances within a natural setting, Anna is clearly a pastoral figure. Nevertheless, we sense that time is working against her. So far Anna seems unaffected by her mother's crime: she sees it, but she understands it only as the signal of another holiday. Thus, when work on the dam stops being play, and the need to hold back the flood begins to seem desperate to her elders, Anna simply walks away. But the dam was built quite literally for Anna's sake, and as it begins to break down we see that Anna is the person who will be most affected by a future which is (in all sorts of ways) getting worse all the time.

One thing that the future will assault her with, of course, is an understanding of Jeanne's crime – or worse, her contamination by it. But Jeanne is in other ways a good mother. She gives her daughter abundant love and fun, she attends fastidiously to Anna's grammar and manners, and she preserves her from the sight of a lover in her mother's bed. There is admittedly an ironic flavour in this last point, since Peter is a considerably better influence than Mr. Arkle, from whose illicit business in the house Jeanne makes no effort at all to shield her child. Stealing the bed is worse than making love in it, by a long shot. And so the irony of Jeanne's complicity with the forces that threaten her daughter's life is clearly present in her belated, increasingly desperate labour on the dam. But that spectacle also suggests that Jeanne is (at least subconsciously) worried about the consequences of her crime for Anna.

Jeanne is never so much a *parent* as at this moment – for parents and teachers must work together to preserve what is good for our children, even if the task seems hopeless, even when the child walks blithely on.

Peter's efforts *in loco parentis* are concentrated in images that carry pastoral themes. He teaches Anna to revere life – to name the various kinds of butterflies, and not to squash the caterpillar that will become a Cinnebar moth. Instead she is to collect and save it, as artists and scholars do in their dealings with the natural world. (Peter's respect for the collector was established in his lengthy reflection upon the work done with badgers by one of his student friends in the first house.) I'm not sure, but I think a very subtle threat is implied by the fact that this caterpillar is 'the fattest' one and is placed in Peter's 'matchbox' (4y). The fattest caterpillar sounds suspiciously like a sacrificial victim, and the matchbox is associated with the cigarettes that do so much damage to wood in Jeanne's houses. It may also be relevant, given the multitude of butterflies that surround Peter and Anna, that what she takes can become at best a moth. (Another image of collection supports this pessimistic view: 'the blue Turf cigarette cards' Peter collected as a boy – 'there had been one he'd never found' (66) – which in return recall the Red Dragon cigarettes collected by Jeanne.)

Anna's own pastoral security and the ghost of her coming insecurity are equally apparent in what Peter sees as he opens his eyes from recalling images of an idyllic holiday with Anna. She is dancing on a grave, 'waving a bunch of flowers' (47). *Et in Arcadia Ego*, we conclude, and rightly. But she is dancing on a Long Barrow, the grave of one of those far-sighted people who '"thousands of years ago"' built the '"big dike"' that Peter had shown to Anna that morning. He must instruct her in the need to respect the dead, their past and significant lives, and so he gives her this small history lesson. (The dike, of course, should be recalled when we come to the contemporary dam that fails.) At the same time he consoles Anna with images of domestic security and collection: the dead are buried '"in high places where they could look out over where they used to live,"' and they have '"all their favourite things with them"' (47).

A similar tension (between security and its imminent loss) can be seen in the very childlike question Anna asks of Peter as she surveys a wide landscape: '"Where's *our* house?"' (46). Anna has generally shown herself to be a child who expects victory in life, like the semi-literate child in Peter's school who intends (although significantly by the mastery of 'JUDO and KARATE') to be *'great great great and great'* (72). And her question about '"*our* house"' does imply an insistence upon establishing her own mark in the world. Indeed, such insistence is clear in something Peter will observe at Gartree: a map of the world on which some other child has placed a dot and a line and 'on the end of the line ... the words: *My House*' (72). But Anna's house is never her own – she keeps moving, the houses keep being destroyed – and so the fact that she asks a *question* ("'Where's *our* house?'"') seems important too.

If, however, a distinction is being made between Anna's question and the other child's firm claim, it is nevertheless clear that *all* these children are in serious trouble. And that is why Peter must abandon Anna. It is why he must go back to work. It is why he must define himself against Jeanne, against the damage she is doing in the world.

§

In losing Jeanne, Peter will lose a great deal: not only the lady herself, but the zest and pleasure of holiday, and the sense of an alliance with those forces of anarchy that have a vast appeal when the authorized version of 'real' life has gone so horribly wrong. Jeanne, as Peter realizes, is in one sense a culturally determined figure, and for him as well as for us there is something heroic in her refusal to accept lying down her status as a victim. She is the feisty under-dog whose anarchic approach to social responsibility is a legitimate judgement upon the class system which has shut her out. Peter is sympathetic to this, and has engaged in minor acts of rebellion against that order himself, acts of playful dishonesty that Jeanne applauds.

Peter is aware of the historical connection between the old world of privilege which he despises and the cultural values, the pursuit of excellence, which he embraces. The world into which he goes with his document case will offer him little of the elegance of mind or living conditions that historically came with an allegiance to high culture. To pursue that now will not lead to the possession of champagne or silk pyjamas – things Jeanne seizes and offers to Peter. Of course one never got these as a *reward* for maintaining cultural values, but there was once a likelihood that the two would come together, since only the rich were well-educated. Naturally enough, Peter (like Jeanne) is attracted to these things; like her, he deplores the connection between class privilege and the possession of good things. Because they are beautiful and give pleasure, these things are allied to the pastoral values for which Peter stands. But they are also tainted as the paraphernalia of the rich – and so Jeanne's seizure of them has a strong attraction for Peter.

In a curious way, it is parallel to his own life's work, the spreading of culture to semi-literate children in a comprehensive school. But their two careers are also opposed, in that hers results in the wanton destruction of beautiful objects, and in that she violates certain ordinary principles of decency, of respect for others, on which his code is also built. Peter's moral and aesthetic principles are deeply related to one another, as they should be in society – which is why he hates the historical connection between privilege and the enjoyment of art. Thus, in the second house Peter passes implicit judgement upon Jeanne over *two* offences: the destruction of beautiful things, and the failure of moral indignation which permits her to exclude the Compton-Smythes from the human race.

The dismantling of the two houses – one near the beginning of the novella, and the other at its close, when the imagery will be more potent – confirms that Jeanne's version of the pastoral (revelry and misrule) is in its working out essentially destructive of the pastoral vision held by Peter. Mainly what gets hurt is *wood.* The cigarettes of Jeanne and her party guests do much of the damage. And the rest is accomplished by Mr. Arkle's poorly-trained assistant crooks. That one version of the pastoral is being destroyed by another is an irony made clear by Mr. Arkle's appreciation of fine wood: '"manogony [*sic*] goes on for ever"' (41). Fine wood and fine craftsmanship represent the marriage of nature and art which is at the heart of the pastoral tradition; and Mr. Arkle is as dismayed by the falling-off of one (the shoddy workmanship on contemporary furniture, the failure of education in his lads) as he is admiring of the endurance of the other (mahogany). Still Mr. Arkle, with his comical complaint that '"There just isn't the honesty for it [craftsmanship] these days"' (41), is as self-deluded as Jeanne with her concern for Anna's grammar. Each has a finger in the dike while using main force to kick it down.

Mr. Arkle's concern with both '"manogony"' and the failure of education in our time should recall to us Peter's attempt to pass on the wealth of a pastoral vision at Gartree. One detail in the Compton-Smythes' house in fact requires us to remember Gartree and its oak tree crest: the 'Hearts of Oak' toiletries in the master's private bathroom. Peter helps himself to these quite liberally *before* the surprise visit by Mr. Arkle and his team of 'wreckers.' But when he understands what is happening, why Jeanne is making no effort to repair the party damage before the return of her employers, he behaves quite differently. In effect, he remembers the honour that is due to wood. He remembers, we might say, what is at the 'heart' of oak – the kernel of his pastoral integrity.

Whereas at Jim's place he had mainly *observed* the devastation, at the Compton-Smythes' he makes various, rather futile moves against it – washing, for instance, 'a carved walnut salad bowl' (86) into which one of the guests had vomited. The juncture of art and nature in the 'carved walnut' is repeated again in the grandfather clock which seems to preside over the end of the novella. It is the one valuable thing that is no good to Mr. Arkle: he can't unload it because '"the maker's name and date"' (99) are engraved on the clock's face. This image suggests that one person can make a difference, can co-operate with time and preserve in time something of value, and that his own identity will be preserved in this way. The grandfather clock *means* that Peter will be returning to labour under the Gartree clock.

But the destruction of beautiful things is not the sole ground of Peter's opposition to Jeanne. He is also, still implicitly, appalled by her failure of moral imagination, her utter lack of concern for the suffering of the Compton-Smythes. We know that Peter is considering this as he examines a silver trophy that has been rejected as not 'weighty' enough for melting down, and reads: *'Presented to Lt. Compton-Smythe by the Officers Mess'* (98). Any anti-military satire – and we do satirically connect Compton-Smythe of the Hussars with Jim of the RAF – yields to a sense of personal history and a pathos which may be supported by our memory of the old soldiers encountered in the pub. They are all *people*, after all. And they do love their things, just as the people buried in the Long Barrows loved theirs and wanted to die with them in safe-keeping, or as an '"old auntie"' of Mr. Arkle's best workman collected and loved her '"*Chinozzery*"' (95), the same chinoiserie that the Compton-Smythes are now in the process of losing. The impulse to preserve – a pastoral impulse present in high and low – is a powerful *human* consideration, and must be placed next to any egalitarian defence of Jeanne's crime.

As Metcalf's brilliant and funny and deeply moving novella comes to an end, we know that Peter Hendricks is miserable over losing Jeanne. We also know that he has no choice in the matter, that his loyalty to what I have called a pastoral vision would have ended things between them even if Jeanne had not. We feel sorry for the lovers and for Anna. We understand that Peter will persevere in his faith at Gartree Comprehensive – and *must* do so, for the sake of nature and of art, for other human beings and for himself – but that he is entering for good now a very grey world. The light of the pastoral has almost gone out, what is left is Gartree, and something very like life itself seems to have gone out the door with Jeanne. When the bastions of culture are so degraded – whether through the privilege of people like the Compton-Smythes or through the parody of true education that occurs in a place like Gartree – life *is* likely to go elsewhere. The pain of Peter's situation is precisely that. The tension in his character (and in Metcalf's sensibility) between anarchic or revolutionary impulses and a deep conservatism is a result of this dissociation of life and art. All that Peter can do – and must do against overwhelming odds – is to attempt what John Metcalf, within the pages of *The Lady Who Sold Furniture*, succeeds in so entirely. And that, of course, is to show us that art and life can be one seamless cloth.

Works Cited

Metcalf, John. *The Lady Who Sold Furniture*, in *Selected Stories*. Toronto: McClelland and Stewart, New Canadian Library, 1982. All references are to this edition and are cited parenthetically in the text.

Between the World and the Word:
John Metcalf's 'The Teeth of My Father'

'The Teeth of My Father' is a story about the writer's father. Or, it is about a story *writer*, and about his construction of stories from the raw material of his father's life. These stories, we are informed by the narrator, pre-date the story we are reading now – which presents itself as a story too, although to a lesser degree. And we get to see them: two brief tales ('Biscuits' and 'A Bag of Cherries') as well as fragments of two others ('Pretty Boy' and another that goes unnamed) which are embedded within 'The Teeth of My Father.' These are 'inner' stories because they are contained within the story's frame and 'outer' because they precede it both in fact and according to the fiction. Because these stories existed as the work of John Metcalf prior to their appearance in 'Teeth,' we may be tempted (if we know this) to take the 'I' of the master-story as Metcalf himself. But we would be tempted to do that in any case. All of the embedded fictions are cast in the third person, with the John Metcalf character (as we will perceive him) being assigned some other name. Thus, we are encouraged to take *this* story as closer to fact, as offering a window upon the writer in autobiographical *déshabille*. Complicating the matter, however, is our recognition of the artfulness, the relentlessly made and dressed-up metafictional quality of the master-story, in contrast to which the embedded stories may seem transparently 'real' or naively mimetic.

Metcalf is pointing in two directions at once: toward the primacy of the word and toward the primacy of the world and the flesh. He is dizzyingly metafictional – but, at the same time, he requires us to acknowledge an extra-literary, human origin for all that is contained within the story. It all goes back conveniently to the father, whose flesh gave him flesh, but who was also his father-in-art; it was the father's imagination, the father's care for words (and almost equally his silence) that set the narrator on to write. Through the 'voices and inflections of his rhetoric' (184), the rise and fall and timing of his father's sermons, the narrator was taught 'what is now [his] craft.' And it all goes back to the *teeth* of his father, as any story should take us back to its title.

The story begins with a boozy afternoon on which, we are told, the narra-tor and a friend traded stories of their dead fathers. We take this occasion as having touched off the words appearing now on the printed page; thus, it seems that *story* rather than memory or experience is signalled as the starting point. And we are struck by the writer's decision not to give us those stories about his father in the context of a conversation with his friend. Metcalf chooses instead to slide from that occasion into a kind of meditation; no further dramatic context is supplied for the voice which addresses us, so that we deduce as a kind of setting only the writer's brain or, perhaps, his study. Again, we are directed away from the ordinary illusions of fiction. In the opening bar scene, certain story topics are named, cryptically; and the three stories cited as having been told by the narrator – about his father's teeth, the loose box, and the consequences of the VD pamphlet – are, in fact, subsequently told. Other topics, however, arise in the narrator's memory as he walks away from the bar; and only one of those will be fleshed out, so that we never learn, for instance, about the enticingly-titled 'tubular steel incident' (174). The effect of this is to remind the reader of all that goes unfinished or unsaid in fiction, of the gap between what imagination or memory may contain and that which finally makes it onto the page. At the same time, Metcalf teases us with a glimpse of treasures the writer may hold in reserve – powers he has still to exercise.

The story-telling session in the bar is important because the stories are not effectively told there, not 'written' there; drinking is only 'a low form of creativity' (174) after all. And it is important because they *are* told, because people always tell stories to each other, because all of us create or fictionalize our lives. The two men talking in that bar are writers; at least I assume that the other man – 'more than an acquaintance, a man I admired and wanted to impress' (175) – is a writer too. The narrator's stories were 'calculated to be funny and to entertain' him, just as when the narrator walks away from the bar (or *writes* of walking away) he walks on 'wilful legs,' plagiarizing Dylan Thomas to impress us. The narrator, in confessing to his plagiarism and the wish to impress and entertain his friend, asserts simultaneously the special case of the writer and the general case of the human being. 'I have decided to tell the truth' (174), he says – reminding us of both ontological realities and of the continuum that runs between them.

But telling the truth is no simple matter, as Metcalf's dedication of this story to Alice Munro may hint. Munro's signature is that moment in the text where she confesses that something has been left out or misrepresented. Like Metcalf in 'The Teeth of My Father,' she is essentially concerned with the interpenetration of truth and fiction, and with the competing claims of world and word. Munro is interested especially in the uses of family history. More than any writer I know, she has made us see how human beings turn life into anecdote – and how creatively, how perfidiously we mine our familial pasts in order to present to others a beguiling persona. She celebrates this tendency, and she castigates herself for it as well. Against her knowledge that we must construct ourselves in this fashion, Munro places her desire to be faithful to the past. She is concerned about exploiting it, about using the other to serve the self. And while she knows that art is a salvage operation, and therefore an act of love, she knows too that it lies and that we cannot finally disentangle the generous and the self-serving elements of art. All of this, I think, is relevant to Metcalf's project in 'The Teeth of My Father.' But the mere fact of this dedication to another writer is useful too; like the story's other beginning, the hidden discourse of those two writers in the bar, it signals the problematic that is known by writers to lie at the heart of their endeavour.

Following this introductory scene, the narrator tells us the 'stories' that were told in the bar – interweaving these with samples of his fiction. The first of the bar stories concerns his father's decision to have all of his 'real' teeth pulled out, since these would necessarily decay, and to replace them with one set after another of artificial teeth fabricated by himself. This choice of art over nature, this passionate and absurd idealism, makes it plain that the narrator is his father's son. The various imperfections of his false teeth continue to 'plague' the father, as the imperfections of art do plague the creator; but the son understands 'that had [his father] produced an undeniably perfect pair it would have broken his heart' (176). Art, which seeks perfection, continues only because we lack it. The teeth which cannot quite conform to the speaker's mouth suggest – of course, but not too crudely – the speech (the writing) which cannot ever precisely match either the truth or the speaker's intent.

Midway in the telling, our narrator interrupts himself to ask, 'The centre of the anecdote?' (175). That question pivots. It may well refer to the making of false teeth, which is the part of the story that follows; or it may refer to what goes before, the image of the father with his teeth torn out and 'blobs of pus that gathered at the corners of his sleeping mouth.' This is a premonitory image, a foretaste of the father's death; it suggests the speechlessness against which writing struggles, the nightmare at the centre of all anecdote. And it reminds us that 'The Teeth of My Father' is finally a story about death, an elegy.

Next comes an embedded fiction called 'Biscuits,' in which a boy meticulously crayons a picture of twenty-eight biscuits as his mother is baking them. That removal of art from reality is intensified by the transposition from visual to verbal art, and by the incorporation of that first story in a subsequent, larger fiction. The child's concern with language is indicated by his asking, twice, how to spell 'biscuits'; by his silent naming of details of the garden, now buried in snow, so that even this early in life he is obliged to do the work of salvage; by his need to name himself both secretly, under the window ledge where no one can see what is written on the plaster, and in public, on his drawing, where David claims the grandeur of his full name and address; and finally, by his interest in the far away sounds of his father's typewriter.

This last point is taken up by the narrator of the master-story, when 'Biscuits' ends. Assuming italics, and the voice of a pompous critic, the narrator expatiates upon the meaning of '*this sample of juvenilia*' (178); he concludes that it suggests identification with the father, and in his other voice acknowledges the piece as '*autobiographical either in fact or impulse.*' Again, Metcalf plays a metafictional game in order to direct us to the story's real heart.

The next section sets up the loose box incident with another embedded fiction, the opening paragraphs of a story called 'Pretty Boy.' Again the boy's artistic sensibility is displayed, together with the domesticity of the mother and the preoccupation of the father: 'Allan's father, remote in his usual silence, did not look up ...' (179). And the family's tea service is patterned with 'impossible orange daffodils,' reflecting once more an intersection of art and nature. We shift them to another family tea, at which the mystery of the loose box is pondered by the narrator and his brother – precisely as if their father, who had caused the conveyance for horses to be dumped in the garden, were not there at all. An explanation comes, by fiat: 'It is not a loose box.... It is a summer house' (180). This pronouncement is made as the father contemplates an etching, which is hung over the mother's head – as if to indicate that matters of art are beyond or above her. Purchased and highly prized by the father, it is an 'atrocious etching'; but he is loyal to it, as he was to the teeth and will be to the summer house. Such confidence in the transformative power of art is dazzling to the narrator, despite and even because of its absurdity in this context.

Before he moves into the third of the bar stories, involving the consequences of the VD pamphlet, the narrator supplies us with another embedded fragment. In this, a man called David recalls the genesis of his love for books – how the father had understood his need for a fresh copy of the book David had stained with his own tears, and how in a 'tobacco-smelling' (181) study David had listened to his father at the typewriter and been ravished by the 'secrets' of the letter 'Q'. David takes intense pleasure in the physicality of such objects – and of Roman numerals, quite apart from the meaning he would just as soon not know; and this is what marks him as a true believer. He is a book man. This is the faith in which he has been installed by the father.

As the tea table was used to shift from one layer of fiction to another, so now the locale of the father's study is repeated in the master-story. And the narrator recalls how he was summoned into that sacred chamber and supplied with a hellish VD pamphlet by his father. His mother, who is characterized by a kindly prudery, has requested that he be given this. The word is passed along wordlessly – so that the narrator is left in terror, to contemplate alone a continuum that runs from his new experience of sex to the consequences promised by the book. He responds in a way that recalls his father's teeth, painting his penis and scrotum with iodine so that 'a perfect slough was cast, a brittle brown replica' (183) of his genitals. Yet artifice is not so easily detached from nature, for this procedure has left him 'as newly pink as a cherub in an Italian painting.' And we know that he will sin again.

The next section begins with an account of the father's tobacco curing, a topic named when the narrator was walking away from the bar; and it proceeds to his cobbling of shoes for all the family. Because this anecdote was not previously announced, it acquires a special status – as if it had materialized from the depths. And in fact it culminates in the moment that seems to me to represent the story's heart. The narrator's father is a man of varied avocations; but through the soles of these home-cobbled shoes we are taken at last into the presence of his *vocation*, which concerns the soul. And I think the pun is intended. All of the tinkering that so absurdly preoccupies the father is connected to his role as a minister of God. In that capacity as in every other, he is concerned with the gap between the real and the ideal, the 'is' and the 'ought.' And the loyalty he exhibits toward his own follies (the noxious tobacco, for instance) only confirms this, for it indicates his faith in perfectability. This is a paradox, of course, one that is applicable equally to the religious man and the artist – who must love *both* the 'is' and the 'ought.'

The sexual matter raised through the story of the VD pamphlet persists to colour this scene in the church. Kneeling at the communion rail, the narrator is alienated from his father by the consciousness of his sexuality; and he experiences 'fierce shame' (184) in the exposure of his own imperfect soles. He cannot swallow the communion bread; and this indicates, I think, that he finds his father's religion unpalatable. But grace descends all the same, when wine (or blood) is offered and his father speaks to him directly: '*A new commandment I give unto you, that you love one another even as I have loved you*' (185). The gap which has existed between father and son is closed. The father's failures in love recede, like his failures in sole-making – and the narrator sees 'swirling dust motes in the shaft of sunlight [that] formed a nimbus around his [father's] feet.' The narrator is blessed, in all his imperfections – even as the father is blessed by an ironic and perfectly serious halo round his feet. The narrator will walk in his father's shoes, for reasons of love as well as art. This is what the story had left out. And beautifully, Metcalf closes in on it – revealing in a moment of high art the primacy of love. He lets the 'other' become radiant. He closes the gap by acknowledging it, by his admission that there are dimensions of the father's being that do not 'fit' the narrator's own design.

The next long section is an embedded fiction called 'A Bag of Cherries,' which recounts the train journey home of a young man who is again called David. It includes the account of a very bookish sexual fantasy, and reveals once more the titillating mix of sex and religion as David invents for his lover's chamber a copy of De Sade 'in a white Bible-binding' (187). In his breast pocket, David carries a letter from his mother which reiterates her concern that he find a 'nice' girl, and which is characterized in fact by reiteration *tout simple.* (We may question this recurrent lack of interest in the mother, her stereotypical reduction – but I shall let that matter go, as Metcalf does.) David's excitement in taking this journey home is two-fold. It involves 'the attic where his past was stored with the *"other lumber"'* (188, my italics), and it involves his father. As David begins to doze, he enters a heavenly dream which is played out beneath 'a sun, perfect with rays, like a child's drawing' (189). This sun recalls the sunlight in the church, but now the father has discarded his clerical collar and put on a red tie. Together, the man and boy consume a sexual and magically innocent bag of cherries; together, they make a pilgrimage to the house of a great writer. It all goes David's way. But the train enters a tunnel, and David wakes to 'the hollow rattle and sulphurous smoke' (190) of hell. This image conveys not only David's loss of innocence, and of perfect communion, but his imminent loss of the father as well.

'A Bag of Cherries' continues with their meeting in the train station and the drive home that will end with a conventional cup of tea. Throughout this scene, with its poignant evasions of intimacy, Metcalf maintains our awareness of the father's coming death. In that light we are especially moved by the father's itch for improvements, with which we are familiar from the master-story, and by his description of a future garden: '"It'll be pretty as a picture"' (182). This cliché, as applied to a garden, supplies us with a summary of the relationship between art and nature that has coloured all of the fictions contained within 'The Teeth of My Father.'

The master-story ends with the narrator's description of his response to his father's death. At the time he did not cry, for his 'thoughts were of the borrowed airfare, the yellowed soles of your feet' (192). But now he has written a story in which the soles of his father's feet are shod anew and regarded otherwise, in which his love and grief have been given space, in which through the myriad layering of art he resurrects the father. He cries, drunkenly, recalling by this device the drunken afternoon on which the story was born; and Metcalf's handling of the several incremental lines concerned with the narrator's tears is also artful. Art holds and art gives way, as this last section of the story is addressed finally to 'you,' the father. And we are left there, in the knowledge of all that fiction can do and all that it cannot.

Work Cited

Metcalf, John. 'The Teeth of My Father,' in *Selected Stories.* Toronto: McClelland and Stewart, New Canadian Library, 1982. All references are to this edition and are cited parenthetically in the text.

Atwood's Hands

In *Margaret Atwood: A Feminist Poetics*, Frank Davey has a chapter called 'An Atwood Vocabulary' in which he treats eight recurrent images (such as mirror and maze). He does not include hands in that brief lexicon. But I found myself thinking most particularly of hands when I came to Davey's concluding remarks, his discussion in the Epilogue of Atwood's recurrent images as constituting (together with various subtexts, symbols, and narrative patterns) 'a "female" sublanguage which rivals and replaces discursive language' (162). Davey, I'm sure, would agree that hands are an important part of Atwood's vocabulary of images or her 'female' sublanguage; but the point I wish to make is that hands are more than just a part of it. In a metonymic sense, they *are* the language through which Atwood attempts to rival and replace the language of men. Hands might be described as nouns on the way to becoming verbs, a lexical item stretching toward and perhaps beyond syntax. They speak *instead* of words, in 'the other language' (202) which the narrator of *Surfacing* acquires in her descent.

Hands are everywhere in Atwood. I'm aware of the hazard attached to looking for them, that they proliferate and swell in significance for that very reason. But I have collected an astonishing number, several thousand of them, and they don't look innocent to me. ('Touch the page at your peril' (45), Atwood says in 'The Page' from *Murder in the Dark*: 'it is you who are blank and innocent, not the page.') The many obvious symbolic occurrences are naturally supported by a vast underground of working hands. These modest little words may not all be aware of what the other hand of Atwood is doing, but they are legion and assist her revolution all the same.

If we look for a moment at English idioms involving hands, we discover that most of them fall into one of two broad categories. On the one hand, there are phrases which suggest co-operation: to go hand in hand with, to lend or give a helping hand, to lift a hand, to turn a hand, or take a hand in, or keep one's hand in. And, on the other hand, we have phrases which suggest control and issues of individual responsibility: to tie the hands of, to get out of hand, at the hands of, to get the upper hand of, to give or have a free hand, to have on one's hands, to soil one's hands or have clean hands, to have well in hand, to play into another person's hands, to hold in the palm of one's hand, to keep a tight hand on, to lay hands on. Only one phrase, with nice gothic Atwoodian irony, strikes me as ambiguous: to ask for a woman's hand in marriage. Is that as in 'go hand in hand with'? Or as in mutilation and disempowerment?

Atwood's own language of the hands reflects these two opposing tendencies. It is also a language that implies a kind of history, and a responsibility on the part of those who use it to become aware of its degenerative and recuperative power. In that sense, it affords a parallel to the language of words. Although I have suggested that hands may speak instead of words in 'the other language' of *Surfacing*, Atwood obviously recognizes as well the necessity of words, and especially contemporary society's need to use them in a redemptive way. In *The Handmaid's Tale*, Aunt Lydia ironically asserts that 'The future is in your hands' (56); but if the Handmaids are to escape the dystopian future that is laid out for them, indeed if they (and we) are to have any sort of future at all, it will be necessary – as the novel makes amply clear – to renew both languages. We need hands *and* words. Thus, as the wilderness gods recede at the end of *Surfacing*, the narrator thinks: 'I regret them; but they give only one kind of truth, one hand' (204).

As George Bowering points out, Atwood's hands often 'grapple with one another as emissaries of the bicameral mind' (48). Sometimes the right hand doesn't know what the left hand is doing; and often hands seem to move with a will of their own, without guidance from the brain. In *The Edible Woman*, for instance, Marian notices a peculiar sensation in her left hand: 'It wanted to reach across and touch him on the shoulder. Its will seemed independent of her own: surely she herself wanted nothing of the kind. She made its fingers grip the arms of her seat. "That would never do," she admonished it silently, "he might scream"' (125). Similarly, in *Life Before Man*, Nate finds that 'He's shaved his beard half off before he knows that it's his intention to destroy it.... His hands have decided it's time for him to be someone else' (43).

Hands can echo or contradict that which is asserted by other means. Atwood uses them to tell us what is really going on, what her characters are feeling at any given moment. But she also uses them in a more stable way to epitomize character. As Anna 'reads' palms in *Surfacing*, so Atwood 'writes' them. Witness this metonymic description of Offred's Commander in *The Handmaid's Tale*: 'His manner is mild, his hands large, with thick fingers and acquisitive thumbs' (97). Or this one, of the Commander's Wife: 'her left hand on the ivory head of her cane, the large diamonds on the ring finger, which must once have been fine and was still finely kept, the fingernail at the end of the knuckly finger filed to a gentle curving point. It was like an ironic smile, on that finger; like something mocking her' (24). This is Offred's first sighting of the Wife, or the only part of her that is available to the Handmaid's lowered gaze. But it's enough. Serena Joy's crippled state, her struggle to retain both self-respect and a measure of power: all this is apparent in her hand.

I'll give just two other examples, both from *Bodily Harm*. Of Daniel, the surgeon who has cut off part of Rennie's cancerous left breast, we are told that 'his soul was in his hands' (198). They are all that Rennie can imagine of him, 'hands with thin fingers and with the marks of a slow dark burning on their backs.' This is a medieval branding, the sign of the martyr – and it captures Daniel entirely. Lora too is represented metonymically by her hands. Thus, Rennie is shown observing Lora's ravaged hands just at the point when Lora introduces herself. This resonates at the end of the novel, when Rennie has overcome her distaste and is trying to pull Lora through, to summon her back into the body which has now been ravaged almost to the point of extinction. Atwood employs a gestural pun here: 'there's an invisible hole in the air, Lora is on the other side of it and [Rennie] has to pull her through' (299). At the moment of incarnation, as life passes from Rennie's hand to Lora's, she will speak her name – 'Lora' – which 'descends and enters the body' as Lora replies, groaning, 'Oh God.' Hand and name (or Word) are one, in this underground version of Michelangelo's masculinist creation, as God's (or Rennie's) finger touches a new Eve. (Again, the languages of hand and word are *both* important for Atwood.) It is also interesting that the torturers have done 'nothing to her hands' (298); symbolically, their hands *could* do nothing to touch the redemptive power of love, which is now finally apparent to Rennie in Lora's hands. Once she saw only 'the dirty blunt fingers with their bitten cuticles.' Now she sees Lora's left hand 'shining and almost translucent in the heavy light. The rest of the body is in darkness ... the hand is in the air.'

Many of the references to male hands in Atwood's fiction convey sexual or mortal threat, invasion, or appropriation. Most commonly these hands are placed on the woman's arm or wrist or around her throat. But sometimes titillation or female complicity is involved. Thus, for example, in 'Murder in the Dark,' turning the lights out 'gave the boys the pleasure of being able to put their hands around the girls' necks and gave the girls the pleasure of screaming' (29). Or, in 'Hair Jewellery,' from *Dancing Girls*, when a young man puts his hand on the narrator's throat and announces himself as the Boston Strangler, that may be regarded as 'a joke which, for one with [her] literary predilections, amounted to a seduction' (119). More often, though, such references involve the woman's sense of forced immobility and her perception of a real threat. Atwood repeatedly exploits the heroine's gothic uncertainty, which is grounded in her fear of men; there is a chance that the hand in question is well-meaning, that it may be the hand of love. And any sex scene by Atwood – whether frightening, ambiguous, or tender – is likely to be choreographed by the play of hands.

'Sunrise,' a story from *Bluebeard's Egg*, may serve here to illustrate the Atwood heroine's fascination with the mystery of male hands – and the constraints which operate with respect to the woman's own willingness to touch. The protagonist of that story is an artist who specializes in men. She is especially interested in their hands, and goes regularly to Sushi bars in order to 'watch the hands of the chefs as they deftly caress and stroke her food. As she eats, she can almost feel their fingers in her mouth' (252). We recognize that these chefs use sharp knives, and may question why she has chosen to emphasize the caress. The answer is partly that Yvonne is a woman who lives on the 'sliding edge' (260), who flirts with an obvious danger that has never quite taken her *over* the edge, as she picks up the men she would like to paint. Hanging in Yvonne's bathroom, positioned so that she can see it while lying in the tub, is the print of a portrait by Holbein. It is of a young man whose hands are particularly important to her: 'each vein in his hands, each fingernail perfectly rendered' (250).

As Holbein's young man is a kind of dream lover for Yvonne – 'He's looking at Yvonne, and he can see in the dark' (264) – so Holbein's art, which she regards as based on a 'language of images ... commonly known and understood' (251), is a dream which attracts her powerfully. She is cut off from this by history, but 'thinks it would be so handy if there were still some language of images like this.... She would like to be able to put carnations between the fingers of the men she draws.' In Holbein's portrait, the carnation is in a vase; it signifies 'the Holy Ghost, or possibly betrothal' (250). Yvonne's wish to place the flower in male hands expresses a wish for 'betrothal,' possibly – for the unifying touch, although she also fears that. Thus, we find Yvonne in a restaurant, 'clutching the tablecloth' (259) in order to avoid touching a man she once loved. She resists because 'To touch his hand ... would be to put herself at risk again.'

The flower she would place in male hands expresses also a wishing away of male violence. As an artist, she moves her pencil like 'a hand being passed over the [male] body, half an inch from the surface' (247). But she does occasionally go to bed with her models, since the danger that may be associated with these men is less painful than the risk of love. In fact, they are tame enough – except for the surly young man who 'puts his hands on her' (262) to initiate sex in the present time of the story. Yvonne has been sketching him with a tulip in his hand, but he makes his move before she can incorporate that. His violence is mostly at one remove, however, as he hisses '"Art sucks"' and shows her some of his own collages, of 'splayed open-legged [female] torsoes with the hands and feet removed.' When Yvonne first sees this punk artist on the street, we are told that 'She'd bet ten dollars he can't draw fingers. Yvonne's own renderings of fingers [like Holbein's] are very good' (261). Thus, his assault on art is understood as a perversion of the hands. Yvonne's landlord, in a comic throw-away line, puts his finger on the pulse: '"Who knows what evil lurks in the hearts of men?" Al says. 'Yvonne [the shadow] knows"' (254). It is why she stays so much in shadow.

But the story ends with light. When her former lover asks Yvonne for the secret of her solitary perseverance and energy, she replies with a smile, '"My secret is that I get up every morning to watch the sunrise"' (259). And at the story's conclusion, following a passage in which Yvonne considers the attractions of suicide, we watch her do this. She never misses a morning: 'It's almost as if she believes that if she isn't there to see it there will be no sunrise' (265). Similarly, we infer, Yvonne herself would die without the sun. Atwood is working here with a complicated image of reciprocity, as she has Yvonne think that 'sunrise is not a thing, but only an effect of light caused by the positions of two astronomical bodies in relation to each other.' Metaphorically, the sun is her lover – 'signifying the Holy Ghost, or possibly betrothal' (250), as in the Holbein portrait which is recalled just before this scene, with the statement that Holbein's young man (the sun's dark counter-part) is 'looking at Yvonne, and he can see in the dark' (264). Each body (astronomical or anatomical) requires the other if the 'effect' of light is to be achieved.

Yvonne knows that 'her dependence is not on something that can be grasped, held in the hand, kept, but only on an accident of the language, because *sunrise* should not be a noun' (265). And she fears the 'sunrise is a fraud,' so that she holds firmly onto the railing of her deck (as earlier she had clutched at the tablecloth) instead of risking a literal enactment of what her heart desires – which is to lift 'her arms as the sun floats up ... an enormous kite whose string she almost holds in her hand.' Thus, in the devious syntax of dreams, and in the language of hands, Yvonne moves away from the noun and toward the linking verb of love.

There are also numerous (frequently metaphorical) references to severed hands, mutilation, and segmentation in Atwood's fiction. And men are often responsible for these, through their wish to diminish, control, and objectify the female body. The collages in 'Sunrise' provide one quite typical example. In *The Handmaid's Tale* women get their hands cut off as a penalty for reading. And in the piece called 'Women's Novels' from *Murder in the Dark*, the speaker remarks that 'Sometimes men put women in novels but they leave out some of the parts: the heads, for instance, or the hands' (34). Actually, it would be hard to beat Atwood's own novels in this regard – though her own intention, of course, is to signal the horror.

The mutilation or absence of hands indicates most often a loss of agency. Elizabeth, in *Life Before Man*, holds 'the veined and mottled stumps' (282) of her Auntie Muriel's hands as the tyrannical old woman is dying, and recalls too 'the ruined hand, still beautiful' of her mother. The power is draining from these aged hands. In *Bodily Harm*, Rennie's grandmother begins to 'lose' her hands. 'I've left them somewhere and now I can't find them,' she says, and when Rennie points out that they are right there, 'on the ends of your arms,' her grandmother replies impatiently: 'Not those, those are no good any more. My other hands, the ones I had before, the ones I touch things with' (57). Significantly, Rennie thinks of her own failure to take and confirm the reality of her grandmother's hands (as her mother does so easily) just before she manages at last to take Lora's hand in her own.

Atwood's women often experience or fear the mutilation of their hands much earlier in life. As a child, the narrator of *Surfacing* was fascinated by Madame, the 'main source of [whose] power was that she had only one hand' (29). Since Madame is a capable adult who can wrap parcels with her stump, and is linked by her exotic Catholicism to 'the cut-off pieces of early martyrs,' that lost hand appears 'miraculous' to the narrator. Yet she is afraid of what this absence might bode for her own future; she wants to know if Madame took the hand off herself (which would paradoxically confirm agency) and 'especially whether [her] own hand could ever come off like that.' Such fears are realized and resisted in the present time of the novel, as the narrator (seeking to overcome the mutilation of an abortion, among other things) feels the power ebb and flow in her own hands.

Gloves are generally a bad thing in Atwood; most often they signify a refusal or an inability to touch. In *Lady Oracle*, for example, the heroine's genteel mother declines to hold her hand because she has her gloves to consider, whereas Aunt Lou (who does touch her) is always losing her gloves. Sometimes gloves signify male power, as in the case of the fascist-seeming leather gloves of the narrator's former lover in *Surfacing*, or the ubiquitous rubber gloves of a doctor conducting an internal examination. The power of the male is in this way defined by his abstraction and the refusal to connect. Sometimes hands *become* gloves too, as in *Life Before Man* where Elizabeth's sense of unreality (her separation from life) is conveyed by the image of her immobile hands: 'she thinks about forcing the bones and flesh down into those shapes of hands, one finger at a time, like dough' (12). Similarly, in *Surfacing*, the narrator says 'The power has drained away, my fingers are empty as gloves' (183).

As this treatment of gloves may imply, the naked hand is for Atwood a potential source for redemption in the world. Gloves, we might say, are excessively and destructively civilized: they *abstract* the hand. What we need is to recover the power of nakedness (or immediacy or intimacy) from an earlier point in our history. Only so can we be healed. Accordingly, Nate in *Life Before Man* puts his faith in Lesje, who seems to him 'the bearer of healing wisdom, swathed in veils' (71). The cigarette smoke in which her magical hands are veiled is decidedly and ironically contemporary, but Lesje herself is a paleontologist; and he imagines her as 'a nurse hurrying over frozen Siberia' (167), to save him from a living death. 'She will put her hand on his forehead and miraculously he will revive.' There are several other important healers in Atwood's fiction, such as Daniel and Elva in *Bodily Harm* – the Canadian doctor who removed her cancerous breast, and the island woman whose ancient healing gift (passed on from her grandmother) is 'in the hands' (193). Elva's more primitive and direct 'magic' seems to Rennie to offer a more thorough cure than modern science can supply; her hands are rough, and Daniel's are unfailingly gentle – but somehow too remote.

Everywhere in Atwood's fiction we encounter this desire to touch and be touched. Our recovery seems dependent on it, just as our sicknesses are imaged by the perversions of touch – alienation and violence. Perhaps the novel in which we feel this most strongly is *The Handmaid's Tale*, where Offred 'hunger[s] to commit the act of touch' (21). All that remains in Gilead is a parody of touch, as in the Ceremony where the Wife grips the Handmaid while the Commander performs his alienated and doomed 'procreative' act. But Offred rebels, at first in such gestures as reaching out to her friend Moira's fingers through the hole in a washroom partition: 'It was only large enough for two fingers. I touched my own fingers to them, quickly, held on. Let go' (100). This scene again recalls the climax of *Bodily Harm*, where Rennie overcomes her long reluctance to touch and takes hold of Lora's hand through that 'invisible hole in the air' (299). In that novel too, prison has been literalized; but Rennie herself is largely responsible for the 'wall' which has separated her from the world. The fear of touch – like the yearning for touch – is endemic in Atwood's fictional terrain.

Atwood's concern with our alienation from nature is also conveyed by the language of hands: our hands should be 'earth-smeared' (*Surfacing*, 185) from touching the natural world. Garden gloves are therefore a distinct mark of Atwood's disfavour. The lady down below in *The Edible Woman* seems especially culpable because she is 'wearing a pair of spotless gardening gloves' (13). And again, in 'Unearthing Suite' from *Bluebeard's Egg*, we are told that 'Gardening is not a rational act. What matters is the immersion of the hands in the earth' (280). But Atwood also gives metonymic hands to nature with remarkable frequency, because it takes two to touch. In the story called 'Polarites' as elsewhere in Atwood's fiction we hear of a 'clenched landscape' (*Dancing Girls*, 67) which is a projection of the character's own closed hands. Human beings in retreat from nature are themselves often described as clenched. The protagonist in 'Scarlet Ibis,' for example, feels the pressure her husband is under 'like a clenched mass … at the back of her own head' (183), and regards him as 'encased in a sort of metal carapace, like the shell of a crab, that was slowly tightening on him … so that something was sure to burst, like a thumb closed slowly in a car door.' Similarly, Marian in *The Edible Woman*'s 'sargasso-sea of femininity' (167) is shown 'clenching her body and her mind back into herself like some tactile sea-creature withdrawing its tentacles.' Other examples of clenching and of nature's metonymic hand occur in *Surfacing*, where on one occasion the narrator hears the 'finger-tapping' (187) of water on the roof. And this functions as a reminder from nature, an invitation to come out and join hands – which the narrator has declined because 'logic is a wall, I built it, on the other side is terror.'

Similarly, in 'Scarlet Ibis' a hole appears in the bottom of a boat: 'It was the size of a small fist. Whatever they'd hit had punched right through the wood, as if it were cardboard' (194). The narrator and most of the other tourists are afraid that this invasion by nature's hand will drown them. But the native guide knows that all will be well. He knows too that if they turn back in fear they will miss something of extraordinary, transcendent beauty: the sight of the Scarlet Ibis, which is the reason they (and presumably all of us) have taken this journey. One other person, a Mennonite woman who is suspect in the eyes of the rational protagonist, is also a model of equanimity. She has taken this trip before, understands the goal, and knows exactly what to do. With a smile, which Christine thinks must be 'a fraud' (197) since she has a 'dead child' and therefore certain knowledge of mortality, she positions her 'large flowered rump' directly over the hole. Nature *can* hurt the one who loves her, but that is not a good enough reason to abandon love. This is the great lesson that Atwood's heroines must learn – and apply as well to their dealings with men, as the relaxed and comic eroticism of the Mennonite woman's point of contact with nature's hand may imply.

Our power seems to begin with nature. It flows into the hand of *Surfacing*'s narrator from the earth, as in this passage: 'when I pick up the brush ... the power is there again in a different form, it must have seeped up through the ground during the lightning' (188). Behind this, I think, is the hint of a creation myth: we began as dust, and the newly creative Word of 'the other language' must be what Atwood in the piece called 'Mute' (from *Murder in the Dark*) calls 'a compound, the generation of life, mud and light' (49). Creation of all kinds requires bare contact, as Atwood indicates in 'The Page' (also from *Murder in the Dark*): 'your hands should be bare. You should never go into the page with gloves on' (45). We know this too from the way that the narrator of *Surfacing* approaches the natural / sexual juncture at which she will attempt to conceive a child: 'My tentacled feet and free hand scent out the way, shoes are a barrier between touch and the earth' (172).

This intercourse between human beings and the natural world is of course non-verbal. And though nature can be threatening in Atwood, on the whole she seems to trust it. Partly, it seems, this is because nature cannot 'talk.' The narrator of *Surfacing* contemplates the disappearance of language, syntax which seems to shrink toward the reciprocal 'compound' referred to above, in the following passage: 'I touched [Joe] on the arm with my hand. My hand touched his arm. Hand touched arm. Language divides us into fragments, I wanted to be whole' (157). This anticipates the collapse of the subject / object distinction that comes when the narrator says, 'I lean against a tree. I am a tree leaning' (195) – after her memory of a language in which 'there are no nouns, only verbs held for a longer moment' and her comment that 'The animals have no need for speech, why talk when you are a word [.]' She thinks that maybe she can trust Joe since he is like an animal, talks so little, and has 'hands at any rate [that] are intelligent, they move over me delicately as a blind man's reading braille' (73).

It is therefore no accident that Atwood repeatedly connects hand with blindness – that is, with people who 'read' by touch – and with an array of mysterious deaf and dumb figures, people who 'speak' only with their hands. In the short piece from *Murder in the Dark* called 'Mute,' Atwood presents herself as a writer who is weary of handling 'bruised word[s]' (49) in a 'fly-specked' market stocked with nouns and verbs. 'How do you wash a language?' she asks. And then:

> Why involve yourself? You'd do better to sit off to the side, on the sidewalk under the awning, hands over your mouth, your ears, your eyes, with a cup in front of you into which people will or will not drop pennies. They think you can't talk, they're sorry for you, but. But you're waiting for the word, the one that will finally be right. A compound, the generation of life, mud and light. (49)

For this reason, the narrator of *Surfacing* decides that she will never teach her baby any words; for this reason too, the mother in 'Giving Birth' (from *Dancing Girls*) waits for her baby's first word, trusting that it will prove 'miraculous, something that has never yet been said' (240).

In another piece from *Murder in the Dark*, called 'Hand,' Atwood the masseuse again obliterates the distinction between subject and object as her hand works to release the tension in the body of another person. That body exists only as 'a fist tightening somewhere at the back of the neck' (59), so that both the Atwood persona and the other are represented metonymically by the hand. This fist, she says, 'is what I must open: to let *you* in.' Here as elsewhere, Atwood associates hands with feet, as extremities and extremists, as fellow travellers in the dark. Thus, she begins by massaging his feet: 'I move my thumbs down between the tendons, push on the deaf white soles of the imprisoned feet.' These feet are deaf, and they are blind: they 'must be taught to see in the dark, because the dark is where they walk. The feet learn quietly; they are wiser than the eyes, they are hard to fool....' Atwood's hand succeeds: 'your body has become a hand that is opening, your body is the hand of a blind man, reaching out into a darkness which may in fact be light, for all you know.... Your eyes are closed but the third eye, the eye of the body, is opening.... Now you see into it and through it.'

In *Bodily Harm*, Rennie is approached by an old and tattered deaf and dumb man who wants to shake hands with her because, as Paul explains, 'he thinks it's good luck' (75). Rennie is frightened by this old man, afraid that his misfortune will prove contagious if they touch hands. She 'feels very suddenly as if she's stepped across a line and found herself on Mars' (74). She regards him as pitiable and dangerous, an alien whom she must propitiate and dismiss, as in 'The Man from Mars' from *Dancing Girls*. In that story another fastidious protagonist suffers from and needs the touch of another unfortunate 'person from another culture' (22). In fact the deaf and dumb man in *Bodily Harm* does not want to shake hands with Rennie in order to acquire her good luck. Rather, he thinks his hand will impart good luck to Rennie. His reason for thinking so is not given, but the novel as a whole makes plain that Rennie does need to touch misery, to feel the pain of others, and that she grows because of it. The deaf and dumb man appears at several other strategic moments in *Bodily Harm*. Once on the street, Rennie sees him beaten by police; in the prison, she watches him being tortured again. Rennie is looking out the window of her cell, and 'the hurt man's face is *on a level* with [her] own' (290, italics mine) – so that she 'understands, for the first time,' that 'she is not exempt.' 'Turned inside out,' aware that 'there's no longer a *here* and a *there*,' Rennie crosses the line to find that 'Mars' is not really another planet. (Neither, of course, is Canada.)

Another shabby deaf and dumb man who 'wants to shake hands with everyone' (20) appears in the prose piece called 'Raw Materials' from *Murder in the Dark*. The speaker and her friends 'smile furiously' (21) as they try to interpret the old man's gestures, but they suspect he is being manipulative and that his disability (his misery) is a fraud. They are wary, as if in keeping with the definition of themselves as tourists in search of 'real experience' (19). The speaker thinks he wants money: 'Isn't it bad luck not to give money to beggars?' (21). And so the irony is made clear: his luck, his experience, are not relevant. But the man becomes insistent, forcing his way across the line: 'When will it stop? If we aren't careful he'll follow us ... turn up some day on our front lawn. He's refusing to play beggar any more, he isn't letting us play tourists, embarrassed but benevolent, he's making us angry, this is too much.' At last they succeed in driving him away, and Atwood ends the piece with a cliché delivered by her speaker to friends at home: 'Don't drink the water' (22), she advises. (Don't get involved. Reality can make you sick; it makes the line dissolve.)

I will give one final example of the deaf and dumb figure, from 'The Sin Eater' in *Bluebeard's Egg*. This is a story about the death of a psychiatrist, one who doesn't charge much, who is shabbily dressed and seems to care about his patients. For years Joseph has been 'eating' their sins, their pain. The speaker, however, one of his patients, was always rather offended at Joseph's desire for reciprocity, the crossing of lines implicit in the psychiatrist's occasional talk about himself. And this is aggravated by his death, a probable suicide. Just when she is most needy, the speaker is obliged to consider him.

So she has a dream about Joseph, which we are able to interpret on the basis of something Joseph had told her: how the person he hated most in the world, and would still kill if given the chance, was the child who out of 'pure bloody malice' (239) picked his one sunflower – the single scrap of beauty he'd had as a kid growing up in a dark slum. In the dream, that malicious child appears as the deaf-mute:

> There's a man standing beside us, trying to attract our attention. He's holding out a small white card covered with symbols, hands and fingers. A deaf-mute, I decide, and sure enough when I look his mouth is sewn shut. Now he's tugging at Joseph's arm, he's holding out something else, it's a large yellow flower. (243-4)

Words are not required. The hand that stole the flower gives it back. And the speaker learns in this way 'the other language' of hands, a symbolic language whose message is reciprocity. The dream itself is the narrator's own reciprocal act, since within it she effectively 'eats' the sin of Joseph's hatred and of the man whose own lips are sewn shut. The story closes with the narrator and Joseph still in the dream, at what seems to be his funeral party. (' "I'm glad you got the invitation," he says,' and with some hesitation she agrees to shake Joseph's 'bright blue' hand.) Although she is afraid of the star- and moon-shaped cookies – thinking 'it's too much for me, I might get sick' (244) – still she reaches out to eat one of the cookies that Joseph has identified as his sins. And she finds that 'thousands of stars, thousands of moons' have begun to shine. The sunflower's light has become manifold because the speaker has reached out with her hand into 'dark space' – which, as the speaker of 'Hand' reminds us, 'may in fact be light; for all you know' (Murder in the Dark, 59).

When Margaret Atwood's hands reach out for something like transcendence or incarnation, two other images are likely to be sparked: flowers and light. 'The Sin Eater,' with its sunflower and star- and moon-shaped cookies, is one example; 'The Sunrise' and The Handmaid's Tale are others. In that novel, the Handmaid's yearning creates brief satisfaction, as the 'sun comes through the fanlight, falling in colours across the floor' (58), and she stretches out her hands to fill them 'with flowers of light.' What Offred must learn, however, is to translate that reaching out into the world of human beings. Like many of Atwood's women, she has reason to be afraid of 'the hands of strangers' (307) – but 'it can't be helped.' She cannot remain separate if she wishes to be whole. She must use her hands and her words: both languages, at whatever risk of being compromised. Care must be exercised, but distrust of strangers and of language must also finally give way. So Offred at the end allows the 'strangers' to 'take [her] by the elbows to help' her into the van – and steps up 'into the darkness within; or else the light.' And then she (or Atwood) goes on to 'write' the book of hands.

Works Cited

Atwood, Margaret. *Bluebeard's Egg.* Toronto: McClelland and Stewart, 1983.

———. *Bodily Harm.* Toronto: Seal Books, McClelland and Stewart-Bantam Ltd., 1982.

———. *Dancing Girls.* Toronto: McClelland and Stewart, 1977.

———. *The Edible Woman.* Toronto: McClelland and Stewart, New Canadian Library No. 93, reprinted 1985.

———. *The Handmaid's Tale.* Toronto: McClelland and Stewart, 1985.

———. *Life Before Man.* Toronto: McClelland and Stewart, 1979.

———. *Murder in the Dark: Short Fictions and Prose Poems.* Toronto: The Coach House Press, 1983.

———. *Surfacing.* Markham: Paperjacks Ltd., 1973.

Bowering, George. 'Margaret Atwood's Hands,' *Studies in Canadian Literature,* 6.1 (1981): 39-52.

Davey, Frank. *Margaret Atwood: A Feminist Poetics.* Vancouver: Talonbooks, 1984.

Interpreting *The Handmaid's Tale*:
Offred's Name and 'The Arnolfini Marriage'

The Handmaid's name is June.

While I'm sure that at least a few other readers must have worked this out for themselves, I haven't seen or heard any reference to Offred's pre-Gileadean name in any interpretation of *The Handmaid's Tale*. I can only assume that the question isn't particularly interesting to the many able critics who have responded to Atwood's novel – and I think it should be. Part of this essay will therefore be concerned with establishing my claim that Offred's true name is June, but my broader concern here is with the imperatives and the attractions of interpretation. I want to explore, in fact, two discoveries that I made in reading this novel: one that I will argue is important and 'called for' by the text, and another that is clearly not. My second discovery, if I may use that term, is that Jan van Eyck's painting 'The Arnolfini Marriage' lurks somewhere in the shadows of *The Handmaid's Tale*; and this discovery might understandably strike other readers (including Atwood) as hallucination. In each case, I want to describe the process and to assess the value or interest of my reading.

I

Chapter One of the novel concludes with a list of names: 'Alma. Janine. Dolores. Moira. June' (14). When I read that for the first time, it occurred to me that the last name (simply because of its rhetorically privileged position) might be the narrator's. I knew only that these women were in some kind of camp, under duress – and that it was important to them, as they lay on cots 'with spaces between us so we could not talk' (13), to 'touch each other's hands across space' (14) and to lip-read, so that they could exchange names, 'from bed to bed.' Perhaps I guessed from previous exposure to Atwood that the narrator's own name might be withheld; if so, that would have given me an extra-textual, 'professional' reason for being alert to the question of names. But the text was enough. I was drawn into the chain and into the necessity of both circumspection *and* naming. My job, I thought, might be to receive and hoard the last name in the series.

As I read on, I felt a conspiratorial interest in the question of these names – especially as it became clear that Offred's real name was a matter of great importance to her, and that it would not be stated openly in the text. The reason for this is obvious, and rests in Offred's hands rather than in Atwood's. The name cannot be stated or hinted at too broadly, because that information in the hands of her enemies could lead to her re-capture. And Offred cares so passionately about her name because it has been stolen away, because she has been issued instead a patronymic tag: she is called Of-Fred, just as our own mothers were Mrs. Fred Whatever. That the narrator's first or 'Christian' name is the one that is important to her can be explained simply on the grounds that last names do not arise in the novel, perhaps because they are more dangerous still. But one's first name is also the most personal or subjectively true of names – as well as the one name a woman has that does not descend from father or husband.

I thought I would test my hypothesis (that Offred was June) by seeing whether the other names on the list would be assigned to particular characters. If they were, and if no one stepped forward with June's name, I thought I could be sure that *she* was the Handmaid who had stretched out her hand to me, and whose lips I had read. Janine and Moira materialized quickly and prominently, but I had to wait for Alma and Dolores; when eventually they appeared (82, 134) I felt sure that these names were inconspicuous precisely so that 'June' would not shine out too brightly, through its absence.

There were other indications of the heroine's name, but these would almost certainly be inaccessible to readers who had forgotten the last name on that list. They do not serve as later points of entry to the secret; instead, they confirm the hypothesis – as if to help us keep the faith, and keep the illicit name alive. The additional evidence I will cite occurs in passages that 'work' without that knowledge, and work better with it. The effect for a reader who is in on the secret is rather like that of being slipped some extra food – or a knife or a flower or a message – by one's fellow prisoner. Some of this aid to my interpretation became apparent only on subsequent readings of the novel.

Perhaps the most striking bit of evidence is an odd, throw-away line delivered by Aunt Lydia: 'Don't let me catch you at it. No mooning and Juneing around here, girls. Wagging her finger at us. *Love* is not the point' (232). Any reader who is looking for traces of 'June' will take this as a conspicuous sign, because it is only the second of three appearances of that word in the novel. And it turns out to be a sign laden with meaning, since 'June' is rhymed with 'moon' – an image that is closely associated with Offred and with the mystery of her true name.

As 'two-legged wombs' (146), in a society that has reduced them utterly to a reproductive function, and that will dispose of them if the menstrual tides flow on too long, the Handmaids 'tell time by the moon. Lunar, not solar' (209). Janine, as she is giving birth, 'glows like a moon in cloud' (135); and

Offred, as she is contemplating her loss of agency – 'I used to think of my body as an instrument, of pleasure, or a means of transportation, or an implement for the accomplishment of my will' (83) – says that now 'I'm a cloud, congealed around a central object, the shape of a pear' (84), which is 'more real than I am.' *Inside* that womb a 'moon' is journeying, as the heart is 'marking time.'

The connection between the moon and Offred's true name is made in a passage where she is thinking of her name as 'treasure I'll come back to dig up, one day' (94). 'This name,' she says, 'has an aura around it, like an amulet, some charm that's survived from an unimaginably distant past.' Like the distant moon with which her name rhymes, 'June' (as the month of brides) has an aura which survives from a time when 'Love' *was* the point (232). Offred's tendency to regard love as 'the point' is of course alarming in relation to the period of her turning away from other women, and from resistance when she establishes a sexual connection with Ned. Love understood more broadly, however, is 'the point'. But the aura around her name is more than this problematic allusion to romantic love, which Gilead has overlooked (231). The name has an aura also and more importantly because it is Offred's 'real' name; the aura is the 'cloud' in which the 'I' lingers – 'I'm a cloud' (84) – and from which agency will be restored. As Offred lies in her 'single bed at night' (94) with her eyes closed, she contemplates another sort of moon within: 'the name floats there behind my eyes, not quite within reach, shining in the dark.' The moon has ceased to be that reductive force by which her womb is regulated, and has become in this configuration a potential source of empowerment.

Shortly afterward, there is another passage that confirms the link between moon and name. Again, Offred is in her single bed; at her window are the white curtains 'like gauze bandages' (108), which in a later passage are 'gauzy as a bridal dress, as ectoplasm' (154), and which in a still later passage surround her 'like a cocoon' (180) or 'a cloud.' She goes to the window because she 'want[s] to see' (108), and Gilead's searchlight makes this difficult: 'but yes, in the obscured sky a moon does float, newly, a wishing moon, a sliver of ancient rock, a goddess, a wink.' The sight of the moon provokes thoughts of her lost husband, of her name, and finally of rebellion:

> I want Luke here so badly. I want to be held and told my name. I want to be valued, in ways that I am not; I want to be more than valuable. I repeat my former name, remind myself of what I once could do, how others saw me.
> I want to steal something.

It seems important that Offred can now see the moon as something outside herself, that she can imagine and desire an outer life for her 'name.' Gilead has tried with its searchlight to obscure the light of the moon, the power of women to feel desire and to act in the world and to exist for their own reasons. But the Goddess of the moon, it seems, is waking up: she – and June, who is most active and most herself in the 'Night' sections of the novel – will find a way to 'TAKE BACK THE NIGHT' (129).

Desire here leads not to paralysis, but to the first glimpse of restored agency. What Offred steals from the sitting room is 'a magic flower' (109), a withered daffodil that she hopes will not be missed, and that she will preserve under her mattress as a message 'for the next woman, the one who comes after me, to find.' In taking this action, Offred is assuming her place in the female chain of resistance. She is repeating the gesture made by the woman who came before her, whose coded message, scratched into the corner of the cupboard, was *'Nolite te bastardes carborundorum'* (62), meaning 'Don't let the bastards grind you down' (197). But on the same night's errand, she also finds Nick – the chauffeur and agent of the resistance for whom she feels immediate desire, and through whom the forces of desire and active rebellion are shown to be aligned. (That they can also be opposed, as when Offred lapses into the erotic trance of which she herself is ashamed, problematizes this alignment but does not, I think, finally destroy it.)

'Mayday' is another clue to Offred's true name. Mayday, from the French *m'aidez*, is the name of the resistance as well as the 'password' (212) by which the Handmaids may signal to one another that they are not what they seem. It is also associated by Offred with May Day, a festival of flowers and rebirth. (Flowers in this novel often signal a natural, anti-utilitarian *riposte* to Gilead's exclusive interest in the fruit.) Offred's rebellion, which will lead to 'June,' begins in May – when she first reaches out with the stolen daffodil to help another woman, and simultaneously establishes contact with the man to whom she will confide her name. Her next steps forward involve the Commander, whom she meets secretly for games of Scrabble; as she assumes control once more of language (which in Gilead is a male prerogative), and gains from the Commander's complicity a measure of power over him, Offred approaches the moment of her rebirth as June.

She breaks through the cocoon and the ectoplasm which are associated with the white curtains, in an image of 'burst[ing]' (156) which occurs when Offred begins to laugh: 'mirth rhymes with birth.' She is laughing at the Commander, at the absurdity of his wanting her to play Scrabble with him and 'kiss him as if I meant it' (154). And she is laughing *after* remembering the mistress of the commandant of a Nazi concentration camp who had denied that her lover was a monster (as Offred will subsequently question the monstrosity of the Commander); so she is laughing also at herself, in part at the absurdity of her request for handcream, for the Nazi's mistress too had taken 'pride in her appearance' (155). Now the laughter is making a fine mess of her, as her restored heart pumps blood and she imagines dying of laughter: 'Red all over the cupboard' (156). If her laughter were heard, she thinks that they might judge her to be suffering from hysteria: 'The wandering womb, they used to think.' And so she is, in the ironic sense that Offred is 'wandering' or moving away from the definition of herself as womb.

Offred then tries to 'compose' herself, to retreat by stifling the laughter which is now mixed with tears in the folds of her Handmaid's cloak. And she seems to despair as in the closet she reads again the message of the Handmaid who preceded her, and died by suicide: 'Why did she write it, why did she bother? There's no way out of here.' But it is too late for retreat. The scene ends with Offred breathing 'as in the exercises, for giving birth' and with her heart 'opening and closing, opening' – so that we know June is on the way.

The next scene extends these images. It opens with a scream and a crash as Cora (one of the 'Marthas' who attend to household chores) drops Offred's breakfast tray. Finding her asleep on the floor, 'still half in the cupboard' (159), Cora thinks at first that Offred too has killed herself. Then, as Offred excuses herself by saying that she must have fainted, Cora leaps to the happy conclusion that she must be pregnant. Thus, in Cora's two suppositions, the images of death and birth from the night before are repeated; and Offred's resemblance to her rebellious predecessor, together with her apparent suicide, signals to the reader that she has indeed died and been reborn as a more heroic woman. (That she is halfway out of the closet may suggest both that the birthing is incomplete and that her circumspection must continue.) When Cora is about to say that she had thought Offred was dead, Offred completes the sentence for her, to suggest that Cora thought she had 'Run off' – as in spirit she has. 'But it was you' (160), Cora says; and Offred says twice that 'it was,' suggesting by this strange emphasis either that it *was* Offred (but now she is someone else) or that she has been restored to the 'you' which elsewhere in the novel is imbued with a sense of immediacy or authenticity.

The breakfast that crashes to the floor extends these images even further. The emphasis (not surprisingly) is on eggs. In an earlier scene, Offred's second egg was kept warm beneath the 'skirt' (120) of an egg-cup shaped 'like a woman's torso.' She had compared the egg of her 'reduced circumstances' (115) in Gilead to the moon, as 'a barren landscape ... [like] the sort of desert the saints went into, so their minds would not be distracted by profusion' (120). But inside the egg is 'glowing ... as if it had an energy of its own,' and Offred reflects that 'the life of the moon may not be on the surface, but inside.'

Now that life is coming out. The broken eggs recall Offred's sense the night before that 'something, inside [her] body' (156) has 'broken, something has cracked.' They also anticipate the Commander's defense of Gilead, 'You can't make an omelette without breaking eggs' (222), and hint at the counter-revolution. And the 'shattered glass' from the orange juice recalls Moira, Offred's rebellious friend from the 'time before' whose escape from the Red Centre in which the Handmaids were indoctrinated had caused the other women to think 'there might be a shattering explosion, the glass of the windows would fall inwards, the doors would swing open ... [because] Moira had power now, she'd been set loose, she'd set herself loose. She was now a loose woman' (143). (In the image of the 'loose woman,' desire and rebellion are again linked.) The shattered glass suggests also the window of Offred's room, which the Gileadeans have supposed is shatter-proof, and beyond which the goddess of the new moon had winked at Offred.

The paragraph after the breakfast scene begins with the statement, 'That was in May' (160). Desire is returning to Offred, as she contemplates 'something subversive' (161) in the garden: 'the swelling genitalia of the flowers' and 'the bleeding hearts, so female in shape it was a surprise they'd not long since been rooted out' and 'a sense of buried things [like her name] bursting upwards, wordlessly, into the light.' She sees in the garden 'metamorphosis run wild' and believes again that 'Goddesses are possible,' as the 'air suffuses with desire' (162). The month of June is not mentioned; but that, I would suggest, is simply a matter of restraint. We know in any case what month follows May, and if we have found out that Offred's true name is June, we will also be attuned to this symbolic use of the calendar.

Atwood gives her narrator this name, and then permits June to conceal it as her circumstances require. In choosing this particular name, Atwood supplies herself with valuable thematic strands for the text she weaves. I raise this point because it seems to matter, if I want to regard myself as the custodian of the narrator's (rather than the author's) secret; and I raise it here because the May / June setting of what I have described as Offred's rebirth may (to adapt a lovely nineteenth-century phrase) smell of Atwood's lamp. Certainly, it can be defended within the illusion of the fictive world: even if these events 'really' happened to transpire in May and June, our linguistically adept narrator might take advantage of that fact and use it as part of the name code she wants *some* of her readers to crack. But inevitably there is slippage; and I am often acutely aware of Atwood's craft operating behind Offred's.

This is always so, of course: it is part of the pleasure of reading. But the relationship into which I entered with the narrator (when I guessed her name) seemed unusually dependent on my suspension of disbelief; I felt that it was important for me to believe in her, in this woman who says 'I feel as if there's not much left of me; they [her husband and child] will slip through my arms, as if I'm made of smoke, as if I'm a mirage, fading before their eyes' (95). I was therefore given a small shock by the following statement in an essay by W.F. Garrett-Petts:

> As the distancing effect of the 'Historical Notes' ensures, by the end of the novel Offred dissolves into the background of thematic patterns and image clusters, leaving the reader to ponder the ontological status of narrative and narration. Focus on character is relegated, of necessity, to the margins of attention. (79)

I had heard others speak of the 'distancing effect' of the novel's epilogue, but what I felt was a profound *resistance* to that effect.

The 'Historical Notes' purport to be Professor Pieixoto's interpretation of *The Handmaid's Tale* to a learned audience, some hundred and fifty years after the flight of Offred. The jolt of another voice, especially of a voice that so cleverly mocks academic pretension (a fresh target for the author's satire) did indeed return me with a resounding thud to Atwood's ontological plane; that effect was increased by an awareness that Offred (if I *insisted* on thinking of her as real) was obviously dead. But as the new professorial voice droned on, offending me with its violation of Offred and her *Tale* – as I knew Atwood intended me to be offended – a curious thing happened. I *desired* Atwood's presence in the text; I wanted to replace this shoddy critic with the author.

I wanted also to replace him with myself. Like Garrett-Petts (who is by no means a shoddy critic) I believe that the 'Historical Notes' serve to 'increase the reader's awareness of his [or her] own interpretive responsibilities' (82): obviously, we want to divorce ourselves from Pieixoto. But I do not agree with Garrett-Petts that 'by treating [Offred's] experiences as an artifact, the "Historical Notes" simultaneously [and intentionally] diminish the vitality of the fictional "dialogue."' Pieixoto's response to the text is clearly not a 'dialogue,' since he has failed to listen well or to be moved by the narrator. Precisely because it is a cool appropriation and not a dialogue, Professor James Pieixoto repeats the Gileadean violation of Offred: in a fresh assault on the narrator, he regards her in effect as a disappointing Ofjames. Her 'turn of mind' (322) is regrettable, since she fails to satisfy his particular desires. He seeks to diminish her vitality, and the dangerous implications of her tale; he declines to pass the 'moral judgment upon the Gileadeans' (314) for which the text cries out. And this is the model we are being asked by Atwood to resist.

What Garrett-Petts has in mind when he suggests that Atwood *intends* the diminished vitality of the fictional dialogue is that the reader's 'focus on character' must (in the Brechtian manner) be replaced by a focus on politics, especially as they impinge on our own time. This is his interpretive imperative. What I would question, however, is the necessity of that choice. What I find particularly impressive about *The Handmaid's Tale* is that it causes me to respond powerfully (and often, as it seems, simultaneously) on both of these ontological planes. It forces the recognition that politics and 'character' go hand in hand. It reminds us that an empathic understanding of the reality of others is the cornerstone of a just society.

I have been trying to suggest that Atwood signals this partly through the mystery of her narrator's name. Somewhere in the middle of my last reading of the text, as I was checking (among other things) for additional appearances of the word 'June' – it suddenly occurred to me that I should check the date of Pieixoto's speech. As I flipped the pages, I felt sure that it would be there, waiting: a message from *Atwood*, ironically and surreptitiously inserted as a rebuke to Pieixoto's pretensions, as a reward for readers who have cracked the code, and as a gesture of solidarity with her heroine. And there it was: 'June 25, 2195' (311), the third and last appearance of the name. (The rhyming word 'moon' is also present, in the name of the convention's female 'Chair: Professor Maryann Crescent Moon', to indicate that female power is still nascent.)

The delicious irony of this last piece of evidence is that Pieixoto's speech is almost entirely concerned with establishing the identity of figures who appear in *The Handmaid's Tale*. (This is his name for the document he constructs from tapes made by Offred after her flight – presumably when she was still in danger, since the tapes are found in Gilead.) Pieixoto's linguistic dexterity and his chauvinism can be gauged by the sophomoric pun he makes on tale / tail as 'the bone, as it were, of contention, in that phase of Gileadean society of which our saga treats' (313). Clearly, *his* 'bone' is still up to its old male tricks of reduction; and just as clearly, he is not man enough for the primary task he sets himself, which is to 'establish an identity for the narrator' (315). He despairs of tracing her 'directly' (316), and so attempts (characteristically) to identify Offred through 'Fred.'

Pieixoto narrows his field to two likely contenders for the role of the Commander – and then he is stymied, since neither of these men was married to a woman called Serena Joy. He concludes that the Wife's name was 'a somewhat malicious invention by our author' (321). And that seems likely. But there is also a more charitable explanation to which (unknowingly) Pieixoto points the way, when he says that '"Luke" and "Nick" drew blanks, as did "Moira" and "Janine,"' and concludes that 'There is a high probability that these were, in any case, pseudonyms, adopted to protect these individuals should the tapes be discovered' (318). Exactly so. And in that case, the narrator might also have been shielding 'Serena Joy,' whom she comes to regard as a kind of doppleganger and another victim of the regime. It is pleasing that this kindness (if it was that) should have the much delayed effect of foiling Pieixoto.

But the recognition that 'Moira' and 'Janine' are likely to be pseudonyms has an even more pleasing effect. It suggests that the narrator's original list of

names contained only one that was 'real' – the one name that she was prepared to risk, since it was her own. And this has consequences for our assessment of the narrator's courage and concern for the welfare of others. It establishes her more clearly as the heroine of her own tale, and confirms the development she has undergone. Repeatedly in the novel, we have had occasion to
feel critical of Offred for her willed blindness or tunnel vision. Indeed, the
headgear which obstructs her vision and the lowered gaze required of her in
Gilead ironically recall the heroine's failure to acknowledge 'the writing on
the wall' of pre-Gileadean society.

June was one of those who 'lived, as usual, by ignoring' (66) – and (as she
begins to understand) 'Ignoring isn't the same thing as ignorance, you have to
work at it.' She describes herself as one of 'the people who were not in the
papers ... [who] lived in the blank white spaces at the edges of print.' But such
'freedom' is illusory; it is neither possible nor desirable to live 'in the gaps
between the stories' (67). And this is what Gilead unwittingly teaches the
Handmaid, as she finds herself confined with a vengeance to the 'gaps' and
denied the world of print. Reduced then to a nearly absolute blankness, she
will begin to use the gaps and to insert her *self* in the story of others.

Interestingly, these reflections on her former 'ignoring' of print are followed immediately by her pleasure in the word 'FAITH' (67) on a petit-point
cushion on her window seat: 'It's the only thing they've given me to read.'
While the reader is likely to think at once of the words 'hope' and 'charity'
which have been denied her, Offred is not yet able to read the gaps or to see
the implications of that absence. Later she does think of the other pillows,
but guesses that they have been assigned to Rita and Cora – whereas the
point, surely, is that hope and charity (or love) have been excised in Gilead.

A measure of her increased but still halting skill at interpretation is supplied in the passage that comes next:

> I sit in the chair and think about the word *chair*. It can also mean the
> leader of a meeting. It can also mean a mode of execution. It is the first
> syllable in *charity*. It is French word for flesh. None of these facts has
> any connection with the others. (120)

Garrett-Petts cites this passage as evidence that Offred is 'interpret[ing] her
world as one might solve a linguistic puzzle' and suggests that she is here
concerned with 'keeping both her intellectual skills and her political will
alive' (85). I would agree that she is trying, but so far without great success –
since it is clear to me that 'these facts' are indeed connected. The statement
that they are *not* operates as an invitation to the reader to discern their connection; it is a covert signal that we may regard as coming from Atwood or
from Offred when she is reconstructing the tale. Decoded, this chain suggests

the need to get out of one's chair, to lead and to meet with others, in order to avoid execution, to preserve love, and to resist the appropriation of one's own flesh.

Offred, however, at this point regards her linguistic musing as a litany which helps her to 'compose [her]self.' Here, as in the passage where she retreats into the folds of the Handmaid's cloak in order to 'compose [her]self' (156), there is a suggestion of withdrawal. Admittedly, Offred *needs* to compose herself: 'My self is a thing I must now compose, as one composes a speech' (76). But she must learn the syntax and the code that will connect the parts of her speech and link her self to others; she must not 'compose' herself in isolation or in resignation, for that is precisely the sort of paralyzing prayer (or litany of negation) that Gilead intends. As the novel proceeds, Offred becomes increasingly adept in the arts of interpretation and communication, and this linguistic development occurs as both a cause and an effect of her developing political will. She unscrambles the Scrabble letters to make words, and to *attach* these words to one another, as the game requires. But she also goes beyond the level of linguistic sophistication that is required for Scrabble or for the similar detecting of merely alphabetical links between 'chair' and 'charity,' to establish syntax and semantic or meaningful connections. The proof of this is in the tapes which are (in a rudimentary fashion) unscrambled by Pieixoto to create the text whose codes he cannot understand.

The Handmaid's Tale asks the reader to do a better job of interpretation, and insists upon the importance both of the name and of the chain that links writer and reader. 'A story is like a letter' (50), Offred says – a letter addressed to *you*. While she regrets the impossibility of naming her reader – 'Attaching a name attaches *you* to the world of fact, which is riskier' – Offred also recognizes the advantage of this:

I will say *you, you*, like an old love song. *You* can mean more than one.
You can mean thousands.

Thus, she extends the link between lover and beloved to forge the chain of resistance. In her deconstruction of the Lord's Prayer, Offred again reaches out to the *you* whose reply (or interpretation of her experience in Gilead) she desires: 'I wish you would tell me Your Name, the real one I mean. But *You* will do as well as anything' (204). I would interpret these passages as a request that I respond intimately to the text, in what Martin Buber would describe as an I / Thou relationship, and also as offering a courteous apology for the narrator's (or the author's) inability to name me or any of her 'thousands' of readers.

Offred's Commander says that 'Women can't add.... For them, one and one and one and one don't make four.... [They] just [make] one and one and one and one' (195). And later she reflects that this 'is true.... Each one remains unique, there is no way of joining them together. They cannot be exchanged, one for the other. They cannot replace each other. Nick for Luke or Luke for Nick' (201-2). This is a loaded passage, pointing in two directions. In one sense, she's wrong – since 'joining them together' is vital, and since the move she makes to Nick in Luke's absence is clearly positive. In another, equally fundamental sense, she's right – since 'Each one remains unique,' even as 'one and one and one and one' mount into the 'thousands.'

The image of the chain reflects both of these truths. It is found in the chain of 'safety pins' (214) made by the narrator's mother, which she regards as one of her mother's useless 'Throwbacks to domesticity' and as 'a road that turns out to lead nowhere.' (I may be reaching here when I suggest that her mother's safety pins suggest a humorous, but auspicious survival of the domestic impulse, which her feminism does not have to preclude.) That chain of safety pins may be recalled when we come to the Underground Femaleroad: 'Each one of them was in contact with only one other one, always the next one along' (258). Here, the linkage of 'one and one and one and one' may or may not add up to 'safety' for the narrator, but the road (and the imaging of its goal) is nevertheless useful. And the underground activity of each unique, anonymous 'one' is clearly valorized.

All of this returns me to the question of my own place on the chain and my responsibility as reader. I have tried to suggest that the act of interpretation which is urged upon me by Offred's example, as well as by the negative example of Pieixoto, should include *both* a careful analysis of society (Offred's and my own) and a caring response to the narrator's unique identity. I should 'add up' the political data of the text, and I should also serve as 'one' who responds to the trust of another 'one.' Both activities are important, and each kind of interpretation (if worthwhile) will be dependent upon the recognition of the value of the other, since society is made up of individuals. This recognition – which I described earlier as an understanding that politics and 'character' go hand in hand – is at the heart of Atwood's aesthetic and her politics. It requires the reader to position herself both within and outside of the fictive world; and it suggests that empathy and the larger perspective are not opposed. In a similar way, Offred must learn to combine her aesthetic response to the world that is 'up close' – 'because where would we be without [flowers]?' (279) – with a broader, political view.

Offred thought of her true name as a treasure she would 'come back to dig up, one day' (94). We don't know if the Underground Femaleroad took her to a place that was safe enough for that, a society in which her singular name could blossom once again. We do know (I think) that she buried it in this text, for someone else to find and pass along. And we know that 'June' is also the secret Atwood would have us uncover – not as idle proof that we can read her lips, but simply because we need to care (as she does) for her character and for what is being whispered in our world. We need to become the 'you' – which 'can mean thousands' (50) – who will really listen to The Handmaid's Tale.

II

The interpretation I have just offered is in my opinion 'called for' by the text. That is, while I would acknowledge that the structure of my argument and some of its details are idiosyncratic, the gist of it seems 'right' – and I would expect my readers and the author to endorse it. That kind of interpretation is always pleasurable for the critic: one feels like an explorer, licensed by the author. There is, of course, always the chance that one is 'wrong' and that self-intoxication has set in. Here, though, both the pleasure and the sense of authorization were increased by a metafictional element in the text which suggests that my reading was 'called for' in another way, since Atwood has clearly thematized the reception of the text and the necessity of interpretation within her fiction. The reading I will venture upon now is of another kind altogether.

I cannot argue that this interpretation is 'called for' by the text, that it should persuade anyone else, or that the author would approve my meddling in these waters. I offer it here simply because it interests me, and to make use of the fishing license which criticism has lately issued to itself. The remarkable thing about this license is that it permits us to invent the fish. We always do a bit of this, in any dull or interesting reading of a text – but lately we have been doing quite a lot more of it. We may begin (as I am doing here) with the merest shifting of the textual water, to discern a fish which then leaps merrily into the extra-textual and inter-textual air. (The license is famous for seducing you into play with metaphors like that one, extended lines in which it is possible to get absurdly tangled up.)

This interpretation too, by a pleasing coincidence, was set in motion through a single point of entry. If I'd missed it – just as if I'd missed 'June' in that initial list of names – I would have read the whole novel without ever again being tempted into an interpretation which has increased my pleasure in the text (if not, in this case, the negotiable value of my reading). What started me off was the mirror in which the Handmaid sees herself reflected when she goes down the stairs near the beginning of the novel: 'round, convex, a pier-glass, like the eye of a fish' (19). I was reminded (on my second reading of the novel) of Jan van Eyck's painting, 'The Arnolfini Marriage,' in which there is a round, convex mirror I've always thought of as a pier-glass.

It doesn't surprise me that it took a second reading for that image to float into consciousness. It did so, I think, because I already had some familiarity with The Handmaid's Tale and could feel the relevance of van Eyck's painting to the text. As soon as the pier-glass chimed, a host of other echoes began to clamour. And I attended to them, with a sense of holiday. I did not in this case expect to find my interpretation 'confirmed' elsewhere in the text; I did not think it was my *job* as reader to pursue this line of thought. What I guessed was that I had happened upon an association that was subliminal for Atwood herself – and I knew that I could easily be wrong about that. (It could be conscious, and it could be absent altogether.)

'The Arnolfini Marriage' is a double portrait, of a man and a woman whose marriage is apparently (and rather strangely) being solemnized in a bedroom. He looks stern and faces front; she, with modestly lowered head, is turned toward him. An elaborately canopied red bed occupies the right-hand frame, and a window the left. The female figure stands closest to the bed, while the male stands near the window – or the outside world. This deployment of the figures has always seemed suggestive to me. The woman's right hand is lying open in the man's left; his right is raised, and her left is holding up the ample folds of her gown at belly level. Perhaps it is only this displacement of her gown that makes the woman look pregnant. We might also speculate, however, that (with the hand that corresponds formally to his raised hand) she is disguising an actual pregnancy, or drawing attention to that portion of her body to which the man's gesture of benediction or promise most particularly refers. Between these figures is the round, convex mirror in which their backs, the window, and the bed are all reflected – as well as two other figures, one of whom we take to be the artist. Above the mirror, written on th wall with a legal flourish, is a Latin phrase: 'Johannes de Eyck fuit hic. 1434 (Jan van Eyck was here).

What, then, are the echoes from this painting that resonate (if only for me) in *The Handmaid's Tale*? The issue of pregnancy is an obvious one, to which I shall return. The costumes (including the woman's white head-dress) also seem vaguely appropriate for Gilead, where indeed it seems that the reactionary mode of dress has been inspired by old paintings. Offred sees such paintings in a church – portraits 'of women in long sombre dresses, their hair covered by white caps, and of upright men, darkly clothed and unsmiling. Our ancestors' (41) – and again in Serena Joy's sitting room, where two stiff portraits 'passing … as ancestors' (90) are positioned on either side of a mirror, 'guarding the room with their narrowed eyes.' The interior of 'The Arnolfini Marriage' makes me think a bit both of that sitting room – which is described as if it were a painting, 'subdued, symmetrical … one of the shapes money takes when it freezes'(89) – and of Serena Joy's bedroom, which has a four-poster bed with a white canopy like a 'sagging cloud' (104) or a 'swollen belly.' Both the Flemish and the Gileadean domestic scenes suggest privilege, solemnity, religiosity, and a preoccupation with the issue of pregnancy. I find myself reaching also for the orange on the window-sill of 'The Arnolfini Marriage,' since oranges are conspicuously prized in Gilead, as well as for the bride's discarded red shoes that match the bed. I'm sure that Offred's red shoes do not descend from these, since there are far more pressing reasons for Atwood to dress her Handmaid in red. I know that such details as these are not finally persuasive. Yet I find them seductive.

When I turned to the art historians, other interesting things came into view. Perhaps the most influential interpretation of 'The Arnolfini Marriage' is Erwin Panofsky's, in 1934. Panofsky was concerned with establishing the painting as a '"pictorial marriage certificate"' (124) witnessed and made by van Eyck, and with analyzing the Christian iconography of the scene. Thus, for instance, the single candle burning in the chandelier represents 'the all seeing wisdom of God' (126). (This may recall both the 'winged eye' of theocratic Gilead and the 'blind plaster eye' (61) of the chandelier which has been removed from Offred's bedroom, so that she cannot hang herself.) Panofsky also says of the figure of St. Margaret, carved on the armchair standing by the bed, that 'this Saint was especially invoked by women in expectation of a child' (126).

Robert Baldwin elaborates on the implications of the mirror's frame, where scenes of Christ's Passion are depicted in miniature. He argues in part that the mirror shows 'the reforming power of matrimony' (67) as a sacrament linked to Christ's sacrifice. The mirror, according to Baldwin, refers to 'the late medieval topos of the human soul as a mirror or image of God, an image soiled by the Fall but cleansed (to a bridal immaculacy) by participation in the sacraments and by meditation on the Passion' (57). Baldwin also refers intriguingly to a lost work by Jan van Eyck: 'a pre-nuptial, ritual bath [that] was likely paired in some way to the "Arnolfini Portrait"' (66). A copy of that lost work shows a naked woman bathing, and another woman – looking very much like a Martha from Gilead – standing grimly by. In Baldwin's discussion of 'The Arnolfini Marriage,' as in Atwood's Gilead, there is considerable emphasis upon the need for a ritual cleansing of woman's body; religious meditation and rituals are in both places seen as means of de-eroticizing Eve, transforming her as far as possible into Mary, the Virgin Mother of God.

Much of the debate about this painting has been concerned with the fact that the man holds out his *left* hand to the woman. Peter H. Schabacker has argued that this 'designates the marriage as a morganatic one, or as it is otherwise called: a left-handed marriage' (377). A morganatic marriage involved a man of high social rank (like a Commander) taking as his 'wife' a woman of inferior status (like a Handmaid); it required her to renounce all manner of claims, as in Gilead the Handmaids were required to give up even the children they might bear. Since there was no disparity in rank between Giovanni Arnolfini and Giovanna Cenami (Fred and Offred?!), Schabacker concluded that some other couple must be represented in the portrait. Others have argued their way out of this dilemma in various complicated ways, since the identity of the figures is reasonably well established – in contrast, that is, to the figures with whom Professor Pieixoto was concerned. (Panofsky had thought the oddity could be explained by the painter's desire to maintain a strict symmetry.)

Obviously, none of this proves that Atwood was thinking (or dreaming) of 'The Arnolfini Marriage' when she wrote *The Handmaid's Tale*. Even if she was, it seems unlikely that issues such as the morganatic marriage were operative in the construction of the *Tale*. That does not, I think, preclude their interest. Other elements of the painting that stand a better chance of having attracted Atwood, whether consciously or not, are the self-referentiality of the artist's signature and his presence in the mirror, the issue of the woman's pregnancy, and the mirror itself. These, at any rate, were the elements that attracted me most powerfully.

In the first part of this essay, I argued that Atwood was 'present' in her text in the sense that she was asking us to interpret it. That is also the effect of Jan van Eyck's tiny image in the mirror, which prompts us to interrogate both the occasion of his painting and its codes. He asserts himself too in the Latin signature above the mirror. And this could be a source for that enigmatic scrap of Latin in the novel, *'Nolite te bastardes carborundorum'* (62), through which Offred's predecessor – who was herself ground down by the bastards to the point of disappearance – paradoxically affirmed her presence. But Atwood's own signature is also in the text: *'M. loves G., 1972'* (123), an inscription that Offred finds on a desk at the Red Centre. For better or worse, I feel sure that this means 'Margaret loves Graeme, 1972.' Like van Eyck, she dates her signature; but the date she chooses marks (I would guess) the beginning of Atwood's relationship with Graeme Gibson, rather than the date of the novel's composition. In Jan van Eyck's case, of course, the two sorts of occasion coincided. That Atwood chooses to inscribe herself in the text in terms of her devotion to Gibson seems important to me: it affirms the value of love between man and woman, even in a society replete with 'bastards.'

The issue of the woman's pregnancy and the mirror are inter-related. The mirror in *The Handmaid's Tale* is convex – like an eye or a pregnant belly. I have thought of the convex mirror in 'The Arnolfini Marriage' as the painter's 'eye' and as an echo of the woman's belly, which to me looks pregnant. I have thought van Eyck might be 'seeing' this too, and suggesting it to the viewer. But because most art historians reject the persistent, popular belief that the woman is pregnant, I have also questioned whether the painting is enlarged or diminished by that view. Perhaps it is a reduction of the woman to assume her pregnancy. In the world of *The Handmaid's Tale*, however, it is clear that the images of eye and belly are associated with the mirror and related in a thematic way.

The eye of Gilead is intensely focussed on the Handmaid's womb: it sees only that function, and reduces her to that. The male eye is 'winged' (225), able to see all and to travel, whereas the female is immobilized by the tattoo of an eye on her ankle, which functions as 'a passport in reverse' (75). 'To be *seen*' (39), Aunt Lydia tells her 'girls,' is to be 'penetrated'; thus, 'Modesty is invisibility.' Yet penetration is a prerequisite of the Handmaids' intended fate; what Aunt Lydia is actually training them for is the kind of 'modesty' (or self-effacement) which will immobilize and blind them. In fact, the penis is a blind eye, 'avid for vision' (98) as it wings its way into woman's 'darkness'; 'woman, who can see in darkness while he himself strains blindly forward.' Woman's power is man's weakness, as when Offred detects a weakness in the Commander: 'It's like a small crack in a wall, before now impenetrable. If I press my eye to it, this weakness of his, I may be able to see my way clear' (146). She needs to see for herself, and to penetrate with her night vision the male's continuing dependency on the female, in order to free herself from the prison of the womb.

An especially poignant passage concerning Offred's lost child suggests another kind of reversal that will be necessary if woman is to assert her own vision, and the right to her own body. Offred has a dream in which, just as her child is being torn from her, her gaze is fixed upon 'a leaf, red, turned early' (85), which is 'the most beautiful thing I've ever seen.' In the darkness of her loss 'nothing is left but ... a very little window, like the wrong end of a telescope,' through which 'I can see her, going away from me, through the trees which are already turning.' The red here (as elsewhere in the novel) signifies blood, the failure of conception *or* the moment of birth; it suggests the fall that must be reversed by spring. Offred's daughter is being 'unborn' through the wrong end of the telescope. Offred herself will become 'Unwoman' (and dead) if her dormancy, her trance-like passivity is not disrupted. Just after this dream, Offred descends on her 'red shoes' (89) past the clock that warns her time is running out, and past the mirror where she sees 'a brief waif in the eye of the glass.' For me, this image recalls the disappearing child and suggests that it is time for Offred to assert herself. She must resist and reverse the process of diminution. In particular, she must be wary of the 'close up' consolations of her 'minimalist life' (120), which are suggested by the womb-like beauty of the egg or that last red leaf.

'What I need' (153), says Offred, 'is perspective.... Otherwise there are only two dimensions. Otherwise you live with your face squashed against a wall.... Your own skin like a map, a diagram of futility, crisscrossed with tiny roads that lead nowhere.' This passage may recall her mother's chain of safety pins, which suggests to Offred 'a road that turns out to lead nowhere' (214); in fact that chain maps Offred's way out of the prison or the mirror in which her face is 'squashed against a wall.' She needs the third dimension or the perspective which is supplied by others, in order to discover a future for herself. She needs to go through the looking-glass. She needs to turn the distorting mirror into a window. She must use her 'eye' to reverse the 'passport in reverse' (75); otherwise, she too will disappear through the wrong end of the telescope.

Atwood refers to the mirror or pier-glass repeatedly in the novel, and often she juxtaposes it with the red and blue fanlight over the front door. This is natural enough, since the mirror is in the front hall – but she also develops a thematic link or progression between the two. Mirrors suggest captivity, while windows and doors signal the possibility of an exit, as when Moira – the 'loose woman' (143) – breaks out of the Red Centre, and the other Handmaids think the windows and doors could open for them too. The fanlight is made of 'coloured glass: flowers, red and blue' (18); it offers a larger spectrum. And flowers, we know, are a sign of progress for Offred. On another occasion – when she sees her face distorted in the mirror, 'which bulges outward like an eye under pressure' (58-59) – Offred stretches out her hands, to fill them with the fanlight's 'flowers of light' (58): 'red and blue, purple.' The 'pressure' has caused her to seek relief, and it may seem that the relief she finds is only aesthetic. But the last two references to the mirror suggest that Offred is learning to conceive of her own fate as involved with that of other people.

The penultimate reference unites the pier-glass and the coloured fanlight, as in the mirror Offred sees 'the two of us, a blue shape, a red shape, in the brief glass eye of the mirror as we descend. Myself, my obverse' (271). Her companion is Serena Joy, glimpsed now as her doppelganger. The earlier reference to 'purple' anticipates this red and blue merger in the glass, which signals a movement toward sisterhood for Offred. Since the occasion of their joint descent is Offred's first visit to Nick, it is also clear that she is on her way to becoming a loose woman. The final reference to the mirror occurs when Offred is about to go out the door with Nick, at the end of the novel; and this time, the mirror is significantly empty. Offred is no longer contained by it. And Serena Joy is standing 'under the mirror, looking up, incredulous' (306).

I said earlier that I had always thought of the mirror in 'The Arnolfini Marriage' as a pier-glass. When I looked that term up in the OED, however, I learned that a pier-glass is 'a large tall mirror orig. one fitted to fill up the pier or space between two windows.' That definition was interesting, in view of the connection between the mirror and the window that I have been exploring – but it seemed also to diminish the possibility of an allusion to 'The Arnolfini Marriage' in Atwood's novel. The roundness and convexity were in both the novel and the painting, but none of the art historians I read called van Eyck's mirror a pier-glass. Just as I was fretting over that, I read *Cat's Eye* for the second time – and found a discussion of 'The Arnolfini Marriage' in which Atwood herself refers to the mirror as a pier-glass.

I had forgotten this fortuitous appearance of the painting in the Atwood canon; I had pursued 'The Arnolfini Marriage' without even that vestige of support for my hypothesis. Yet since my second reading of the *Tale* was preceded by my first reading of *Cat's Eye*, perhaps I really did remember it, subliminally. And if, as it seems, both Atwood and I have been wrong in referring to the mirror as a pier-glass, my discovery (or hallucination) is all the more beguiling. *Cat's Eye* confirms Atwood's knowledge of this celebrated painting, which I would not have questioned in any case, and it removes the difficulty I was having over the pier-glass. But it still doesn't prove my case. At most, it lends support to my guess about the 'presence' of 'The Arnolfini Marriage' in *The Handmaid's Tale*, since it makes an obvious sort of sense that such a shadowy presence would surface in the author's next book.

The use that Atwood makes of 'The Arnolfini Marriage' in *Cat's Eye* is interesting in a number of ways. Perhaps most intriguing, for my purposes, is the inter-textuality of the fact that van Eyck's painting inspires her heroine – the painter, Elaine Risley – to create a series of works based on reflection. By analogy, then, we might suggest that Atwood herself was inspired to re-work and reflect 'The Arnolfini Marriage' in *The Handmaid's Tale* – as Elaine does in a painting called 'Cat's Eye.' The more reliable point to be made is simply that in Atwood's work (as in Elaine Risley's) mirrors proliferate. Certainly the mirror is what most impresses Elaine about 'The Arnolfini Marriage,' though she is struck too by the self-assertiveness of the signature, '"Johannes de Eyck fuit hic. 1434,"' which she says is 'disconcertingly like a washroom scribble, something you'd write with spray paint on a wall' (327). She calls the pier-glass 'an eye, a single eye that sees more than anyone else looking,' and refers to the figures who are reflected by that eye as 'locked in, sealed up as if in a paperweight.' She does not allude to the issue of pregnancy or indicate any particular interest in the central figures.

In the painting Elaine calls 'Cat's Eye,' the pier-glass which is 'like an eye' (327) appears again. And this time the figures are very important to her. The upper half of Elaine's head is in the foreground; behind her, 'in the centre of the picture ... a pier-glass is hanging, convex and encircled by an ornate frame. In it, a section of the back of my head is visible; but the hair is different, younger' (408). She is developing here the notion of 'curved space' in which an earlier time may reappear. In this pier-glass, as in van Eyck's, other 'small figures' are reflected; we recognize them as Cordelia, Grace, and Carol, whose tormenting of Elaine in childhood had led her to withdraw trust and to seal herself up 'as if in a paperweight' (327) or a blind eye. Now, though, she has begun to see: both front and back, two 'sides' of the story. Her fear of persecution is 'like a mirror that shows you only the ruined half of your face' (410). As that recedes, she can 'almost believe' (411) that others wish her well, and she can see herself and Cordelia as 'twins.'

Nearly all of this seems relevant to *The Handmaid's Tale*. We recall, for instance, that for Offred, as for Elaine Risley, it is necessary to be wary – and even more necessary to trust. But that dialectic is apparent throughout Atwood's work, which is unusually rich in such inter-textual echoes. The narrative occasion of *Cat's Eye* is a Risley retrospective, and *Cat's Eye* itself may strike the reader as an Atwood retrospective. (Thus, for example, the parents and brother of *Surfacing* are re-worked in Elaine's family, the Royal Porcupine of *Lady Oracle* reappears as her first husband, Jon, and the childhood tormenters of *Lady Oracle* achieve new prominence.) The complex transmigration of images or figures or ideas between texts often entails those which are incidental or incipient in one text 'coming out' or appearing more conspicuously in a later text. There are, for instance, two references to the 'cat's eye' in *The Handmaid's Tale* (155, 165), and there is also a discussion of 'falling women' (237) that is relevant to Elaine's painting of that name. It seems, then, quite possible that 'The Arnolfini Marriage' journeyed from *The Handmaid's Tale* to *Cat's Eye* in a similar way.

But there is one last image I thought I'd glimpsed in the 'curved space' of that pier-glass in *The Handmaid's Tale*, and I will end my fishing expedition with that. I end, as it happens, where Atwood's fiction began – with the staircase that Marian McAlpin descends at the start of *The Edible Woman*. I was reminded of that staircase when Offred walks downstairs at the beginning of *The Handmaid's Tale*. Both novels mark the house in which the protagonist lives as old-fashioned space, to suggest woman's incarceration in traditional roles. Very like Offred, Marian lives on the top floor of a large house in 'one of the older and more genteel districts' (12), in what she supposes must have been the 'servants' quarters.' She too must endure the puritanical supervision of the mistress of the house, 'the lady down below' (13) whose gardening gloves and obsession with 'the child' may remind us of Serena Joy.

As Offred's room contains a braided rug because 'This is the kind of touch they like: folk art, archaic, made by women.... A return to traditional values' (17), so the stairwell in *The Edible Woman* is endowed with touches like 'pioneer brass warming-pans' (12), a 'spinning wheel,' and the 'row of oval-framed ancestors that guards the ... stairway' (12). Although the staircase in *The Edible Woman* does not culminate in the pier-glass of *The Handmaid's Tale*, in both novels it is clear that the heroine descends that staircase into reactionary space and time. And Marian is herself associated with distorting mirrors – as when she bathes before her ritual engagement party, and sees in the taps and spout disturbing images of 'her body suddenly bloated or diminished' (218). In both novels, the heroine is threatened by diminution and by her own complicity in that diminution.

§

I have argued that the two interpretations offered in this essay are different in kind, that one is 'called for' by the novel and the other is not. Both lead into speculations and explications of imagery that have their own interest, quite apart from this essay's insistent claim that the heroine's name is June, or its hesitant suggestion that 'The Arnolfini Marriage' had some role to play in the making of *The Handmaid's Tale*. That is a common enough occurrence in literary criticism; we all know that even the most thoroughly wrong-headed essay may have attractive or useful spin-offs. The reader of the novel and the reader of criticism may both profit in unexpected ways. But I want to close with some further consideration of the value of the propositions themselves, and the issues of obscurity and authorial intention.

What do I make of the fact that while I think the heroine's name is so important, no one in my vicinity has said a word about it? I may conclude either that I have been over-subtle and (not to put too fine a point upon it) *wrong*, or that Atwood wanted to make this discovery hard for her readers. I can repeat my argument that the author was constrained by the narrator's constraints, so that she could not lead the reader more forcibly into the secret of Offred's name. But the main point I would make is that the name is obscure because this is a book *about* the necessary rigours of interpretation; and the name is important because the public world that Atwood would have us enter and interpret is one that can (if we remain quiescent) efface us as private individuals. Of course it is possible to read the novel well without this information, and to profit from it – thousands of people have done so.

I would dismiss, however, any suggestion that the name is a kind of minor in-joke for the author herself. In 'The Page,' from *Murder in the Dark*, Atwood makes clear that the important things in a text are not always the obvious ones. This extraordinary piece does not specify whether Atwood's instructions for entering the page are aimed at the writer or the reader; for both, then, 'The question about the page is: what is beneath it? … *Beneath the page* is another story' (45). You have to enter with bare hands; 'You should never go into the page with gloves on,' because the page 'can feel you touching it.' Light or darkness may be waiting at the point of incision, just as it is for Offred when she exits the page. She has 'given [her]self over into the hands of strangers, because it can't be helped' (307). She who has 'hunger[ed] to commit the act of touch' (21) is now committed to our hands, which must be bare, which must (as always in Atwood) learn how to touch in the dark. And so I continue to believe that 'June' is important, that we really *ought* to bring into the light the buried name. (Thus Rennie – who is analogous to Offred and to us, as the 'reporter' of *Bodily Harm* – at last takes Lora's hand, realizing at that moment that 'there's no such thing as a faceless stranger, every face is someone's, it has a name' (299). And then she *speaks* the name, to raise Lora from the dead.)

In fishing for Offred's true name, I used the bait Atwood herself had attached with some care to the end of a line – or so I think. (I see this metaphor obliges me to be the fish who took the bait, but let that pass.) In pursuing the 'fish eye' of the pier-glass, however, and relating it to 'The Arnolfini Marriage,' I was operating without the author's license or implicit approval. I thought I knew that if Atwood had intended her readers to consider van Eyck's painting, she would have signalled it more strongly. Clearly, there was nothing to prevent her in this case. But neither was there anything to prevent me: no 'ought' or 'ought not' seemed to apply. I was not obligated by any imperative in the text, or constrained by the probable lack of intention. I felt free to speculate upon what Atwood *might* have been thinking or dreaming about, and to develop my own line of thought. The 'spin-offs' of this angle of vision pleased me and enriched my reading of the novel. But whether my discussion of 'The Arnolfini Marriage' will have value for other readers I cannot say.

One problem remains. In both cases, I have been interested in the question of authorial intention or in second-guessing Atwood. And the license on *that* (as issued by the academy) has lately expired. Those waters are murky at any time, and perhaps they really are better left alone. I do realize that I could be wrong: theoretically, at least, 'The Arnolfini Marriage' might be 'intended' and June the hallucinated fish. (And the patterns I have seen could still independently apply.) For many critics today that would not matter. To me it does – not ultimately, perhaps, but it matters. I would be interested to learn whether Atwood has thought at any point about the links I see between the painting and the novel, or would find them of interest now, and I would be very unhappy to learn that she had not consciously named the heroine June. I realize that I am much less vulnerable if I cast my lines another way, without recourse to the author. But I cannot help reading in this way. Reading is not for me a solitary act. Whatever idle or auspicious day-dreaming it may entail, reading is also a response to another person's urgent speech. As in life, it is a response as well to what may (or may not) be written between the lines.

Works Cited

Atwood, Margaret. *Bodily Harm.* Toronto: Seal Books, McClelland and Stewart-Bantam Ltd., 1982.

———. *Cat's Eye.* Toronto: McClelland and Stewart, 1988.

———. *The Edible Woman.* Toronto: McClelland and Stewart, New Canadian Library No. 93, reprinted 1985.

———. *The Handmaid's Tale.* Toronto: McClelland and Stewart, 1985. All references are to this edition and are cited parenthetically in the text.

———. *Murder in the Dark: Short Fictions and Prose Poems.* Toronto: The Coach House Press, 1983.

Baldwin, Robert. 'Marriage as a Sacramental Reflection of the Passion: The Mirror in Jan van Eyck's *Arnolfini Wedding*,' *Oud Holland* 98.2 (1984): 57-75.

Garrett-Petts, W.F. 'Reading, Writing, and the Postmodern Condition: Interpreting Margaret Atwood's *The Handmaid's Tale*,' *Open Letter* 7.1: 74-92.

Panofsky, Erwin. 'Jan van Eyck's *Arnolfini* Portrait,' *The Burlington Magazine* 64 (1934): 117-127.

Schabacker, Peter H. '*De Matrimonio ad Morganaticam Contracto*: Jan van Eyck's '*Arnolfini*' Portrait Reconsidered,' *The Art Quarterly* 35.14 (1972): 375-391.

Acknowledgements

'Fear of the Open Heart' appeared in *A Mazing Space: Writing Canadian Women Writing*, ed. Shirley Neuman and Smaro Kamboureli (Edmonton: Longspoon / Newest, 1986).

'Waiting for a Final Explanation: Mavis Gallant's "Irina"' appeared in *Writers in Aspic*, ed. John Metcalf (Montréal: Véhicule Press, 1988).

'A Feminist Reading of *The Stone Angel* appeared in *Canadian Literature*, no. 93, Summer 1982.

'Hagar's Old Age: *The Stone Angel* as *Vollendungsroman*' appeared in *Crossing the River: Essays in Honour of Margaret Laurence*, ed. Kristjana Gunnars (Winnipeg: Turnstone Press, 1988).

'Dog in a Grey Room: The Happy Ending of *Coming Through Slaughter*' appeared in *Spider Blues: Essays on Michael Ondaatje*, ed. Sam Solecki (Montréal: Véhicule Press, 1985).

'P.K. Page: The Chameleon and the Centre' appeared in *The Malahat Review*, no. 45, January 1978.

'Approaching P.K. Page's "Arras"' appeared in *Canadian Poetry*, no. 4, Spring / Summer 1979.

'Pastoral Restraint: John Metcalf's *The Lady Who Sold Furniture*' appeared in *The Malahat Review*, no. 70, March 1985.

'Between the World and the Word: John Metcalf's "The Teeth of My Father"' appeared in *The New Quarterly*, vol. VII, nos. 1 & 2, Spring / Summer 1987.

Several of the essays in this book contain ideas that were developed by or in concert with women who were my students at the University of Victoria. I wish to acknowledge and thank Barbara Burkhardt, Gail Harris, Michele Holmgren, Marlene Goldman, and Carol Matthews. I also want to thank Barbara McLean and my colleague Linda Marshall from the University of Guelph for their advice and support.

For a list of other books,
write for our catalogue
or call (416) 979-7374.

Coach House Press
401 (rear) Huron Street
Toronto, Canada M5S 2G5

- Mrs. Leon R.
  — met at BC's Sept. '98 book launching
  (meal at Biglierdi's — chat across table)
    - nervous before academic papers
      (not creative — with Leon)
    - troubled with duties of chair